DE FACTO FEDERALISM IN CHINA

Reforms and Dynamics of Central-Local Relations

Series on Contemporary China (ISSN: 1793-0847)

Series on Contemporary China – Vol. 7

DE FACTO FEDERALISM IN CHINA

Reforms and Dynamics of Central-Local Relations

Zheng Yongnian

University of Nottingham, UK

World Scientific

NEW JERSEY · LONDON · SINGAPORE · BEIJING · SHANGHAI · HONG KONG · TAIPEI · CHENNAI

Published by

World Scientific Publishing Co. Pte. Ltd.

5 Toh Tuck Link, Singapore 596224

USA office: 27 Warren Street, Suite 401-402, Hackensack, NJ 07601

UK office: 57 Shelton Street, Covent Garden, London WC2H 9HE

Library of Congress Cataloging-in-Publication Data
Zheng, Yongnian.
    De facto federalism in China : reforms and dynamics of central-local
relations / by Zheng Yongnian.
        p. cm. -- (Series on contemporary China ; v. 7)
    Includes bibliographical references and index.
    ISBN 13 978-981-270-016-2 -- ISBN 10 981-270-016-1
        1. Federal government--China. 2. State-local relations--China. 3. Decentralization
in government--China. 4. China--Politics and government--2002–   I. Title.
II. Series.

JQ1506.S8 Z54 2006
320.451--dc22

                                                        2006050096

British Library Cataloguing-in-Publication Data
A catalogue record for this book is available from the British Library.

Typeset by Stallion Press
Email: enquiries@stallionpress.com

Contents

Preface

China's central-local relations have interested me for years. In the 1980s, China's reformist leadership implemented radical decentralization. While promoting economic development, it also generated enormous problems. In the late 1980s, encouraged by the then liberal environment associated with the political reform initiatives under Deng Xiaoping and Zhao Ziyang, a national debate relating to neo-authoritarianism took place among Chinese intellectuals and government officials. Among other issues, decentralization became a major target of criticism. The proponents of neo-authoritarianism focused on why power should be and how it could be centralized in the hands of the central government. Many argued that the decentralization initiated by Deng's reform since the late 1970s had led to the decline of central power; and as a consequence, the central government had lost its control over the provinces. One major spokesman for neo-authoritarianism, Wu Jiaxiang, then a researcher at the Office of Central Policy Studies under the Central Committee of the Chinese Communist Party (CCP), argued that decentralization had eliminated an eagle with one head (i.e., the central government), but had given birth to a bird with nine heads (i.e., the provincial governments) (Wu, 1989: 31). Others warned that China had become a country of various dukedoms (e.g., Shen & Dai, 1992).

The rise of the 1989 pro-democracy movement and the subsequent crackdown by the government interrupted the debate. The debate on neo-authoritarianism was seen by many conservatives as a platform to justify Zhao Ziyang's efforts to struggle for greater political power. Nevertheless, concerns over the decline of central power never disappeared. The collapse of the former Soviet Union in the early 1990s led Chinese intellectuals to question the long-term viability of the state built by the Communist Party. They were afraid that China would follow in the Soviet Union's footsteps since the decentralization in China was more radical than in the Soviet Union. The fear of a possible collapse of the Chinese nation-state thus led the Chinese government to tighten its control over the provinces by reorganizing its nomenklatura system after the pro-democracy movement. Many intellectuals began to try to justify why China needed a highly centralized central state; no consensus, however, was reached as to what central-local relations China should build.

In 1993, the Princeton-based Modern China Center organized a symposium on central-local relations. China scholars from various parts of the world, as well as many who served under Zhao Ziyang and are now living in exile in the United States and Europe, participated in the conference. The discussions were extremely fruitful, given the fact that both academic researchers and former policy makers or practitioners were involved. Among others, two opposite schools of thoughts emerged, i.e., decentralization versus centralization. Scholars such as Wang Shaoguang and many others presented strong arguments in favor of centralization. Wang concentrated on how economic decentralization had weakened central power. His fear of a possible breakdown of the Chinese nation-state was supported by his comparison between China and other former Communist states, especially former Yugoslavia (Wang, 1994). Wang and others believed that radical decentralization had become a major barrier to the formation of an integrated national market economy. Wang also argued that a highly centralized state was not necessarily totalitarian or authoritarian. Instead, according to Wang, in order to build a strong democratic China, the country had to have a centralized state (Wang, 1992).

Wang and his collaborator, Hu Angang, had then finished the draft of their book on the capacity of the Chinese state. The book was soon published in Hong Kong and China, and was widely read in academic circles and by government officials (Wang & Hu, 1993). In 1994, the central government began to implement a new taxation system, called the tax-division system, in an attempt to recentralize its fiscal power. Though it was uncertain whether there was a direct link between the Wang-Hu report and the government's new fiscal measures, the report undoubtedly justified efforts by the central government to recentralize the country's fiscal power.

On the other hand, scholars such as Zhang Xin and others presented strong arguments in favor of decentralization. They attributed China's rapid economic development to Deng's decentralization strategy and argued that the main obstacle to China's push for more rapid reform was that the country's system was still too highly centralized. To these scholars, deepening the reform meant further decentralizing power. To accelerate economic reform, Zhang argued, China had to establish a system of regional economic autonomy, which would allow local people to have total freedom to choose their own economic systems. Each region should have the right to issue its own currencies; to establish their own development strategies; to implement their own foreign trade policies; and to conduct their relations with other regions. Simply put, each region should serve as an independent "economic state". The central government's role would then be to coordinate economic activities among the regions (Zhang, 1991). In response to Wang Shaoguang's "strong state and strong democracy" argument, Zhang pointed out that a strong democratic state could not be based on a highly centralized state; instead, power had to be decentralized first, and only after each region became developed could a foundation for a democratic state be created. In other words, a democratic state could not be built from above, but from below (Zhang, 1995).

I found myself caught in between the two camps. My initial study in 1993 had shown that decentralization had benefited the country tremendously. Decentralization had given rise to local developmentalism, i.e., development-oriented local states. Local states, motivated by local economic and political interests, became major actors in promoting China's economic development. Compared to the central government, local states played a more important role in China's economic life (Zheng, 1993, 1995). But at the same time, my study also revealed that radical decentralization had resulted in enormous unexpected consequences in central-local relations. Despite its authoritarian nature, China's central-local relations were characterized by *de facto* or behavioral federalism. It was behavioral and *de facto* since it was not institutionalized. This was why a collapse in central-local relations was possible. What the central government should have done was to recognize the critical role of the provinces in China's political system and to institutionalize *de facto* federalism (Zheng, 1993).

Overall, I feel that all these discussions, so far, were quite normative. Both the centralization and decentralization scholars were actually making efforts to answer what kind of central-local relations China should have and, consequently, their studies were policy-oriented. To me, whether the central government should centralize or decentralize power further would depend on how central-local relations have actually worked since the post-Mao reform began. To explore how this central-local relationship worked in post-Mao China has since become the theme of my own studies.

Whether China as a nation-state would collapse was also a major concern among scholars and policymakers in the West in the early 1990s after the breakdown of the Soviet Union. Many scholars believed that China would collapse, just as the Soviet Union had. In practice, no communist country had departed more rapidly from the institutional core of the pre-existing economic order than China. To many, it was rather ironic that China, where the tide of popular political protest first crested in the spring of 1989, had remained united. Great changes associated with reforms had led to the collapse of the Soviet Union and many other former communist nation-states. Why didn't China follow suit?

In examining China's central-local relations, my initial interest had been to look at the impact of radical decentralization on central-local relations. But over the years, my research interest gradually extended to cover the issues relating to why China did not collapse. While many scholars have made efforts to discover the various elements that could cause a collapse in China's central-local relations, I attempt to figure out what has kept the center and the provinces together.

In explaining why the central government was able to govern the provinces, many scholars have placed an emphasis on the formal organizational structure of China's political system, the nomenklatura system of the Chinese Communist Party and other coercive measures adopted. I do not deny the role that these coercive measures played in maintaining China's central-local relations, but I also realize the limits of such measures. In discussing central-local relations, we not only need to look at the relations between the central government and provincial governments; more importantly, we need to look at the relations between the provincial government and lower levels of government, due to the vast size of China's provinces. Big provinces could be as large as medium-sized countries. In terms of population, big provinces such as Shandong, Guangdong, Sichuan and Henan can be easily ranked among the top ten countries in the world. In other words, we can see the nature of the central-local relations by observing how a given province is governed. If we pay careful attention to what happens at the provincial level and below, we can find the limitations of all the coercive measures taken by the central government. This is especially true in the post-Deng era when coercive measures are increasingly unwelcome among Chinese party cadres and government officials. There is thus a need to look for other non-coercive measures in mediating the relations between the center and the provinces. This book identifies rules and norms, both coercive and non-coercive, in regulating the relations between the center and the provinces. It attempts to examine how limited coercive measures by the central government are; what advantages and disadvantages non-coercive measures such as bargaining and reciprocity have in governing central-local relations.

THE RESEARCH

This research takes the approach that anthropologist Clifford Geertz called "thick description" (Geertz, 1973) to interpret the nature of China's central-local relations. Over many years of research on China's central-local relations, I found that no social science approach can replace the "thick description" approach to catch the essence of China's central-local relations and enable us to interpret the meanings embedded in the interactions between the center and the provinces. Many years of conducting personal fieldwork, doing interviews and collecting local information (documents and statistics) have enabled me to create such a "thick description." Briefly speaking, this project has gone through several periods.

Since the mid-1980s, I have paid close attention to the evolution of central-local relations and gathered substantial information at a local level, including local newspapers, journals, interviews with local officials and statistics. From 1981 to 1990, I lived in Beijing and witnessed the changing economic and political landscape in the provinces and Beijing's reactions to these changes. In 1983 and 1987, I conducted fieldwork on China's rural reforms in two poor provinces, Yunnan and Shanxi, respectively. In talking with local officials and peasants, I saw the limits of the reach of central power. I began to make sense of the old Chinese saying, "the sky is high, and the emperor is far away." Although I did not choose these two provinces for my case study in this book, my initial ideas on central-local relations, were formed from these two research trips.

In 1989 during the so-called neo-authoritarian movement, central-local relations became a focal point of intellectual debates in Beijing. I gained many chances to discuss central-local relations with dozens of local officials. Their bottom-up views contrasted with the top-down views from the proponents of neo-authoritarianism. I was a part of this debate and learned that neither a top-down approach nor a bottom-up approach could enable us to have a proper understanding of China's central-local relations. An approach that focused on the interaction between the center and the provinces was needed.

In the summer of 1993, I spent three months in Beijing, Zhejiang, Jiangsu, and Guangxi. In Beijing, I conducted interviews with economic officials and intellectuals at the Development Research Center of the State Council and many other institutions. These interviews were very valuable because, generally, both government officials and intellectuals in Beijing provided a top-down perspective of China's central-local relations and they represented, to some extent, the center's attitude toward local governments. This was especially true in the summer of 1993 when the central government called for the recentralization of economic power in order to exercise greater control over the provinces and to reach a more balanced development among the regions. The intellectual circles provided central officials with various ways that power, especially fiscal power, could be recentralized, and localism, in which local governments no longer kept in line with the central government, managed.

But when I went to two coastal provinces (Zhejiang and Jiangsu) and then to the provinces in Southwest China, I met a very different intellectual climate. Local officials and intellectuals in these places expressed their concerns about the center's recentralization efforts. They felt that, instead of recentralization, further decentralization was necessary for local governments to sustain rapid economic growth. This was especially true in Zhejiang and Jiangsu — two of the richest provinces in China. In Southwest China, government officials and intellectuals also felt the necessity of decentralization. But they showed the same concerns about income disparities between the Southwest and other regions. It seemed to them that some measure of recentralization was needed to enable the center to balance regional development. In Nanning, the capital city of Guangxi province, I was able to gain access to various documents regarding the Economic Coordination Association of Southwest China. These documents, together with many interviews with provincial officials and association staff, provided me with basic information on how the provincial governments in Southwest China, as a coalition, responded to decentralization.

Between late 1997 and early 1998, the central government under Zhu Rongji initiated a campaign against Guangdong localism in an attempt to recentralize power. I believed Guangdong provided us with a new case study to examine central-local relations in the post-Deng era. In 1999, I spent two months in Guangdong, interviewing provincial officials concerning localism and the campaign by the central government. From these interviews and field investigations, I gradually came to realize more clearly the advantages and disadvantages of the Chinese way of dealing with central-local relations. The Zhu Rongji government employed some coercive measures to bring localism under control, but it seemed to me that the reach of central power became very limited due to the fact that the central government had to recentralize power very selectively.

From 2001 to 2003, I led a research project — Singapore-Suzhou Industrial Park: An Assessment, commissioned by Singapore's Ministry of Trade and Industry. The China-Singapore Suzhou Industrial Park (SIP) was launched in February 1994 with great enthusiasm and much fanfare, amidst pledges of strong support from the top leadership of the two countries. The project was supposed to take 10 to 15 years to complete. However, soon after its inception, the project underwent many twists and turns. Problems associated with bureaucratic bickering, commercial wrangling and clashes of personality kept surfacing. Increasingly, the project, instead of becoming a symbol of China-Singapore friendship, threatened to become a major source of a China-Singapore spat. Frustrated by the slow progress and problems, Singapore opted to get out of the driver's seat. In January 2001, almost exactly half-way towards the completion date, the Singapore-led consortium handed over majority-ownership and management of the project to its Chinese partner.

This research project gave me a unique opportunity to understand China's central-local relations. The research team was able to interview all the important decision-makers in both Singapore and China (the central government, the Jiangsu provincial government and the Suzhou city government). The team was also able to go over all the relevant documents and records. Many factors contributed to

Singapore's unsuccessful story in China. But China's complicated relationships between the central government and the Jiangsu provincial government, and between the Jiangsu provincial government and the Suzhou city government, were undoubtedly a major factor.

As my research evolves, so does the revision of the manuscript. In 1995, I submitted my doctoral dissertation (Zheng, 1995). Since then, I have continuously revised the manuscript by refining the main arguments and incorporating new information. Still, I am not able to incorporate the case of the China-Singapore Suzhou Industrial Park. My research team submitted a 500-page report to the Singapore government. Due to its sensitivity, the report is unlikely to be released in the near future. Despite this difficulty, this research experience has greatly enhanced my arguments on China's *de facto* federalism and some of the findings from the SIP project have now been implicitly expressed in various parts of the book.

THE ORGANIZATION

The study is organized into eight chapters. Chapter 1 discusses three major approaches to China's central-local relations including structural, procedural and cultural. It examines the advantages and disadvantages of each approach in explaining China's central-local relations. I believe that with the progress of new scholarship in social sciences, especially new institutionalism, it has become possible to develop a new paradigm to explain China's central-local relations by combining major elements of these three approaches.

Chapter 2 attempts to develop a new institutional explanation of China's central-local relations by integrating the structural, procedural and cultural factors. This chapter first discusses the nature of China's central-local relations — the *de facto* federalism — and delineates the main characteristics of this *de facto* federal structure. It then identifies three main institutional factors — coercion, bargaining and reciprocity — which have been associated with the *de facto* federal structure and explains how each factor works in mediating the relationship between the center and the provinces.

The interactions between the three institutional factors identified, coercion, bargaining and reciprocity, are complicated. While these factors can independently mediate the interaction between the center and the provinces, they are often linked to one another. Through the history of the interaction between the center and the provinces, some coercive elements have transformed themselves into reciprocal elements. Chapter 3 examines how reciprocity has been formed and developed over the course of China's changing central-local relations. Although reciprocity was formed historically, this does not mean that there is a need to go too far back in time. Instead, recent experiences are more important than historical events in the making of reciprocity. This chapter focuses on how Mao Zedong's way of dealing with provincial officials has affected central-local relations in the reform era.

Chapters 4 to 7 discuss how the center and individual provinces have interacted with each other. Chapters 4 and 5 deal with how Jiangsu and Zhejiang responded to inter-governmental decentralization respectively. Jiangsu and Zhejiang, two neighboring provinces, are the richest areas in China. The two provinces have also been regarded as being "loyal" to the central government, because they never challenge central authority. However, their loyalty to central authority does not mean that the provincial government and the governments below it will always follow central policies. Local interests are frequently in conflict with those of the central government. What is important is how the two actors — the center and the provinces — mutually accommodate each other's interests while pursuing a common goal — economic development.

The two provinces had very different sources of economic growth in the early stages of the reform. This situation has continued even until today. What interests me here is how the center and the provinces interacted in pursuing a common goal when the two provinces had different paths of development. When the reform began, the two provinces had very similar industrial structures, but their ownership structures were very different. The collective sector was dominant in Jiangsu, while the private sector was developed rapidly in Zhejiang. Both achieved high economic growth under post-Mao decentralization. Although the two provinces had rather different ownership structures, both were able to cooperate with the center in promoting economic growth. For provincial officials, cooperation with the central government does not necessarily mean that they should not be self-interested. In their policy making, provincial officials could be motivated by local interests, but they would also need to take the center's interests into consideration.

While the Jiangsu and Zhejiang cases described in Chapters 4 and 5 deal with how the provinces responded to decentralization, Chapter 6 presents a different case. It looks at how the central government responded to growing localism in Guangdong. Guangdong has been regarded as having a tendency towards localism. This chapter attempts to "deconstruct" localism in Guangdong. It explores the kind of localism the central government did not want to see develop, and the kind of localism it could accept and even promote. The case shows how the transition from radical inter-governmental decentralization to selective recentralization took place in the province. It shows that while the central government had to apply coercive measures such as the nomenklatura system to initiate such a transition, the role of these coercive measures is limited in soliciting provincial compliance, which led to the emergence of a new type of central-local relationship. Selective recentralization does not mean that the central government wanted to and could eliminate interests-associated localism in Guangdong; instead, it means that the central government not only had to consolidate its power via new means, but also to adjust the boundary to accord with local interests.

Chapter 7 is a case study of the formation of a provincial coalition in Southwest China. It examines how the provinces collectively interact with the central government and explores the nature of local collective action. Individually, the provinces in Southwest China were weak and were not able to bargain with the central government. An inter-provincial coalition was formed in order to maximize local interests; but provincial officials had refrained from using the coalition to impose unilateral demands on the central government. Instead, they were able to take priorities of the central government into account in their decision-making. On the other hand, the central government did not need to satisfy all the demands from the provinces, but it could not be too self-interested. The case also shows that with the evolution of inter-governmental decentralization, provincial governments not only had authority over matters that were local in nature, but also gained the authority to influence decision-making at the central level.

The concluding chapter summarizes the major findings of this study and discusses in what possible direction China's central-local relationship is heading. It shows that China's *de facto* federal structure provided an institutional foundation for rapid local economic growth that in turn empowered local governments. The rise of local power led the central government to adjust the current frame of central-local relations via selective recentralization. While in economic areas such as taxation and finance, institutional innovations have taken place, they have not been in place in the political arena. The central government has employed conventional measures to solicit local compliance. While the central government continues to appeal to coercive measures to deal with the provinces, such measures involve increasingly high costs, and their role has become increasingly limited. Although China is facing insurmountable difficulties for the transition from a *de facto* to a *de jure* federal structure, a new frame associated with *de facto* federalism has emerged in China's central-local relations. In the long run, various reform measures such as selective institutionalization will lay an institutional foundation for China's transition from *de facto* to *de jure* federalism.

Acknowledgements

This research has now lasted almost one decade. During this prolonged process, I have benefited enormously from individuals both inside and outside China; without their help, this project could not have been done as it stands now. But there is no way for me to list them all. I hope that those with whom I have communicated will have a chance to read this book and find in it their contribution to this research.

There are several individuals I must acknowledge, including Lynn While, Gilbert Rozman and Atul Kohli at Princeton; Ezra Vogel at Harvard; Wang Gungwu and John Wong at the East Asian Institute, Singapore; Wu Guoguang at the University of Victoria, Canada; and Kjeld Erik Brodsgaard at the Asian Institute of Copenhagen Business School, Denmark. Without their intellectual and moral support, I would not have been able to sustain my efforts over the years.

Katherine and Nevin were born when this research was started and written up. Now they have entered their teenage years. Their sacrifices have been the source of my courage for this research. This book is dedicated to Katherine and Nevin, and their mother.

List of Figures

List of Tables

1

Approaches to Central-Local Relations in China

During the 1989 pro-democracy movement, the power struggle between Zhao Ziyang, then the General Secretary of the Chinese Communist Party (CCP), and conservative leaders was intensified; consequently, the so-called unified central leadership was no longer viable. Provincial officials who seemed to have lost contact with the central government apparently gained greater autonomy in dealing with local issues since they were not informed by the central leadership of what should be done.

Nonetheless, interestingly, they were not prepared to make independent decisions. Instead, they tried to figure out what the central government's intention was and what was going on inside *Zhongnanhai*. Local officials also turned to their colleagues in other provinces in an attempt to find out what action they should take. Jiang Zemin who was summoned to Beijing to replace Zhao Ziyang recalled that when he was not able to get information from the Central Committee, he turned to Li Ruihuan, then the party secretary in Tianjin, to discuss what they should do.

In telling this story, Jiang was implicitly criticizing Zhao Ziyang, since it had been Zhao's decision during the 1989 student movement that had led to a split in the top leadership and caused local officials to lose their identity towards the central government, i.e., that represented the center. What is of interest in Jiang's story is a serious question: Why did the provinces not take independent action to deal with the central government? At the height of the 1989 movement, all provincial governments did take action quite independently from the central government to bring the student movement in their territories under control. They exercised their authority in managing local affairs. Nevertheless, when they faced their relations with the central government, they did not use this autonomy. What mentality did Chinese provincial officials have when they dealt with the central government? How did such a mentality form? How has this mentality affected central-local relations?

Indeed, one single important puzzle that has preoccupied Western observers since the early Jesuits first began to write about China is: How was it possible for a country of continental dimensions, inhabited by people who speak mutually unintelligible languages and exhibit an amazing array of regional differences, to be organized by a unitary state and governed by one power center (Watson, 1993: 81)? The question has been repeatedly asked among scholars in the West since China began its reform in the late 1970s. *The Economist* (1998: 75) asked, "in a world of almost 200 countries, is it likely that a quarter of humanity (1.3 billion people) will remain citizens of just one nation-state — China?" The issue was raised largely because of China's rapid economic development in the past two decades. An immediate question is whether the established institutions of central-local relations can accommodate such unprecedented drastic economic growth and consequent sociopolitical changes in the human history.

The issue was not raised without sound reasons. In the Soviet Union and Eastern Europe, radical reform not only brought down the communist regimes there, but also resulted in the collapse of nation-states that had been built up for years under the rule of communism. The breakup of the Soviet Union and Czechoslovakia and the civil war in Yugoslavia led scholars to realize that these communist regimes that were once regarded as indestructible were in fact very fragile. Reconstructing these post-communist nation-states has become the most difficult issue confronting political elites there (e.g., *Daedalus*, 1993; Linz & Stepan, 1996).

Will the Chinese nation-state follow the Soviet Empire and collapse? In the aftermath of the crackdown on the 1989 pro-democracy movement and the breakup of the Soviet Empire, not a few observers, both at home and abroad, predicted an imminent Chinese collapse. In their study of the capacity of the Chinese state in the early 1990s, two Chinese scholars, Wang Shaoguang and Hu Angang, claimed that the decline of Beijing's ability to amass revenue was leading the country to follow Yugoslavia's fate, i.e., breakup (1994a, 1994b). According to W. J. F. Jenner, "the state, people and culture known in English as China are in a profound general crisis... The very future of China as a unitary state is in question" (1992: 1). Similarly, Gerald Segal (1994) argued that excessive decentralization in the post-Mao era transformed China from a Middle Kingdom into a muddle state. Jack Goldstone even claimed that "we can expect a terminal crisis within the next 10 to 15 years" (1995: 99).

Why and how could a Chinese collapse happen? Among others, three major views can be easily identified. First, the impending collapse could result from excessive decentralization. For Wang and Hu (1994a, 1994b), this was due to Deng Xiaoping's strategy of decentralization that led to the weakening of the capacity of the central state. Two well-known Chinese economists Shen Liren and Dai Yuanchen (1990) believed that decentralization promoted the formation of independent dukedoms at different administrative levels. According to Segal (1994), decentralization enabled local governments to nullify central authority; Beijing now could only pretend to rule the provinces, while the provinces only pretended to be ruled by Beijing. Indeed, China as a nation-state needs to be redefined.

Second, there is the argument of the contradiction between economy and politics. According to this argument, a Chinese collapse could be a consequence of the Chinese model of reform, i.e., "economic reform without political reform." According to Susan Shirk (1993), who has theorized this model, the very success of

Chinese reform is due to "economic reform without political reform." But for others, it is this model of reform that will contribute to the collapse of the central authorities. According to Goldstone (1995: 41–46), without political reform, the communist regime has shown four major vulnerabilities like those associated with the collapse of earlier Chinese regimes, including the split within the ranks of the Party leadership; the rift between the Party leaders and China's other elites; the decline in the Party's direct control of Chinese society; and discontent among the foot soldiers of the revolution (peasants and workers). Similarly, according to James Miles (1996), China will split apart, as it has repeatedly from the dim beginning of time through the warlord period of the 20th century. The very nature of the authoritarian regime creates a myriad of destructive emotions that will spill over just as they did in some of the former communist countries of Eastern Europe and parts of the former Soviet Union.

Third, there is the cultural or civilizational argument. Lucian Pye, who has developed this theme, argued that China is a civilization pretending to be a nation-state, which if left to take its own course, could fragment into separate political entities (1990: 60). The argument consists of two main points. First of all, while modern nation-states are based on nationalism, the Chinese state is based on culturalism. The Chinese do not have a strong national identity; what they identify with is their culture rather than their nation-state.

Furthermore and related, while modern nation-states are highly organized and institutionalized, China as a civilization lacks institutional coherence. This applies not only to the relations between the center and the provinces, but also to the center of the country and the peripheral regions. At its peripheries, until this century, the west and northwest were dominated by a mosaic of peoples whose cultures were more closely linked to India, Persia and Turkey than to coastal China. Geographically and culturally, the contrasts between Inner Asian China and heartland China are sharper than those between North and South America or Eastern Europe (Nathan & Ross, 1997). Three areas, Tibet, Xinjiang and Inner Mongolia, have demonstrated their "splittist" or independent tendencies for years. Even in the most heavily populated and wealthy areas, the relations between the center and the provinces have not been easy. The issue here is not ethnicity, but central control vs. local autonomy. The struggle between central authorities in Beijing and provincial governments in prosperous places such as Shanghai and Guangdong still continues. It is still uncertain whether "provincial authorities [will] eventually tire of taking orders and giving tax revenues to far-away Beijing" (*The Economist*, 1998: 76).

A coming collapse, however, is not the only image that scholars both at home and abroad have presented to us. There are arguments, based on substantial evidence, that the Chinese state is becoming more integrated, rather than disintegrating. For those who argue for a more integrated China, the impending collapse argument puts too much emphasis on the (negative) economic aspect of central-local relations. There are signs that even with rapid decentralization, the central government has not lost its control over the provinces.[1] The center-province relationship is not a zero-sum game (Li, 1998). The center has been able to bring provincial economic behavior under its control (Huang, 1996). Decentralization is not a matter of who gains and who loses. More importantly, it is about how the two actors, the center and the provinces, interact with each other. Furthermore, the economic (and fiscal) approach is not the only means by which the center controls the provinces. There are many other capacities in which the central government can keep central-local relations on an even keel. Though the central government did not introduce radical changes into central-local relations, it had continuously adjusted its relations with the provinces in order to accommodate rapid changes in the provinces. Consequently, the center has been able to solicit provincial compliance amidst radical decentralization (Huang, 1996).

---

[1] There has been a debate among Chinese scholars over whether the central government has lost control over the provinces, for instance, see Wang Shaoguang and Hu Angang (1994a, 1994b); Wu Guoguang and Zheng Yongnian (1994); Yang Dali (1994); Rao Yu-qing and Xiao Geng (1994); and Yasheng Huang (1996).

There are also arguments against the China-as-a-civilization argument. There have been powerful civilizational or cultural forces supporting the unity of the Chinese nation-state. Though the Chinese people's identity towards the nation-state is rather weak, their strong identity towards the unity of the state is undeniable. For centuries, China as "a great systemic whole" (*da yi tong*) has been one important theme of Chinese political values, in terms of central-local relations, and thus a cultural force behind the unity of the Chinese state (Bockman, 1998).

The Chinese did often show their apathy towards the disunity of their state, as the opening passage of the historical novel, *Romance of the Three Kingdoms* (*Sanguo Yanyi*), states: after a long separation, there is bound to be unity; after a long unity, there is bound to be separation (*fen jiu bi he, he jiu bi fen*), or as Arthur Wright summarized: "While political disintegration was thought of — in terms of various life-cycle analogies — as periodically inevitable, reunification, by the same analogies, was regarded as inevitable" (cited in Bockman, 1998: 328). Nevertheless, under the influence of the mindset of China as a great systemic whole, unity was regarded as normal, and disunity not. As a matter of fact, even though China is still an empire-state, powerful cultural forces make it impossible for China to disintegrate like other empires.

Moreover, realizing that the worldwide failure of the communist ideology and the associated legitimacy crisis are undermining the capacity of the government to rule the country, the Chinese government has "eagerly embraced Chinese nationalism as a new fount of legitimacy" (Huang, 1995b: 57). Various studies have shown that the Chinese government has initiated waves of nationalistic education movements aimed at cultivating or reinforcing the Chinese national identity (Zheng, 1999; Clausen, 1998; Dong, 1997). These deliberate efforts by the government indeed have brought about a new national identity among the political elites and the general public. Implicit in this argument is that so long as the government is consciously making efforts to foster national identity, localism or regionalism will not become excessive and impose a major threat to China as a nation-state.

How can these conflicting images of central-local relations be reconciled? In effect, both are supported by substantial evidence and can be regarded as two different interpretations of changes in central-local relations in the reform era. Certainly, it is changes in central-local relations, which are themselves often contradictory with one another, that have led observers to reach conflicting conclusions. Efforts have to be made to reinterpret central-local relations to reconcile these images. Changes are contradictory, but forces that have led to these changes have coexisted for years. We need to identify what these forces are and how they have affected and will affect central-local relations in China.

This brings us to a methodological issue. Different images of central-local relations were largely reflections of changes in the scholarship of Chinese studies over the past few decades. In general, three main approaches have been widely used by scholars of central-local relations: structural, procedural and cultural.[2] This chapter discusses these approaches and provides a critique on each of them. The next chapter attempts to develop a new institutional perspective to explain China's central-local relations.

THE STRUCTURAL APPROACH

The structural approach has dominated the study of China's central-local relations for several decades. Its emphasis is on the formal organizational (or structural) distribution of resources and authority between the center and the provinces. According to this approach, it is the formal institutional arrangements between the center and the provinces, which determine how the center and the provinces interact with each other. Within this approach, three sub-models can be identified, namely, the totalitarian model, the cellular model and the pluralist model. What model one takes to study China's central-local relations depends on which actor, the center or the provinces, is the analytical focus. A brief discussion of each of these models follows.

---

[2] For a discussion of this classification, see Lieberthal (1992) and Chung (1995).

The Totalitarian Model

Initially developed to analyze the overthrow of the old order and the rapid consolidation thereafter of the new communist regime, the theory of totalitarianism gave explanatory primacy to the Chinese state and ideology. The Chinese state included the Chinese Communist Party, the government, the People's Liberation Army and other organizations, which mobilized the populace. This system, modeled after the Soviet Union and Eastern Europe, was described as totalitarian and highly coercive.[3] In terms of central-local relations, the proponents of this model did not believe that the provinces possessed any real autonomy in such a highly-centralized system. The provinces carried out central policies to the letter. Decentralization did happen, but only took place when the center wanted it to. Power thus could easily be recentralized if the need arose (Barnett, 1967).

Furthermore, the center not only monopolized all aspects of political power, but also exercised direct control over the Chinese economy. The state owned and managed the major means of production. Private property was strictly limited and the allocation of strategically significant resources occurred through state command, rather than the marketplace. The state sought to regulate the economy through five-year and annual plans, rather than through monetary and fiscal instruments of control. Prices of key commodities were bureaucratically administered, rather than set in the market.

Various studies showed how the Chinese state sought to manage economic growth through non-market mechanisms. Dwight Perkins (1966) emphasized state control of the market. Other authors (Lardy, 1983; Parish & White, 1978) examined how the Chinese state controlled the rural economy. Though these studies differ in their assessments of the effectiveness of bureaucratic allocation, they shared a common assumption that the Chinese state was hostile to the allocative role of the market. China was pictured as effectively

---

[3] Classic studies on totalitarianism include Friedrich (1954); Friedrich and Brzezinski (1956); Ulam (1963); and Schapiro (1967). On China, major works include Barnett (1967); Lewis (1963); and Perkins (1966).

organized and led. The top political leaders had sufficient power to extract compliance from lower levels on almost any issue at any time. This perspective focused on the top leaders and the bureaucratic apparatus at their command. Leaders like Mao Zedong and Deng Xiaoping were able to obtain the desired response from officials through the vast Chinese party and government apparatuses.[4]

Within this framework, there existed a modified centralist vision of central-local relations (Schurmann, 1968; Lardy, 1975). According to this view, though China's political power was highly centralized, there was a balance between political initiatives at the center and those that originated from the provinces. General policies were formulated at the center, but the provinces were allowed flexibility in their implementation. Nevertheless, the center could either decentralize or recentralize according to its own perceptions of the need to adjust central-local relations.

Two important aspects can be summarized. First of all, the analytical focus of the totalitarian model is on the central level such as the party, the government and its bureaucracies. Second, the provincial (local) government is merely the agent of central control in Beijing (Barnett, 1967). Since the center serves the central nervous system in China's political hierarchy, it is able to bring the provinces under control. On the other hand, as agents of the central government, the provincial governments do not enjoy territorial autonomy, but only have "operational autonomy." According to Franz Schurmann, "Regional government has a unique importance in Communist China... Though there have been few separatist tendencies in China, most of the provinces have a distinctive character, the product of long historical development... There are thus historical reasons for the operational autonomy of provincial government in Communist China" (1968: 174–175).

The totalitarian model, according to Walder (1986), places too much emphasis on the role of coercion, impersonal ideology and social atomization. Even before the post-Mao reform, the central

---

[4] Roderich MacFarquhar presents a sophisticated example of this image (see MacFarquhar, 1974, 1983).

government did not always use coercion to govern all localities. Great diversities among different regions posed a serious obstacle to state control and often disabled the center from soliciting provincial compliance. Even if the center did not always consult with the provinces in the formation of national policies, it would have been extremely difficult for the center to implement its policies without provincial cooperation.

Furthermore, the totalitarian model sees local governments as mere instruments of policy implementation, thus overstating their administrative functions and neglecting their political functions. Economic decentralization in the post-Mao era has introduced great changes into local-central relations. The central state is no longer able to control every aspect of Chinese society and local governments as well. In terms of policy formation and implementation, the state tends to resemble "fragmented authoritarianism" (Lieberthal & Oksenberg, 1992) or "consultative authoritarianism" (Harding, 1986). The local-central relationship thus needs to be redefined.

Also, although the totalitarian model sheds light on the role of the Chinese state in the evolution of the Chinese political economy, it neglects the role of the state in economic transition, more specifically, in the development of the market mechanism in the post-Mao era. The model is not able to explain new developments in the Chinese political economy. As Victor Nee (1989) points out, the argument that the Chinese state was hostile to the allocative role of the market needs to be reconsidered. According to Nee (1989), before the current market reforms, there was little reason to question this view. Nevertheless, this assumption continues to color the discussion of the Chinese state, even after the post-Mao reformers launched their program of economic reforms, and consequently, "the analysis of state interventions to encourage market arrangements has been overlooked by analysts through force of habit: we have grown accustomed to thinking about the socialist state as inherently hostile to markets" (Nee, 1989: 170).

More importantly, the totalitarian model has overlooked the institutional basis of local dynamics in China's development. Most advocates did not realize that local governments have their institutional instruments to serve local interests and thus to change the power distribution between the center and the provinces.

It is also worth noting that the defects of the totalitarian model are also due to the fact that China was not open to outside researchers for a long period after the establishment of the People's Republic in 1949. To do research on China, scholars had to rely heavily either on interviews with former lower-level government officials, especially those who fled to Hong Kong, or extensive readings of the Chinese press, especially officially released documents. Therefore, it was almost impossible for outside scholars to develop a deeper understanding of central-local relations. Instead, they had to take it for granted that what happened to the Soviet Union would necessarily happen to China. In some sense, the totalitarian model was not developed out of the Chinese experience, but was imposed onto China from outside. Consequently, a distorted image of central-local relations became inevitable.

The Pluralist Model

While the totalitarian model focuses on the central government, the pluralist model sees the provincial (local) governments as its analytical unit. The formation of the pluralist model was heavily influenced by various theories of interest groups. Many studies of communist political systems argued that, as political terror and mass mobilization subsided, there was an accompanying revival of genuine political competition within the framework of political control. Thus, "real" political activities are based on groups that share common interests, and these groups act through formal or informal political institutions.[5]

As reflected in the study of China's central-local relations, the group theory puts much emphasis on the importance of local government. David Goodman argued that provincial party first

---

[5] For original group theories on the communist countries, see Skilling (1966, 1983); Skilling and Griffiths (1971). On Chinese politics, see Goodman (1984, 1986) and Falkenheim (1987).

secretaries played an important role in the decision-making process. According to him, "the importance of the provincial party first secretary undoubtedly stems from his position as the key link in the spatial hierarchy between policy formulation and policy implementation... The identification of the provincial party first secretary as a 'political middleman' thus highlights not only the spatial dimensions of decision-making in the PRC, but also the possible group dynamics of that process" (1984: 76). To Goodman (1984), provincial territory or space is of more than passing significance to decision-makers in China.

The simple fact that China is such a huge country requires that provincial government, as a middleman, plays an essential part in policy-making process. National policy-making in China is almost always an incremental process. Guidelines are generally drafted and policy then implemented on an experimental basis. Central directives frequently specify only the general aims of a policy and leave the specific arrangements to each province. Furthermore, the choice of "experimental points" is crucial to the emergence of policy. The period and mechanisms of experimentation provide an access to influence in not only the implementation, but also the formulation of national policy. Political power is thus not an undifferentiated commodity. The central government is tolerant toward provincial variations in the implementation of national policy. The principle of "do the best according to local conditions" means that the central government lays down the broad outlines of a policy, while the provinces adopt specific provincial measures for its implementation. This process allows considerable potential for deviation from central policy. A province might claim to be adapting a central policy to local conditions when, in fact, its provincial implementation is intended to achieve some other goals. In other words, the power of the provincial government comes from the very fact that, due to great diversities among different provinces, the central government is not able to make a decision applicable to all regions. Provincial government, therefore, has an important, even a crucial, say, both in the formation and the implementation of national policies.

Several authors have pointed out the shortcomings of the pluralist perspective on Chinese politics. According to Shue, who has also questioned seriously the totalitarian model, the pluralist model does not tell us about politics and the power of the state vis-à-vis society. The model "quite missed the point in a realm of other issues where the underlying understanding of politics is not a problem of allocation but a problem of control, or rule, of us against them" (1988: 19). The pluralist model simply cannot be applied to China's development in the post-Mao era. Instead, "the Chinese party/state must be seen as a modernizing dictatorship, seizing resources from some segments of society to serve its planned goals of economic development and social transformation... As a self-described dictatorship it has necessarily sought domination over certain elements in society" (1988: 19).

According to the pluralist model, the provincial government can be a protector of provincial interests by negotiating with the central government on provincial affairs. They are also creators of provincial interests, however. This means that they are not only agents of policy implementation of the central government, but more importantly, they also frequently initiate policies that are often not in line with the central government's priorities. In other words, they are actors with their own interests and passions. Therefore, taking the provincial government as the analytical unit helps us to understand the dynamism of changes in central-local relations in post-Mao China.

The pluralist model, however, overlooks the impact of the central government on the local government. The local government does have autonomy in its decision-making, but its decision-making process is constrained by given institutional conditions. Provincial governments formally exist within the structure of the state. They pursue their own interests, but their behavior is constrained by this structure. The role of the central government is to provide institutional settings in which the local government behaves. These institutional conditions are an important power resource for the center because it can change the behavior of the provincial government by changing institutional backgrounds.

Moreover, on the provincial government's side, it also has its own power resources to initiate policy within its jurisdiction and influence the formation and implementation of policies of the central government. So, what is important is not to see which is more powerful, the center or the local government, but to examine their respective power resources and policy constraints, and the interplay between the two within the Chinese political-economic system.

The Cellular Model

The cellular model has been provided by a group of scholars writing about decentralization, with its emphasis on the problematic interaction between the center and the provinces. According to this perspective, the center and the provinces do not interact in accordance with a formal organizational formula. Though the center possesses institutional advantages, it is not always able to get its policies implemented. The local government is not only the leader of the province, but also its acknowledged representative to the center and in discussions with other provinces. Though much emphasis was put on the role of coerciveness and the impersonal ideology of the Chinese state, many authors do not think that provincial governments are merely agents of the central government. Therefore, at the operational level, there is a balance between the center and the provinces, and decentralization was an inevitable process.

Audrey Donnithorne, one main advocator of the cellular model, argued that "China is not a monolithic society, but a cellular one" (1967: 506) and the center cannot always solicit compliance from the province. There are always loopholes left, and there are plenty of examples of the free way in which law is interpreted, or ignored, according to local requirements. According to Donnithorne (1967: 506–507),

> The real limit on the expansion of central revenues lies in the relations between the center and the major local authorities. The center depends on the cooperation of these authorities in many different ways and only in an extreme situation can it afford openly to use crude force — i.e., its control over the armed forces — to secure increased levies of revenue or

commodities. The tension between the center and provinces in respect to transfers in cash and kind must be seen in the context of their mutual dependence.

Donnithorne (1967) here primarily refers to China's economic system. But later, Vivienne Shue (1988) formed a more systemic expression of the cellular model and extended it to the political system. She focused on the spatial aspect of the Chinese political economy and suggested that we should pay attention to the importance of the non-market economy in shaping a pattern of local-central relations. Her analysis proposed "less direct and unmediated central penetration ... than is frequently supposed" (1988: 54). Rather than dividing the populace into new, irreconcilable political factions, Mao's anti-capitalist policies buttressed "cell-like communities" and a "sub-culture of localism" that had predated the revolution by centuries. Shue (1988) uses the term "honeycomb polity" to describe the character of Chinese politics caused by the tension between center and periphery. The "honeycomb polity" refers to the segmented, parochial structure of politics that was prevalent in China over the centuries. According to Shue, although the Chinese government was highly centralized and was of a coercive nature, "the Chinese party/state,... a self-described dictatorship..., has provoked resistance; sometimes outright resistance, sometimes indirect or evasive resistance, and sometimes only privately internalized resistance, or alienation" (1988: 19).

Under the cellular model, the provincial government tends to be an extremely important factor in the Chinese economy. Localities act like entrepreneurs: developing local industries, providing coordination, and finding customers. As a result, central ministries and planning organs lose major sinews of financial and material allocation powers; important centrally-managed industries find themselves in competition with localities for needed materials; local investment soars; and protectionism hampers the movement of goods between localities (Donnithorne, 1972). According to this image, policies made in Beijing bear little resemblance to reality at lower levels. There is a great concentration of power in the hands of provincial-level officials and leaders of lower-level units. China is thus a cellular economy and polity, with the territorial components of the system surprisingly self-sufficient and capable of frustrating and subverting Beijing's demands.

Within this school, some scholars even go further to argue that the Chinese system is highly decentralized (Whitney, 1970). The center is nothing more than an amalgam of local representatives in competition, or an arbiter of competing local interests. As a result, decentralization is a natural state that the center cannot control.

Differing from both the totalitarian and pluralist models, the cellular model has enabled us to see enormous practical conflicts between the center and the provinces during the process of their interaction. Nonetheless, the model is not without criticism. Many observers reject the cellular model and maintain that China has actually had an integrated national economy. Earlier on, Nicholas Lardy (1975) concluded that economic growth after the decentralization during the 1957–1958 period was not characterized by a strong pattern of regional self-sufficiency. According to William Snead (1975: 305), Donnithorne's explanation is very questionable, and "her conclusion that China was moving towards a cellular economy... is incorrect." Similarly, for Alan Liu (1975: 174–177), national integration could be seen in the penetration of a single governmental and party system into every region and in the establishment of a nationwide communication infrastructure.

The debate between Donnithorne, Lardy and others was mostly due to changes in local-central relations over time. Donnithorne (1967) raised the conception of cellularity to characterize what she saw as the relative fragmentation of the Chinese economy in the wake of the Cultural Revolution's attacks on central and local party/state bureaucracies. But Lardy (1975), after carefully observing the organization and management of the economy before the Cultural Revolution, found little evidence of entrenched cellularity in the 1950s, and emphasized the relatively high degree of centralized state control over planning and finance in that era. Even for individual scholars, their perceptions of central-local relations change from time to time. For example, before the Cultural Revolution,

Schurmann (1966) strongly argued for the role of organization and ideology in governing the country. But after Mao Zedong began to attack the Party during the Cultural Revolution, Schurmann (1968) revised his earlier judgment and found the continued vitality of Chinese traditions and social organizations beneath the formal organizational facade. All these scholarly exchanges happened decades ago, but they suggested to us the importance of the dynamic aspect of local-central relations in China.

Recent Development of the Structural Approach

Even with drastic changes in the reform era, the structural approach still dominates the study of central-local relations. As in the past, how the center and the provinces interact depends on what perspective the individual scholar takes. Though scholars now do not use old terms such as totalitarianism or pluralism, the study of central-local relations, generally speaking, is still characterized by the dichotomy of the top-down approach and the bottom-up approach. While the bottom-up approach stresses how rapid development at local levels has enabled local governments to nullify central policies or not to take orders from central authorities, the top-down approach highlights how the central government has utilized its organizational advantages to bring the provinces under its control.

Given the fact that China's post-Mao development has been characterized by decentralization, scholars have overwhelmingly concentrated on decentralization and its impact on central-local relations.[6] A common argument is that after a decade of decentralization, the central government's economic capacity has declined, while that of localities has increased. Great local power has frustrated many of the goals of the reform movement by protecting inefficient industries, feeding high rates of investment and inflation, depriving

---

[6] The literature of the impact of decentralization on central-local relations continues to grow. An incomplete list would include the following: Li (1998); Wong (1997); Yang (1997); Breslin (1996); Jia and Lin (1994); Wang and Hu (1994); Goodman and Segal (1994); Agarwala (1992); White (1989); Perry and Wong (1985).

the center of funds and raw materials for high priority projects, etc. (Shirk, 1985). So, decentralization, rather than promoting reform, limits its progress (Naughton, 1987; Bachman, 1987). Consequently, "to save decentralization, the reform coalition must first recentralize" (Kelliher, 1986: 480).

A structural analysis of the impact of decentralization has often led scholars to conclude that an impending collapse of central-local relations is possible and recentralization becomes imperative in order to maintain China as a nation-state. Take the study of Wang Shaoguang and Hu Angang (1994a, 1994b) as an example. According to Wang and Hu (1994a, 1994b), radical economic decentralization in the Deng era has resulted in a major power shift between the center and the provinces. The decline of the central government's share of national income has had serious consequences for China's "state capacity" (central power). With "extractive capacity" falling, other capacities of the state would inevitably fall too: the capacity to steer the use of resources; the capacity to legitimate itself in the eyes of the people; and the capacity to force obedience. Wang and Hu argued that the breakup of Yugoslavia could not be blamed on ethnic hatred, but rather on the fiscal weakness of the central state. With central power seriously weakened, a mere push was enough to bring the whole regime crashing down into a heap of rubble. This could happen to China due to excessive decentralization. "If the center is weakened to the point where it cannot control the advancing power of the regions, there is no avoiding civil wars" (1994b: 13–14). Recentralization thus should be given the highest priority to maintain the unity of the country.

In contrast, other scholars take a top-down approach (Huang, 1996; Naughton, 1995; Shirk, 1993). Even though these scholars acknowledged the impact of decentralization on central-local relations, they argued that the central government has been able to solicit provincial compliance by using various economic and political means. According to this approach, since the center and the provinces coexist in the same political hierarchy, the center has enormous organizational capacities to influence the provinces. For instance, Yasheng Huang (1996) still regards provincial government officials as agents of the center with only limited operational autonomy. According to Huang (1996), under China's highly centralized political system, the central state is equipped to bring local officials into line through a variety of bureaucratic carrots or sticks such as the nomenklatura (personnel) system, various monitoring means and administrative control. So long as the central government possesses various organizational advantages, it is able to achieve successful control of local authorities, while retaining the incentives and dynamism of rapid local development through decentralization.

Central to the structural approach is the assumption that the interaction between the center and the provinces is institutionally dictated. The approach enables us to examine the formal institutional aspects of China's central-local relations. Since its emphasis is on the distribution or arrangement of the power between central and local governments, it tends to focus overwhelmingly on how various economic factors affect central-local relations. Certainly, according to the formal organizational charts, the center without doubt occupies a dominant position and the provinces have to subordinate themselves to the center. Therefore, the proponents of authoritarianism or centralization prefer to look at how the center has utilized its economic and political power to solicit compliance from the provinces. By contrast, the proponents of decentralization tend to focus on how decentralization has resulted in a major power shift between the center and the provinces, and how the provinces are utilizing growing economic power to nullify central policies and defend their own interests.

Undoubtedly, most studies within the structural approach on central-local relations of post-Mao China are concerned with fiscal and planning arrangements.[7] Nonetheless, changes of central-local relations are not solely economically determined. As one scholar pointed out, "budgetary figures are an imperfect indicator at best of the relative powers of central and local governments and therefore, attention needs to be more diversified to personal, information

---

[7] For a survey of the literature on central-local economic relations, see Chung (1995: 491–492).

control and implementation issues" (Chung, 1995: 491). In effect, simply identifying how various forms of source are distributed between the center and the provinces prevents us from seeing how the center and the provinces have interacted. A more dynamic approach is needed to reflect the nature of China's central-local relations in the reform era.

THE PROCEDURAL APPROACH

While the structural approach examines the formal structure of the Chinese system, the procedural approach focuses on how the system works at the behavioral level. It is only until recently that enormous efforts were made to examine the inner dynamics of the Chinese system. The development of this approach is attributable to several major factors.

First, the reform that began at the end of the 1970s resulted in drastic socioeconomic changes in China. Certainly, it is important to see how these changes have occurred. To do so, scholars cannot simply look at formal organizations and institutions. From an organizational point of view, the Chinese political structure almost remains intact. But it is certain that the political system behaves differently now than it did in the past. Organizational changes have lagged behind behavioral changes. There is a need to understand the behavior of the Chinese political system.

Second, the open-door policy has created tremendous opportunities for unprecedented scholarly access to government agencies in China. Except for organizations relating to national security and national defense, the Chinese system has been opened gradually to outsiders. This is especially true in various economic areas. Given the fact that foreign investment has played an important role in pushing China's economic development, the Chinese leadership has had to allow outsiders access to not only general economic formation, but also to how Chinese bureaucrats make economic decisions at different levels. Nowadays, outsiders can interview pertinent Chinese officials, staff in the country's enterprises and foreign businessmen in China. Moreover, the decision by the Chinese government to allow international organizations such as the World Bank to play a role in the country's economic decision-making has provided outsiders with a legitimate way to access inside-bureaucratic information (Jacobson & Oksenberg, 1990). All these changes have removed, to a great degree, the limitations of the documentary sources and émigré interviews, which scholars had relied on in the pre-reform period and enabled us to understand China from within.

Third, the development of the procedural approach is also due to scholarly developments in social sciences. Recent decades have witnessed a growing literature of organizational and decision-making theories (for instance, Allison, 1971; Grindle, 1980; March & Olson, 1989), from which the procedural approach to China is heavily drawn. This still-growing intellectual enterprise has shown why in all organizations and polities, there is a disjuncture among leadership intention, organizational behavior and the actual results of action; and how such a disjuncture forms. In the 1970s and early 1980s, scholars made great efforts to understand the difficulty in assuring congruence between policy intent and actual outcomes. Summarily, these factors included: the scope of affected interests; the character-istics of implementing agencies; the level of available resources and elite attention; the clarity and complexity of policy; the time span over which policy must be implemented; incentives for compliance; capacity to monitor policy implementation; and the relationship of implementors to clients.[8]

These newly-developed theories have enabled scholars to develop a procedural approach to the Chinese politics (for instance, Lampton, 1987; Lieberthal & Oksenberg, 1988; Lampton & Lieberthal, 1992; Shirk, 1993). The procedural approach has had a profound impact on the study of central-local relations in China. As discussed above, with the structural approach, scholars look at Chinese politics either from the "top down" or from the "bottom up." But with a procedural approach, scholars want "both strictly 'top down' and 'bottom up' views of Chinese politics" (Lieberthal,

---

[8] See Pressman and Wildavsky (1973); Bardach (1979); Leichter (1979); Nakamura and Smallwood (1980); Ripley and Franklin (1982); and Williams (1982).

1992: 12). The structural approach tends to identify the strengths and weaknesses of the center and the provinces in terms of the formal distribution of power. According to Lieberthal, a major advocate of the procedural approach, the structural approach provides "at best an inexact guide to the real operations" of the Chinese political system, and the focus of much scholarly analysis should be "the actual policy process that characterizes decision-making and implementation." In other words, scholars have to pay attention to "the effects of the interactive processes among the constituent elements of the Chinese polity" (Lieberthal, 1992: 12).

The procedural approach enabled Lieberthal and others to have a modified assessment of China's central-local relations, i.e., "fragmented authoritarianism", an assessment different from those by scholars of the structural approach. On the one hand, China's political system is not as coherent as many (e.g., Huang, 1996) have argued; instead, it is quite fragmented. According to Lieberthal, "authority below the very peak of the Chinese political system is fragmented and disjointed" (1992: 8). This is due to several factors (Lieberthal, 1992: 7–9). First of all, the post-Mao reform has resulted in a major structural change in the distribution of basic decision-making in the country's economic arenas: a significant devolution of economic authority, with the party and government officials at lower levels greatly increasing their influence over economic decision-making. Second and related, the coexistence of the functional and vertical division of authority has produced a situation in which no single body has authority over the others. Third, the reform has led to many procedural changes, such as reducing the role of ideology as an instrument of central control, decentralizing personnel management, and encouraging different policy proposals. These changes, originally designed to produce more effective information and incentive systems, had contributed to the fragmentation of authority.

On the other hand, the fragmentation model does not mean that the Chinese leaders at the top of the system are helpless. While many (e.g., Wang & Hu, 1994) warned that decentralization could lead to a collapse of the political system, the fragmentation model concluded that the system still retained some important elements of coherence. As Lieberthal (1992: 10) summarized,

> The fragmented authoritarianism model thus did not present the Center as helpless, the bureaucracies as unable to cooperate, or the localities as all-powerful. But it did seek to identify the causes of fragmentation of authority among various bureaucratic units, the types of resources and strategies that provide leverage in the bargaining that evidently characterizes much decision-making, and the incentives of key individuals in various units, in order to gain a better grasp on the ways in which bureaucratic structure and process affect Chinese policy formulation, decision-making, and policy implementation.

The procedural approach regards central-local relations as the function of discrete strategic interactions between the center and the provinces to achieve consensus. By looking at the inner dynamics of central-local relations, the approach enables us to see how central-local conflicts are produced and how they are resolved. Therefore, the approach has not only provided a new way of understanding China's central-local relations, it has also opened a new area of the field.

Nevertheless, the approach also suffers from some limitations. First of all, the model is drawn from three groups of literature, the rationality model, the power politics model, and the cellular model (Lieberthal & Oksenberg, 1988: 11–16; Lieberthal, 1992: 10–11). Central to this model is that central-local relations are about politics in which rational actors (the center and the provinces) interact to maximize their own interests and power. Since all actors are self-interested, conflicts become inevitable among them and fragmentation is a natural result of the interaction between the two actors. Without doubt, the emphasis of the procedural model is the conflicts between the center and the provinces, albeit in a modified version. As we will see later, both the center and the provinces are not only motivated by self-interest, but are also culturally motivated. Without taking cultural or ideational factors into account, the model is still very weak in explaining the nature of China's central-local relations.

Second, in explaining Chinese politics in general, and central-local relations in particular, scholars of the procedural approach have focused on particular sets of policy issues or bureaucratic clusters. This, of course, enables us to see the very inner dynamics of the operation of the Chinese political system. The approach *per se*, however, often generated some "fragmented" pictures of central-local relations. I argue that central-local relations are not only about power politics; more importantly, they are about the structure of governance in which the center and the provinces interact. In order to see the nature of central-local relations, both the center and the provinces need to be taken as a whole. We have to look at not only how the center governs the provinces, but also how the provincial governments govern their territories.

Third, most studies of this approach have predominantly focused on central-local resource relations. Scholars have identified the resources that the center and the provinces own and how these resources affect the interaction between the two actors. However, the model has failed to show why the two actors utilized their resources in the way they actually did. In other words, the model does not answer the question: What is the ideational rationality behind a particular pattern of the interaction between the center and the provinces?

THE CULTURAL APPROACH

The cultural approach is heavily influenced by various theories of modernization developed in the 1950s and 1960s. According to the modernization paradigm and its branch theory of national integration (relevant to central-local relations), cultural transformation or value change is the key to a given country's political development. It assumes that successful national integration, which is symbolized by effective governance over localities by central authorities, is dependent on successful value transformation on the part of the locality, since parochial and primordial values, such as localism and regionalism, prevent the cultivation of loyalty for the nation as a whole (Binder *et al.*, 1971).

The cultural approach to politics in the PRC is as old as the structural approach. When scholars of totalitarianism (both centralists and decentralists) argued that the structure determined the behavioral pattern of the Chinese politics, Lucian Pye (1968, 1981, 1988) and others (e.g., Solomon, 1971) proposed a cultural approach to Chinese politics. According to authors of totalitarianism, the Chinese leaders established its governance system according to the Soviet Union system. By contrast, Pye (1968) and Solomon (1971) argued that the Chinese communist system was unmistakably Chinese. According to this perspective, an understanding of Chinese culture is crucial for scholars to have a proper understanding of the behavior of the political system in the PRC, since culture can explain the nature of political alliances; expectations of political behavior; attitudes towards authority relations; and even the fundamental strength of political organizations.

The cultural approach has had a major impact on the understanding of China's central-local relations. According to Pye (1968) and Solomon (1971), the organizational apparatus that so impressed scholars of totalitarianism was indeed vulnerable to rapid breakdown, and localism or regionalism could be inevitable. This is the case because of two major cultural factors.

First, even though the Chinese communists established a totalitarian political system, its operation was largely in accordance with Chinese cultural practices such as patron-client relations and patrimonialism, rather than formal institutional rules. Subordinates placed excessive faith in the capacity of their patrons. Nevertheless, when their hopes were dashed, anger came to the fore.

Second and more importantly, as mentioned at the beginning of this chapter, the Chinese do not have a strong national identity and the nation-state is, therefore, not as well-organized as nation-states in Europe are. Under the strong influence of culturalism, central sovereignty over the provinces becomes symbolic. According to Pye (1990: 59–60),

> Although government in the People's Republic involves more concerted policy efforts, it is one of the great illusions of the day that Chinese authorities are as omnipotent as they pretend to be. In a host of fields, from tax collecting to controlling economic activities in Guangdong, Fujian and other dynamic provinces, central authorities know that feigned

compliance still reigns and that it is best not to attempt the impossibility by demanding precise obedience. Sovereignty, after all, calls for theatrical representation.

The cultural approach has been used to deal with issues of national integration in China (Solinger, 1977; Goodman, 1986). Interest in this approach seems to have grown rapidly recently (e.g., Dittmer & Kim, 1993; Friedman, 1994, 1995). Scholars have begun to examine the pluralistic nature of the Chinese political culture and its impact on national integration (e.g., Friedman, 1995; Yang *et al.*, 1994; White & Li, 1993; Goodman, 1992; Waldron, 1990). White and Li (1993) argued that the post-Mao reform has reinforced the multiplicity of Chinese cultural identities, especially in coastal areas. According to them, national identity in coastal areas becomes situational, since it is not the only identity option open to coastal Chinese. In other words, the Chinese nation-state is not the only, or even the most important, experienced reality in their psycho-cultural consciousness and historical time. State-centered political identity is less salient in Guangdong with the rise of a more assertive commercial civil society. Consequently, the concept of one China seems like a myth that papers over economic, political, and identity disparities, and tensions between coastal and inland China. The center can hardly exercise its rule over the localities, but go back to a more traditional form of governance, i.e., doing less and less is really achieving more and more.

Edward Friedman (1994) goes even further to raise the prospect of China being divided into a northern and a southern part as a result of the modernization processes. According to Friedman, the North can be uniformly regarded as Leninist and be subject to procrastination, while the South is dynamic and modern. He seems to suggest that the theory of the Yellow River region as the cradle of Chinese civilization is a Communist construction, and that the ancient near-coastal cultures of Wu and Yue belonged to the ancient inland Chu culture (1994: 85). Friedman (1994) concluded that given the importance of the south in the construction of a modern Chinese identity, southern culture would be the main constituent part in a new Chinese national identity, instead of the existing Leninist ideology.

Nevertheless, at the subjective level, we can find substantial evidence against the above-discussed disintegration argument. For example, as mentioned earlier, one major theme of Chinese political culture (in terms of national integration) is "a great systemic whole," a political value that has survived from the *Chunqiu* (Spring and Autumn) period, through various dynasties, to the Communist regime. Though the rise of regional forces often led to the break-down of the Chinese Empire, the aim of all local power pretenders was always to restore the imperial order, a political value that was embedded in the popular saying "striving to gain the political order of the Central realm" (*zhulu zhongyuan*). This is also true of the Chinese warlords in the 1920s and 1930s. As one commentator pointed out, "one sign of the strong tradition of centralization is the way in which the warlords asserted provincial sovereignty... The warlords fought each other in order to unify the country; the territo-rial divisions came about only because they disagreed over who should do the unifying" (Huang, 1995b: 58–59). Such historical developments enabled Bockman to conclude that "within this con-ceptual framework (i.e., China as a great systemic whole), there has been no room for a notion of developing different nation-states within the Chinese cultural realm" (1998: 312).

This political value is still relevant in China today. When compared to national states in Europe, China still looks like an old empire. Nonetheless, powerful cultural forces make it impossible for China to disintegrate like other empires. According to Harald Bockman, the Chinese Empire differs from the Romanov/Soviet Empire, arguing:

> Those who extended their analysis to the Chinese scene after the breakup of the Soviet Union did so primarily from a "Communist systems" approach. They tended to forget that the Chinese Communist also inherited — as a deliberate policy — the geographical configuration of the former empire... the Chinese imperial tradition is infinitely more entrenched and durable than the brief Romanov empire (1998: 310).

Other authors have argued that there has been a transformation from cultural identity to national identity (Levenson, 1964; Schwartz, 1964; Whitney, 1970). According to this argument, the modern Chinese national identity that came to the Chinese around the turn of the

20th century is radically different from earlier forms of Chinese identity. The high culture and ideology of pre-modern China were principally forms of cultural consciousness — an identification with the moral goals and values of a universalizing civilization. Without regard to national boundaries, Confucianism was said to represent a universal ethic; highlighting a "civilized" way of life accessible to any population through education, virtue and good government. On the other hand, modern Chinese nationalism sees the nation-state as the ultimate goal of the community. Culturalism is a natural conviction of cultural superiority that seeks no legitimation or defense outside the culture itself. Only when culturalism was challenged in the late 19th century was there a transformation to nationalism.

When Chinese leaders saw the role of nationalism in the development of the modern nation-state, building a new national identity became their central concern. This is especially true in post-Mao China. As Bockman pointed out, "What we have witnessed during the past decade or so is that ethnic Chinese nationalism has not only been given freer rein, but has been used more actively by the political leadership as a lever for implementing the politics of economic reform, as a lever in the efforts to regain Hong Kong and Taiwan, and finally as a source of legitimation for the ailing regime" (1998: 323). It is found that though nationalistic voices inside China have been pluralistic, the regime has made enormous efforts to build up an official nationalism aimed at bringing all of the population within the national boundaries under its control (Zheng, 1999).

The significance of cultural factors in explaining Chinese politics can be hardly denied. As discussed above, there are arguments both for and against central control over localities. To a great degree, how cultural factors influence central-local relations depends on how we interpret them. Since culturally, there exists both centrifugal and centripetal forces, how one assesses whether the center can bring the provinces under control depends on which force is emphasized.

Since the cultural approach meets enormous methodological difficulties in linking the subjective factors of values and cultures to institutional dynamics, most studies within this framework "have been content with producing results that are either too abstract to be analytically useful or that are interesting yet insignificant or irrelevant" (Chung, 1995: 490). We know that cultural factors have an important impact on central-local relations, and make efforts to "dig" them out and conceptualize them. But this is not enough. An analytically useful cultural argument has to be empirically relevant. In other words, in order to see how culture affects central-local relations, we have not only to conceptualize cultural factors, but also to operationalize these cultural concepts.

SEARCH FOR A NEW PARADIGM

I have discussed three main approaches or paradigms in the study of China's central-local relations. All these perspectives have contributed to our knowledge, but we are still unclear about the nature of their relations. While scholars use terms such as "unitary state" or "federalism" to refer to central-local relations in other countries, they have failed to find such terms to conceptualize China's central-local relations.

Certainly, simply looking at the formal institutions of central-local relations will not enable us to see the nature of China's central-local relations since formal organizational adjustments have lagged far behind informal behavioral changes. This requires a proper understanding of China's central-local relations beyond an examination of formal institutions and tautological cultural variables. Following the call for behavioral studies, the procedural approach has enabled scholars to examine changes in central-local relations at the operational level. This approach has enriched our knowledge of how the system of central-local relations operates. While previous studies of the procedural approach have overwhelmingly focused on the economic side of central-local relations, scholars (e.g., Chung, 1995) have called for greater attention to other issue areas such as governance policy (e.g., personnel and communication), resource policy (e.g., allocation and distribution), and substantive policy (e.g., provincial compliance).[9] Recently, scholars have made enormous efforts to study provincial China; research designs of these studies combine provincial histories, single-province case studies, comparative case studies, statistical analyses and so on.[10] But by focusing on some specific policy issues or provincial cases, these studies tend to either be lost in rich empirical descriptions or provide us only with some fragmented pictures of central-local relations.

This study takes a new institutional approach to integrate all three approaches discussed above, i.e., the structural approach, the procedural approach and the cultural approach. It conceptualizes China's central-local relations as *de facto* federalism, identifies main institutions that are embedded in this *de facto* federal structure, and examines how these institutions mediate the interaction between the center and the provinces.

---

[9] Lieberthal (1992) identified six bureaucratic clusters, including economic bureaucracies, propaganda and education bureaucracies, organization and personnel bureaucracies, civilian coercive bureaucracies, the military system, and Communist Party territorial committees. While previous studies have focused on the economic bureaucracies, Lieberthal called for greater attention to the rest, especially the military system, the security apparatuses and the territorial Party leaders (Lieberthal, 1992: 2–4).

[10] The Institute for International Studies at the University of Technology in Sydney has organized a series of annual workshops to examine China's regional developments since the mid-1990s, and some primary research results have been reported in the newsletter, *Provincial China: Research, News, Analysis*. Also see Goodman (1997), and Hendrischke and Feng (1999).

2

De Facto Federalism: Organizations, Procedures and Norms in China's Central-Local Relations

A new approach to China's central-local relations requires a combination of all three of the approaches discussed in Chapter 1. This study takes a new institutional approach, especially its historical branch, towards the issue by attempting to achieve the aforementioned goal. The concept of institutions is used in this study to include both formal organizations, and procedures and informal rules or norms, which structure the behavior of both the central government and provincial governments. An institutional interpretation attempts to illuminate how the interaction between the center and the provinces is mediated by the institutional setting in which it takes place.

In this chapter, I first sketch out an overall structural environment of China's central-local relations, namely, *de facto* federalism. I then discuss briefly three sub-structures of the central-local relations, namely, formal organizations, procedures and norms, and how they can interact with each other in influencing the interaction between the center and the provinces. Finally, I identify three main institutions that are embedded in China's *de facto* federal structure, namely, coercion, bargaining and reciprocity, and discuss how these institutions regulate the interaction between the center and the provinces.

DE FACTO FEDERALISM AND STRUCTURAL ENVIRONMENT FOR CENTRAL-LOCAL RELATIONS

Before we can identify institutions that regulate and mediate the interactions between the center and the provinces, we need first to sketch out the overall structural environment that helps to generate these institutions. I define such an overall structure of China's central-local relations as *de facto* federalism.

Defining Federalism: Formal Institutional vs. Behavioral

China does not have a federalist system of government — it has neither a constitutional division of power between the different levels of government nor a separation of power within the branches of government. Nevertheless, with the implementation of the post-Mao reform characterized by inter-governmental decentralization, China's political system, in terms of central-local relations, functions like federalism. This study defines China's central-local relations as *de facto* federalism.

In academic circles, federalism is usually defined in two ways. First, it can be defined from a formal institutional perspective. In this context, federalism is often regarded as a form of government that differs from unitary forms of government, in terms of the distribution of power between central and sub-national governments; the separation of powers within the government; and the division of legislative powers between national and regional representatives. In this sense, a true federation has both a distribution of political power specified in the constitution and a direct relationship between political power and the individual citizen. Only a few countries fit an ideal type of federalism. For example, K. C. Wheare (1964) regarded the United States, Canada and Switzerland as federal countries, while

Malaysia and India only as "quasi-federal". This is so because states and local governments in the United States, Canada and Switzerland are not totally dependent on their central government for matters that are local in nature, while in Malaysia and India, they depend heavily upon their national government, despite the fact that these nations possess a federal structure.

Federalism presents itself in various forms of institutional arrangement. There are lesser forms of federalism, and those forms can be divided into parliamentary federalism (for example, Canada and Germany) and presidential federalism (for instance, the Latin American countries). A new form of federalism — executive federalism — is also emerging, where major constitutional issues are decided by executives, instead of by legislatures.

Needless to say, federalism works better in some countries than in others, and the performance of federalism is often subject to local historical trajectories and institutional arrangements. Germany is an example where federalism works well. This is due to several important historical characteristics that preceded the founding of the Federal Republic in 1949, including a socially and culturally homogeneous population; a tradition of federalism going back several centuries; a strong sense of nationalism; and institutional experience with federal processes. World War II accentuated strong regionalism and resulted in social leveling that stemmed from the massive movement of the German population. The war experience also provided strong incentives for the creation of a system of checks and balances to prevent the rise of dictatorships in the future.

Constitutionally, Germany is a parliamentary state that is a fusion between the functions of the executive and legislative branches, as well as a cooperative and interwoven distribution of executive, legislative and judicial powers among three branches of government. There is a fixed revenue-sharing system specified in the Constitution and a true multi-party system that makes gridlock a distinct possibility on contentious issues. At the same time, the size and scope of German entitlement programs has led to executive federalism on some issues. Firstly, the 1990 reunification created financial strain because of the large resource requirements of former

East Germany. Secondly, the membership of Germany in the European Union may have created additional federalist issues, since some of the provisions of the EU actually contradict specifications of the German Constitution.

In the developing world, federalism has worked less satisfactorily. For example, in Brazil, many of the difficulties stem from several key elements of a federalist system, which constrain presidential initiative and contribute to policy gridlock: a symmetric bicameralism in which the strong Brazilian senate forces the president to explicitly consider a regional balance of partisan forces; severe regional disparities in the legislature; a Constitution that embeds many policies and procedures, which other countries treat via ordinary law; a very high share of fiscal resources that remain with the sub-national governments; very strong gubernatorial positions coupled with strong propensities for political leaders to seek gubernatorial vice national careers; and an extremely poor nationalized party system. This form of federalism has seriously constrained reform efforts by the national government. Given the strength of state interests within the national congress, the balance of forces in terms of inter-governmental relations in Brazil is unlikely to change in the near future.

Among the post-communist countries, Russia is evolving into a federal state. Historically, Russia was a "tribute" state, with a strong impulse toward centralization. Moscow dominates Russia in a way that no other central government dominates its regions, and the party lists a guarantee that Muscovites will get elected. The president has too much power, and it will be important to obtain a functioning system of checks and balances in the face of a strong impulse toward centralization. Possibilities of countervailing forces in Russia will include competitive elections; a functioning central state that can distribute revenue; along with a functioning court and legal system to define and enforce a process for dealing with conflict. As a form of transition, Russia is developing a federal state structure. Nonetheless, Russia today does not fit well into any existing category of federalism.

Apparently, federalism is a concept in flux, and presents itself in various forms of political arrangement. If the Chinese state is defined in terms of formal institutions, it cannot be considered federal. The country has constitutionally remained a unitary state, whereby all local governments are subordinate to the central government. The principle of a territorial distribution of power has not been changed since 1949 when the People's Republic was established. According to China's Constitution, all provincial governments are local state administrative organs; they must accept the unified leadership by the State Council; implement administrative measures, regulations and decisions by the State Council; and be responsible and report to the State Council (Pu *et al.*, 1995: 223). On the other hand, the State Council can define the specific functions and powers of the local governments; nullify their decisions; impose martial law in the localities; and direct its auditing agencies to conduct inspections of financial discipline.

Similarly, while provincial people's congresses have the right to make local laws, the Standing Committee of the National People's Congress can annul this legislation if it conflicts with national laws. There is also no clear demarcation regarding the scope and content of the respective legislative authority between the central and provincial congresses.

Nevertheless, this should not prevent us from classifying China as a model of *de facto* federalism. Formal institutions alone cannot guarantee the powers of local governments vis-à-vis the national governments. Constitutional federalism guarantees the power of local governments such as in Australia, Canada and the United States, where local governments have a considerable amount of legal authority to determine their governmental form, as well as legislative power to make and revise their own laws (Nathan & Balmaceda, 1990). In many other countries with constitutional federalism, especially developing countries, local governments do not have such authority. For example, in India and Brazil, constitutions assign extensive powers to the national government that has the right to veto state legislation and take over the administration of states under emergency conditions. In Brazil, the federal constitution explicitly specifies how the internal political institutions of the states are to be organized. In India, state powers are constrained by the fact that the governors of the states are appointed by the country's president on the recommendation of the Prime Minister (*ibid.*). This is also true in the former Soviet Union. Even though there was a federal political structure, little autonomy was granted to local officials, and the central government retained virtually all authority over major economic and political decisions.

More importantly, a formal institutional perspective can hardly help us understand China's central-local relations properly simply because of the lack of a sound legal infrastructure in the country. In the developed world, laws, regulations and contacts often mean the end of business. Once made, they are binding and local governments have to follow. But this is hardly the case in China. China has never developed a system of rule of law. For China's local governments, laws, regulations and contracts often mean the beginning of business. Bargaining in different forms between the center and the provinces is a must in the enforcement of laws, regulations and contracts. Legal fragmentation is an essential part of China's political system. Therefore, a better understanding of China's central-local relations can begin with a behavioral perspective. Such an approach will enable us to see how China has actually developed *de facto* federalism and how this system is actually functioning.

There is a behavioral tradition in understanding federalism. Since the 1960s, scholars have attempted to look at different political systems from a behavioral perspective. Scholars find that local governments, even in unitary systems, have not only a considerable degree of autonomy on matters of local policy choice and in setting local policy priorities, but also have influence over national policy frequently. From a behavioral point of view, they criticized the centralists who often perceived central-local relations from a formal organizational point of view, thus misperceiving central-local relations in a unitary system. Douglas Ashford (1977: 491) argued that the centralist perspective does not discuss the relation of local to central power, but only central to local policy. Theo Toonen (1983: 247) also pointed out that "among the community of policy or implementation analysts, there seems to be some kind of implicit and broadly accepted assumption that in unitary systems... policy and implementation processes are comparatively less problematic — and therefore perhaps can be considered less intriguing — than in federal systems."

Scholars in the behavioral school also found that the *de facto* power of local government officials is often much greater than their constitutional authority. Local officials can always defend their local interests in the face of the central power through the use of various local resources such as: social identities; a shared local-political culture; distinct economic activities and interests; the statutory powers of local authorities; and the interests of local political party organizations (Schulz, 1979: 18). Studies of local power in Europe, Latin America, Africa and Japan have all suggested the persistence of local power and local initiative in rather centralized political systems.

Even in the former communist countries, essential local autonomy also existed. Daniel Nelson (1980: i) argued that "the processes of making and implementing public policies in communist systems ... cannot be understood unless we observe the roles in these processes, which are performed by local party and state organs that constitute day-to-day government for the citizenry." Jan F. Triska (1980: 2) also found that local governments in communist countries were not mere local extensions of superior governments. They should not be perceived as simply convenient arrangements for national governance, mere local tools of national administration.

Scholars of the behavioral school argued that even though constitutionally well-defined, federalism is so broad and inchoate as a governmental arrangement that it defies close specification. M. D. Reagan and J. G. Sanzone (1981) even argued that federalism as an operational concept is almost bankrupt. Diverse approaches to federalism have led to great differences in judging which country belongs to the club of modern federalism. So when K. C. Wheare (1964) published his study on comparative federalism in 1946, he believed that the club consisted of only four or five countries. Nevertheless, Daniel Elazar (1987) argued that as high a proportion as 70 percent of the people in the world live in countries with federal state structures and federal arrangements of some description.

However, all the above controversies have not prevented scholars from defining federalism in specific contexts. I argue here that federalism can be regarded as an instrument to resolve conflicts between governments at different levels through various measures such as interest representation and decentralization. All political systems have to confront the problem of interest representation, that is, the manner in which local interests can best be expressed and how the central government responds to them. Political systems also confront the problem of policy implementation. If the central government wants to impose its own will on society, it must have policy implementers. Whether policy implementers are bureaucracies or governments, the central government needs a mechanism of interest representation internal to itself because organizations, bureaucracies or local governments have their own interests, which may not necessarily be synonymous with central interests. Obviously, most political systems depend upon intermediary levels of government organizations or political bodies to provide contact between citizens and the central government. How these government organizations or political bodies should be organized is another important question.

Federalism is one means of resolving conflicts of interest between governments at different levels. But a key question that involves the structure of the federal system and the division of power and authority among different levels of government is whether we define federalism as a system of multiple centers of power in which the central and local governments have the broad authority to enact policies of their own choice, or whether we define federalism as a system of decentralization in which the central and local governments essentially implement uniform national policies (Kenyon & Kincaid, 1992: 4). If we take the first interpretation, then federalism could be the outcome of bargaining or a negotiated working agreement between political actors with conflicting goals, as William Riker (1964) understood it. As a matter of fact, federalism has been widely regarded as a means for resolving conflict in a fragmented society and for reducing the burden of the central government.

Moreover, there is a dynamic aspect involved in organizations. A behavioral approach is to look at China's central-local relations in a dynamic way. It helps us to understand how changes in local socio-economic environments will generate changes in the relationship of the provinces to the center. China's political system is not a status quo. Various factors such as economic development, changes in the power distribution of different levels of government and changing expectations of different actors within the system ultimately lead to changes in the way the political system is organized. In this sense, the role of local governments in economic development must be taken into account in understanding changes in China's central-local relations.

Following the behavioral tradition, I define China's central-local relations as *de facto* or behavioral federalism. One caveat must be added here first. The term "Federal China" is gaining popularity among Chinese dissident scholars (for example, Yan, 1992; Wu, 2003, 2004). These scholars suggest that China should adopt federalism to solve the issues of national integration such as those related to Taiwan, Hong Kong, Tibet and Xinjiang. This paper does not deal with these issues. Instead, it investigates how China's existing central-local relations are characterized by *de facto* federalism. In other words, it only looks at the issue in terms of the power distribution between the center and the provinces. Other factors such as ethnicity, Hong Kong identity and Taiwan nationalism are important in moving China towards federalism, but these factors are beyond the scope of this study.

In a behavioral sense, China's *de facto* federalism can be defined as follows:

> A relatively institutionalized pattern which involves an explicit or implicit bargain between the center and the provinces, one element in the bargain being that the provinces receive certain institutionalized or *ad hoc* benefits in return for guarantees by provincial officials that they will behave in certain ways on behalf of the center.

More concretely, China's central-local relationship can be defined as *de facto* federalism because it satisfies the following conditions:

I. A hierarchical political system in which the activities of government are divided between the provinces and the center in such a way that each kind of government has some activities on which it makes final decisions.

II. Inter-governmental decentralization is institutionalized to such a degree that it is increasingly becoming difficult, if not impossible, for the national government to unilaterally impose its discretion on the provinces and alter the distribution of authority between governments.
III. The provinces have primary responsibility over the economy and, to some extent, politics within their jurisdictions.

Figure 2.1 illustrates China's *de facto* federalism. China's constitution does not describe such a division of power between the center and the provinces, but at a practical and behavioral level, power is divided between the two actors. Some powers such as foreign policy, national defense and birth-planning belong exclusively to the central government, and it is very difficult for local governments to have a say on these matters. Some other matters are exclusively dictated by local governments such as local public security, road construction and school building. Most economic matters are exclusively handled by local governments. For example, foreign direct investment (FDI) and out-flowing investment below a certain limit is decided by local governments. Other powers are shared by the center and the provinces. There are policies that are made by the center, but implemented by local governments. The central government also has to consult local governments in the formulation of

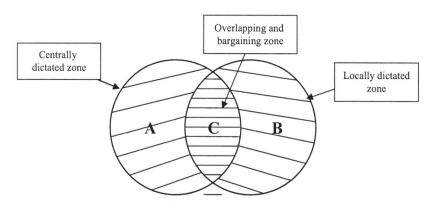

Figure 2.1 The Division of Powers between the Center and the Provinces

certain policies. Actually, there is no essential difference between China's *de facto* federalism and other forms of federalism in the world, in terms of policy formation and implementation, except that China is not democratic.

Inter-governmental Decentralization as a Source of *De Facto* Federalism

In the era of reform and openness, inter-governmental decentralization is the main source of China's *de facto* federalism. Not much has been done to discuss the impact of inter-governmental decentralization and its impacts on central-local relations. The term "decentralization" has been used widely by the reformist leaders in communist and post-communist countries to resolve economic and political problems resulting from over-centralization in the past. Nevertheless, different methods of decentralization engender different consequences. I summarize four major types of decentralization in Table 2.1. This typology is not intended to simplify the complicated processes of reforms in China. I use it here to show the links between inter-governmental decentralization and *de facto* federalism.

In the discussions on reforms in China and other former communist countries, much emphasis has been placed on decentralization between the state and society in the literature of comparative politics, i.e., economic decentralization, in terms of state-enterprise relations, and political decentralization, in terms of state-society relations. As one author (Hasegawa, 1992: 62) summarized it, "transition from the communist system ... involves two interrelated and interdependent processes: transition from a command economy to a market economy and transition from Communist Party dictatorship to democracy."

Economists appreciate the economic decentralization from the state to individual enterprises because there is an important value that is enhanced by decentralization, i.e., economic efficiency. Efficiency is defined as the maximization of economic profits. In order for profits to be maximized, individual preferences have

Table 2.1 Types of Decentralization and Their Outcomes

Decentralization	Stage I Inter-governmental	Stage II State-Society (enterprise)
Economic	*Central-local* Outcomes: • Local or regional property rights • Jurisdictional competition • Limited marketization • Local intervention • Local protectionism, etc.	*State-enterprises* Outcomes: • Private property rights • Privatization • Marketization • Competition among individual enterprises • No government intervention, etc.
Political	*Central-local* Outcomes: • "Areal democracy" • Perforated sovereignty and *de facto* federalism • Limited individual rights, etc. • Governmental "NGOs"	*State-society* Outcomes: • Democratization • Popular sovereignty and individual rights • Political participation • NGOs and civil society, etc.

to be expressed accurately. Within a private economy, individual preferences are expressed through market mechanisms. Economic decision-making should reflect as accurately as possible the aggregated preferences of consumers. Because individual preferences for economic goods differ, there will be a divergence between individual preferences and the economic policies adopted by the government. Consequently, the greater the centralization of economic decision-making authority at the level of the national government, the greater will be the average divergence of the individual preferences for the economic policies adopted by the government. By contrast, if economic decision-making authority is decentralized, each local unit can adapt its economic policies to the preferences of its local residents. The greater the number of economic units to which economic decision-making authority is decentralized, the lower will be the average divergence of individual preference for economic policies. Economic efficiency is thus likely to be maximized under highly decentralized economic structures.

Economists thus emphasize decentralizing economic decision-making authority from state organizations to individual enterprises. By doing so, economic efficiency can be maximized by competition among individual enterprises. The corollary is that economic reforms in communist countries should aim at marketization and privatization. To reform their economies, the reformist leadership has to introduce drastic changes in property relations. A legally-recognized private sector has to be established. Individual enterprises have to be given a large sphere of decision-making authority with regard to production, sales, price setting, wages, etc. Although passing decision-making power to local government is necessary at early stages of reforms, economic reforms are incomplete until individual enterprises gain full authority. Decentralization only transforms a planned economy to a mixed market economy. The ultimate goal of economic reforms is a *laissez-faire* economy where the state does not intervene in the economy.

Similarly, the literature on political transition in communist countries has focused on the decentralization from the state to society. Political transition means democratization and the decentralization of power from the state to society. The logic of political reforms follows. The communist state has to "modify the decision-making mechanism by including a broader portion of the society in the political process, and it must modify the ideology to accommodate new economic measures. This leads to redefining and extending rights and tolerating spaces for free expression and collective action for individuals and groups in society" (Hasegawa, 1992: 63–64). Furthermore, political transition can be divided into two major stages. Liberalization is the first stage of political transition, and democratization, the next. Liberalization refers to the process of making effective certain rights that protect both individuals and social groups from arbitrary or illegal acts committed by the state, while democratization refers to the processes whereby the rules and procedures of citizenship are applied to political institutions previously governed by other principles; expanded to include persons not previously enjoying such rights and obligations; or extended to cover issues and institutions not previously subject to citizen participation. Further, democratization is ultimately signaled by elections (for example, Di Palma, 1990; O'Donnell & Schmitter, 1986).

The impacts of inter-governmental decentralization have largely been ignored in the transition literature. As a matter of fact, inter-governmental decentralization can not only significantly change inter-governmental relations (e.g., central-local relations) but also can generate dynamism for changes in state and society (enterprises) relations in later stages. Figure 2.2 shows the flow of power among the central government, local governments and society resulting from inter-governmental decentralization.

With inter-governmental economic decentralization, the center decentralized economic decision-making authority to local governments. Even though the reformist leadership aimed to give individual enterprises more authority over economic decision-making, the previous economic structure made it virtually impossible for governments at different levels to withdraw completely from individual enterprises for a long period of time. It was also difficult for individual enterprises to make economic decisions according to markets because there were no such markets. During the early stages of reforms, individual enterprises still relied heavily on the state for protection. Consequently, instead of privatization, with inter-governmental economic decentralization, property rights were decentralized to local governments, rather than to individual

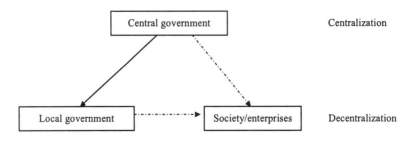

Figure 2.2 Inter-governmental Decentralization

enterprises or individual entrepreneurs. Local governments became *de facto* owners of state enterprises.

Thus, even though the center gradually withdrew from economic affairs of individual enterprises, local governments became highly interventionist. Inter-governmental decentralization actually created an institutional setting and legitimacy for local governments to intervene in economic activities under their jurisdictions. Nonetheless, inter-governmental decentralization does not mean that marketization becomes unlikely. Instead, marketization was highly encouraged. This was not only because the reformist leadership was market-oriented. More importantly, it was because intense competition existed between different jurisdictions, and between enterprises with different forms of ownership. Local protectionism existed during the early stages of economic reforms, but with the deepening of decentralization, it was constrained.

With inter-governmental political decentralization, even though the political space for free expression and collective action for individuals and social groups were extended and the communist regime turned to consultative authoritarianism, political participation was very limited. The focus of inter-governmental political decentralization was power shifts, not between the state and society, but between the center and the provinces. The reformist leadership did not want to decentralize political power to society. Instead, it believed that political participation should be constrained and mass mobilization could not help the transition to an efficient government.

But with the deepening of economic reforms, great changes occurred in the power bases of local governments. Central-local relations became highly interdependent. While previously the center still held great power over local governments, cooperation from the provinces now became essential in the governance of the country. Increasingly, the decentralization of power was not merely at the discretion of the central government; indeed, it became inevitable. As a result, while the provinces developed and strengthened their own power basis, the center also adjusted its relations with the provinces. The center recognized the *de facto* independent power of the provinces on the one hand, and made efforts to develop its own independent power to constrain local behavior on the other. Mutual adjustment in the relations between the center and the provinces resulted in changes in the state structure. What Arthur Maass (1959) called "areal democracy" took place. The provinces had not only the authority to deal with local affairs, but also to influence decision-making at the national level. Democracy in terms of state-society relations may emerge, but vary in different regions. Political participation was very limited and depended on local factors such as the levels of economic development; local political cultures; the attitude of the local leadership toward democracy; and the measures of political reforms introduced locally.

Inter-governmental political decentralization was significant for economic reforms, since economic decentralization did not, in itself, generate momentum toward marketization and had to be implemented by an authoritarian regime, as one scholar (Hasegawa, 1992: 69) has already pointed out:

> It seems almost impossible for pockets of privatized economic entities or decentralized economic decisions to develop spontaneously into a market economy. The roots of a command economy are so resilient that they are bound to stifle such incipient, fragile development from below. Thus, strong leadership from above is necessary for decentralization to lead to marketization. And yet strong leadership, buttressed by strong machinery to implement its decision, can be created only by the Communist Party apparatus, which is the greatest impediment to political transition.

Inter-governmental political decentralization alleviated this contradiction between economic and political reforms. Decentralizing political decision-making power to the provinces strengthened local power in initiating economic reforms and creating a counter-power to central bureaucracies, which often served as a major impediment to economic reforms in communist countries. Moreover, political decentralization itself was an important aspect of democratic changes in China. Powerful provinces exerted a serious constraint on the power of the center and protected local societies from arbitrary central power, even though local governments were often reluctant to share political power with society.

DE FACTO FEDERALISM: ORGANIZATIONS, PROCEDURES AND NORMS

So, how does the *de facto* federal structure affect the interaction between the center and the provinces? We can look at the issue from an organizational approach. Although it has been controversial whether organizational theories or administration theories can be applied to the study of Chinese politics (see Pye, 1995; Tsou, 1995), they are helpful in understanding China's central-local relations. This is because, even though, as I will show below, the relations between the center and the provinces are not just administrative in nature, both actors co-exist in the same hierarchical system, and both actors are constrained by China's *de facto* federal structure.

According to organizational theories, organizations consist of three structural aspects (Benson, 1977; Zeitz, 1980; Benz, 1987). First, the political-economic basis of the organizational structure is the power and resource structure formed by the distribution of legally defined authority; financial resources; political support; and information among different levels of government. Second, the interaction structure comprises the individual attitudes, action strategies, interests and goals of the actors in the system, which are integrated in collective action. Third, the organizational paradigm that comprises both the rules of the game and the institutionalized thought structure provides the principles of coordinating and regulating individual actions.

The three levels of the structure normally tend to achieve a state of equilibrium, but they are not totally dependent on one another. Instead, they can vary autonomously, and tensions and contradictions are thus created. All structural variations are determined by the existing power and resource structure, but the system is not deterministic. The political and economic bases can be altered by changes in the organizational paradigm or the processes of resource-flow between the organization and its environments. Because the government system depends on resource acquisition from the economic system and needs political support from society, state organizations at different levels affect each other in different ways; shifts in resource-flow directly influence the power and resource structure of the political and administrative system.

Changes in the organizational paradigm are also significant for the power and resource structure and the interaction structure. As long as the organizational paradigm is constant, changes in the power and resource structure and the interaction structure will be latent, or the impulse to change will not be effective. According to Benz (1987: 131), "if the tensions in the inter-organizational political and administrative system rise to a level at which they are evident to all actors and, therefore, cannot be concealed, they will generate a climate of reform which creates the conditions for a paradigmatic change." Furthermore, competing ideologies or "paradigmatic approaches" of governments at different levels can also bring about changes in the organizational paradigm. Thus, "the formulation and implementation of reform conceptions should be regarded as a political process in which the aspirations and interests of different levels of government are at stake as well as maintenance or realization of power position" (Benz, 1987: 136).

These three structural aspects of organizations can help us to clarify many issues in China's central-local relations. The *de facto* federal structure empowered local governments, and power shifted from the center to the provinces. Inter-governmental decentralization not only meant that the provinces were able to share the economic power that previously was monopolized by the center. More importantly, it implied that the provinces could develop their own independent power bases by increasing their local wealth. Since local governments themselves became economic planners, and local wealth was locally created, the operation of local power, to a great degree, became irrelevant to the center. Changes in the power structure of central-local relations also had a major impact on the second level of structural aspects, i.e., the interaction structure between the center and the provinces.

With increasing power and wealth, local government officials changed their perceptions of interests and their action strategies in their dealings with the center. They could not only plan local development independently from the center, but also bargain with the center to pursue greater power. Furthermore, all these changes were not reflected in the formal institutions of central-local relations. In other words, changes in central-local relations at the operational level did not result in any formal organizational changes. While the behavioral patterns between the center and the provinces are different from the past, the organizational structure of central-local relations remains intact. However, changes in both the structure of power of central-local relations and the interaction between the center and the provinces could gradually generate new rules and norms of central-local relations in the long run, and eventually, lead to a new paradigm. These are the dynamics of China's central-local relations.

To identify institutions that regulate and mediate the interaction between the center and the provinces, we can go one step further to look at new institutionalism that drew much from organizational theories. New institutionalism informs us how collective choices or individual choices are made with the presence of the constraints from these structural factors. Institutionalism aims to explore the impact of both the existing structure and its predecessor, i.e., culture, on human behavior. As Berger and Luckman (1966) pointed out earlier on, institutions imply historicity and control, but they cannot be created instantaneously. According to them (1966: 54–55),

> Institutions always have a history, of which they are the products. [Institutions] control human conduct by setting up predefined patters of conduct, which channel it in one direction as against the many other directions that would theoretically be possible. It is important to stress that this controlling character is inherent in institutionalization as such, prior to or apart from any mechanisms of sanctions specifically set up to support an institution.

In order to see how cultural factors affect behavior, two important aspects still need to be clarified, i.e., what are institutions and how do they affect human behavior? Actors (the center and the provinces in this study) seek their goals under given institutions that in turn, provide the context in which actors define their strategies and pursue their interests. In seeking their goals, actors form their own preferences. The formation of their preferences, however, is mediated by institutions. As Thelen and Steinmo pointed out, "Not just the strategies but also the goals actors pursue are shaped by the institutional context" (1992: 8).

In defining institutions, scholars usually include both formal organizations and informal rules and procedures. But in using "institution" as an analytical tool, some emphasize the formal organizational context, while others emphasize the informal rules or the cultural context. According to Peter Hall (1991: 19),

> Institutional factors play two fundamental roles... On the one hand, the organization of policy-making affects the degree of power that any one set of actors has over the policy outcomes... On the other hand, organizational position also influences an actor's definition of his own interests, by establishing his institutional responsibilities and relations to other actors. In this way, organizational factors affect both the degree of pressure an actor can bring to bear on policy and the likely direction of that pressure.

What Hall emphasizes here is the impact of formal organizations on human behavior. Once an organization is created, it not only establishes formal rules and procedures, but also generates informal ones. But those who took a more cultural approach argued that this will permit scholars to investigate more closely the context in which actors exercise power. Even though many scholars also defined institutions as particular combinations of principles, norms, rules and procedures, they, nevertheless, insisted on the importance of historical experience (e.g., Katzenstein, 1996b; Thelen & Steinmo, 1992). As Katzenstein (1996b: 23) argued, "history is a process of change that leaves an imprint on state identity."

"Institutions" are used in this study to include not only formal organizations, formal rules, compliance procedures and standard operating practices related to the operation of organizations, but also historically-formed informal ones. In other words, this study defines culture as norms that include organization-generated and historically-formed rules.

The next important question is how norms affect behavior. Traditionally, scholars defined culture as a body of attitudes and beliefs. Many implied that there was a one-to-one correspondence between attitude and behavior, that is, one set of attitudes leads consistently to one type of behavior. Clearly, such mechanically-deterministic theories are unable to explain disjunctures between practice and thought. A new institutional approach attempts to avoid this trap by defining culture as a body of norms. According to Katzenstein (1996b: 5), norms can be used to:

> ... describe collective expectations for the proper behavior of actors with a given identity. In some situations norms operate like rules that define the identity of an actor, thus having "constitutive effects" that specify what actions will cause relevant others to recognize a particular identity. In other situations norms operate as standards that specify the proper enactment of an already defined identity. In such instance norms have "regulative" effects that specify standards of proper behavior. Norms thus either define (or constitute) identities or prescribe (or regulate) behavior, or they do both.[1]

Culture, defined as norms, affects behavior due to its nature of instrumentality. Using Ann Swidler's term, cultural norms affect behavior by providing actors with a "tool kit" of habits, skills and styles from which people construct strategies of action. From this point, we can see that the institutions of central-local relations can affect the interaction between the center and the provinces in at least the following three ways.

First of all, since norms consist of shared decision rules, recipes, standard operating procedures, and decision routines, they provide assumptions about the orderliness of the political universe, the nature of causality, principal goals in political life and the trustworthness of other political actors (Elkins & Simeon, 1979: 132). In this sense, norms allow both the center and the provinces to interpret the game being played, and to figure out what others know, believe and mean. Therefore, norms help them to predict what reaction will follow, if a given strategy is used in their interaction.

Second, norms have a direct effect by defining collectively-shared standards of appropriate behavior, which validate social identity. This implies that behavior is shaped not only by goals,

---

[1] Also see Katzenstein (1996a: 18–22).

alternatives and rules of maximization or satisfaction, as the rationalist model of politics suggested. More importantly, behavior is shaped by roles and norms that define standards of appropriateness. Since norms are what the center and the provinces have learned from their interaction in the past, they help the center and the provinces not only in what action they should take, but also in what action they should not take in their interaction. In other words, norms help the center and the provinces to reduce, even eliminate, inappropriate behavioral options. Norms and behavior patterns are not the same, but norms affect behavior by presenting limited options. In this sense, the interaction between the center and the provinces is not only motivated by self-interest, but also constrained by their identification with appropriateness. The importance of the instrumentality of norms lies in the fact, as March and Olsen (1989) argued, that obligatory action is different from consequential action.

Third, we can understand the instrumentality of norms in a Gramscian way, that is, norms are ideational mass products of symbolic manipulation by political actors aimed at creating mass support for their particular choice. This points to two aspects of the interaction between the center and the provinces. On the one hand, this can imply that the center (the dominant power actor) can escape from, or rise above, the constraints of norms that it manipulates. On the other hand, since political leaders in the center are also socialized by the norms they produce, and thus, over time, are constrained by the symbolic or textual myths that they or their predecessors created. In other words, discourses that the center employs to pursue its interests can be used by the provinces to seek their local interests. As we will see, decentralization is one such discourse. It is created by the center to achieve its goals, but is often utilized by the provinces to promote their local interests.

By incorporating norms into the model of central-local relations, this study attempts to provide a more effective explanation of central-local relations in the reform era than the ones provided by both the structural approach and procedural approach. We will see that norms promote and reinforce cooperation between the center and the provinces.

COERCION, BARGAINING AND RECIPROCITY: HOW *DE FACTO* FEDERALISM WORKS

The *de facto* federal structure affects all the three levels of structural aspects, including the political-economic basis, the interaction structure and the organizational paradigm of China's central-local relations. Many institutions are implicitly and explicitly embedded in such a *de facto* structure, institutions that affect relations between the state and society, and between the center and the provinces. This study only deals with those institutions that have governed the interaction between the center and the provinces. In this regard, three main institutions can be identified, including coercion, bargaining and reciprocity.

As discussed in the last chapter, scholars have emphasized the role of coercion and bargaining in regulating central-local relations. Having recognized the importance of coercion and bargaining, I, nevertheless, argue that without a third institution, i.e., reciprocity, central-local relations cannot work smoothly. The interaction between the center and the provinces, be it coercion or bargaining, contains elements of reciprocity. Coercion, bargaining and reciprocity have formed a coherent body of institutions, and governed central-local relations throughout the whole reform process. While coercion and bargaining govern aspects of central-local relations, reciprocity regulates the daily businesses of central-local relations. It is worth noting that coercion and bargaining *per se* contain reciprocity, but, generally speaking, when coercion and bargaining end their functions, reciprocity begins. In Table 2.2, I outline some main characteristics of these three institutions and how they affect central-local relations.

Broadly speaking, these three institutions can be defined as follows:

- *Coercion* can be defined as a process in which the center employs coercive means such as the nomenklatura system and massive campaigns to solicit compliance from the provinces. Coercion is unilateral, aiming at guaranteeing central control over the provinces and strengthening the unity of the nation.

Table 2.2 Institutions Governing Central-Local Relations in China

Institutions	Justification	Motives	Process	Goal
Coercion	Necessity of unified leadership and centralization	Central control and coordination	Personnel appointment and campaign, etc.	Forced local compliance
Bargaining	Mutually advantageous	Self-interest	Negotiations	Conflict resolution
Reciprocity	Mutually acceptable	Justification to other, obligation	Self-adjustment, deliberation	Voluntary Cooperation

- *Bargaining* can be defined as a process in which the two actors (the center and the provinces) resolve conflicts between them through various forms of bargaining. It is bilateral and both sides utilize their resources to promote their mutual interests or to maximize their respective interests.

- *Reciprocity* can be defined as a process in which the two actors (the center and the provinces) achieve voluntary cooperation between them through self-adjustment and deliberation. Reciprocity is based on obligation, with each side behaving in a mutually acceptable way or with each side's behavior justifiable to the other side.

Coercion

Coercion, as an institution, can be formally institution-embedded and informally practice-embedded. Besides these two types of coercion, coercion also can be formally-defined. Regarding central-local relations, China's constitution regulates that the country is organized as a unitary state, under which certain aspects of power, e.g., powers over foreign affairs and national defense, should be and are exclusively monopolized by the central government (Diao *et al.*, 1989). Given that provincial officials are to be punished if they step into these fields, they are not likely to do so, unless they are allowed and encouraged by the center to do so. On the other hand, if they are punished for having done so, they are likely to regard the punishment as a legitimate action by the central government. These different types of formally-defined coercion actually point to the formal distribution of authority between the center and the provinces. Since provincial officials will not step into these fields, these forms of coercion do not function daily. To a great degree, using them to explain central-local relations will not enable us to see how the center and the provinces have actually interacted with each other. Therefore, it is necessary to search for institutions and norms, which regulate daily interactions between the two actors. More concretely, we need to examine institution- and practice-embedded norms.

Institution-embedded norms that play a role of coercion are formulated in China's economic system and in the political system as well. China's old planned economic system was highly centralized and, in principle, the central government monopolized all aspects of economic power and left provincial governments no leeway for local autonomy. But the economic reform that Deng Xiaoping initiated in the late 1970s dramatically changed the structure of power centralization. Until Zhu Rongji initiated selective economic recentralization in the mid-1990s, the whole reform era was characterized by excessive decentralization. Many scholars and policymakers believe that excessive decentralization led to a serious crisis of state power and a crisis of national integration. Even though there still existed various economic monitoring systems in which the central government solicited provincial compliance (Huang, 1996: 101–107), decentralization shifted economic power from the center to provinces, thus implying that the center was no longer able to use economically- coercive means against the provinces (Lieberthal, 1992). In other words, economically-coercive means were no longer available to the central government. How, then, has the center been able to control the provinces? Scholars turned to the political side of China's central-local relations. They found that, while economic power was drastically decentralized, the political structure remained intact. Indeed, an examination of the political structure of central-local relations is the key to an understanding of how coercion affects provincial behavior.

In terms of the daily interaction between the center and the provinces, coercion is expressed in both China's structural hierarchy and the nomenklatura system. Constitutionally, China is a unitary state, in which virtually all organizations, whether formally part of the state or not, are assigned particular bureaucratic ranks. The general principle of central-local relations is: provincial governments derive their authority and decision-making rights solely from the central government and their duties at the provincial level are performed on behalf of the central government (Huang, 1996: 28). But one point needs to be emphasized regarding the hierarchical relationship between the center (e.g., the State Council) and the provinces (e.g., provincial governments). To say that the relationship between the State Council and provincial governments is one of direct subordination does not mean that all provincial officials have to take orders from the State Council as a whole. According to the system of the bureaucratic rank, central ministries and provincial governments are on the same bureaucratic level. Therefore, though provincial bureaus are lower in bureaucratic rank than their ministerial counterparts in Beijing, provincial bureaus do not necessarily take orders from their ministries. As shown in Table 2.3, provincial bureaus have to answer to two superior units, i.e., the central ministry and the provincial government that are at the same administrative level.[2]

The structural hierarchy means that provincial officials are subordinate to the central government, but subordination *per se* does not imply coercion. To see how coercion is executed is to see how the system of subordination functions. This requires an investigation of how provincial officials are actually managed. The two most important principles of China's political system are: party

---

[2] For a discussion of the complicated relationship between the provincial government and the ministry, see Huang (1996: 28–32).

Table 2.3 Rank Equivalents among Government Organs

Center	Province	County
State Council		
Ministry (*Bu*)	Province (*Sheng*)	
General Bureau (*Ju* or *Si*)	Commission	
	Provincial department	
	(*Ting* or *Ju*)	
	Prefecture	
Division (*Chu*)		County
Section (*Ke*)		County department

Source: Lieberthal & Oksenberg (1988: 143).

control of the government, and party management of cadres.[3] The two principles are embedded in the nomenklatura system, under which important provincial leaders and cadres are appointed and managed by the central government (see Table 2.4). The nomenklatura system "consists of lists of leading positions, over which party units exercise the power to make appointments and dismissals; lists of reserves or candidates for these positions; and institutions and processes for making the appropriate personnel changes" (Burns, 1989: ix). The system established was based on the Soviet model. Changes occurred from time to time, but not drastic ones.[4] In terms of central-local relations, a significant change was introduced into the system in 1984.

From the mid-1950s until 1984, the nomenklatura system allowed the Central Committee appointments two ranks "down" in the system, meaning that the central government had not only the leaders of ministries and provinces on its nomenklatura list, but also ministerial bureaus and provincial departments. In 1984, the two-rank down system was changed to a one-rank down system, meaning that the Central Committee only managed directly leaders at the

---

[3] For discussions of these two principles, see Lieberthal (1995: Chapter 6), Huang (1996: Chapter 4) and Shirk (1993).
[4] For the development of the nomenklatura system, see Burns (1989, 1994).

Table 2.4 Provincial Officials Managed by and Reported to the
Central Committee (1990)

Provincial Leaders Managed Centrally

Position	Unit
Secretaries, Deputy Secretaries, Standing Committee Members	Party committees of provinces, autonomous regions and centrally-administered cities (Beijing, Tianjin and Shanghai)
Chairmen, Deputy Chairmen	Party advisory committees (small groups) of provinces, autonomous regions and centrally-administered cities
Secretaries, Deputy Secretaries	Party discipline inspection commissions of provinces, autonomous regions and centrally-administered cities
Governors, Deputy Governors	Provincial governments
Chairmen, Deputy Chairmen	Autonomous region governments
Mayors, Deputy Mayors	Centrally-administered city governments
Chairmen, Deputy Chairmen	Standing committees of people's congresses of provinces, autonomous regions and centrally-administered cities
Chairmen, Deputy Chairmen	Chinese People's Political Consultative Conferences of provinces, autonomous regions and centrally-administered cities
Presidents	Higher-level people's courts of provinces, autonomous regions and centrally-administered cities
Chief Procurators	People's procuratorates of provinces autonomous regions and centrally-administered cities

Provincial Cadres Reported to the Central Committee

Position	Unit
Secretaries General, Deputy Secretaries General, Department Heads, Deputy Department Heads, Bureau (office) Heads, Deputy Bureau Heads	Party committees of provinces, autonomous regions and centrally-administered cities

(Continued)

Table 2.4 (*Continued*)

Position	Unit
Presidents, Vice-Presidents	Party schools of provinces, autonomous regions and centrally-administered cities
Editors-in-Chief, Deputy Editors-in-Chief	Newspapers of provincial, autonomous region and centrally-administered city party committees
Secretaries General, Deputy Secretaries General, Commission Heads, Commission Deputy Heads, Bureau (*Ting, Ju*) Heads, Bureau Deputy Heads	People's governments of provinces, autonomous regions and centrally-administered cities
Vice-Presidents	Higher People's Courts of provinces, autonomous regions and centrally-administered cities
Deputy Chief Procurators	People's Procuratorates of provinces, autonomous regions and centrally-administered cities
Chairmen, Deputy Chairmen	Provincial autonomous region and centrally-administered city branches of the ACFTU
Secretaries, Deputy Secretaries	Provincial autonomous region and centrally-administered city branches of the Youth League
Chairmen, Deputy Chairmen	Provincial autonomous region and centrally-administered city branches of the Women's Federation
Presidents (Managers), Vice-Presidents (Deputy Managers)	Provincial autonomous region and centrally-administered city branches of the People's Bank of China, various specialized banks, and the People's Insurance Corporation of China
Secretaries, Deputy Secretaries	Party core groups (committees) of the above banks and insurance company
Secretaries, Deputy Secretaries, Standing Committee Members	Party committees of cities under central planning (Shenyang, Dalian, Changchun, Harbin, Xi'an, Chengdu, Chongqing, Qingdao, Nanjing, Ningbo, Xiamen, Wuhan, Guangzhou and Shenzhen)

(*Continued*)

Table 2.4 (*Continued*)

Position	Unit
Mayors, Deputy Mayors	People's governments of cities under central planning (see above list)
Secretaries, Deputy Secretaries	Party committees of prefectures (*di*), cities, districts (*zhou*) and banners
Commissioners (*Zhuan Yuan*), Deputy Commissioners	People's governments of prefectures
Mayors, Deputy Mayors	People's governments of cities
Heads, Deputy Heads	People's governments of districts
Heads, Deputy Heads	People's governments of banners
Secretaries, Deputy Secretaries	Party committees of districts directly administered by Beijing, Tianjin and Shanghai
Heads, Deputy Heads	People's governments of districts directly administered by Beijing, Tianjin and Shanghai

Sources: The DOO (1990). The table is adopted from Burns (1994: 479–480, 484–485).

ministerial and provincial levels. This change greatly reduced the number of cadres directly managed by the Central Committee. It is important to point out that by decentralizing nomenklatura authority, the Central Committee aimed to strengthen its power and management efficiency over provincial leaders. The huge numbers of cadres under the two-rank down system had, too often, resulted in *pro forma* consideration and *de facto* approvals of whomever the lower territorial unit nominated (Lieberthal, 1995: 211). The system was thus rather inefficient. By contrast, the one-rank down system enables "the central authorities to exercise their nomenklatura powers in a more serious fashion" (*ibid.*).

Scholars have used the nomenklatura system to explain central-local relations, especially why radical decentralization did not lead to the collapse of an already fragmented relationship between the center and the provinces. Nevertheless, the change, i.e., from the two-rank down to one-rank down system, showed the limitations of the nomenklatura system in explaining the interaction between the center and the provinces. The change was significant for central-local relations. One point needs to be emphasized, specifically, that is, to manage top provincial leaders is not to manage provincial affairs. As emphasized earlier, central-local relations mean not only relations between the central government and provincial governments, but also relations between provincial governments and their territories. Using the nomenklatura system enables us only to see the one level of relations, i.e., the central government and provincial governments; nonetheless, it underestimates the second level of relations, i.e., the provincial government and their territories. To explore how China's provinces are governed requires examining this second level of relations. It is in this sense that this study does not regard the provincial government as an agent of the central government, but as a level of government within its *de facto* federal structure.

The change from the two-rank down to one-rank down system has complicated the second level of relations. First of all, the change means that only the very highest officials at each territorial level, i.e., the provincial party secretaries and deputy secretaries, as well as the governors and vice governors, would be appointed and managed by the Central Committee. The new system also enabled provincial leaders to gain almost complete control over appointments and dismissals of officials within their territorial jurisdiction. The 1984 change created the possibility that provinces would increasingly become in-grown since appointments to all, but the top-level positions, were controlled from within. According to Lieberthal (1995: 211), there was a general increase in the percentage of provincial appointments below the top level in which the appointee's previous position was in that same province. An early study of China's mayors also showed this trend (Li & Bachman, 1989). According to the study, differing from the mayoral recruitment pattern of Mao's time, 70 percent of Chinese mayors were natives or were born in a neighboring province in the late 1980s (*ibid.*: 86).

Second, while the nomenklatura authority over posts previously controlled by the Central Committee was decentralized to provincial party committees, the latter, in turn, decentralized their control over the nomenklatura to prefectural, city and county party committees. Although the new system reduced greatly the number of centrally-managed cadres, it did not reduce the total size of the nomenklatura. Rather, it changed the distribution of authority over the same number of posts to lower-level party committees. Therefore, while economic decentralization shifted economic power from the center to the provinces, the new nomenkaltura system changed the structural distribution of political power between the two. This shift, in turn, reinforced the role of the provincial governments in governing provincial affairs, be it economic, political, or social. In this sense, Lieberthal argued that "the decentralization of personnel decisions under the reforms has increased the chances of local despotism" (1995: 212). Put in another way, though the central government still controls top provincial leaders tightly, within the boundary of a given province, the provincial government behaves like an independent actor with total autonomy.

Indeed, by changing the two-rank down system to a one-rank down system, the central government aimed at not only strengthening its control over provincial officials. More importantly, the central government also wanted low-level governments to function as a government. According to Burns, who has written the most thorough analyses of China's nomenklatura system,

> By granting more autonomy to local party authorities on personnel matters, the reforms sought to "spur their initiative" to appoint high-quality local officials and to supervise them efficiently. If local officials had the authority to make more personnel appointments, they would ... be in a better position to complete their responsibilities. Finally, decentralization of cadre management was necessary to implement new economic reforms, which, among other things, emphasized increased autonomy for enterprises and other local units (1989: xix).

This major change points to a methodological deficit in using the nomenklatura system to explain central-local relations. To control provincial leaders and to manage provincial affairs are two different matters. Take the transfer system as an example. With the implementation of this system, provincial leaders are frequently transferred from one province to another. Frequent turnover of provincial personnel does not allow consistent provincial policies (i.e., policies by provincial leaders). But in reality, as will be shown in later chapters, provincial policies have been consistent, and provincial affairs have been managed in quite similar ways. This means that the nomenklatura system as a variable is incapable of providing a satisfactory explanation of central-local relations. Therefore, we need to go beyond the nomenklatura system to search for a more effective explanation of how central-local relations have actually worked.

Bargaining

Coercion explains why radical economic decentralization did not lead to a collapse of central-local relations. Since the central government has tightly controlled the appointments of provincial leaders, it is hard for the latter to develop independent forces to threaten the center. The role of coercion in regulating central-local relations depends solely on the position of the central government in China's political hierarchy. As shown in Table 2.2, the aim of coercion is to achieve forced provincial compliance. Therefore, coercion hardly explains how provincial leaders make use of local resources to interact with the center, and how the provinces are actually governed by provincial leaders. The provincial government is not just an agent of the center, acting on behalf of and subordinate to the latter. It is a government with its own resources and interests. To see how the center and the provinces have interacted, it is important to explore other variables. In other words, coercion only tells us one side (the center) of the story of central-local relations; other variables are needed to tell the two sides of the story.

Scholars such as Lieberthal, Oksenberg and Lampton, among others, have developed a new concept, i.e., bargaining, to explore how the center and the provinces have interacted with each other. I have summarized the main characteristics in Table 2.2. The aim of bargaining is to resolve conflicts between the center and the provinces. The process of bargaining is rather different from coercion. Coercion is justified by the necessity of centralization and central control. Provincial leaders do not have any other choice, but to be subordinate to the center, since the central government can force them to do so through its nomenklatura system. In the process of bargaining, both central and provincial officials are self-interested actors, and the interaction between the two actors is mutually advantageous. Differing from coercion, bargaining refers to a situation in which both the center and the provinces recognize that negotiations between them can resolve their conflicts while promoting their mutual interests. In this sense, David Lampton (1992: 37) argued that bargaining occurs because both central and provincial leaders believe that "the gains to be made by mutual accommodation exceed those to be made by unilateral action or by forgoing agreement altogether."

According to Dahl and Lindblom (1976), bargaining commonly means reciprocity among representatives of hierarchies, and it is a form of reciprocal control among leaders; bargaining occurs because they disagree and expect that further agreement is possible and will be profitable (as cited in Lampton, 1992: 37). I should like to emphasize two main factors in Dahl and Lindblom's (1976) definition of bargaining. First, bargaining is form of reciprocal control. Second, it aims to resolve conflicts among actors and promote mutual interests.

Bargaining has increasingly become the dominant form of authority relationship in Chinese politics. In the writings of scholars of the procedural approach, this is so because of structural, procedural and cultural factors:

- Structurally, China's bureaucratic ranking system combines with the functional division of authority among various bureaucracies to produce a situation in which it is often necessary to achieve agreement among an array of bodies, where no single body has authority over the others. Moreover, inter-governmental economic decentralization has enabled locales and bureaucratic units to accumulate resources to bargain with the central government (Lieberthal, 1992: 8).
- Procedurally, the reform has changed the way of policy formation and implementation, and thus encouraged bargaining to emerge.

The leaders have reduced the use of coercion against those who propose ideas that are eventually rejected, thus emboldening participants to argue forcefully for their proposals. The stress laid on serious feasibility studies encouraged various units to marshal information to support their own project preferences. The general decline in the use of ideology as an instrument of control increased the "looseness" of the system, and decentralization in personnel management permitted many bureaucratic units to have their own initiatives (*ibid.:* 9).

• Culturally, an enduring aspect of the Chinese political milieu is that there has existed a deeply-shared value, i.e., fairness, among both superiors and subordinates, fairness that requires consultation and just compensation through bargaining among actors (Lampton, 1992: 39).

All these changes have made the Chinese bureaucratic system more fragmented, and thus increased bargaining among bureaucratic units. As Lieberthal pointed out,

> Fragmentation of authority encouraged a search for consensus among various organs in order to initiate and develop major projects. This consensus, in turn, required extensive and often elaborate deals to be struck through various types of bargaining stratagems (1992: 9).

Since bargaining as an analytical tool focuses on how actors actually interact, it enables us to see how the central-local relationship functions in the reform era. Bargaining as a paradigm has been widely used to study China's policy-making processes and generated many scholarly works (e.g., Lampton, 1987; Lieberthal & Oksenberg, 1988; Lieberthal & Lampton, 1992). Nevertheless, the limitations of this paradigm in explaining central-local relations are also obvious.[5]

---

[5] Indeed, Lampton himself emphasized that "bargaining is one of several forms of authority relationship in China," and there are other forms of authority relationship such as hierarchy and command, market relations, patron-client ties, pleading and rent-seeking or corruption, etc. (1992: 34). This is certainly true. But my reservations are not about the paradigm leaving out many other forms of authority relations, but over bargaining *per se.*

First, though scholars have pointed out how structural, procedural and cultural factors have affected bargaining in China, their analytical framework is not well-integrated, especially because cultural factors are not an internal part of the paradigm. Overall, bargaining is still structurally determined. Lieberthal argued that "the structures that link the top and the bottom of the system ... require negotiations, bargaining, exchange, and consensus building" (1992: 12). This inevitably leaves out cultural factors that enable the paradigm to see how cultural factors affect central-local relations. Indeed, cultural factors affect and adjust central-local relations in many areas.

Second and related, since weight is given to structural factors, the focus of bargaining is still on the relations between the central government and provincial governments. Like coercion, bargaining is still not capable of explaining how a given province is governed. Without an examination of how provincial officials govern their territories, it will be difficult to explore the nature of China's central-local relations.

Third, not everything is negotiable in China's central-local relations. There are fields such as national defense and foreign policy that provincial governments will not become involved with. In using bargaining as an analytical tool, scholars have first to identify "bargaining areas." In choosing "bargaining areas," scholars have to focus on the areas where the center and the provinces interact. So far, studies on bargaining have all focused on some major policy issues in which both the center and the provinces are involved. In such policy areas, without negotiations, neither the center nor the provinces can make or implement a policy. However, the central-local relationship is more than policy-making. The center governs the provinces through making policies, but policies cannot cover all aspects of central-local relations. How the center and the provinces interact in policy-making is not the same as how a given province is governed.

Fourth and more important, there are also areas that the provinces do not negotiate with the center. This is so, not because the provinces are not eligible to negotiate with the center as in the cases of national defense and foreign policy-making, but because they do not need to. That means that the provincial governments can govern their territories without central intervention. There is a "tacit agreement" (*moqi*) between the center and the provinces. Provincial officials can exercise their power at will, but will not deviate greatly from what the center expects. The central government does not use coercion against the provinces and does not negotiate with the provinces, but it is still capable of soliciting compliance for provincial officials. So, the questions become: What is a "tacit agreement"? And how does it work to regulate central-local relations? To answer these questions, I turn to a third institution — "reciprocity."

Reciprocity

A third institution, reciprocity, is needed to explain central-local relations — a paradigm that will incorporate cultural factors into its analytical framework. Central to reciprocal behavior is obligation. It is formed during the long process of the interaction among actors. It is a process of invisible or tacit interaction among actors, a process regulated not by coercion as in the process of coercion, and explicit negotiations as in the process of bargaining, but by an appropriate standard of behavior by which actors adjust their respective behavior toward each other voluntarily. The questions are: How does an institution of reciprocity produce voluntary cooperation between the center and the provinces, and how does it regulate central-local relations?

Scholars have searched for how cooperation among egoistic social members can be achieved without coercive intervention from government authorities; how cooperation between governments and people can be achieved without appealing to external forces; and how international cooperation among sovereign states can be achieved without any supra-sovereign authority. Many have found that reciprocity has played a crucial role in facilitating cooperation among egoists. In domestic politics, Robert Axelrod (1984) has advised people and governments to practice and teach reciprocity in order to foster cooperation. Similarly, in international relations, Robert Keohane (1984: 214) strongly argued that reciprocity "seems to be the most effective strategy for maintaining cooperation among egoists."

Though reciprocity has been used as an analytical tool in sociology, anthropology, and international politics and law for years, its meaning is still vague as scholars often define it in specific contexts. Individual scholars often define the term in accordance with their theoretical purposes. Thus, it still remains an ambiguous term.

Reciprocity is used in this study in a sociological sense (see, Blau, 1964; Gouldner, 1960; Sahlins, 1972). Applying this approach to central-local relations, I argue that reciprocal obligations hold the center and the provinces together since reciprocity helps the two self-interested actors (the center and the provinces) to cooperate. Reciprocity can function in this way because it is an ongoing series of sequential actions, which may continue indefinitely, never balancing, but continuing to entail mutual concessions within the context of shared commitments and values.

In his classic study of social exchange, Peter Blau (1964) distinguished two types of exchange, i.e., economic exchange and social exchange. Social exchange involves somewhat indefinite sequential exchanges within the context of a general pattern of obligation, while in economic exchange, the benefits to be exchanged are precisely specified and no trust is required (Blau, 1964: 8, 93–97). Robert Keohane (1986) applied Blau's concepts to international politics and distinguished two types of reciprocity, i.e., specific reciprocity and diffuse reciprocity. According to Keohane, specific reciprocity refers to "situations in which specified partners exchange items of equivalent value in a strictly delimited sequence." In diffuse reciprocity, "the definition of equivalence is less precise, one's partners may be viewed as a group rather than as particular actors, and the sequence of events is less narrowly bounded" (*ibid.*: 4).

From this distinction, bargaining can be regarded as specific reciprocity or an economic exchange. In the process of bargaining, both the center and the provinces are motivated by self-interest. Bargaining occurs because both the center and the provinces believe that it helps resolve conflicts between them and promote their mutual interests. Indeed, in constructing bargaining as an institution regulating Chinese politics, scholars have heavily relied on rational choice literature and power politics literature (e.g., Lieberthal & Oksenberg, 1988). The strength of bargaining in explaining central-local relations is specific policy areas where the center and the provinces negotiate to increase their own interests. Bargaining is a form of reciprocity since both actors are involved in negotiating over something like "the price of a house." Nevertheless, it is game-like or economic bargaining, since actors here behave "in a reciprocal fashion respond to cooperation with cooperation and to defection with defection" (Keohane, 1986: 6). This form of game-like bargaining seems to be inefficient in explaining voluntary cooperation between the center and the provinces. As mentioned earlier, there are areas in which the center and the provinces do not negotiate with each other.

In this study, "reciprocity" refers to what Keohane (1986) has called "diffuse reciprocity" and distinguish it from bargaining, which belongs to what Keohane (1986) called "specific reciprocity." While the emphasis of bargaining is on self-interest, the type of reciprocity that I emphasize in this study is less based on self-interest, but more on shared concepts of rights and obligations. This implies that the central-local relationship entails obligations of one actor toward another. In a sociological sense, reciprocity can be identified with mutual obligation (Moore, 1978: 506). According to Gouldner (1960: 169–171), there are norms that help impose obligations. For example, people should help those who have helped them, and people should not injure those who have helped them. With this type of norm, mutual obligation does not require that the actors involved be altruistic, since norms consist of standards of behavior, which are widely regarded as legitimate. In this sense, Keohane argued that diffuse reciprocity "involves conforming to generally accepted standards of behavior" (1986: 4).

While how reciprocity affects central-local relations will be discussed in the later chapters of case studies, some significant points can be derived from the above basic assumption of reciprocity.

First, reciprocity is a conditional action. It usually refers to mutual dependence, mutual influence, and mutual exchange of privileges. According to Blau, reciprocity implies "actions that are contingent on rewarding reactions from others that cease when these expected reactions are not forthcoming" (1964: 6). In the context of central-local relations, reciprocity is also conditional, but whether cooperation can be achieved does not depend on any particular interaction between the center and the provinces. Rather, it is based on a series of continued interaction between them. In other words, since the interaction between the center and the provinces is a continuous process, both actors behave not necessarily in accordance with the principle of "ill for ill, and good for good," which is prevalent in a condition of anarchy.

Second, since the center and the provinces have to interact with each other continuously, they are not always motivated by self-interest to bargain with each other. If you become a loser in time A, you will not necessarily lose again in time B. You may give up something in time A in order to gain something in time B. You do so because you believe that your altruistic behavior today will be rewarded in the future.

Furthermore, reciprocity is not equivalent to benefits. In practicing reciprocal interaction, both the center and the provinces do not have identical obligations. It would be misleading to regard the two actors as rationally self-interested. If the center treats the provinces to a dinner today, it will not necessarily ask the provinces to treat it to a dinner too, in the future. For example, in patron-client relationships, the center and the provinces exchange mutually-valued, but non-comparable goods and services. But practitioners of obligation-based reciprocity know that they should discharge, in the interest of continuing to receive needed services, their obligations for having received them in the past. This implies that both the center and the provinces can develop an appropriate standard of behavior. The formation of such a standard promotes voluntary cooperation between them and contributes to the stability of their mutual relations. The one side does to the other side just what is in accordance with the appropriate standard of behavior. In other words, both sides know: "What should I do and in what way?"

Third, a further point can be made here. In the context of central-local relations, reciprocity involves not only standards of behavior, but also moral codes that supersede self-interest. Reciprocity does not reject the self-interest assumption, but egoists can also undertake obligations. As Keohane pointed out (1984: 57), egoists can also conform to obligations. This is especially true for provincial officials. Under an anarchical condition, no authority exists to enforce moral obligations. But central-local relations are different, the center and the provinces exist within the same political hierarchy, provincial officials will voluntarily behave in accordance with what they previously obligated.

Fourth and related, the center and the provinces practice bargaining, but since both the center and the provinces live in the same institutional framework, bargaining, a form of specific reciprocity, tends to turn itself into diffuse reciprocity. Bargaining between the center and the provinces is not a one-time game, but a series of sequential games. In other words, bargaining is a form of reciprocity. More importantly, it is sequential reciprocity that promotes long-term cooperation between the center and the provinces.

CONCLUSION

Three institutions have played their unique roles in different policy areas and in different historical periods. Since changes in China's central-local relations are mainly driven by local economic development, reciprocity has become an increasingly self-sufficient institution in regulating central-local economic relations. But this does not mean that the other two institutions are irrelevant. Just as coercion-based interactions between the center and the provinces can generate unwanted consequences, so do reciprocity-based interactions. To solve the problems resulting from reciprocal interactions, coercion and bargaining can come in. Moreover, the efficacy and effectiveness of reciprocity in the reform era is also due to the fact that it is affected by the other two institutions, i.e., coercion and bargaining. Over the long history of the interaction between the center and the provinces, all three of these institutions have intertwined to affect central-local relations. While coercion and bargaining contain elements of reciprocity, many elements of coercion and bargaining now present themselves in the form of reciprocity. How reciprocity has come to play a dominant role in regulating central-local relations is the theme of the next chapter.

3

Reciprocal Interaction in *De Facto* Federalism

This study argues that coercion, bargaining and reciprocity have regulated the interaction between the center and the provinces in China. There are many forms of power-relationship between the center and the provinces. China's hierarchical political structure determines that the provinces have to subordinate themselves to the center. The center does use coercive measures to solicit (forced) compliance from the provinces. The two actors also negotiate to resolve conflicts between them and to promote their mutual interests. All these interaction patterns undoubtedly are power-relationships. I argue that reciprocity regulates central-local relations, but this does not mean that reciprocity is power-free. Many forms of reciprocity may be hidden domination and exploitation. Indeed, as reciprocity can be based on self-interest, it does not need to be power-free (Keohane, 1986: 8).

Nevertheless, the center and the provinces also practice obligation-based reciprocity. With the development of a *de facto* federal structure, not every interaction between the center and the provinces can be explained by coercion and bargaining. Many forms of the authority relationship between the center and the provinces contain coercion and bargaining, but cannot solely be interpreted by either coercion or bargaining. Since the center and the provinces coexist within the same system, many forms of interactions produce norms and shape the identity, thus enhancing the solidarity between the two actors. Neither coercion nor bargaining can explain norm- and identity-based interactions.

Consider the following two examples. According to the assumption of power politics, the center should never decentralize its power to the provinces since decentralization undermines, even threatens, central authority. But in fact, decentralization was implemented continuously before Premier Zhu Rongji's recentralization movement in the mid-1990s, even though it did undermine central authority. Similarly, we can assume that the provinces would never give up their power and would make use of their resources to negotiate with the center, even resist central authority, in order to maximize their power. Nevertheless, the reality is more complicated. On the one hand, the provinces have struggled for what they thought should belong to them, i.e., local autonomy and independent power. On the other hand, they have given up powers that they thought should belong to the central government. Conflicts often arise between the center and the provinces, but cooperation is also achieved. In some cases, cooperation is realized by coercion and bargaining, but in other cases, voluntary cooperation emerges. That means that there exists a sense of mutual obligation and identity between the center and the provinces, a sense that leads one actor to take the interests of the other into account when pursuing self-interests.

Voluntary cooperation reduces conflicts, and promotes solidarity between the center and the provinces. How does voluntary cooperation occur? How have mutual obligation and identity grown from the interaction between the two self-interested actors and become a norm in regulating central-local relations? These are the central questions this chapter tries to address.

This chapter is divided into several sections. The first section applies a new institutional approach to see how self-interest-based reciprocity (economic exchange) can become obligation-based reciprocity (social exchange) over a long period of time. The second section attempts to examine how the practices of central-local relations during Mao's time have been institutionalized, thus promoting the formulation of obligation-based reciprocity. The third section discusses the impact of the pre-reform practice of central-local relations on the interaction between them in the reform era. Summarily, this chapter aims to look at how "the shadow of the past" is transformed into "the shadow of the future."

THE SHADOW OF THE PAST VS. THE SHADOW OF THE FUTURE

Two important and relevant points can be drawn from the literature of new institutionalism. First, the past practice of central-local relations matters in explaining how the two actors interact today. Second, time matters in explaining how self-interest-based reciprocity can generate obligation-based reciprocity. Moreover, in terms of the relationship between structures and norms, two aspects need to be emphasized. First, in any political system, formal structures change over time, but the norms that these structures generated over a period of time remain. In other words, the structure of the past can be turned into today's norms, and today's structure can be turned into norms of the future. Second, once generated, norms are relatively autonomous in a given period of time and affect the choices of individuals acting within that society. All these aspects of social life point to the linkages between the past, the present and the future. Thus, an understanding of how reciprocity affects central-local relations requires an examination of how it was formed in the past.

Central to an examination of how reciprocity was formed in the past is to examine how the past structure or practice that was characterized by self-interest, power and domination was transformed into reciprocity characterized by obligation, voluntary cooperation and compliance. One caveat needs to be reemphasized here. To say that reciprocity regulates central-local relations is not to argue that the interaction between the center and the provinces is free from coercion and bargaining. By emphasizing reciprocity, this study attempts to explore three main aspects of central-local relations in China: (1) how have past experiences been internalized by the two actors and generated a sense of obligation that fosters voluntary cooperation? (2) how has the central government been constrained by the structure that it created itself? and (3) how has reciprocity governed central-local relations in the present?

The literature of new institutionalism, especially its historical (cultural) version, helps to explore these aspects of central-local relations. A central assumption of new institutionalism is that both the center and the provinces are constrained by the institutions (including formal structure, rules and informal norms) of central-local relations, regardless of who has created these institutions. From this point of view, two working hypotheses can be made.

First, the central government is likely to be constrained by the institutions that it initially created to control the provinces. The central government undoubtedly was the initiator of the institutions of central-local relations in the People's Republic. Initially, the system was created to control the provinces in order to maintain a unified state. The use of political coercion such as the nomenklatura system and political campaigns was designed to solicit compliance from provincial officials. Moreover, the center also used the provinces to achieve its own goals (e.g., economic development). In this case, the center decentralized its power to the provinces in order to provide provincial officials with economic initiatives. In using political and economic means to deal with the provinces, the central government created various forms of political and economic discourse to justify its own behavior. These discourses actually established guidelines for both the center and the provinces in their daily interaction. Nevertheless, the fact that these discourses were used by the central government as instruments to control the provinces and to solicit provincial support does not necessarily mean that the central government could escape from these ideational constraints. This is because both the center and the provinces were socialized in the same structure. Over time, forms of practice and discourse were internalized and tended to appear as norms and identities. I will show later that past experience has constrained the choices of the central government.

Second, the provinces are likely to use what the center has used to solicit provincial support to constrain the center. It was the center that established the institutions of central-local relations, but both the center and the provinces were involved in the process, even when the center solicited compliance from the provinces. The process of mutual interaction is important. Original institutions of central-local relations were modified and even reconstructed during the process in order to improve their efficiency. Meanwhile, both actors internalized forms of practices during the same process and accepted the previous "right" practices as norms and generated identities towards these norms.

Consequences for both the center and the provinces are complicated. For the center, on the one hand, once such norms are produced, the center will not only lose control over them, but also is constrained by them. On the other hand, once norms come into existence, the center does not always need to appeal to coercion and bargaining to solicit provincial compliance. For the provinces, on the one hand, norms constrain their choices, that is, they could not go beyond the boundary that these norms would allow. The provinces do so not only because they are afraid of being punished, but also because they have benefited from doing so. On the other hand, the provinces are likely to use these norms to justify their own behavior, while restraining the center from violating these norms.

From this point of view, the initial structure of central-local relations is important to explain how the center and the provinces behave. Nonetheless, one cannot solely rely on this initial structure, since the functioning of this structure involves both the center and the provinces, and generates norms and identities between them. So, what is more important is to see how the interaction between the center and the province generates norms and identities.

In his influential work on human behavior, Robert Axelrod (1984) showed how cooperation was achieved between two players under the condition of no external intervention. The starting point of Axelrod is the rationality assumption that human beings are motivated by the maximization of self-interest. Axelrod (1984) focused on the game of Prisoner's Dilemma. In playing the game, both players benefit more from cooperation than from mutual defection, but each player achieves the most successful outcome by defecting, provided that the partner cooperates. Since there is no external force to enforce the two players' promises, it is always rational for an egoistic player to defect. But in reality, cooperation does occur. How can cooperation be explained?

Sequence explains that. When the game is played a known finite times, the players have no incentive to cooperate. According to Axelrod, "on the next-to-last move neither player will have an incentive to cooperate since they can both anticipate a defection by the other player on the very last move" (1984: 10). However, when an indefinite sequence of games is played, cooperation becomes rational for the players. Because the interaction between the two players is a continuous process, the rationality of cooperation depends not only on the immediate payoff facing the players but also on the "shadow of the future." In other words, the more important outcomes of future games are, the more sensible it is for players to forgo maximal current payoffs by defecting, and choose to cooperate instead. Such an interaction strategy fosters cooperation in future games. Axelrod thus calls for people to practice reciprocity in order to achieve cooperation among egoists (*ibid.*: 214).

Axelrod's (1984) analysis also makes sense in the interaction between the center and the provinces. The interaction between them (e.g., exchange, bargaining) takes place sequentially, rather than simultaneously. Since the interaction is a continuous process, both actors have to take the "future" into the current game. Both actors cannot be too selfish in interacting with each other. The center cannot use its coercion too often to exploit the provinces and negotiate with the latter without taking the interests of the latter into consideration. Otherwise, it will meet explicit and implicit resistance from the provinces. Similarly, the provinces cannot deceive the center and make full use of the resources under their control to bargain with the center without taking the interests of the latter into consideration.

Furthermore, since both the center and the provinces coexist and both actors are socialized in the same structure, we can go beyond Axelrod's (1984) assumption of self-interest-based rationality. Because interaction occurs sequentially, both actors are likely not to defect because of an unsatisfactory result in time *A*. Norms resulting from their past interaction tell them that their altruistic concession in time *A* will be rewarded in time *B*. To put it simply, frequent and sequential interaction generates a sense of moral obligation between the center and the provinces. As Keohane (1986: 21) pointed out,

> In the long run, reciprocity based on self-interest can generate trust based on mutual experience as a result of the recurrent and gradually expanding character of processes of social exchange. That is, by engaging successfully in specific reciprocity over a period of time, governments may create suitable conditions for the operation of diffuse reciprocity.

THE SHADOW OF THE PAST: CENTRAL-LOCAL RELATIONS UNDER MAO

Norms and identity are the products of historical experience. This does not mean that they are deeply rooted in history. Instead, they come from recent practice and experience. When norms guide individual behavior, they have to be relevant to the current situation. Ideas guide actions, and the "right" ideas are those that have been tested in recent practice. Mao Zedong once asked, "Where do correct ideas come from?" According to Mao, they do not fall from the sky, nor are they initiated in the minds of men. Instead, they emerge from social practices, and social practices alone (1986: 839). Of course, this study is not to examine whether Mao himself behaved according to his dictum, but to explore how the experience of central-local relations under Mao has affected the choices of the leaderships of both the center and the provinces in their mutual interaction in the reform era.

Although the post-Mao reform was a radical departure from the previous system, the reform, in many ways, has been a continuity, rather than discontinuity, in terms of the strategies of adjusting central-local relations. In other words, it is from the past experience of central-local relations that the leadership has gained ideas to deal with central-local relations. It is worthwhile reemphasizing that to examine central-local relations is to explore two layers of relationship: first, relations between the central and provincial leaderships; and second, relations between the provincial leaderships and provincial affairs. Therefore, an examination of central-local relations needs to cover these two levels of relationship.

Economic Decentralization under Mao

Institutionalism assumes that historically-developed economic institutions have a significant impact on economic behavior. Mao Zedong and Deng Xiaoping initiated waves of decentralization in different periods, but what Mao did had a major impact on Deng's choices of strategies.

After the CCP defeated the Nationalist Party and became the political party in power on the mainland, it was successful in establishing a hegemonic regime following the Soviet model, and achieving an overall control over local society. However, due to the very size of China and the Chinese polity, the tension between centralizing and decentralizing forces could not be relaxed. The capacity of the state to develop the economy depended not only on the will and skill of the top leadership, but also on lower-level governments or state organizations, as well as non-state organizations. Without the cooperation of lower-level organizations, the state leaders could hardly get their job done or get people in society to do what they wanted them to do.

So, once centralization was achieved, it quickly became evident that a high degree of centralization carried its own burden of problems, and there were distinct advantages to decentralization (Cohen, 1988). Mao soon found some major shortcomings in the highly centralized system. In the wake of the unparalleled centralization achieved in the early and mid-1950s, Mao turned to focus on the relations between the center and the provinces because how the incentives of the provinces could be aroused became a major problem in the centralized regime. The result was a significant devolution of the decision-making power from the center to the provinces after 1957. Mao's decentralization also aimed to weaken bureaucratism. It seemed to Mao that decentralization could avoid a large bureaucratic system by building various local self-sufficient economic systems, and render a market mechanism that might lead to inequality and the rise of social classes unnecessary (Riskin, 1988).

The first wave of decentralization took place in 1958. In its Third Plenary Session of the Eighth Congress in 1957, the CCP adopted three decisions about local-central relations. First, nearly all state-owned enterprises were delegated to local governments for management at different levels. Second, central planning was changed from a national to a regional basis. Third, revenue-sharing schemes were fixed for a period of time and local officials gained authority over taxes.

Beginning in 1958, the central government implemented various measures to decentralize power to local governments. First, state enterprises were decentralized to provincial authorities. Enterprises formerly managed directly by central bureaucracies were reduced from 9,300 in 1957 to 1,200 in 1958, decreasing by 88 percent, and industrial output by the centrally-managed enterprises declined from 40 percent to 14 percent in the same period (Zhou, 1984: 70). In practice, provincial authorities further decentralized enterprises to the prefecture, county and even commune levels.

Second, the central government decentralized the central planning system in order to create conditions for local self-sufficiency. Centrally-planned products were reduced from 300 categories in 1957 to 215 in 1959 — about 58 percent of the total industrial products in the country. That meant the remaining 42 percent were planned by local governments. Meanwhile, taxes collected directly by central bureaucracies decreased from 40 to 20 percent of the total central revenue in the same period. Fully 80 percent of central revenue was collected by local governments. Also, former centrally-allocated materials decreased to 132 categories — a drop of 75 percent (*ibid.*: 72).

Third, the power of approval for capital construction projects was also decentralized; local autonomy in seeking local economic development was expected to increase. Local authorities gained greater power over projects in their territories. To a great degree, the central government became a real "rubber stamp". After 1958, the central government further implemented the investment contract system under which local governments could develop local projects of any size as long as they were able to collect the capital. These policies led to a rapid expansion of local industries. For instance, in 1960, there were 380 extra-plan large and medium local projects — about 20 percent of the total for such projects in the country. Investment in capital construction increased from 14.33 billion *yuan* in 1957 to 38.9 billion in 1960 (Zhou, 1984: 73).

Fourth, fiscal and taxation decentralization led to greater fiscal power in the hands of local governments. Before decentralization, local governments could not share with the central government the revenue from enterprises managed by the central bureaucracies. With decentralization, most provinces shared about 20 percent of total enterprise profits with the central government. On the expenditure side, provincial governments could now gain 70 percent of the total capital from the central government for local state-enterprises. Meanwhile, local taxation power also increased. The simplification of the taxation system left local governments greater leeway in collecting taxes for local uses. Decentralization thus shifted power between the central and provincial governments. During the First Five-Year Plan period, the central government received about three-quarters of the total revenue annually; now its share was reduced to half of the total revenue. The extra-budgetary revenue by local governments increased from nine percent of the budgetary revenue in 1957 to 21 percent in 1960. Decentralization thus generated a greater incentive for provincial governments to lower local tax rates in order to stimulate local economic development by enterprises and communes (*ibid.*: 74–75; also see Wu and Rong, 1988).

Decentralization soon led to the decline of the central government's control of China's overall economy. The rise of the provincial governments' economic power put the central government in a very weak position to coordinate economic development among regions. In effect, decentralization resulted in a deficit crisis due to the decline of the central government's capacity to collect revenue. Within four years (1958 to 1961), decentralization gave the central government a deficit of more than 18 billion *yuan* (ZGTJNJ, 1991: 12).

After 1961, the central government reorganized central control over China's economy. The central government increased its economic power gradually in the next few years (Zhao, 1988). But Mao maintained his opinions regarding the central bureaucracy consistently. After the economic crisis was gone, he again wanted to redirect China's economic system. On 12 March 1966, Mao wrote a letter to Liu Shaoqi and stressed, "It is not a good way to have everything centralized." On 20 March, Mao reemphasized in an extended conference of the Political Bureau held in Hangzhou that the central government had to make some general policies and let local authorities do more. He complained that the central government and its bureaucracies had recentralized too many enterprises that had to be "redecentralized," and the central bureaucracy must also be decentralized (*ibid.*).

Apart from the chaotic changes during the Cultural Revolution in the late 1960s, decentralization began again in 1970. In a short period of time, more than 2,600 centrally-managed enterprises including the Anshan Steel mill, the Daqing oil fields, the Changchun Auto Plant and the Kailan Coal mine were decentralized to the provincial or prefectural level. In 1965, there were 10,533 state enterprises managed directly by the central bureaucracy, which produced more than 42 percent of the total industrial output in China. After the 1970 decentralization, only 142 such enterprises remained centrally-managed, and they produced only about 8 percent of total industrial output (Zhou, 1984: 137).

The decentralization of enterprises changed central-provincial fiscal relations. Direct central government revenue was reduced to custom duties and profits of enterprises under central control. Meanwhile, the central government's expenditures were restricted to national defense, foreign aid, strategic reserves and expenses for basic construction projects, as well as enterprises and undertakings of science, culture, education and health agencies under central ministerial control. All the remaining revenue sources and expenditure categories became those of provincial governments and below.

The provinces now could control a much larger share of the state revenue and expenditure. This, in turn, led provincial officials to expand local enterprises rapidly. Extra-budgetary revenue again skyrocketed. Such revenue increased from 15 percent of total budgetary revenue in 1970 to 36 percent in 1976. Further, provincial governments implemented very favorable taxation policies in their territories in order to provide incentives for local economic development. Decentralization thus led to the birth of numerous local self-sufficient economic systems and the central government became incapable of implementing macro-economic control (Lyons, 1987). On the other hand, decentralization also provided an opportunity for local industrial expansion, the institutional legacy of which has had a major impact on post-Mao local economic development.

The two waves of decentralization have had a significant impact on the post-Mao reform from various perspectives. First, decentralization provided an initial power and resource structure for the post-Mao reform, a structure that was characterized by cellularity (Donnithorne, 1972). Compared to other former communist countries, local governments in China had greater autonomy in decision-making in local affairs. Even if the cellular economy effectively delayed the formation of a nationwide marketplace after 1978, thus adding to the unevenness of development, this initial structure also constrained the post-Mao policy alternatives. It rendered any unified policy ineffective and decentralization became an unavoidable trend.

Second, the cellular system made it impossible for the central government to integrate local economies into a highly centralized management system. This in turn led to the existence of local officials' "territorial interests". Local officials were often able to resist the central mandates and implement favorable policies in their locales.

Third, the two waves of decentralization determined, by and large, the policy choices of the reformist leadership after 1978. Even though various policy options were available at a given time, the choice that the leadership made depended on institutional circumstances. The reformist leadership chose decentralization as the strategy for reforming the economy because it was embedded in previous experiences of local-central relations. Decentralization became an institutionalized mindset among major leaders at different levels who experienced the two waves of decentralization under Mao. It was easy for the reformist leaders to build a consensus regarding decentralization and translate such a policy idea into specific outcomes. Also, institutions mediated between economic policies and changes. Although the two waves of decentralization under Mao resulted in chaos, decentralizing economic decision-making in effect became a norm among Chinese local officials, i.e., to resolve economic problems, economic decision-making power had to be decentralized to local governments. Thus, once decentralization was chosen as an economic policy, it soon spread over the whole country.

Economic Decentralization under Deng

The process of economic reform in the Deng era has been documented in detail (e.g., Naughton, 1995; Shirk, 1993). It has been widely believed that rapid growth in post-Mao China was due to the new development strategy. In some sense, it is true since the new leadership deviated from the old planned economy and put much emphasis on the role of markets in leading development. Nevertheless the perception and strategy of the economic reform of the leadership are also constrained by past experiences and historically developed economic institutions.

The two waves of decentralization under Mao had a major impact on the actual structure of China's political economy. As noted, before the post-Mao reform, China's economy already acquired a "cellular" quality and local officials formed varying power networks that were not necessarily in line with the central government (Donnithorne, 1967; Shue, 1988). This characteristic of the Chinese system largely determined the reform leadership's alternatives for economic reform. For the leadership, a new wave of decentralization was part of a continuous effort for reform, based on past experiences of reforming the Chinese economic system. The central government faced a dilemma: decentralization meant that local governments gained greater decision-making power, but increasing the power of localities would lead to a greater possibility of their deviation from the center. Local cooperation was thus imperative to guarantee that local leaderships kept in line with the central government's grand goals of reform, i.e., economic growth and political stability.

How could the reform program be implemented? The mass mobilization strategy was no longer acceptable due to the disasters resulting from such a strategy during the Cultural Revolution. Further, political liberalization had to be very limited. What alternative was available for the reform regime to achieve rapid economic growth and political stability? Both Mao and Deng called for local initiatives for economic development. But a crucial question still remained: Did local officials have an incentive to promote economic development? Mao treated local officials as mere instruments of policy implementation. He imposed great ideological, as well as political pressures on government officials for their economic initiatives. Deng also called for local initiatives. But Deng no longer regarded government officials as only instruments of implementing policy, but actors who had their own interests. Deng thus employed a materialist strategy for government officials' economic initiatives, namely to devolve fiscal power and property rights to local governments — tools that Mao used before Deng.

China's economic system under Mao was already complicated in terms of property rights. Compared to other socialist countries, China's property rights were localized and local governments at different levels owned *de facto* property rights. A study by the World Bank (1988: 59–60) found that "the share of state enterprises in the total number of industrial enterprises in the USSR and Eastern Europe is surely much higher than in China, where it was only 8 percent in 1980 and not much higher than that in the immediate pre-reform period."

Even before the reform, the non-state sector was already controlled by local governments of different levels. The post-Mao reform continued to localize the property rights of state-owned enterprises. Numerous formerly state-owned enterprises were decentralized to local governments at different levels. These enterprises were no longer managed directly by the central government or its agents, but jointly by the central and local governments, or by the latter alone.

Fiscal decentralization was another institutional factor of post-Mao rapid growth. Fiscal decentralization was significant for China's economic growth mainly for the following reasons. First, fiscal decentralization was a materialist approach to inspire local economic initiatives. Since the reform, the center no longer implemented a unified fiscal policy to localities, and the latter was encouraged to initiate its own fiscal policies that were appropriate to their own arenas and from which they could benefit more. Second, in order to achieve rapid local growth, provincial governments had to have their own financial resources and used these resources freely without direct interference from the central state. Fiscal decentralization satisfied such an institutional prerequisite.

With the implementation of various fiscal reforms, the responsibilities for economic growth were shared between the center and governments at lower levels, especially the provincial governments. Local governments were assigned great autonomy in policy-making, and there were frequently tacit agreements by the center to permit local governments to make decisions in separate arenas. Local governments, partly because of their relatively small size and scale of operation, and partly because of their know-how about their own territories, were more successful in coordinating the internal activities of their executive-administrative branches, and relations between government organizations and enterprises. Fiscal decentralization and relatively efficient economic management by local governments brought about further changes in local-central relations.

Property rights localization created an institutional setting for local governments to intervene in local economic affairs, while fiscal decentralization provided governments at different levels with a very strong incentive to pursue local economic development. Since government officials could gain great benefits from economic growth, "local state corporatism" or local developmental state, was developed in China, that is, "local governments have taken on many characteristics of a business corporation, with officials acting as the equivalent of a board of directors" (Oi, 1992: 100). It is the rise of local developmental state that has changed the structure of power distribution between the center and the provinces and weakened central power in governing provinces.

Historical Legacy of Central-Local Political Relations

Certainly, to judge central-local relations solely from an economic point of view would be too economically deterministic. Rapid economic decentralization did not lead to the collapse of central-local relations, since it was accompanied by tight political control over provincial officials. Tight political control was the instrument of stabilizing central-local relations, but costs were paid for the control over the provincial leadership. Although the post-Mao reform continues to be characterized by rapid economic decentralization and central political control, the way of controlling provincial officials has been changed. To see how the central government interacts politically with provincial officials requires an examination of how the two interacted during the pre-reform period.

Scholars have emphasized the importance of the nomenklatura system in central-local relations. But a further question is: Why has the center relied heavily on the personnel system to exercise its control over the provinces? To raise this question is important for central-local relations, and it will enable us to see the weaknesses of the nomenklatura system that is widely believed to play a dominant role in keeping an increasingly diversified China integrated. It will also enable us to see the role of reciprocity in regulating central-local relations.

Throughout modern Chinese history, the central theme of all waves of political reform, even revolution, was to build a strong unified nation-state (Hunt, 1993). This theme continued in the post-Mao reform period (Zheng, 1999). But this has not been an easy task. A modern state refers to "an organization, composed of numerous agencies led and coordinated by the state's leadership (executive authority) that has the ability or authority to make and implement the binding rules for all the people as well as the parameters of rule making for other social organizations in a given territory, using force if necessary to have its way" (Migdal, 1988: 19). To build a stable central-local relationship is undoubtedly an internal process of state building. Centralization does not necessarily lead to a strong state, even if it means the central leadership centralizes all aspects of power in its own hands. As the above-cited definition implies, state capacity does not only involve decision-making power. More importantly, it involves power for policy implementation. In terms of central-local relations, it is clear that without provincial cooperation, it is almost impossible for the center to have its policies implemented. Radical economic decentralization under Mao was aimed at providing local officials with incentives to develop local economies, and indeed, Mao Zedong overwhelmingly stressed the importance of building a balanced central-local relationship.

Nevertheless, there are often contradictions (or in Chinese, *mao-dun*). A political system does not necessarily function in accordance with the initial ideas of its designer(s). Consequences can be opposite to what has been expected. After 1949, many layers of territorial administrations (*kuai-kuai*) and vertical functional organizations (*tiao-tiao*) were established in order to exercise control over society and mobilize social forces (Schurmann, 1968). Initially, this way of organizing the state enabled the regime to implement such profound tasks of social engineering as land reform, collectivization, and nationalization of business and commerce. The functioning of the system, however, generated enormous institutional space for government officials in different organizational frameworks to pursue their local interests.

The *tiao-kuai* system *per se* embodies a variety of institutional interests (Schroeder, 1987). In order to enable this system to function, local leaders have to play an important role. As Lampton (1992: 39) pointed out, "local leaders not only are advocates for their own territory's interests, they also are mediators of disputes among the autonomous, but interdependent, vertical hierarchies that intersect in their localities." More seriously, the functioning of the system further expands and strengthens the power of the provinces. Put simply, the development of China's system is a process of economic and political "cellularization."

In economic terms, bureaucratic devices embedded in the *tiao-kuai* system, plus rapid decentralization under Mao, permitted the provinces effectively to block upward flows of information and to blunt higher-level initiatives that cascaded down on local leaders. A highly-centralized planned system did not bother the provinces too much in pursuing their own ways of governing their territories (Donnithorne, 1978).

"Cellularization" also occurred to the political relationship between the center and the provinces. The *tiao-kuai* system divided China into millions of miniaturized cell-like socioeconomic units. Local cadres and people living and working in these effectively isolated units could resort to deception to deal with the barrage of edicts emanating from the state. Consequently, according to Vivienne Shue (1988, 1994), what began as a sweeping social revolutionary movement linked to a well-organized and highly efficacious party-state gradually deteriorated into a regime of ideological obsession, which lacked almost any genuine social base beyond that of the party-state apparatus itself.

Exactly because the party-state became the only instrument for the central regime to achieve its goals, the central leadership had to control provincial personnel tightly and treat them coercively. Two further points need to be clarified. First, the capability of the center to exercise personnel power over provincial officials does not mean that it is all-powerful. Instead, it shows that the center is seriously constrained by the system of its own creation, that is, the center has no institutionalized means to have its policies implemented. Second, it also does not imply its capability of governing the provinces; instead, it only means that, without the cooperation from the provinces, the system will not be able to function.

This is what happened to provincial officials under Mao. The CCP regime effectively eliminated local political forces through the land reform campaign of the early 1950s. The movement removed a major obstacle in the path of China's state-building efforts. The party-state was successful in establishing a hegemonic regime and achieving overall control over the local society through its coercive organization and ideology (Schurmann, 1968). Nevertheless, political conflicts between governments at different levels occurred frequently within this hegemonic regime.

Immediately after the PRC was established in 1949, local governments were built on the bases of the guerrilla army and governments, and were staffed largely by local residents. Six regional administrations were established in order to strengthen the center's control over the provincial governments and the coordination between the provinces. The center, however, had neither the administrative personnel nor the experience to impose a tight central administration all over China. A great deal of local autonomy in effect existed. The party central committee enacted its nomenklatura system, but the system was quite decentralized, with party organs at each level having their own nomenklatura (Burns, 1989: ix).

Great *de facto* regional autonomy frequently challenged the central leadership in the early 1950s. Consequently, Gao Gang and Rao Shushi, heads of the two regional bureaus, were purged for disagreeing with the central committee in different policy areas. An important cause of the purge was that the two purgees struggled for greater power. Gao Gang believed that some regions were underrepresented in the central government. He wanted to be a representative from Northeast China and competed with Liu Shaoqi for the leadership in Beijing (Bo, 1991). Centralization followed the purge. The six regional government bureaus were abolished. The nomenklatura system was centralized and the provincial governments' nomenklatura was constrained by the central government. According to the 1954 Constitution, the provincial authorities were the agents of the central government, with limited powers to implement the plans and directives from the center.

From 1953 to 1957, power was highly centralized. The central government executed excessive control over the provinces through its various central bureaucracies. Consequently, ministerial autarky occurred, in which "a ministry became an independent economic system that tightly controlled the supply of materials and the allocation of resources under its jurisdiction. Instead of regional, independent fiefdoms, there were centralized, ministerial, independent kingdoms which interfered with provincial and local administration, drew up ill-conceived plans, and made repeated revisions of the plans" (Wang, 1989: 164).

Mao Zedong quickly realized the high costs of centralization. Centralized ministries constrained provincial initiatives, on the one hand, and began to challenge Mao's policies, on the other hand. Decentralization was thus initiated. By advocating the return of power to the province, he expected to receive support from provincially-based political forces and thus create a counterweight to other party-government officials at the top (Chang, 1990).

During the Great Leap Forward (1958–1960), Mao overwhelmingly emphasized local economic autonomy. As discussed in the last section, Mao initiated radical economic decentralization. It could be expected that economic decentralization would make the provincial leadership more stable since decentralization was meant to assign more autonomous power to the latter. But this was not the case. Instead, the personnel turnover of provincial leaderships became more frequent during this period. Teiwes (1972: 126–127) found that purges of leading provincial personnel occurred in 12 provinces in the period from late 1957 to 1959; among those who were purged, most (eight cases) were charged with localism and local independence. That meant that those who had reservations about the Great Leap Forward and were cautious in practicing radical policies were removed and attacked. After the great famine resulting from the Great Leap Forward, the leadership began to adjust its policies. The policy adjustment was accompanied by another purge. This time, those who followed radical central policies closely were purged. In 1960 and 1961, purges occurred in six provinces.

This pattern of central-local relations was repeated throughout the Cultural Revolution (1966–1976), during which a new wave of radical economic decentralization was initiated. Again, this did not mean in any sense that Mao was prepared to let local officials have a say in national decision-making. He initiated decentralization mainly because he disliked the central bureaucracy and favored a mass mobilization strategy (Harding, 1972). Once Mao felt that his power was challenged by local leaders, he turned to attack provincial leaders. Throughout the Cultural Revolution, Mao replaced almost all provincial first secretaries (Chang, 1972; Baum, 1972). Robert Scalapino (1976: 21) found that over 20 of provincial secretaries in 1975 had been victims of purges between 1966 and 1969 when radical economic decentralization was implemented.

In effect, political localism, a major danger to the central authority in China's long history, did not come to an end because of the establishment of the CCP regime. With the lack of effective institutions, the regime overwhelmingly relied on the nomenklatura system (e.g., appointments, dismissals, etc.) to exercise its control over the provincial leaders. The system enabled the central regime to constrain the build-up of excessive local forces to challenge central authorities. The implications of the nomenklatura system on central-local relations are complicated. It is an important institutional link between the center and the provinces. The system prevents excessive localism or local independence from rising and thus avoids the breakup of central-local relations. The frequent use of the system, e.g., dismissals and purges, however, can be seen as a sign not of central strength, but of weakness. Put simply, the use of these coercive means implies the failure of normal institutions between the center and the provinces.

Furthermore, the system reflects more on the relations of leadership between the center and the provinces than general central-local relations. Scholars have regarded the nomenklatura system as a serious constraint on provincial autonomy. For example, Falkenheim (1972: 202) argued that "the case [for provincial autonomy] is difficult to make in the face of the clear ability of the central government historically to exact compliance of provincial leaders when desired and to remove them from office when deemed necessary." To a degree, this is true. But it should not be over-exaggerated. The use of coercion against provincial leaders often reflected a divide in the central leadership over specific policy packages. As Breslin (1996: 14) pointed out, "provincial purges in the pre-reform era were more often a consequence of leadership conflicts that cut across the center-province divide rather than a result of a direct center-province conflict." In other words, provincial officials were only victims of power struggles among top leaders.

Third, even if the nomenklatura system signals a tight control of the center over the provincial leadership, it does not mean that the center can exercise effective control over provincial affairs. The central-local relationship is more than the central-local personnel relations, and to control the provincial leadership and manage provincial affairs are two different matters. Indeed, the more the center relies on the provincial leadership, the greater the power the provincial leadership enjoys. This study thus argues that the central-local relationship cannot be judged by the nomenklatura system alone, and it has to be examined in the context of how provincial affairs have actually been managed.

RECIPROCITY: CENTER-PROVINCE RELATIONS IN THE REFORM ERA

Changes were introduced into central-local political relations when Deng Xiaoping and his coalition took over power in the late 1970s. As discussed above, the post-Mao reform was characterized by radical economic decentralization — a strategy similar to that of Mao's time. But the shadow of the past has functioned and the lessons of the past have been learned. Reciprocity has come to replace coercion to regulate central-local political relations.

The mass mobilization strategy that was used by Mao to attack central bureaucrats and provincial government officials, was regarded as harmful for both economic development and political stability. New ways had to be constructed to regulate central-local relations. For those who regard China's reform as "economic reform without political reform," China's central-local political relations have remained intact. This is indeed confirmed by the fact that the post-Mao central leadership has continued to use extensively the nomenklatura system to exercise control over provincial leaders. According to Huang (1996: 119),

> The reform era has witnessed a number of important institutional developments in the areas of personnel management and administrative and economic monitoring that, on balance, have given the Center a greater degree of control. Chinese central authorities have retained a firm grip over the vital aspects of personnel allocations: selection, promotion, and removal.

Does this mean that the center has tightened its control over the provinces? Does it mean that the post-Mao reform has posed more serious political constraints on provincial leadership? Or, does it mean that the central-local relationship has become more coercive? This study argues that the still frequent use of the nomenklatura system in the post-Mao era needs to be reinterpreted. It is true that provincial personnel adjustments have been a regular feature of China's nomenklatura system, meaning that the nomenklatura system "may have become an institutionalized practice" (Huang, 1996: 111). Yet, this fact *per se* means that reciprocity, rather than coercion, has become a norm in regulating relations between the center and the provinces.

The use of the nomenklatura system is based more on the consideration of development strategy than political control over the provincial leadership. The highest priority of the post-Mao reform is undoubtedly given to economic growth. What Deng Xiaoping and his fellow leaders wanted to do was to transform the Maoist exploitative state into a productive or a developmental state. The Maoist state created non-market failure, as politics dominated economic activities. In order to promote economic development, political intervention into the economy had to be reduced. But this did not mean transforming the state into a neutral one. The issue was not state interference or non-intervention, but what kind of intervention. For Deng, what China needed was a "right" kind of state intervention. In order to make intervention "right," it was necessary to restructure the leadership and make it suitable and favorable for economic growth.

The restructuring of the leadership did not mean political reform in a Western sense, i.e., democratization. Deep commitment to economic growth made the reform leadership conclude that political democratization should be subordinate to economic growth. In order to provide a stable political environment, the state had to not only abandon the mass mobilization strategy, but also to constrain civil society or spontaneous social forces, so long as they would endanger political stability. This, however, did not mean that the leadership opposed some forms of political reform. The reformist leadership believed that political reform or political development itself was desirable, since as Deng Xiaoping (1984: 138) argued that "without political reforms, the achievements of economic reforms cannot be secured. Also, economic reform will not be able to continue further."

Nevertheless, political reform did not mean a sudden opening up of China's political process or policy-making process to competing social forces. The state had to remain autonomous in policy-making, and had to be able to impose its rational plans on society. Social forces were important in promoting the country's economic development, but this goal could be realized through economic decentralization, since it would provide social forces with great economic initiatives. More importantly, a developmental state required an efficient leadership capable of making "right" economic policies. These goals could be achieved by recruiting technocrats into the government and encouraging them to take part in the economic decision-making process. In other words, to build a developmental state requires partial openness, that is, opening the political process to a particular social group, i.e., technocrats or the educated elite.

These strategic considerations led the leadership to adopt a technocratic approach to development. Technocracy refers to a system of governance in which technically-trained experts rule by virtue of their specialized knowledge and position in dominant political and economic institutions (Meynaud, 1969). The technocratic approach to development is in accordance with Deng Xiaoping's concept of political reform, i.e., restructuring the state leadership and modernizing state agents (e.g. party cadres and government officials). The state needed a competent leadership so that it could provide good service to people. In other words, personnel changes were an integral part of political reform. One observer (Morey, 1993: 117) pointed out:

> In the Chinese context political reform does not generally embrace issues concerning civil liberties and the extension of the basic tenets of democracy (e.g., popular sovereignty, political equality and majority rule), but rather the area receiving the most attention concerns reform of the public sector. Regardless of the nature of the economic system or of the emphasis of political reform in a given country, the need for a public service that is competent, professional, honest and more responsive to public needs is of paramount importance. Reform which will lead to the creation of such a civil service can be seen as political reform in the broader sense and it will be more conducive to further and more extensive reform efforts throughout China.

The technocratic movement is significant for central-local relations. First, the nomenklatura system has been used to achieve its goal of modernizing state agents. The reform years have witnessed waves of personnel changes (Li, 1992; Li & White, 1998; John & Zheng, 1999). The nomenklatura system is still used, but more for reaching the standards of technocracy than simply for controlling. Second, changes over the nomenklatura system, i.e., from two-rank down to one-rank down system, can be seen as a process of localization of politics or inter-governmental political decentralization, that is, political power is decentralized from the central government to local governments. All these changes mean that the central leadership relies on provincial governments for both economic growth and political stability.

An analogy can be used here. In rural areas, the government implemented a reform measure called the "responsibility system," under which peasants had *de facto* ownership rights over the land that the government distributed to them, while the government retained only *de jure* ownership rights. Therefore, as long as peasants acted in accordance with the contracts they signed with the government, the latter would not intervene in their decision-making.

The central-local relationship in the reform era can also be regarded as a form of a political responsibility system in which the provincial government is no longer seen as merely an agent, but a government. As long as the provincial government does not go beyond the boundary (the contracts) that it has signed with the central government, it will enjoy total autonomy in decision-making over provincial affairs. Bargaining between the center and the provinces will occur in negotiating a contract. But reciprocity becomes more important after that contract is assigned.

Under the political responsibility system, political power no longer flows only from the center to the provinces. Even though the central government often structures the interests of local governments and provides policy choices for provincial governments in negotiating "contracts" with the provinces, it will not impose excessive conditions on the contracts, since the center needs strong local support for the initiation and implementation of reform policies. Provincial governments are allowed to design economic plans and implement provincial policies to promote local growth. For the central government, while economic decentralization allows great diversities among localities, the new pattern of reciprocity is expected to serve as a mechanism to integrate provincial governments into its political system.

This definition of local-central relations differs from both pluralism and totalitarianism as discussed in Chapter 1. First, it recognizes the active role of the central government in rebuilding local-central relations. But this does not mean that the center is totalitarian or highly authoritarian, in which the provincial government has to act on behalf of the center without considering its own interest. The central state devolves decision-making power to the provinces, but provincial officials must behave in a manner that is still, to some extent, dictated by the central governments, that is, they cannot go beyond the boundary. Put in another way, provincial officials can take policy initiatives, even make policies independently, but the policies they make need to be legitimated by the central state, at least formally.

Second, it recognizes that provincial officials have their own independent interests within the boundary. But provincial leaders still cannot be seen as a cohesive interest group. Practically, frequent personnel changes resulting from the nomenklatura system make it difficult, if not impossible, for provincial leaders to form an interest group. Also, provincial leaders have to take central interests into account when defining their own interests. Otherwise, their interests cannot be legitimated by the center.

Since China still lacks a clear institutional definition of central interests and provincial interests, all these behavioral patterns are established by a reciprocal interaction between the center and the provinces. Reciprocity thus becomes very important in regulating central-local relations. It is a mechanism in which the conflict between the center and provinces is resolved. Because provincial officials are actors with their own interests, their behavior is not always necessarily in line with that of the central government, even if they behave within the boundary. Deviation is allowed. The center no longer imposes absolute authority on provincial officials, and disagreements between the center and the provinces are resolved through explicit bargaining and implicit reciprocity.

Reciprocity and Interest Representation

For scholars who put an emphasis on the nomenklatura system, the provincial government is merely an agent, acting on behalf of the center, meaning that the center is able to impose its policies on the provinces, simply because it can remove those provincial leaders who are reluctant to follow central authority. But here, the issue becomes complicated. The questions are: Does the center take provincial interests into account when central policies are made at the top level? Do central policies only reflect central interests? How are provincial interests reflected in central policies?

This study argues that except for a few areas such as national defense and foreign relations, central policies are formed in the process of the reciprocal interaction between the center and the provinces. We do not need to focus on enormous economic policies that were practiced by the provinces and legitimated later by the center and became national policies. Reciprocity also takes place in political relations between the center and the provinces. Even though China's political system is still hierarchical and coercive, political reciprocity has become embedded in various aspects of institutional practice and process of decision-making.

The Nomenklatura System

Since the nomenklatura system has been widely regarded as the only effective means for the center to exercise its tight control over provincial leaders, it is important to examine whether this system *per se* is reciprocal. Though the central leadership makes final decisions on who will be chosen as provincial leaders, the latter are also involved in the process of selection. In other words, provincial interests are also represented in the selection process.

I only deal with how government officials at provincial (ministerial) level and below are chosen by higher authorities. With the decentralization of the nomenklatura system (i.e., from two-ranks down to one-rank down), provincial leaders actually have a more important say over personnel changes below the provincial level than the center, and this, in turn, affects the provincial leadership's relations with the center. To see how reciprocity is embedded in the nomenklatura system is to examine the process of selecting leaders at the provincial level and below; as emphasized before, the party management of cadres is the most important rule that the party exercises in its control over the provinces. The Communist Party regulates,

> Organization department shall be established at the central and local levels of Party committees and these organization departments are in charge of cadres who hold major leadership posts in the Party, the government, mass organizations, enterprises and undertakings. Personnel department shall be established at all levels of the government to assist the Party's organization departments to manage cadres (Cao, 1985: 426).

In other words, the party's organization departments are in charge of leading cadres, whereas the personnel departments at different levels of the government manage ordinary cadres. After the decentralization of the nomenklatura system in 1984, the CCP has implemented the system of administration by different levels, and of one level taking charge of the next lower level (*fenji guanli, xiaguan yiji*), in which major provincial leaders are controlled by the Central Organization Department (COD).[1]

The COD is the most important department in China's political system.[2] Its main functions are to assist the Standing Committee of the Central Committee of the CCP in controlling the principal cadres in all central-level organs under the party, government and military system,[3] and to manage thousands of provincial (ministerial)-level leading cadres.

A change of leading personnel at the provincial (ministerial) level could take place as the result of the following: (1) when the term of the Party Congress and the People's Congress expires at the end of five years; (2) when a nationwide reshuffle of leading personnel takes place; (3) when serious problems occur in a province and the provincial leadership has to be changed. Normally, the process of selection will be as follows:

1. Initiative taken by the center. The Central Committee would issue a notice on the principles governing the appointment of provincial-level cadres of the main provincial leading organs,[4] drafted

---

[1] More concretely, the Central Organization Department (COD) controls all the cadres at the central and provincial levels: a provincial organization department is in charge of all the cadres at the prefectural level in the province; a prefectural organization department manages all the cadres at the county level in the prefecture; and a county organization department controls the cadres at the township level in the county. The central, provincial, prefectural and county level organization departments together form a so-called "system of organization departments," which controls every leading cadre from the center to the localities.

[2] For a discussion of the Central Organization Department, its structure and functions, see Yan Hui (1995).

[3] They include: the Central Committee, the Central Discipline Inspection Committee, the National People's Congress, the State Council, the National Committee of the Political and Consultative Conference, and the Central Military Commission.

[4] They include: the provincial party committee, the provincial discipline inspection commission, the provincial government, the provincial people's congress, and the provincial political consultative conference.

by the COD, specifying the number of cadres to be appointed, their educational qualifications and age limits.

2. Report by the provincial party committee. Secretaries of the provincial party committee and heads of provincial organization departments would come to Beijing to report on the reshuffle plans.

3. Internal study. The COD would take initial suggestions on promotions, retainment of positions or dismissals.

4. Consultation with old leading cadres. Many old leading cadres, who had worked in the locality in question, often have an important say on the change of personnel of this locality. On appointments in these localities, the COD has to personally consult these old leading cadres and take directives from them.

5. On-the-spot investigation. The COD would form a three- to four-person group to carry out an on-the-spot investigation in the locality in question. The investigation groups first listen to the reports made at the COD by heads of provincial organization departments on how they decided on the name-lists of nominees, and then proceed to study each candidate's personal dossier to decide a priority list. The investigation would focus on the candidates' morality, capability, diligence, performance, personal history and their potentialities. The means of appraisal includes:

- At the unit (*dan wei*) where a candidate works, the investigation group would carry out an opinion poll by secret ballot among a certain number of cadres.
- The group would also carry out private talks with the candidates' superiors, colleagues and subordinates to gain more information about the candidate.
- The group would go to his previous unit to investigate the performance of the candidate during the Cultural Revolution.
- The group would also assess the work performance of the candidate at all the units where the candidate used to work.
- Finally the investigation group would talk to the candidate personally to assess his awareness of his own strengths and weaknesses, and to test his capability in person.

For each vacancy of the provincial leadership, the investigation group would have to consider three to four candidates. The results would not be revealed even to the provincial leadership.

6. Decision by the COD. After the investigation group returns to Beijing, it would report to the COD. After the approval by the COD, the plan would be reported to the center.

7. Approval by the center. The Secretariat of the Central Committee would first study the plan and report it to the Political Bureau for approval. After approval, the center would finally issue the decision as a document of the CCP.

The process of selecting leading cadres below the provincial level is similar to that of selecting provincial leaders. As discussed above, the Central Committee, since 1984, has decentralized the power of appointing and dismissing leading cadres of the prefectural level to the party groups of the provincial party committees, while retaining the power of appointing and dismissing cadres holding the rank of deputies at the provincial level and above. Thus, in selecting leading cadres below the provincial level, the standing committee of provincial and city party committees play a key role in the nomination of cadres holding the deputy rank (*fu zhi*) at the same level and those holding the substantive rank (*zheng zhi*) at the lower level.

At this point, it is important to clarify the concept of a "city" in China. Cities in China are divided into cities at the provincial level (e.g., Beijing, Shanghai, Tianjin and Chongqing), cities at the sub-provincial level (whose heads are of the rank of vice-provincial governors), cities at the prefectural level, and cities at the county level. I will only deal with cities at the sub-provincial level, whose leaders are controlled by the provincial leadership.

New candidates for vice-mayoral posts are determined by the standing committee of the city party committee and then reported to the organization of the provincial party committee. The organization department will, on behalf of the provincial party committee, appoint a team to carry out an assessment of the candidates and then give an opinion. This opinion is reported to the provincial party committee and at the same time, discussed with the standing committee of the city party committee itself. When there is an agreement between the provincial and city party committees, the candidates will be regarded as members of a reserve team. Sometimes this has to be reported to the Central Organization Department for the record. It may also be used as a reference by the central authorities for the transfer of cadres across provincial boundaries and to the central ministries.

In 1984, the Central Organization Department, acting on Hu Yaobang's proposal, tried out the nomination and election of the provincial leadership through secret balloting among cadres. This system has been gradually institutionalized. The present practice normally consists of taking a poll among the cadres, democratic nomination (nomination based on a secret ballot in a party conference or among cadres), differential election, and final appointment by the superior organizations.

This description of the process of selecting leaders at the provincial level and below shows that the provincial leadership is an internal part of the selection. In selecting provincial leaders, the central government formally makes the final decisions regarding who will be chosen, but due to the complicated process of selection, the provincial leaders, in effect, have an important say over who should be chosen. Without provincial leaders providing information on individual leaders, the central government can hardly make evaluations on them and make decisions over provincial personnel changes. Similarly, formally, the provincial leadership has a final say over the selection of leaders below the provincial level, but it cannot dictate the process and has to consult with leaders at lower levels.

Simply speaking, with the implementation of the principle of administration of cadres by different levels and of one level taking charge of the next lower level, the nomenklatura system has become increasingly reciprocal. The system, indeed, is the means for the center to control the provinces, but without provincial cooperation, the system will not function normally. The provincial government is in a subordinate position in China's political hierarchy, but this does not imply that it is not able to affect central personnel decisions. The nature of reciprocity is that each side can benefit from mutual cooperation, rather than confrontation. Therefore, reciprocity guides both the center and the provinces, constraining their own behavior in dealing with each other.

Reciprocity: "Play to the Provinces" and "Play to the Center"

Reciprocity is not only reflected in the process of selecting leaders at the provincial level and below. To a degree, it is also embedded in the selection of central top leaders. According to Susan Shirk (1993), the interaction between top leaders and provincial leaders is reciprocal. The Chinese Communist Party (CCP) has the ultimate authority over the provinces, but top leaders (including the Communist Party general secretary, Political Bureau members, or Political Bureau standing committee members) are chosen by an "elite selectorate" that consists of the members of the Central Committee, the revolutionary elders and top military leaders. The operational procedure that the Party, the government and military officials in the selectorate are appointed by top CCP leaders, and vice versa creates a relationship of "reciprocal accountability". Shirk observed (1993: 83), "reciprocal accountability is a relationship in which neither side has a definitive right. The lines of authority run in both directions." Reciprocal accountability is a distinctive institutional feature of the Chinese Communist system and shapes the interaction between the center and the provinces. On the one hand, assuming that a rational provincial official will seek to be promoted in the Chinese political hierarchy, central authorities could "play to the provinces" to gain political support from provincial officials by providing them with political incentives through the appointment system or the central nomenklatura. On the other hand, provincial officials can also "play to the center" because they are the majority of the selectorate and their votes are an important source of a given top leader's political legitimacy (Shirk, 1993).

In Shirk's (1993) explanation, individual leaders' preferences are seen as resulting from their rationality. As rational politicians responding to career incentives, policy-makers competing for the top positions have to play to the selectorate, and especially to the largest block within it, i.e., provincial officials. Shirk (1993) indeed showed why and how the provinces can also play to the center. But given the fact that reciprocity is asymmetrical, the model is not able to explain why the center as a rational actor does not maximize its power vis-à-vis the provinces. In other words, the model does not give a sound explanation of consistent decentralization that, to a large extent, has weakened central power. Certainly, as a power maximizer, the center would not have had such a reform strategy that would lead to the decline of its power. It seemed to Shirk (1993) that the center has to behave as it does. Her only major reason was that numbers matter because the largest block in the selectorate is provincial officials.

But this is not a satisfactory answer. Numbers change. While provincial leaders made up the largest power block in the Central Committee in 1987, the 1990s changed the power configuration between the center and the provinces. After the crackdown of the 1989 pro-democracy movement, the central government made great efforts to recentralize its power (Burns, 1994). As shown in Table 3.1, in the 14th Party Committee (1992), the leaders from various central bureaucracies became the largest block (40 percent), while the power of local leaders declined (30 percent). Although the power of local leaders was strengthened at the 15th Party Committee in 1997 (32 percent), leaders from central bureaucracies were still the largest power block (42 percent). Even with such a change, reciprocity between the center and the provinces continues.

Why should the provinces "play to the center"? It is not because provincial officials are the largest block in the selectorate, but because of the role they play in governing their territories. The simple fact that provincial officials are the largest block in the selectorate does not explain their capability of playing to the center since they are not a cohesive interest group. As this study argues, decentralization means that the center withdraws its institutional power

Table 3.1 Power Configuration of the Central Committee
(Full members) (13th–15th)

	13th (1987) No. (%)	14th (1992) No. (%)	15th (1997) No. (%)
Central organizations (Party & government)	62 (35)	76 (40)	81 (42)
Local organizations (Party & government)	67 (38)	62 (33)	62 (32)
Military	28 (16)	41 (22)	42 (22)
Others*	18 (10)	10 (5)	8 (4)
Total	175 (99)**	189 (100)	193 (100)

*The "Others" category includes: mass organizations, intellectuals, model workers, etc.
**The percentage does not add up to 100 due to rounding.
Sources: *China News Analysis*, no. 1347 (15 November 1987), p. 3; *China News Analysis*, no. 1471 (1 November 1992), p. 7; and *China News Analysis*, no. 1594 (1 October 1997), p. 4.

from the provinces and provincial governments become *de facto* independent players in dealing with provincial affairs. Without provincial cooperation, the center will not be able to govern the country. The fact that the provinces are governed by provincial governments plays an essential role in conducting reciprocity between the center and the provinces.

This can be confirmed by the "rewards" that the center has given to the provinces. We have seen that provincial leaders who are from developed areas that have contributed economically more to the center are appreciated and recruited into the top leadership. Table 3.2 shows that, during Mao's time, the majority of the Party elite came from Central China, especially Hunan, Jiangxi and Hubei. Since 1978, more and more power elites in the Central Committee (CC) are from eastern coastal areas, where rapid economic growth has been seen. In other words, a leadership transition in terms of geographic distribution has occurred.

Furthermore, local leaders have also become increasingly important in the national political arena. If so, their political interests

Table 3.2 Distribution of Birthplace, by Province, of Full Members of the Central Committee (8th–15th)

Native Province	8th CC: N: 97(%)		9th CC: N: 163(%)		10th CC: N: 181(%)		11th CC: N: 216(%)		12th CC: N: 266(%)		13th CC: N: 175(%)		14th CC: N: 189(%)		15th CC: N: 193(%)	
North																
Beijing	Nil	Nil	1	1	2	1	1	0.5	1	0.4	2	1	4	2	5	3
Tianjin	Nil	Nil	Nil	Nil	1	1	3	1	4	2	2	1	5	3	3	2
Hebei	4	4	9	6	14	8	19	9	29	11	20	11	22	12	10	5
Shanxi	7	7	7	4	8	4	15	7	14	5	5	3	7	4	6	3
Neimenggu	1	1	1	1	2	1	2	1	2	1	1	1	1	1	2	1
Subtotal	12	12	18	11	27	15	40	19	50	19	30	17	39	21	26	13
Northwest																
Liaoning	1	1	6	4	7	4	3	1	6	2	6	3	8	4	10	5
Jilin	Nil	Nil	1	1	2	1	Nil	Nil	2	1	5	3	8	4	10	5
Helongjiang	1	1	Nil	Nil	Nil	Nil	1	0.5	2	1	2	1	3	2	2	1
Subtotal	2	2	7	4	9	5	4	2	10	4	13	7	19	10	22	11
East																
Shanghai	1	1	3	2	4	2	Nil	Nil	3	1	3	2	2	1	2	1
Jiangsu	3	3	4	2	10	6	16	7	32	12	22	13	28	15	29	15
Shandong	3	3	12	7	14	8	16	7	31	12	25	14	24	13	24	12
Zhejiang	2	2	6	4	8	4	6	3	11	4	13	7	15	8	11	6
Anhui	4	4	5	3	7	4	6	3	9	3	4	2	6	3	10	5
Fujian	4	4	7	4	3	2	8	4	12	5	5	3	2	1	4	2
Taiwan	Nil	Nil	Nil	Nil	Nil	Nil	2	1	1	0.4	1	1	1	1	1	1
Subtotal	17	18	37	32	46	25	54	25	99	37	73	42	78	41	81	42

(Continued)

Table 3.2 (*Continued*)

Native Province	8th CC: N: 97(%)		9th CC: N: 163(%)		10th CC: N: 181(%)		11th CC: N: 216(%)		12th CC: N: 266(%)		13th CC: N: 175(%)		14th CC: N: 189(%)		15th CC: N: 193(%)	
Central																
Henan	3	3	11	7	9	5	9	4	12	5	6	3	5	3	5	3
Hubei	9	9	20	12	18	10	16	7	13	5	7	4	10	5	4	2
Hunan	30	31	17	10	22	12	28	13	18	7	9	5	9	5	11	6
Jiangxi	4	4	25	15	16	9	22	10	18	7	3	2	3	2	5	3
Subtotal	46	47	73	45	65	36	75	35	61	23	25	14	27	14	25	13
South																
Guangdong	5	5	7	4	8	4	5	2	7	3	11	6	5	3	5	3
Guangxi	Nil	Nil	3	2	3	2	2	1	3	1	1	1	1	1	Nil	Nil
Hainan	Nil	Nil	Nil	Nil	Nil	Nil	Nil	Nil	Nil	Nil	Nil	Nil	Nil	Nil	Nil	Nil
Subtotal	5	5	10	6	11	6	7	3	10	4	12	7	6	3	5	3
Southwest																
Sichuan*	10	10	10	6	10	6	15	7	14	5	8	5	10	5	7	4
Guizhou	Nil	Nil	Nil	Nil	1	1	Nil	Nil	3	1	1	1	1	1	1	1
Yunan	Nil	Nil	Nil	Nil	Nil	Nil	Nil	Nil	1	0	1	1	2	1	Nil	Nil
Tibet	Nil	Nil	Nil	Nil	1	1	1	0	2	1	1	1	1	1	1	1
Subtotal	10	10	10	6	12	7	16	7	20	8	11	6	14	7	9	5
Northwest																
Shaanxi	5	5	4	2	7	4	16	7	12	5	6	3	3	2	4	2
Gansu	Nil	Nil	3	2	2	1	1	0.5	1	0.4	2	1	1	1	1	1
Qinghai	Nil	Nil	Nil	Nil	Nil	Nil	1	0.5	Nil	Nil	Nil	Nil	Nil	Nil	Nil	Nil

(*Continued*)

Table 3.2 (*Continued*)

Native Province	8th CC: N: 97(%)		9th CC: N: 163(%)		10th CC: N: 181(%)		11th CC: N: 216(%)		12th CC: N: 266(%)		13th CC: N: 175(%)		14th CC: N: 189(%)		15th CC: N: 193(%)	
Ningxia	Nil	Nil	Nil	Nil	Nil	Nil	Nil	Nil	Nil	Nil	Nil	Nil	Nil	Nil	Nil	Nil
Xinjiang	Nil	Nil	1	1	2	1	2	1	3	1	3	2	2	1	2	1
Subtotal	5	5	8	5	11	6	20	9	16	6	11	6	6	3	7	4
Unknown	Nil	Nil	Nil	Nil	Nil	Nil	Nil	Nil	Nil	Nil	Nil	Nil	Nil	Nil	18	19
Total	97		163		181		216		266		175		189		193	

*Chongqing is included.

Sources: For the 8th to the 14th Central Committees, see, Li Gucheng, "Zhonggong Lijie Zhongyang weiyuan Shengji Fenxi" ("An Analysis of the Provincial Origins of the Central Committee Members of the CCP"), in *Yanzhou yanjiu* (Asian Studies), Hong Kong, No. 22 (April 1997), pp. 28–101; For the 15th Central Committee, see, Cheng Li & Lynn White, "The Fifteenth Central Committee of the Chinese Communist Party: Full-Fledged Technocratic Leadership with Partial Control by Jiang Zemin," *Asian Survey*, Vol. 38, No. 3 (March 1998), p. 246.

must be satisfied to some extent. Indeed, since the establishment of the reform regime, interest representation has occurred in the political realm. Many local leaders have been recruited into the most important positions in the central government and central party committee. Zhao Ziyang (Sichuan) and Wan Li (Anhui) in the 1980s; and Jiang Zemin (Shanghai), Zhu Rongji (Shanghai), Li Ruihuan (Tianjin), Li Changchun (Guangdong) and Wu Guanzheng (Shandong) in the 1990s are good examples. Actually, more and more local leaders tend to occupy major institutions of the central government.

Although local power in the central government and party committee should not be overestimated, local leaders' recruitment into the top leadership is significant. As one observer noted (Wu, 1993: 14),

> This change [the recruitment of more local leaders into the top leadership] first means that economic reforms have led to the rise of local force, and that rising local force is recognized by the central leadership. Local force must have more say in top decision-making from now onward.

CONCLUSION

Three major factors may account for the increasingly reciprocal nature of central-local relations in the post-Mao era. First, major reforms were initiated by local leaderships, and implemented nationwide after the coalition between the central reform regime and local leadership was established. The inability of the central bureaucracy to start any effective reform put local officials in an important position during the reform, especially during the early stages. The effectiveness of local initiative in the reform process forced the central government to legitimate it. What is important is that the central government legitimated local autonomy, but the basis of local autonomy was not in the central government; instead, local autonomy had a territorial base. Moreover, great local initiative facilitated further disparities among provinces, which, in turn, increased local autonomy because of the increased difficulty of the central government in forming and implementing any unified policies. The central government was no longer able to impose great power on localities, or to destroy localism as Mao did. This is confirmed by the fact that in 1992, Deng Xiaoping went to South China and used local forces to initiate another wave of reform when the conservative faction became increasingly powerful after the crackdown of the 1989 democratic movement in Beijing.

Second, the basis of authority of major leaders in Beijing was redefined, and the role of party ideology was reduced greatly. The reform years saw a decline in the importance of charisma and ideology, and a rise of more secular and pragmatic forms of political authority. Leaders no longer had the charismatic authority Mao did. Changes in the authority basis led to the inability of major leaders to deal with localism even if they thought such localism was harmful for central policies.

Also, now the reform leadership no longer regards ideology as a dogma that provides specific and infallible solutions to immediate political, as well as economic issues. Thus, both central and local leaders have become increasingly pragmatic, and their policies are problem-solving in their orientation. This is especially true of the young generation of leadership, which consists mainly of technocrats. Although it is uncertain whether politics can be reduced to technocratic solutions, technocrats do have a pragmatic attitude toward reality. As David Bachman (1992: 1050) observed,

> The area of expertise for the successor generation is the economy, not ideology or organization, suggesting that ideological issues will be less important than they have been with the older leaders. Because of their training and experience in economic work, the successors are likely to be even more pragmatic than Deng.

In effect, pragmatism of the new leadership is determined to a large extent by their technocratic background. They are able to overcome difficulties to achieve a consensus, because it is simple pragmatism necessary to get the job done (Suleiman, 1974: 380). In his study of Chinese technocrats, Hong Yung Lee (1991: 404) found,

> Technocrats evaluate even political decisions in terms of actual outcome rather than ideological value. In developing a range of policy options, each of which carries only different costs, benefits, and feasibility, this

way of thinking inclines the bureaucratic technocrats toward compromise and bargaining.

Learning from past experiences, ruthless power struggles within the government, and between different levels of government, is no longer acceptable. The top leadership has attempted to revive the traditional norms of political life. Harding (1986: 26–27) earlier on observed that China had undergone a process of moralization of elite politics:

> Party members agree to follow party discipline, to implement even those party decisions with which they disagree, and to advocate their preferred policy through orderly and peaceful procedures. In return, they are guaranteed that they will be governed by a system of collective leadership, that the power of individual leaders will be limited, that those whose interests are involved will be consulted in the determination of policy, and that the rights of those who take minority positions will be safeguarded.

This is the general political background against which new norms concerning the relations between officials at different levels have developed. The central leadership no longer forces the local leadership to keep in line with the central government by attacking or removing them. Instead, because new leadership tends to be problem-solving, a reciprocal relationship has been established between the center and the provinces. The territorial power of local officials is seen as legitimate, even though there is no institutional guarantee. In effect, the decline of the fiscal power of the central government puts the provincial government in a favorable position in its dealings with the central government.

Third, the establishment of the local election system brought about a legal basis for local authority. Before the reform, the only government officials directly elected by their constituents were the delegates to the people's congresses at the lowest levels of society. Since the reform, delegates to the middle-level people's congress are selected through direct election. The CCP also claimed that the use of direct elections would be extended to higher levels of government in the future. More importantly, elections now involve competition for office. Such elections are significant because local officials now can base the legitimacy of their authority on the people, rather than the high-level government or the party. So, even if an official is a non-native outsider, he or she must gain enough local votes. That means that he or she must take the local people's preferences into account. The central government is gradually finding that it cannot remove locally elected officials arbitrarily. For instance, in the 1993 provincial elections, the provincial people's congresses in Zhejiang and Guizhou selected their own candidates, rather than those appointed by the central government as their governors, and the central authorities recognized these results without great hesitation.

I, so far, have examined the important role of reciprocity in regulating central-local relations and how reciprocity has formed from recent experience (the shadow of the past). I have also discussed how reciprocity can mediate the interaction between the center and the provinces in general. Now I turn to case studies to examine how reciprocity is actually embedded in central-local relations by examining how individual provinces are governed and developed in the reform years.

Autonomous Development in *De Facto* Federalism: Jiangsu under Decentralization

I have argued that the relationship between the center and the provinces in China is not only governed by coercion and bargaining, but also by reciprocity. While coercion and bargaining are often used to resolve conflicts between the center and the provinces, reciprocity tends to become increasingly important in governing central-provincial relations. As discussed in the previous chapters, scholars who put an emphasis on coercion and bargaining have explored central-provincial relations by looking at how the center and the provinces interact in policy formulation and implementation. I do not want to underestimate the importance of coercion and bargaining; nevertheless, this study aims to highlight how reciprocity works in governing central-local relations.

"Reciprocity" implies that the provincial governments govern the provinces on behalf of the central government, but this does not mean that the provincial governments have to strictly follow central policies; nor does it mean that the central government has to execute its control over the province through coercive measures and intensive bargaining with the latter. Since reciprocity is based on obligation, the center and the provinces interplay with one another in a mutually acceptable way and each side is willing to justify its own behavior to the other side.

This chapter examines how the center and the province interacted in a reciprocal way in the context of local economic development in Jiangsu in the 1980s. Certainly, central to the political economy of central-local relations in post-Mao China is how decentralization resulted in rapid economic growth, while maintaining a rather stable central-local relationship.

Jiangsu has been known for its rapid economic growth. The province achieved an average annual growth rate of 12.7 percent in its gross domestic product (GDP) from 1979 to 1997. It produced about 9 percent of the national GDP in 1997 (The Statistical Bureau of Jiangsu, 1998: 23–24). While the province developed a strong collective sector in the 1980s, it has successfully transformed into a major manufacturing center in China since the mid-1990s. It is important to note that such a great transformation has taken place without any intervention from the central government. China's *de facto* federalism has provided an institutional setting for the provincial government to engage in such a transformation autonomously.

It has been argued that China's economic progress has originated from the market-oriented reform under which governments at all levels withdraw from economic affairs and enterprises gain autonomy in their decision-making.[1] Differing from this explanation, this case study will show that the market-oriented reform *is* significant, but more important is government entrepreneurship resulting from local autonomy. In Jiangsu, rapid economic growth in the early stages of the reform did not result from a radical market-oriented reform. In contrast, the government played an important part in promoting economic growth.

The very fact that the provincial government in Jiangsu played an entrepreneurial role had an important impact on central-local relations. With radical decentralization, the center was no longer able to impose absolute authority on provincial officials, even though there

---

[1] See most essays in Dorn, James A. and Wang Xi (1989).

were disagreements between the center and the provinces. In contrast, provincial government officials gained greater autonomy, which enabled them to modify policies made in Beijing and initiate new policies to develop their local economies. Since the provincial government actively took part in creating new local wealth, it was able to execute firm control over local economic resources, while the central government gradually lost its leverage over local development.

A common assumption has been that the control of the provincial government over economic resources enabled provincial officials to deviate from central policies and thus created tension between the center and the provinces. Nevertheless, even with the decline of central power, the center was still able to elicit compliance from the provincial governments to a great degree. Therefore, it is important to explore how the provincial government in Jiangsu played the role of entrepreneur in promoting provincial economic growth, while maintaining cooperation with the central government.

A caveat is to be added. Though more rapid development in Jiangsu took place since the 1990s, the emphasis of my discussion is on the development in the 1980s when the reform was characterized by radical decentralization, since, as discussed earlier, much tension between the center and the provinces was caused by decentralization. In 1993, Zhu Rongji, then Vice Premier, was appointed by Deng Xiaoping to be in charge of China's overall economic affairs. Since then, the central government has formed a rather consistent policy of recentralization regarding central-local relations. An emphasis on the 1980s will enable us to see how the provincial government responded to decentralization. More concretely, we will see whether the provincial government utilized fully the strategy of decentralization by the central government to pursue local interests without taking central interests into account.

ADJUSTING DEVELOPMENT STRATEGIES

History

Jiangsu has been a rich area for several centuries, and due to its richness, it has always been important to the central government.

As early as the Tang dynasty (618–907), Jiangsu was already contributing a large portion of state revenues. From the Song (907–127) and Yuan (1279–1368) dynasties, Jiangsu developed into one of the most commercialized provinces. Jiangsu and its neighboring province, Zhejiang, contributed about 70 percent of total state revenues. In the Qing dynasty, the commercial handicraft industry grew rapidly. Numerous townships emerged. In some places, only 20–30 percent of residents were engaged in rice-growing, and another 70–80 percent engaged to a notable degree in light industry such as cotton and silk production (Liu *et al.*, 1989: 1–13). During the 50 years before the Sino-Japanese War (1894–1895), Jiangsu became noted for its modern industries. National governments established some major enterprises such as the Nanjing Mechanical Production Bureau, the Qinglong Mountain Coal Mine (Nanjing) and the Xu Zhou Coal Mine. At the beginning of this century, Jiangsu had 155 modern enterprises, and numerous entrepreneurs were emerging. By 1932, Jiangsu had 4,652 modern enterprises with about 108,000 employees (not including the mining industry, transportation and construction). There were 103 textile mills, producing 19.2 percent of the total national textile production, and 19 flour mills, producing 11.4 percent of the total national flour products (*ibid.*). In 1949, before the establishment of the PRC, the province had 3,000 enterprises that employed more than 25 workers (*ibid.*: 314) and produced a total industrial output of 1.59 billion *yuan* (94.5 percent from light industry and only 5.5 percent from heavy industry) in the same year (The Statistical Bureau of Jiangsu, 1988: 93, 96).

Maoist Legacy

After its establishment in 1952, the Jiangsu provincial government gradually extended its control over economic affairs. At the end of 1952, there were 355 state-owned enterprises that had 71,000 employees and produced 17.3 percent of the total industrial output of Jiangsu; 341 cooperatives with 20,000 employees; and 47 state-capitalist enterprises with 24,000 workers (Liu *et al.*, 1989: 58). With a capitalist tradition in Jiangsu, the private economy was still dominant up to the end of 1952. There were 10,723 private enterprises, maintaining about 196,000 employees. Fully 83 percent of the total industrial output in the province came from capitalist enterprises, including state-capitalist and private enterprises, compared to 56 percent in the nation as a whole. In 1953, Jiangsu had 4,520 enterprises, each of which had more than ten employees, about 308,000 workers, and produced 2.18 billion *yuan* (fixed price) of industrial output. Of these enterprises, 3,523 private enterprises, nearly 80 percent of the total, had 169,000 employees, about 55 percent of the total, and produced 1.18 billion *yuan* in industrial output, about 54 percent of the total (*ibid.*: 73). But from 1953, the private economy declined rapidly. The central government gave the highest priority to state-owned enterprises and imposed strict constraints on private economic activities. As a consequence, private enterprises did not have incentives to develop because the state controlled the whole market system and private business became unprofitable. In 1982, several years after the reform began, of Jiangsu's total 50.3 billion *yuan* in industrial output, only 1 percent came from non-state and non-collective enterprises, compared to 61 percent from state-owned enterprises and 38 percent from collective enterprises (The Statistical Bureau of Jiangsu, 1988: 188).

During the First Five-Year Plan period (1953–1957), high priority was given to heavy industry. The output of heavy industry in the total industrial output more than doubled between 1952 and 1957 (The Statistical Bureau of Jiangsu, 1990: 179). Many industrial enterprises were also established in underdeveloped North Jiangsu areas — an attempt by the provincial government to balance regional development within the province. Meanwhile, small enterprises supporting agriculture grew quickly. It was found that "most of the counties in the province had their own repair shops and mechanical factories for agricultural machines" (Liu *et al.*, 1989: 85).

In 1956, Mao, aiming at achieving a high rate of economic growth, called for radical decentralization in an attempt to depart from the Soviet model. All provincial governments were encouraged to use their greater power to pursue self-sufficient and independent industrial systems within their domains. In Jiangsu, the Great Leap Forward brought about a high growth period (1958–1960). Total industrial output more than doubled between 1957 and 1960 (see Table 4.1). Nevertheless, the growth rate declined rapidly in the following years, including a period of retrenchment. In rural areas, a radical communization was implemented. At the end of 1957, Jiangsu had 34,367 agricultural cooperatives, each of which had 260

Table 4.1 Total Outputs of Agriculture and Industry in Jiangsu
(1953–1975) (billion *yuan*)

Year	Total	Agricul.	%	Indus.	% of which	Light Indus.	%	Heavy Indus.	%
1953	6.21	3.32	52.0	2.98	48.0	2.77	92.8	0.22	7.2
1954	6.41	3.24	50.6	3.17	49.4	2.90	91.6	0.26	8.4
1955	6.90	3.62	52.2	3.28	47.5	2.96	90.1	0.32	9.9
1956	7.22	3.36	46.5	3.86	53.3	3.35	86.9	0.51	13.1
1957	7.78	3.68	47.3	4.10	52.7	3.48	84.8	0.62	15.2
1958	11.40	3.87	34.0	7.52	66.0	5.81	77.2	1.71	22.8
1959	13.34	3.74	28.0	9.60	72.0	7.18	74.8	2.42	25.2
1960	13.71	3.68	26.8	10.03	73.2	6.87	68.5	3.16	31.5
1961	9.82	3.57	36.4	6.25	63.6	4.74	75.8	1.51	24.8
1962	9.35	4.02	42.9	5.34	57.1	4.29	80.5	1.04	19.5
1963	10.14	4.68	46.1	5.47	53.9	4.29	78.6	1.17	21.4
1964	12.48	5.66	45.4	6.82	54.6	5.36	78.7	1.45	21.3
1965	14.54	5.73	39.4	8.81	60.6	6.63	75.2	2.18	24.8
1966	17.03	6.61	38.8	10.42	61.2	7.46	71.6	2.96	28.4
1967	14.60	6.12	41.9	8.48	58.1	6.33	74.6	2.15	25.4
1968	15.09	6.54	43.3	8.55	56.7	5.95	69.6	2.60	30.4
1969	16.84	6.56	39.0	10.28	61.0	6.91	67.2	3.37	32.8
1970	20.68	7.13	34.5	13.55	65.5	8.31	61.4	5.23	38.6
1971	24.71	7.99	32.3	16.72	67.7	9.40	56.0	7.36	44.0
1972	26.66	8.32	31.2	18.34	68.8	10.11	55.1	8.23	44.9
1973	29.78	8.97	30.1	20.81	69.9	11.49	55.2	9.32	44.8
1974	29.53	8.99	30.4	20.54	69.9	11.75	57.2	8.79	42.8
1975	32.69	9.17	28.0	23.53	72.0	13.3	55.4	10.50	44.6

Source: The Statistical Bureau of Jiangsu, *Jiangsu Tongji Nianjian 1990* (Statistical Yearbook of Jiangsu, 1990), Beijing: Zhongguo Tongji Nianjian Chubanshe, pp. 93–97.

households on average. In 1958, the provincial government announced that communization was achieved in rural areas. It was reported that 1,490 communes were established and more than 94 percent of all households joined these communes (*ibid.*: 95). Rapid communization, however, did not result in high growth in agriculture. Total agricultural output increased a little in 1958 and then declined in the following three years (see Table 4.1). Famine occurred from 1959 to 1961. An official report recognized that due to that serious problem, the birth rate declined and the death rate increased rapidly in these years. The total population decreased by 1 percent in 1959 and another 0.1 percent in 1960 (*ibid.*: 98).

During the Great Leap Forward, small-scale industrial enterprises developed rapidly. The provincial government required that every commune open 15 to 25 small enterprises in three to five years in order to achieve its goal of rapid expansion of industry. It is not clear how many such enterprises were established in these years. But the number must be very large. In the adjustment period (1961–1962), many small enterprises were closed. In effect, 5,238 industrial enterprises were closed or "rectified" in 1961 alone. Half of all urban and rural collective enterprises were closed and state-owned enterprises were reduced by 40 percent (most of them were small-scale) in the same year. Another 773 state-owned enterprises were "rectified" in 1962.[2]

Also, after communization, the private economy was almost eliminated and collective ownership became dominant in the province. Individuals no longer owned any production elements; all were owned by collectives of various forms. Meanwhile, the system of the "unification of government and enterprises" (*zhengqi heyi*) was prevalent. Formally, commune or brigade property was owned by all members in the commune or in the brigade, but actually managed and used by government officials who had the greatest authority over commune or brigade property, and connected to higher-level governments through indirect channels, mainly through taxation and fiscal revenues. This form of property rights created a condition

---

[2] Liu *et al.* (1989: 106). Also see, the Government of Jiangsu (1984).

for government officials in some circumstances to violate, even deprive, peasant property rights on the one hand, and to play the role of entrepreneurs on the other. It was still dominant in rural areas, especially in south Jiangsu after several decades, as shown in various studies (Li, 1988; Zhou, 1988).

The impact of the Cultural Revolution on Jiangsu's development is complicated. During this period, economic growth still took place in Jiangsu, as shown in Table 4.1.[3] Some other major changes also occurred. Agricultural outputs actually increased continuously, but because the industrialization level rose, its percentage of total agricultural and industrial output decreased from 38.8 percent in 1966 to 28 percent in 1975. The percentage of the industrial output in the total agricultural and industrial output increased from 61.2 percent in 1966 to 72 percent in 1975 (The Statistical Bureau of Jiangsu, 1990: 96–97). During this period, high priority was given to heavy industry in order to develop a self-sufficient industrial system. Most investments were channeled from light to heavy industry. For example, in the 1950s, the ratio of investments between light and heavy industry was 1:3.5, and it was increased to 1:11 in the 1970s. Throughout the whole period, an annual growth rate of 20.4 percent in heavy industry was achieved, compared to 9.4 percent in light industry (Liu *et al.*, 1989: 124). Light industry output increased from 28.4 percent in 1966 to 44.6 percent in 1975 (The Statistical Bureau of Jiangsu, 1990: 96–97). In rural areas, the provincial government placed an emphasis on grain production, and other sideline products were overlooked. This policy resulted in serious consequences. People's living standards were rather low. For example, among 300,000 production teams in the province, 23,000 had less than 40 *yuan* annual per capita income (Liu *et al.*, 1989: 124).

After 1970, rural industry expanded rapidly in Jiangsu. Decentralization granted greater power and incentives to local officials to develop rural enterprises. In 1975, the total output of rural industry reached 2.28 billion *yuan*, twice that of 1970 (*ibid.*: 317). More

---

[3] Also see Prime and Penelope (1991).

important is that a new method of organizing production was gradually formed. With a rapid expansion of the rural industry, enterprises faced a serious shortage of material supplies for production. Local officials and entrepreneurs had to seek materials from outside the state planning system and established various forms of connections with numerous production units outside the province from which they obtained extra-budgetary materials and to which they sold their products. This form of production activity was rather controversial then, but had a great impact on the operation of rural industry in the era of reform.

Reform: Policy Adjustment and Industrial Expansion

It is difficult to tell when the Jiangsu province started the reform that is still continuing today. During the ten years of the Cultural Revolution (1966–1976), the annual growth rate of the total agricultural and industrial output reached 9.6 percent (see Table 4.1). Although the Cultural Revolution (CR) lasted 10 years, serious disorder in Jiangsu occurred only for a short time in 1967, 1971 and 1976, and it also did not spread to the whole province. According to an official report, disorder occurred in four out of 14 major cities, and six out of 68 counties of the province (Liu *et al.*, 1989: 134). Also, the CR did not have a significant impact on rural areas. As mentioned earlier, after communization, collective ownership was dominant in rural areas. Both local officials and peasants were not involved in the CR, because rural units were basically self-sufficient. From 1968 to 1974, the annual growth rate of the total agricultural output reached 4.6 percent (see Table 4.1). Although high priority was given to grain production, agricultural sideline production also increased gradually. Agricultural development provided rich supplies of raw materials for light industry, especially for rural enterprises. In 1975, rural areas provided raw materials that generated 9.4 billion *yuan* — about 76.8 percent of the total light industrial output. More than 50 percent of total provincial revenue was provided by agricultural production in the same year (Liu *et al.*, 1989: 135).

One major goal of Mao's CR was anti-bureaucratism. Participants in the CR in Jiangsu generally focused on large state-owned enterprises and high-level bureaucracy, and leaders in small-scale enterprises, especially collectives, did not feel great political pressure. Due to the fact that most enterprises were small, the CR did not have much impact on them. For example, the province owned only 360 enterprises that had more than 1,000 workers — about 1.1 percent of all enterprises (Liu *et al.*, 1989: 135). During the CR, small-scale enterprises and collectives had a higher growth rate and better economic efficiency than state-owned ones. Also, while bureaucrats in high-level organizations were attacked by Mao's Red Guards, production team leaders in rural areas were able to concentrate on developing the economy and opening new factories. The rural industry gained a great impetus for development during the CR, especially in the later period.

Great adjustments, both economic and political, took place after the post-Mao reform began. Adjustment strategies were rather diverse within the province, and overall, the provincial government was able to take a pragmatic stance to implement policies appropriate to the province.

In rural areas, Jiangsu did not develop the private economy as the Zhejiang province did (see the next chapter). The provincial government gave priority to collectives. Due to the fact that collectives had been dominant in Jiangsu, the household responsibility system that was initiated in the Anhui and Sichuan provinces before 1979 was not implemented arbitrarily. The provincial government of Jiangsu carried out the contract system as an experiment in 56,000 production teams — about 13.1 percent of the total in the province — between 1979 and 1980. But only 37 percent of them actually implemented this system during this time period. The government thus changed its strategy of agricultural reforms. During the 1981–1982 period, the household responsibility system was implemented in poor areas, mostly in north Jiangsu, while various collective contract systems were implemented in rich areas, mostly in south Jiangsu. Up to 1982, 82 percent of all production teams continued to be active, carrying out various forms of the collective contract system (Liu *et al.*, 1989: 148).

For rural industrial reforms, emphasis was put on leadership, rather than on ownership. In 1984, the Yanqiao township (Wuxi county) created a system of "*yibao sange*" (one contract and three changes) for rural enterprises. Under this arrangement, an economic contract system was implemented effectively with three other measures, i.e., cadres were no longer appointed by the higher-level government, but recruited by the contract system; workers were no longer allocated by the government, but recruited by the contract system; and a worker's income was no longer determined by the former rigid wage system, but by a floating wage system. This arrangement was approved and implemented within the province (The Commission of Economic System Reform of Jiangsu, 1988).

What was important was that the provincial government did not apply the south Jiangsu model to north Jiangsu. In the early 1980s, local officials in north Jiangsu tried to implement the south Jiangsu model, but did not produce positive economic effects. The provincial government thus encouraged local officials in 13 counties of north Jiangsu to pursue appropriate models, while using favorable policies in the areas of investment, finance and taxation toward these localities. Differing from the south Jiangsu model, collectives were not dominant in north Jiangsu, as shown in the "Gengche model." Ownership was more complex in north Jiangsu, where the private economy and cooperatives were dominant, while collectives (township and village ownership) also played a part (Hu, 1988: 123).

In urban areas, the economic management system reform was treated as an important political agenda of the provincial government. After 1953, the province implemented the system of the coexistence of the municipal administration and the prefectural government. These two kinds of government organizations had no close relations and had their own ruling domains. From 1971 to 1983, the province had seven municipal governments and seven prefectural administrations. In principle, the municipal governments were supposed to be in charge of industrial development, while the prefectural governments were in charge of agriculture. In May 1982, the provincial government held an urban working conference and called for the reform of this system. In early 1983, major provincial leaders such as Xu Jiatun, Zhu Jiangxian and their colleagues went to the Liaoning and Zhejiang provinces, looking for information about the system of "municipal administration direction of counties" (*shi guan xian*). The provincial government formulated a proposal, attempting to apply the *shi guan xian* system to Jiangsu. This proposal was approved by Beijing, and the system was implemented at the same time. In 1985, the whole province was divided into 11 municipal governments, 40 city-managed areas and 2,052 townships (275 *zhen* plus 1,777 *xiang*), with new types of link among them (Liu *et al.*, 1989: 152–153).

The new system was expected to provide an organizational condition for the provincial government and its low-level agents to coordinate economic development between urban and rural areas. Labor mobility and industrial integration were encouraged through various government policies. Rural areas were thus able to meet various needs with the help of cities in such fields as industry, technology, communications, transportation, education and information. Numerous enterprise groups, including both urban and rural enterprises, were established. For example, as of 1988, the Changzhou municipal city organized 80 enterprise groups that consisted of 450 urban and rural enterprises — about 75 percent of all enterprises in this municipal area. A variety of markets were organized under the *shi guan xian* system. By 1988, 60 big exchange markets for industrial and agricultural outputs, and more than 3,000 special markets, were established. Benefits from the integration of urban and rural industries also provided leaders with incentives to make efforts in building small townships. Township development reduced the municipal government's burden for the employment of rural residents. From 1984 to 1988, townships absorbed 70 percent of the rural surplus labor. On the other hand, township industries also contributed to the municipal government greatly. In the same period, 70 percent of the total industrial output of this municipal area was created by township industries (The Commission of Economic System Reform of Jiangsu, 1988: 46–50).

Changes also occurred to the system of macro-economic management. After the 1950s, Jiangsu implemented a distinctive industrial management system in which the provincial government did not manage enterprises directly, while the municipal and county governments participated actively in industrial construction. This system had a major impact on the province's industrial structure. The municipal and prefectural governments gained incentives to develop non-state industrial enterprises because of benefits they could gain from this sector, even before the reform. As a consequence, the state sector was never dominant in the province. At the beginning of the industrial reform, only 1 percent of the total industrial enterprises was state-owned. The rest were either urban collectives or rural enterprises. This structure insulated the provincial industry from the great damage caused by the CR chaos. But the structure also constrained the government's choice for a development strategy. Collectives were a major industrial sector, even after almost two decades of reforms, while the private sector was only a small portion.

After the reform began, the provincial government "decentralized" industrial management to lower-level government organizations. In 1984, 34 provincial enterprises were transferred to the municipal governments for management. The provincial government also reduced its mandatory plans and encouraged the market to influence enterprise production. In 1985, two-thirds of the 60 mandatory indices were removed. It is reported that, by 1985, the market regulated half of all industrial output (*ibid.*: 156).

Meanwhile, the provincial government adjusted its fiscal relations with lower-level governments in order to provide an incentive for them to develop local economies. A fiscal contract system was implemented. Municipal and county governments could have independent revenue sources that they could use for local projects. Municipal and county revenue increased quite dramatically, from 0.4 billion *yuan* in 1982 to 1.3 billion in 1985 (Liu *et al.*, 1989: 613). More importantly, township governments were allowed to establish their own relatively independent fiscal institutions. Due to the fast development of the rural industry in the province, the provincial government decided to establish the township fiscal regime in 1985 based on various experiments. Up to the end of 1985, 1,571 township governments — about 85.3 percent of total townships in the provinces — had their own fiscal systems (*ibid.*: 614).

After the reform began, high priority was shifted from heavy to light industry. The Maoist development strategy encouraged every province to develop a self-sufficient industrial system. In line with this strategy, the provincial government in Jiangsu had to put an emphasis on heavy industry before the reform. For example, in 1978, heavy industrial output was 229 times that of 1949, compared to only 13.3 times for light industry output in the same period (The Statistical Bureau of Jiangsu, 1990: 95). During the adjustment period (1979–1983), the government channeled a great proportion of investment into light industry. Investments for light industry were increased from 9.2 percent of the total in 1979 to 15.3 percent in 1983, while those for heavy industry decreased from 47.7 percent of the total to 38.9 percent in the same period (Liu *et al.*, 1989: 145). Meanwhile, structural adjustment also occurred within heavy industry. Great emphasis was put on the development of those sectors that could support light industry. Adjustment was quite successful. Light industry output was increased by 100 percent from 1979 to 1983, while heavy industry output increased by 52.3 percent in this period (*ibid.*).

The provincial government's strategy toward market development also changed. The economic reform meant that the government would not interfere in economic activities, thus letting the market govern enterprise production. But that did not necessarily mean that government organizations had nothing to do with market development. Actually, due to the absence of a marketplace, market development was a major task for government organizations. The provincial government in Jiangsu was rather successful in organizing such a marketplace. A strategy called "internal connection and external introduction" (*neilian waiyin*) was established at the beginning of the reforms. In 1984, major provincial leaders visited Guangdong and Fujian provinces and found that governments in these two provinces played an important role in developing favorable conditions for absorbing overseas Chinese and foreign capital, and also for market formation. In 1986, Governor Gu Xiulian visited Wenzhou (Zhejiang province) and concluded that government organizations could not stand idle, but should actively participate in creating markets

(1987). Jiangsu had seen a shortage of production materials. Even before the reform, the province "imported" a portion of such materials from other provinces. With reforms, horizontal cooperation (internal connections) became an important political agenda of the provincial government. Up to 1985, the province formed close ties with 1,600 stable industrial material bases in other provinces. A large proportion of production materials were imported into the province. During the Sixth Five-Year-Plan, Jiangsu had 3,500 joint economic projects with 28 provinces (Liu et al., 1989: 159). According to a statistic in 1987, the province imported 1,861 tons of coal and 188.7 tons of steel — about 49.1 percent and 41.7 percent of the total industrial consumption for both materials — respectively. Meanwhile, Jiangsu also "exported" a large proportion of its industrial production. Nearly 7 percent of the total industrial products on the nationwide market came from Jiangsu in that year (The State Statistical Bureau, 1989: 43).

Further, favorable policies were implemented toward foreign trade in the province. In 1984, the central government decided to open two major cities in Jiangsu (Nantong and Lianyungang) for foreign trade. In the same year, the provincial government suggested opening three other major cities (Wuxi, Suzhou and Changzhou) and the proposal was approved by the central government in 1985. Meanwhile, the provincial government "decentralized" decision-making over foreign trade to lower-level government agents and enterprises. The latter could now retain a portion of foreign exchanges earnings, bargain directly with foreign businessmen, and engage in above-quota exports. Further, these open cities were able to obtain production materials at lower prices and the necessary investment loans. Incentives were thus provided for local government agents to organize and develop foreign trade. During the Sixth Five-Year-Plan, Jiangsu introduced 500 technological projects, and exports increased from 0.85 billion *yuan* in 1981 to 1.55 billion in 1985, achieving a 13.3 percent average annual growth rate (Liu et al., 1989: 161).

The adjustment of the development policies contributed to fast growth in the Jiangsu economy. During the first decade of economic reforms (1978–1989), Jiangsu reached a 10.8 percent average annual growth rate of GNP, and 6.6 percent in provincial revenue growth (The Statistical Bureau of Jiangsu, 1990: 59, 320).

The first decade of reforms laid down a rather sound institutional foundation for a real take-off of the province's economy in the second decade. Though Jiangsu achieved even more rapid economic development in the 1990s, without reforms that occurred in the 1980s, it would have been very difficult for the province to achieve such rapid development in the second decade. These important reforms can be summarized into four aspects.

First of all, the highest priority of development was given to rural industry in the countryside and light industry in urban areas. The two supported each other and reinforced the momentum of economic growth. Second, the provincial government restructured organizational links between urban and rural governments in an attempt to coordinate economic activities in these two areas. Given the fact that government organizations played an important role in promoting economic development in Jiangsu, the restructuring was essential in initiating the take-off of the provincial economy. Third, the provincial government adjusted the distribution of economic interests among different government units by decentralizing fiscal power further to lower levels of governments, and thus provided them with greater incentive for development. Fourth, the provincial government adopted a pragmatic approach to relations between the government and the enterprises. While reforms required that government units unlink themselves from enterprises, the provincial government did not force government organizations to do so. As a matter of fact, the industrial structure both in the rural and urban areas made it impossible for the government not to unlink itself with economic affairs. The provincial government did so, not only because of the existing industrial structure, but also because the provincial government believed that the government had to be an active actor in economic affairs. All the above-mentioned policy adjustments enabled lower levels of governments to play the role of enterprise managers.

FISCAL REFORMS, CHANGING INVESTMENT PATTERNS AND INDUSTRIAL STRUCTURE

Fiscal Reforms and Changing Local Incentives

Since the establishment of the PRC, the province of Jiangsu never had deficits, and it was able to contribute most of its revenues to the central government (see Table 4.2). From 1949 to 1985, the province contributed 69.27 billion *yuan* to the center — about 59.8 percent of the total provincial revenue during this period. The province also contributed an additional 7.1 billion *yuan* from 1978–1985 — about 60 percent of the province's total revenue (Liu *et al.*, 1989: 595–596). In 1989, the province created 12.4 billion *yuan* in revenue — about 4.4 percent of the national total (The Statistical Bureau of Jiangsu, 1990: 29). Due to the great budgetary contribution to the center, the province faced a heavy revenue burden, compared to other developed areas. For example, in 1988, the province had 11.5 billion *yuan* in revenue, ranking third among all the provinces. But the province's contribution to the center ranked second (after Shanghai).

Table 4.2 Jiangsu's Revenue Contribution to the Central Government

Period	Revenue Contribution (billion *yuan*)	Contribution as % of Total Provincial Revenue
The Recovery period (1949–1952)	1.23	76.0
The 1st Five-Year Plan (1953–1957)	2.75	61.6
The 2nd Five-Year Plan (1958–1962)	4.20	42.2
The Adjustment Period (1963–1965)	2.83	56.1
The 3rd Five-Year Plan (1966–1970)	6.35	59.0
The 4th Five-Year Plan (1971–1975)	11.78	59.7
The 5th Five-Year Plan (1976–1980)	16.7	59.8
The 6th Five-Year Plan (1980–1985)	23.5	64.2
Total	69.27	59.8

Source: Liu *et al.*, *Dangdai Zhongguo de Jiangsu*, Beijing: Zhongguo Shehui Kexue Chubanshe, 1989, p. 596.

Roughly speaking, Jiangsu and Guangdong had the same-sized GNP, but Jiangsu's revenue contribution was about four times that of Guangdong in the 1980s. Wuxi, one major city in Jiangsu, had an economy the same size as that of Foshan, a major city in Guangdong province. However, Wuxi's revenue contribution was 15 times that of Foshan and was equal to that of Guangdong's total contribution. Zhenjiang, another city in Jiangsu, had revenue contribution almost the same size as Shandong's total (not including that of Qingdao) (The Investigation Group of Industrial Efficiency, 1990).

Fiscal reforms in Jiangsu began in 1977 when the provincial leadership proposed a reform package to the central government, stating that the province should go a step ahead in reforming China's economic management (The CCP Provincial Committee of Jiangsu, 1977). In November, Yu Qiuli and Gu Mu, two major leaders in Beijing, chaired a special meeting, attended by the heads of Jiangsu's Planning Bureau and those of the central government's First Ministry of Machinery, the Ministry of Finance, and the National Bureau of Material Supply. The meeting discussed a reform package that would give greater leeway to Jiangsu in economic planning, material allocation and fiscal management, and decided that a new fiscal system of "fixed rate contracts" (*guding bili baogan*) be implemented in Jiangsu beginning in 1977.

The new system was expected to give the province much greater fiscal autonomy. Instead of annual fiscal bargaining between the province and the center in determining the province's revenue contribution base, the rate of sharing was fixed for a period of four years. The province could thus be able to retain a growing portion of its increased revenue. Also, the central government would no longer issue mandatory fiscal plans to the provinces. Instead, the provincial officials could determine the spending levels for specific expenditure categories within an overall expenditure plan. But the provincial government's budgetary plan had to be in line with central policy and the central government still had authority in approving the province's budget and final accounts. Once the rate of sharing was set, the province had to balance its own budget. According to this new system, the province would contribute 58 percent of its total revenue and retain the other 42 percent in 1977. During the 1978–1980 period, the figures to contribute were 57 percent of its total and 43 percent retained. In 1978, the central government provided financial and material aid for those projects that originally were assigned to Jiangsu. The province submitted 61 percent of its total revenue and retained the other 39 percent after that year (Zhou, 1988: 653–654; Zuo & Song, 1988: 456–457).

Similarly, in 1977, the provincial government implemented a system of fixed-rate contracts to lower-level governments including municipal, county and township governments. In 1982, the provincial government adjusted its fiscal policy, under which lower-level governments could retain more of their increased revenues. Various experiments were also implemented. In Changzhou, the municipal government, after 1979, retained 3 percent of industrial and commercial benefits, which originally had been transferred to the provincial government. In 1980, the city administration was allowed to retain 20 percent of depreciation funds. After 1983, the city government could retain another 30 percent of depreciation funds, which had been previously given to the central government. In the same year, the city government proposed to the central government that Changzhou implement a system of "incremental contracts" for every three-year period. The proposal was approved by the central government and Changzhou became a model of economic reforms (Zhou, 1984: 672–680). In 1985, Nanjing city also implemented a similar experiment. All those reforms provided greater benefits for those governments and higher-level ones as well. The provincial government legitimated them because those reforms were able to provide greater incentives for local governments to develop their local economies, which, in turn, increased government revenue sources. So did the central government.

More importantly, such fiscal reforms were also applied to grass-roots government organizations such as township administrations. In 1981, the provincial government allowed communes to establish their own fiscal systems, but with no institutionalized authority. With the fast development of rural industry and agriculture, townships (former communes) accumulated enormous wealth, and township governments were soon allowed to establish formal fiscal systems. By the end of 1985, 85.3 percent of all townships in the province had them. Correspondingly, the Nanjing municipal government even established a district-level fiscal system, which was rather successful in generating and increasing government revenue. Because of benefits from increased revenue, grassroots administrations had incentives to promote economic development. In 1985, township governments collected 110.9 percent of their assigned revenue — an amount increased by 24.5 percent, compared to that of the prior year. Further, the system provided township administrations with the financial conditions to improve local education, housing, health care, and other welfare services. Those efforts, in turn, provided a source of social stability.

Overall, the new fiscal arrangement provided great incentives for local officials to develop the local economy. According to two local economic officials, the system played the following functions: first, the new arrangement enabled the province to establish its own relatively independent fiscal system and developed its own capacity to formulate and implement an economic growth plan based on local circumstances. Second, to some extent, the new arrangement hardened local budgetary constraints and reduced bargains between the center and the province, and between the provincial government and its lower-level governments on investment and material allocation because the new system institutionalized relations among governments at different levels. Third, because of institutionalized fiscal relations among them, local governments could gain direct benefits from increased revenues, and thus had a strong incentive to develop the economy and raise revenues. Finally, the new system provided the financial conditions for horizontal economic cooperation among industrial units within and across the province (Yu & Zhu, 1987).

How, then, did government officials deal with enterprise managers? Governments did unto enterprises as their higher-level governments did unto them. Various management responsibility or contract systems were implemented in both state-owned enterprises and collectives, and enterprise managers were given greater financial power; enterprises established many small account units, and the system of "cooking in separate kitchens" was also applied to them; the link between rewards or bonuses and individual performance was established. Up to 1984, fully 70 percent of all state enterprises carried out these reforms in the province (Liu *et al.*, 1989: 155–156). In 1987, the enterprise contract system was widely implemented in the province. Out of a total of 1,966 state-owned enterprises, 1,730 enterprises, or 87.9 percent of the total, implemented such a system.

Incentives for Local Growth and Changes in Investment Patterns

Fiscal decentralization increased the capability of the provincial government to accumulate capital for investment and for local economic development. Investment policy became a reflection of the intention of the provincial government to interfere in local industrial structure. An examination of local investment behavior enables one to see whether the provincial government deviated from the central government's priority of industrial policy.

With economic reforms, the provincial budgetary revenue increased continuously, from 6.2 billion *yuan* in 1978 to 12.4 billion in 1989 (The Statistical Bureau of Jiangsu, 1990: 320). The banking system reform increased the capacity of the provincial government to raise savings and deposits, which had grown rapidly since the reform. Bank savings increased more than eight-fold from 1979 to 1989, while total savings by residents (urban and rural areas) increased from 1.67 billion *yuan* to 33.2 billion in the same period (The Statistical Bureau of Jiangsu, 1990: 322–323).

Moreover, fiscal decentralization granted the provincial government greater autonomy in investment decision-making. A stable growth of budgetary revenue and bank savings led to a fast growth of investments in the province. Fixed asset investments in state-owned enterprises increased from 8 billion *yuan* in 1985 to nearly 13.5 billion in 1990, and that in collectives increased from 6 billion *yuan* to 7.5 billion in the same period. See Table 4.3 for details.

Table 4.3 Composition of Total Fixed Asset Investment in Jiangsu
(1985–1997) (100 million *yuan*)

	State-owned		Collectives		Others*		Total
	Amt	%	Amt	%	Amt	%	
1985	80	42	59	31	52	27	192
1986	101	42	61	25	79	33	241
1987	128	40	80	25	108	34	317
1988	154	41	93	25	124	33	372
1989	124	39	67	21	129	40	320
1990	135	38	75	21	147	41	356
1991	172	39	110	25	158	36	440
1992	288	40	276	39	148	21	712
1993	404	35	493	43	247	22	1144
1994	478	36	418	31	435	33	1331
1995	603	36	491	29	586	35	1680
1996	709	36	465	24	776	40	1950
1997	827	38	448	20	929	42	2203

*"Others" refers to the private sector and other non-state and non-collective sectors.
Sources: The Statistical Bureau of Jiangsu, *Jiangsu Tongji Nianjian*, various issues.

The question of whether the province deviated from the central government's priority becomes complicated when we turn to examine where fiscal and financial revenues were used. Generally speaking, the provincial government made a great effort to keep investment patterns in line with the central government's priority. As shown in Table 4.4, investment in agriculture declined drastically, from 8 percent of the total in 1980 to 3 percent in 1990; investment in light industry and heavy industry did not change greatly from 26 percent of the total to 21 percent, and from 58 percent of the total to 59 percent in the same time period, respectively. Investments in transportation, post and telecommunications increased rapidly from 8 percent in 1980 to 17 percent in 1990.

The provincial government attempted to put more budgetary investment in priority sectors such as energy and transportation, but this was overshadowed by the fact that extra-budgetary investments that largely went to profitable sectors such as processing industries

Table 4.4 Budgetary Investment in Capital Construction
in Jiangsu (1980–1997)

Year	Agriculture		Light Industry		Heavy Industry		Trans., Post & Telecommun.		Total
	Amt	%	Amt	%	Amt	%	Amt	%	
1980	1.91	8	6	26	13.63	58	1.92	8	23.46
1985	1.16	2	13.29	25	30.47	58	7.4	14	52.32
1990	2.58	3	19.31	21	54.55	59	15.92	17	92.36
1995	9.94	2	86.57	20	205.97	48	125.87	29	428.35
1997	24.91	4	92.49	14	323.8	50	204.89	32	646.09

Source: The Statistical Bureau of Jiangsu, *Jiangsu Tongji Nianjian*, p. 111.

increased throughout the 1980s. For example, according to the 1987 central government plan, Jiangsu could have a fixed investment of 10.75 billion *yuan*; of those, 8.69 billion was invested in state enterprises, and 2.08 billion in urban collectives. But, in effect, investment in state enterprises reached 11.75 billion, and 2.84 billion in urban collectives — 26 percent and 27.6 percent above the state quota, respectively (The Statistical Bureau of Jiangsu, 1988: 232). The increasing amount of investment, especially extra-budgetary investment, was mainly due to the fact that financial resources that were beyond the control of the provincial government were now available for lower-level governments and state enterprises. The banking system that frequently had close relations with local government organizations often became a major investment source for enterprises. An official report stated,

> Every occurrence of disproportional economic development in Jiangsu is mainly due to an expanding fixed-asset investment. Every economic adjustment must first control and reduce the size of fixed-asset investment. The Jiangsu Branch of the Construction Bank manages the province's fixed investment size, and mismanagement often brings about great loss to the national economy (Liu *et al.*, 1989: 629).

Indeed, the provincial government faced a dilemma. On the one hand, there was a strong motivation to develop profitable sectors that needed less investment and could produce a quick return.

The fiscal burden also required the government to invest in short-term projects. On the other hand, long-term development required the government to invest in long-term projects such as transportation, communications and energy.

Changes in investment policies resulted in considerable changes in the industrial structure in Jiangsu. Before the 1960s, agriculture was dominant. Agricultural output was 47.5 percent of the total in 1964, while industrial output was 26.8 percent of the total. Industrial output increased once during the Great Leap Forward, but dropped afterward. From 1964 to 1972, agricultural development was quite stable, but due to the fast development of collectives, especially of rural industry, during the later period of the Cultural Revolution, industrial output was above that of agriculture for the first time in 1972. After 1972, the percentage of agricultural output, in total, declined continuously from 38.3 percent in 1972 to 26.4 percent in 1989. On the other hand, industrial output in total increased rapidly from 39.2 percent to 53.4 percent in the same period (The Statistical Bureau of Jiangsu, 1990: 62–63).

The post-Mao industrial structure in Jiangsu was characterized first by the predominance of light or processing industry. In 1985, more than 85 percent of the total industrial output came from the processing industry. Second, collectives were dominant within the processing industry. Up to the end of the 1980s, more than 90 percent of all industrial enterprises were collectives and more than 55 percent of the total industrial output was created by collectives. Third, small-scale enterprises were dominant. The province had about 46,900 small-scale enterprises — about 98 percent of the total of industrial enterprises. These enterprises produced about 68 percent of total industrial output (Li, 1990).

This industrial structure had a major impact on economic development and political stability. Jiangsu is rich in its labor force and poor in its natural resources. Population pressure is always a major concern in government decision-making. After the late 1970s, numerous agricultural laborers were transferred to industry. In 1989, there were 6.6 million persons registered as agricultural laborers in rural industry, about a quarter of the total agricultural labor in the province. Additionally, a portion of agricultural laborers migrated to cities. Urban residents increased from 7.3 million in 1978 to 13.7 million in 1989 (Shao, 1991). The fast development of the processing industry was mainly a result of an increasing surplus in the agricultural labor force as farming became more efficient.

Although the processing industry absorbed a large surplus in the agricultural labor force and created favorable conditions for political stability, it also generated difficulties for the provincial government to adjust its industrial policy. The fast development of the processing industry increased the tension between the demand for and supply of industrial materials. In 1987, overall industrial growth reached an annual rate of 23.8 percent, but the growth of coal, transportation, electrical power, steel and cement was only 2.8 percent, 4 percent, 14.2 percent, 13.3 percent and 14.7 percent respectively. About one-third of industrial capacity thus could not be used fully (Yi, 1990: 35).

Furthermore, the rapid expansion of the rural industry generated various criticisms among different groups.[4] The fast development of collectives absorbed raw materials essential to state enterprises. Since labor was cheaper in collectives (especially rural collectives) than in state enterprises, products by the former were more competitive than those by state enterprises. Also because of the great demand from consumers, due to product selection and quality, products by collectives were very profitable in the 1980s. Collectives absorbed significant agricultural surplus and promoted industrial progress in the provinces. Nevertheless, a fast expansion of collectives led to low economic efficiency; because of the popularity of their products, collectives were unwilling to use new technologies, let alone invest in them.

Although Jiangsu's products were still profitable during the initial stages of post-Mao reform, Guangdong and Fujian soon posed a serious challenge. Guangdong and Fujian opened their doors earlier

---

[4] Among others, see Yi Jiafu (1990); Li Yun (1990); Shao Jun (1991); Yu Guan (1990); The Investigation Group of Industrial Efficiency (1990); and Yu Guan *et al.* (1990).

than Jiangsu, and absorbed advanced technologies from their neighbors — Hong Kong and Taiwan, respectively. Their products became very competitive in the market and rapidly invaded the markets originally occupied by products from Jiangsu and Shanghai. Compared to those at the beginning of the reform, various profit indices in Jiangsu declined dramatically by the end of the 1980s (see Table 4.5).

The nationwide industrial expansion put Jiangsu in a weak position. Jiangsu was no longer able to gain raw materials as easily as before, because every province was able to process its own raw materials for profits. Jiangsu thus had to pay much higher prices for the raw materials that its industry needed. More seriously, the market coverage of Jiangsu's products declined as other provinces

Table 4.5 Major Industrial Indices in Jiangsu (1980–1988)

	1980	1981	1982	1983	1984	1985	1986	1987	1988
Size of enterprises that suffer losses %	6.17	9.70	12.52	9.59	19.17	13.67	17.51	14.71	18.04
Size of enterprises losses (billion, *yuan*)	1.11	1.65	2.36	1.47	2.13	1.95	5.0	5.57	6.82
Profit rate of industrial output %	18.86	16.67	18.15	17.93	16.86	16.39	13.09	12.14	11.30
Profit rate of sales %	20.48	19.61	19.48	19.34	18.60	18.15	14.91	13.56	12.53
Profit rate for capital %	33.35	30.04	28.61	28.06	29.18	29.69	22.55	20.73	21.11
Profit rate for original fixed assets %	40.15	35.49	33.28	32.70	33.23	35.03	27.61	25.53	26.65
Profit rate for net fixed assets %	58.42	52.45	47.84	47.01	48.17	49.82	38.43	34.89	35.95
Profit rate for hundred *yuan* wage		280	269	295	223	218	202	196	191

Source: The Investigation Group of Industrial Efficiency, The Commission of Science and Technology of the Conference of Political Consultant, Jiangsu, *"Jiangsu Sheng Gongye Jingji Xiaoyi Kaocha Baogao"* ("An Investigation Report of Industrial Enterprise Economic Efficiency of Jiangsu"), in *Nanjing Shehui Kexue* (Nanjing Social Sciences), 35: 1 (1990), p. 47.

Table 4.6 The Ratio between "Imports" and "Exports" in Regions
of Province ("Imports" as 1)

Region	1978	1986	Increase (+) or decrease (−) during 1978–1986
Southwest	1: 0.49	1: 0.81	+0.32
Northwest	1: 0.54	1: 0.71	+0.17
Central	1: 0.56	1: 0.92	+0.36
North	1: 0.91	1: 0.70	−0.21
Northeast	1: 0.86	1: 0.93	+0.07
East	1: 1.08	1: 1.12	+0.04
Jiangsu	1: 1.09	1: 1.02	−0.07

Source: The State Statistical Bureau, *Yanhai Jingji Kaifangqu Jingji Yanjiu He Tongji Ziliao* (Economic Studies and Statistical Data of Coastal "Open" Economic Areas), Beijing: Zhongguo Tongji Chubanshe, 1989, p. 55.

expanded their markets (see Table 4.6). The ratio between "imports" and "exports" declined from 1: 1.09 in 1978 to 1: 1.02 in 1986.

STRUGGLES FOR AN EXPORT-LED DEVELOPMENT STRATEGY

The Initiation of the Export-Led Policy

One of the major goals of the reform leadership was to establish an open economy. After the establishment in South China of four special economic zones (SEZs) at the beginning of the reform, the reform leadership considered opening more cities in the coastal areas of China in order to integrate China into the international economy. As early as April 1981, the State Council initiated a proposal called the dialogue between the eastern and the western parts of China. The proposal stated that China's economic development was very uneven; east China had a relatively developed economy, while the economy in the west was backward; therefore, China had to establish a long-term economic development strategy that took into account the division of labor among different areas in order to achieve fast economic growth. In November, the state council held a conference attended by local leaders from nine provinces. The conference proposed that each province make use of its own comparative advantages and play a role in the national economic development.

In early 1984, Deng Xiaoping visited economic zones in South China and called for further development of China's international economy. Between 26 March and 6 April 1984, the Secretariat of the CCP and the State Council held a joint conference in Beijing, attended by local leaders from Tianjin, Shanghai, Dalian, Yanta, Qingdao, Ningbo, Wenzhou and Beihai. Local leaders from the four SEZs emphasized that one of their major experiences in developing international trade had been that the central government decentralized financial power dealing with international trade to localities, and local leaders gained greater autonomy and incentives to seek development. Deng gave very positive comments on the SEZs and called for further decentralization of financial power in international trade. Hu Yaobang, then the General Secretary of the CCP, argued that Shanghai, Jiangsu and other coastal provinces had many advantages and local leaders should consider how to make use of those advantages fully. He then asked them to open their minds and have the courage to develop their local economies. Zhao Ziyang suggested that local leaders in coastal areas go to the SEZs to learn lessons from them in order to speed up their own development. Many major policies were formed at the conference. The coastal areas were assigned great autonomy in their decision-making in developing international trade. The central government decided to carry out favorable fiscal and investment policies for these areas (The Editorial Bureau of the Economic Management of Contemporary China, 1987: 534–535).

In 1984, the State Council sent investigation groups to the Changjiang (Yangtse) delta and Zhujiang delta. The group members discussed with local leaders widely about how economic growth in those areas could be accelerated. After their investigation, the groups wrote a report, entitled "Some Issues Concerning Economic Development in the Coastal Areas," and recommended opening the Changjiang and Zhujiang deltas first, and the Liaodong and Jiaodong peninsulas later, so that an open Economic zone could be integrated along the country's coastlines. The proposal was supported by Zhao Ziyang who recommended it to Deng Xiaoping. Deng responded positively and suggested to the concerned leaders that they study how to get the job done (Wang *et al.*, 1989: 563).

Based on Deng's suggestion, the State Council held a conference about formulating and implementing policies toward open areas in January 1985. The conference recommended a major development strategy for the Changjiang delta. The delta includes the Shanghai area and almost all the important cities in Jiangsu and Zhejiang provinces. The suggested strategy was "to earn foreign exchange by exports, to lift economic and technological levels by introducing technologies, and thus to increase exports" (*ibid.*: 493).

In 1987, Wang Jian, an economic official in the State Planning Commission and one of the writers of the report of the 13th Congress of the CCP, proposed the "Theory of Grand International Circulation" (*Guoji Da Xunhuan Lilun*). Wang strongly proposed that China employ an export-led development strategy, following other East Asian economies. According to him, the government needed to channel numerous surplus agricultural laborers into international circulation by developing labor-intensive industries. An increasing surplus agricultural labor force was a serious issue in China, both economically and politically. Labor-intensive industries could absorb numerous surplus laborers on the one hand, and could earn more foreign exchange on the other. The acquisition of foreign exchange was important for China's economic development. The government could use it to gain the capital and technology needed for the development of heavy industry, and thus lift China's overall level of industrialization (Liu & Wang, 1988; Wang *et al.*, 1989: 495–503).

Wang's proposal was supported by some major leaders including Deng Xiaoping and Zhao Ziyang during the 13th Congress of the CCP. Deng emphasized that China could no longer lose such an opportunity and that the leadership should have the courage to implement such a strategy (Wang *et al.*, 1989: 505). Various measures were taken soon after Deng's suggestion. In January 1988, the Planning Office of the Shanghai Economic Zones under the State Council held a conference in Shanghai, and suggested that the Zhujiang delta model should be transferred to Shanghai. In March, the State Council held a working conference, discussing how the coastal area development strategy could be implemented. Local leaders, especially those in Guangdong, Shandong and Shanghai, responded that they would make great efforts to implement such a strategy (*ibid.*: 506).

Any development strategy could be a dead letter without cooperation from local leaders, especially those in the provinces. The central leadership initiated an export-led development strategy, but implementing such a policy is a matter for leaders at different levels. In order to provide incentives for local leaders to develop China's international economy, the reform leadership decentralized international trade policy and provincial leaders were authorized with greater decision-making power. Politically, under new policies, the provinces could gain more benefits from increased exports than before.[5] However, local performance in foreign trade was very diverse. Foreign trade development was much faster in the Zhujiang delta than in the Changjiang delta. A 1986 report by the *Open Newspaper* (*Kaifang Bao*) reached the conclusion that "both the industrial base or the technological and management level are much higher in the Changjiang delta than in the Zhujiang delta. However, in past years, economic performance in terms of exporting industrial output, making use of foreign capital and introducing foreign technology has been better in the Zhujiang delta than in the Changjiang delta" (cited in Zhao *et al.*, 1989: 21).

From November 1987 to January 1988, Zhao Ziyang, the General Secretary of the CCP, visited the Changjiang delta and tried to build a consensus among provincial officials about the implementation of the center's export-led development strategy. Zhao held various conferences (*zuotanhui*) with major local leaders in Jiangsu and Zhejiang in order to secure further provincial cooperation in developing foreign trade. Zhao called for local leaders to seize various opportunities to accelerate foreign trade in the area. Zhao also

---

[5] On decentralization in decision-making in China's international trade, see Chong Pengrong (1990: 135–160).

proposed concrete measures. First, development could be labor-intensive. There are rich and highly-qualified labor forces in the area compared to other regions, and local leaders needed to make use of this advantage. Second, the delta had to develop the strategy of "two heads outside" (*liang tou zai wai*), i.e., gaining raw materials outside China and building markets outside China. Third, local governments needed to put emphasis on developing various enterprises in order to absorb as much foreign capital as possible. Enterprises could be established and managed by foreign businessmen independently. They could also be joint ventures. Further, local leaders could also invite foreign businessmen to manage Chinese enterprises according to their own experience so that economic efficiency could be expected to improve. Zhao especially emphasized the role that rural industry in Jiangsu and Zhejiang could play in developing foreign trade because, compared to state enterprises, rural enterprises or collectives were very competitive. Local leaders should provide strong incentives for rural enterprises to play their role fully (Xinhua News Agency, 1988).

Provincial Responses to Central Initiatives

Jiangsu's progress in international trade was not made without difficulties. The central government allowed Nantong, Lianyungang, Suzhou, Wuxi and Changzhou in 1984 to become open areas. In 1987, the province generated foreign trade of US$2 billion, reaching an annual growth rate of 23.4 percent. This figure was about four times that of 1978. But compared to Jiangsu's economic development level, this performance fell short of expectations. In 1986, Jiangsu generated 8.37 percent of the total national output, 8.54 percent of the total GNP, and 11 percent of the total national industrial output (ranking first). But the province only had 6.35 percent of the total national exports (ranking fifth), and just 151 joint ventures and foreign enterprises — only about 2 percent of the national total. From 1981 to 1985, the province achieved an annual growth rate of 13.7 percent for the national output, 15.3 percent for the total industrial and agricultural output, but had only a rate of just

12.2 percent for foreign trade, whereas in many other areas, foreign trade led in growth. In 1986, the province's exports amounted to only one half that of Guangdong. Jiangsu's purchase of foreign trade commodities was 5.1 percent of the total industrial and agricultural output, compared to 13.4 percent in Guangdong, 7.4 percent in Liaoning, and 6.6 percent in Shandong. In the same year, the purchase of foreign trade commodities in three cities (Suzhou, Wuxi and Changzhou), which were the most advanced areas in Jiangsu, was about 5.6 percent of the total industrial and agricultural output, compared to 12.3 percent in the counties in Shanghai suburbs, and 7 percent in the Jiaxing and Huzhou areas in Zhejiang (Zhao *et al.*, 1989: 20–21).

One major reason for Jiangsu's relatively low level of foreign trade in the 1980s was that Jiangsu's products were very profitable in domestic markets. A relatively solid base of industry created a situation where Jiangsu would be in an advantageous position in competition with most other provinces. But after the mid-1980s, how Jiangsu's foreign trade could be speeded up became a hot topic among different groups. The provincial government was criticized for not implementing effective policies to promote Jiangsu's foreign trade.

According to a group of investigators, various reasons led to such a situation in foreign trade. First of all, the leadership's mindset was not open enough and the leadership did not realize the significance of developing foreign trade for overall economic progress in the province. In contrast, leaders in the Guangdong and Fujian provinces were playing an important role in the fast growth of foreign trade and they were making full use of favorable policies. But the leadership in Jiangsu did not employ the central government's favorable policies quite as well. Second, the leadership did not make great efforts to reform Jiangsu's system of foreign trade, which was still too centralized. Guangdong's success had been due to two reasons — decentralization and the separation of government from enterprises. Decentralization provided local units and enterprises with incentives to seek growth in foreign trade, and the absence of the government's interference gave enterprises greater autonomy in decision-making (*ibid.*: 21–22).

The government was criticized for not adjusting Jiangsu's industrial policies, thus leading to the declining competitiveness of Jiangsu's products even in the domestic market. The government was thus asked to implement new and effective policies to initiate the development momentum of foreign trade. Xue Jiaji, the president of the Jiangsu Academy of Social Sciences, argued that because Jiangsu had a heavy fiscal burden compared to Guangdong and Fujian, the province did not have many financial resources to invest in foreign trade; therefore, the province should use foreign capital to develop foreign trade. The leadership could not be limited by the constraints set forth by the central government that foreign capital needed to be kept within 20–25 percent of the total foreign exchange controlled by the government. Jiangsu also needed to develop foreign direct investment (FDI) because FDI could enable the province to make use of the central government's favorable policies fully, or even overuse them, as other provinces had done (Xue, 1988).

A careful reading of the province's policies toward foreign trade shows that the provincial government made great efforts in promoting it. Nonetheless, the provincial government was not all-powerful. Government behavior was seriously constrained by the province's existing industrial structure and other important factors. As mentioned earlier, the province's industry had been organized around various processing industries that "import" an essential portion of raw materials from other provinces and also "export" its products to them. By the mid-1980s, the province "imported" about 60 percent of raw materials and "exported" 60 percent of its products. A government report strongly recommended that if the province ignored further development of the domestic market for Jiangsu's product in order to seek a pure export-led development strategy, there would be a very negative impact on the province's economy. So, the government needed to be cautious in implementing an export-led strategy (The Statistical Bureau of Jiangsu, 1989).

The provincial government did implement various measures to promote fast growth in foreign trade. After the mid-1980s, numerous effective methods were sought to speed up the province's pace in foreign trade. Many special offices were established at different levels of government to deal with businesses engaging in foreign trade. Increasing exports became a major goal of the government. At the beginning of every year, the government set forth a specific goal that had to be achieved. Economic performance became a main standard for the provincial leadership to judge the political achievements of government officials at lower levels. Very preferential policies were carried out toward open areas because:

> If there is no policy difference toward open and non-open areas, in reality there will be no such thing as an open policy.... The state assigns different tasks and requirements to the open areas, certainly the state needs to have preferential policies toward them. The government organizations need to give open areas higher priority when they design plans, make policies, distribute financial and material resources, and plan college student and cadre training. An overall favorable condition needs to be created for them in order to help them to speed up their pace [in developing foreign trade]" (The CCP Provincial Committee of Jiangsu, the Government of Jiangsu, 1986a).

Further, the provincial government encouraged major cities to establish their own branches of international trade companies and decentralized decision-making power to those companies. In 1986, the government authorized international trade decisions to the branches in five major cities, i.e., Suzhou, Wuxi, Changzhou, Nantong and Lianyungang. Those companies were allowed to establish direct trade relations with foreign partners, engage in direct exports, and decide almost all major aspects of production. Although those companies still formally belonged to the state enterprise category, they had much greater autonomy in decision-making compared to other state enterprises (The Government of Jiangsu, 1986a). This regulation was extended to most cities in the province later.

Decentralization, nevertheless, did not mean that the government isolated itself from the economy for foreign trade. Instead, the government tried to make its policies penetrate grassroots production units for international trade. Government organizations at different levels were devoted to coordinating the relations between international trade companies and production units. Trade companies were encouraged to give overall support to production units including opening new products; introducing new technologies; engaging in technological updating; providing information about international markets; suggesting reliable adjustments in production, etc. (The CCP Provincial Committee of Jiangsu, the Government of Jiangsu, 1986b).

Very detailed financial plans were decided for production units in order to provide them with greater incentives to develop international trade. For example, a 1986 government regulation showed that with the 1985 performance as the base, production units could retain 3 cents *yuan* for each US$ they earn within the base, and they could retain 20 cents *yuan* for each US$ above the base. Newly-opened enterprises could retain more from their profits in international trade (The Government of Jiangsu, 1986b, 1986c).

The provincial government also sent investigation groups led by major provincial leaders to the Guangdong and Fujian provinces to examine how those provinces had promoted foreign trade. From these investigations, government officials in Jiangsu realized that without the very favorable circumstances that the Guangdong and Fujian governments created for foreign businessmen, foreign capital would not have flowed into those provinces. The Jiangsu provincial government thus established various regulations, under which foreign businesses were in a very privileged position (The Government of Jiangsu, 1986d, 1986e, 1986f). The provincial government gave foreign businesses high priority when they distributed raw materials and financial resources. Local government organizations were required not to assign the same burden to foreign businesses as to other types of enterprise.

Jiangsu's economic performance in international trade after the mid-1980s was quite impressive. Total domestic purchases for foreign trade increased from 5.31 billion *yuan* in 1985 to 13.62 billion in 1989. Direct provincial exports increased from US$155,851 million in 1985 to US$244,111 million in 1989 (The Statistical Bureau of Jiangsu, 1990: 305, 308).

GOVERNMENT ENTREPRENEURSHIP
AND RURAL INDUSTRY

What was the dynamic in the rapid development of rural industry in Jiangsu before the mid-1990s? Did the market-oriented reform provide the province with this dynamism? Could collective ownership provide incentives for development as private or individual ownership has done? Having examined the role of the government in continuous adjustment of development policies, I now turn to the rural industrial sector. By investigating this sector, I shall show how local autonomy enabled the government to play the role of entrepreneur in developing the province's rural industry.

The fast post-Mao pace of rural industrial development was rooted deeply in the province's history after the establishment of the PRC. Due to the pre-existing solid foundation, the rural industry gained strong momentum in the early 1970s. But the structure of the rural industry also constrained the reform leadership's alternatives for adjusting development strategy in this sector. As shown in Table 4.7, township collectives produced about 55.5 percent of the total rural industrial output in 1970. The percentage did not change much (52.9 percent) in 1988. So, a full understanding of the post-Mao development of rural industry and the role that the government played in this process require us to take a look at the history of rural industry in Jiangsu.

The first short boom of rural industry in the province occurred during the Great Leap Forward (1958–1959). Mao, driven by his desire to catch up with advanced Western countries, called for rapid industrialization of rural China. In Jiangsu, up to the end of 1958, 39,000 commune enterprises were established.[6] There were about 1.1 million peasant workers in those enterprises — about 2.28 percent of the total rural laborers. Commune enterprises created 1.48 billion *yuan* in industrial output — about 17 percent of the total for

---

[6] In 1984, after abandoning the commune system in rural China, former commune enterprises were renamed as township enterprises, and brigade enterprises as village enterprises.

Table 4.7 The Growth of Rural Industry in Jiangsu (1970–1988) (billion *yuan*)

Year	Total Indus. Output	Change (%)	Township Indus. Output	Change (%)	Village & Private Output	Change (%)
1970	0.70		0.39		0.31	
1971	0.93	33.47	0.55	43.0	0.38	21.61
1972	1.14	22.71	0.69	26.08	0.44	17.77
1973	1.36	19.56	0.89	27.29	0.48	7.43
1974	1.67	22.45	1.08	22.10	0.59	23.06
1975	2.28	36.84	1.44	33.08	0.84	46.02
1976	3.37	47.67	2.04	41.52	1.34	58.17
1977	5.20	54.22	3.09	51.85	2.11	57.90
1978	6.34	21.83	3.85	24.53	2.49	17.88
1979	7.64	20.54	4.68	21.43	2.96	19.15
1980	11.03	44.30	6.63	41.76	4.39	48.32
1981	12.57	14.05	7.68	15.82	4.89	11.36
1982	13.42	6.72	8.32	8.30	5.10	4.19
1983	16.21	20.79	10.05	20.72	6.16	20.89
1984	23.63	45.80	13.84	37.37	9.79	58.95
1985	38.33	62.19	20.96	51.41	17.38	77.43
1986	49.63	29.47	26.88	28.27	22.75	30.92
1987	66.54	34.06	35.91	35.58	30.63	34.63
1988	90.56	36.09	47.88	33.32	42.68	39.34

Source: Wu Xiangjun, (ed.), *Jiangsu Xiangzhen Qiye Guanli Jingjian Qianli Xuan* (The 1373 Cases of Management Experiences of Rural Industry in Jiangsu), Beijing: Zhonggong Zhongyang Dangxiao Chubanshe, 1990, p. 908.

the province in this year. But this boom lasted for only a short period of time. In September 1960, the central leadership in Beijing called for an adjustment period. After the adjustment, there were 841 commune enterprises left and they produced only 34 million *yuan* in rural industrial output (Mo & Liu, 1990: 899–900).

After three years of economic adjustment (1963–1965), the rural industry again gained a development momentum. Numerous urban workers were sent to the rural areas by the regime, but they were not familiar with rural work. In order to support them, local leadership silently allowed them to open new enterprises or revive the enterprises banned by authorities at higher levels. Due to the profitability of rural enterprises, many local leaders actually encouraged the development of rural industry. By 1965, the rural sector produced 0.32 billion *yuan* in industrial output. But this time, most rural enterprises were owned by brigades, rather than communes (*ibid.*: 900). Also, the rise of brigade enterprises did not result from a movement initiated by the regime as before, but by local leaders' material incentives. More importantly, brigade enterprises now were "market"-oriented. That meant that their activities were beyond state planning, and enterprises needed to adjust their production according to supply and demand in the "market."

Another real boom in the rural industry happened in the early 1970s. In 1970, Zhou Enlai, then the Premier of the State Council, presided over the conference of agricultural development in northern China. The conference called for the rapid development of agricultural mechanization. The provinces were encouraged to open new enterprises to make agricultural tools. This conference had a major impact on the state of industry in Jiangsu. Jiangsu's already relatively-developed rural industry was thus legitimated and gained further momentum, as shown in Table 4.7.

Importantly, even long before the post-Mao reform began, provincial leaders and those in lower-level government organizations already had greater autonomy in decision-making regarding rural industrial development. Great autonomy made it possible for the leadership to adjust development strategies appropriate to local circumstances, rather than mechanically following the central leadership's mandates. In the early 1970s, the provincial leadership modified the collective ownership system. The government clearly claimed that commune and brigade enterprises belonged to two different forms of ownership. Commune leadership could not give mandatory orders to brigade enterprises and the latter had relatively independent decision-making power. In effect, decommunization occurred to some extent, with the rural industry clearly being treated in the category of agriculture. Members of the commune had equal rights to become involved in the industry. Enterprises and enterprise members, and other commune or brigade members, could gain an essential portion of the profits. Further, because most rural enterprises were beyond the state planning system, they had to rely heavily on the market to gain raw materials and sell their products. Also, rural enterprises could not gain financial support from the state planning system and had to raise funds by themselves. The formation of a system for raising these funds increased the capacity of the province to open more new enterprises and promote faster development later on.

Due to these changes, the rural industry gathered momentum in the mid-1970s. Rural industrial growth reached an annual rate of 36.84 percent, 47.67 percent and 54.22 percent in 1976, 1977 and 1978, respectively. In 1978, Jiangsu's rural enterprises produced 16.6 percent of the total rural industrial output of the whole country. The rapid growth of the rural industry created numerous job opportunities for urban workers, the unemployed and educated youth who were sent to rural areas. Rural enterprises employed 2.49 million rural workers, compared to 2.77 million urban workers in state enterprises and urban collectives in 1978 (*ibid.*: 902).

How much change was introduced into the rural industrial sector after the national reform began in the late 1970s? Rural industry boomed during this period (see Table 4.7). Nevertheless, the provincial government was criticized for not being able to change the collective ownership of most rural enterprises, and for the government's frequent interference into enterprise businesses.[7] While the provincial government was constrained by various institutional factors in adjusting development policies toward rural industry, its policies were very flexible and pragmatic, and thus effective in promoting the rapid development of rural industry.

The province did not develop as many private enterprises as the Zhejiang province did in the 1980s. Collective ownership was dominant in Jiangsu, but this form of ownership was rooted in the institutional evolution of the pre-existing rural enterprises in the province. Compared to other provinces, the rural enterprise took off much

---

[7] For examples, see Guo Xiaoming *et al.* (1987); Chen Zhizhong and Wang Shalin (1990); Li Zongji (1988).

earlier in Jiangsu. Various factors made it very difficult to change the collective ownership. Mao's regime did not allow a private sector in the rural areas to develop. In the early 1960s, many forms of owner- ship, such as household contracts, briefly emerged around the coun- try, but soon disappeared due to high political pressure from Beijing. In the eyes of the leadership, only collectives had the legiti- macy to develop. Further, at the early stage of the rural industrial development, there was a major financial problem. The absence of state investment in the rural industry forced communes and brigades to rely heavily on commune and brigade members to finance rural enterprises. The ownership of enterprises based on such finances was very complicated. Enterprises did not belong to the state, local state organizations, or enterprise managers, but to the enterprise members collectively. But due to the small size of such enterprises, incentives were still provided for both managers and enterprise members. After the reform began, with the separation of ownership from management, various contract systems were introduced into the rural enterprises where collective ownership was still very effec- tive. In effect, collectives were expanded. The income of township collectives (initially commune level one) increased from 26.95 per- cent of the total rural income in 1978 to 41.59 percent in 1986, while the income of brigade collectives decreased from 41.61 percent to 15.83 percent during the same period of time in the Suzhou area (see Table 4.8). Cooperatives and private enterprises remained quite constant. However, it is important to note that the provincial govern- ment also encouraged the development of other non-collective ownership, such as household cooperatives and private enterprises. Table 4.8 shows the development of ownership structures in the areas under Suzhou municipal city.

Compared to south Jiangsu, household cooperatives and private enterprises developed rapidly in north Jiangsu. North Jiangsu did not have a developed rural industry as it began the reform. The area was also poorer than south Jiangsu. For example, in Gengche town- ship, where the Gengche model originated, per capita income was only 41 *yuan* in 1978 (The Economic Research Center of Suqian City Government, 1988: 80). In the early 1980s, some places in north

Table 4.8 The Ownership Structure in the Suzhou Area (percentage)

Year	Township Collective	Village Collective	Bridge Collective	Cooperative & Private
1978	26.95	17.88	41.61	13.56
1979	26.87	18.70	42.14	12.29
1980	33.84	24.76	29.47	11.93
1981	36.13	25.85	26.33	11.69
1982	35.94	24.77	28.88	10.41
1983	39.91	25.22	23.79	11.08
1984	39.03	25.20	22.42	13.35
1985	43.25	28.48	15.57	12.70
1986	41.59	27.80	15.83	14.78

Source: Li Xuegen, "*Sunan Nongcun De Jiti Suoyouzhi*" ("Collective Ownership in Rural Areas of South Jiangsu"), in Tao Youzhi, (ed.), *Sunan Mushi Yu Zhifu Zhidao* (The South Jiangsu Model and the Road to Wealth), Shanghai: Shanghai Shehui Kexueyuan Chubanshe, 1988, p. 37.

Jiangsu attempted to use the south Jiangsu model to promote economic development. But most of these did not succeed. The local government in Gengche thus turned to many other models. Local leaders visited Zhejiang and Shandong provinces, and drew lessons from their development experiences. Eventually, multiple, but household-centered ownership, was generated in the township. There were four different levels of ownership: township, village, household cooperatives and individual households. In 1986, 19.9 percent of the total township laborers were in township and village enterprises (collective ownership); 5.3 percent were in household cooperatives (private ownership); and 74.8 percent were in individual household enterprises (private ownership). In the same year, within the boundaries of Gengche, township enterprises generated 29.5 percent of the total industrial output; village enterprises produced 15.2 percent; cooperatives generated 16.9 percent; and individual households produced 38.4 percent. Individual households enterprises also provided the biggest portion of township revenue — about 64 percent in the same year (Hu, 1988: 123). This very flexible multiple-ownership system was adopted by many places in north Jiangsu.

In effect, government entrepreneurship was a major source of dynamism in the rapid growth of rural industry. Given the fact that capitalism was not legitimate when the reform began, whether or not the provincial government held a pragmatic attitude toward the rural industry became significant. Between 1976 and 1978, it was very controversial whether rural industry belonged to the category of socialism or capitalism. Facing numerous conflicting ideologies, the provincial government was very pragmatic. In this period, the government held many conferences attended by government officials at different levels and justified the significance of rural industry in the province's economy. Various regulations were implemented to promote the rural industry (Tao, 1988).

One of the main bottlenecks faced by rural entrepreneurs and small-scale enterprises was to get the financial capital they needed to start operations and to expand. A major role the government played was to use various measures to provide support in financial resources for the rural industry. But a chief goal of government investment in the rural industry was to gain benefits from this sector. Without returns, investment could not last long. The question was how the government adjusted its financial policies and whether those policies were able to promote economic growth, while increasing government revenues.

In Jiangsu, various tax reforms toward the rural industry were carried out in order to provide incentives for local leaders or enterprise managers to develop the local economy and to increase government revenues simultaneously. In 1977, based on the central government's general policy toward rural areas, the provincial government decided to reduce peasant burdens in an attempt to provide incentives to develop the local economy. Except those enterprises that produced cigarettes, wine and textiles, newly-opened rural enterprises were exempted from commercial and income taxes for two years. In 1979, the tax-free period for such enterprises was extended to three years. Meanwhile, the State Council issued regulations that those rural enterprises that provided services for agriculture could be exempted from commercial and income taxes. These policies had a major impact on the expansion of the rural industry.

For example, in the Suzhou area, enterprises increased from 10,663 in 1976 to 14,937 in 1980; the total industrial output increased from 921 million *yuan* to 3,510 million; enterprise profits increased from 172 million to 773 million during the same period (*ibid.*: 165).

In 1981 and 1982, the State Council repeatedly adjusted its fiscal policies toward rural enterprises because the central government encountered serious deficits in those two years. Consequently, many forms of tax-exemption no longer applied to rural enterprises. Instead, tax rates were raised. The rural industry declined rapidly in Jiangsu. The rate of growth in the rural industrial output declined from 44.30 percent in 1980 to 14.05 percent in 1981 and 6.72 percent in 1982 (see Table 4.7). Facing difficulties, the provincial government focused on adjusting the rural industrial structure. Departing from the central government's general policy, the provincial government implemented some special tax policies toward its rural enterprises. Taxes were removed or reduced toward those enterprises that had financial difficulties in operation (*ibid.*: 167). Economic growth in this sector recovered gradually.

The provincial government and lower-level government organizations also frequently bargained with local banks and required them to make loans to rural enterprises that government officials believed would be profitable. Banks were still not independent entities in China. Government officials at different levels had great authority over the banks, especially over rural financial cooperatives. Due to the fact that bank savings heavily depended on local economic development, local banks were willing to make loans to rural enterprises. For example, in the Changjiagang area, banks started to issue a small portion of loans to rural enterprises in 1970. From 1980 onward, bank loans increased rapidly. In 1980, banks lent 31 million *yuan* to rural enterprises — about 24.2 percent of the total working capital in this area. The figure increased to 192 million in 1985 and 512 million in 1988 — about 34.4 percent and 48.7 percent of the total working capital of rural enterprises in the area respectively (The Office of Local Chronicles of Changjiagang City, 1990: 83). Also, as in many other areas in the province, the local government was in charge of borrowing money from banks and from many other local organizations for rural enterprises after 1981. Local governments also encouraged enterprises to use various channels to collect financial resources they needed. Many forms of household financial cooperation were established, and absorbed an essential portion of financial resources in the area. Finally, local officials were very active in absorbing foreign capital. Up to 1988, 40 rural enterprises absorbed US$14 million (*ibid.*: 84).

Organizing Markets

China's reform was market-oriented, but the development of the marketplace took different paths in different circumstances. Due to the absence of an integrated marketplace during the early stages of the reform, the role of the government in creating such a market became significant. The provincial government in Jiangsu was very effective in adjusting the leadership structure in the face of changing circumstances. At the early stages of the rural industry, numerous local party secretaries were appointed as enterprise managers. Later, those who were good at financial management were appointed as enterprise managers; because with rural industrial development and the expansion of enterprise size, enterprise finance became complicated. After the reform began, local governments turned to put an emphasis on those who had wide know-how about markets and those who had special knowledge concerning rural enterprises.

In the Suzhou area, the city government began adjusting the leadership structure in rural enterprises in 1982. Up to 1985, 1,936 enterprise leaderships were rectified. Among 263 enterprises, 147 out of 1,077 enterprise leaders were forced to retire and 210 new leaders were appointed.[8] According to an investigation of 1,140 enterprise leaders, after the adjustment, the average age was 33.8; 74.3 percent of them had middle-school or higher education (25 percent of them had high-school education) (*ibid.*: 84). An investigation of the leadership of nine townships in a developed area in the Suzhou showed that from 1984 to 1986, 168 major leaders were

---

[8] Tao Youzhi, ed., *Sunan moshi*, p. 151.

forced to retire because of the following reasons: (1) too old to be leaders (n. 102); (2) no great accomplishments (n. 46); and (3) corruption (n. 20). Most of the newly-appointed major leaders were younger. Among the nine township leaderships, 35.1 percent of the major leaders were below 39 years old; 46 percent were between 40–49 years old; and only 19 percent were above 50 years old. Also, they had higher education backgrounds or special skills. Among them, 39 percent were good at industrial management; 32 percent were good at agricultural and sideline management; and the rest of them had different administrative experiences (Lu, 1986).

Raw material supply was problematic in the development of the rural industry in Jiangsu. Because the rural industry was beyond state planning, rural enterprises could not gain raw materials from the state. They needed to rely heavily on the marketplace. However, an integrated marketplace had not been formed in China; so rural enterprises had numerous difficulties in gaining raw materials from such a "market." Before the post-Mao reform, the rural industry in other provinces was not developed and rural enterprises in Jiangsu were able to get raw materials through various "market" channels. After the end of the 1970s, the rural industry expanded nationwide as it had in Jiangsu. The tension between raw material supply and great demands of enterprises thus increased rapidly.

A major cause of the fast growth of the rural industry was that local governments acted as entrepreneurs and market organizers. Numerous measures were implemented to relax the supply and demand tension. First, the provincial government used different regulations to promote horizontal economic cooperation among different enterprises within the province and between organizations within and outside the provinces. For example, the Suzhou area from 1983 to 1985 established various economic relationships with economic organizations in 20 provinces and 34 enterprise groups. In the Changshu area, 1,500 out of 3,400 enterprises had economic cooperation with enterprises in Shanghai. In the city of Wuxi, up to the end of 1985, 3,520 rural enterprises established economic relations with other enterprises, research centers, universities and colleges. Through these relations, the city created more than 1,000 new products, established 350 raw material and energy bases, and 14 enterprise groups that had 252 formal members and 500 informal members (Tao, 1988: 90–91).

A fairly well-integrated market was created for Jiangsu province. This market, or more correctly, the economic network, consisted of five forms of horizontal economic cooperation: (1) cooperation among enterprises within the area (such as the Suzhou and Wuxi areas); (2) cooperation with other enterprises within the province; (3) cooperation with economic organizations in Shanghai; (4) cooperation with economic organizations in other provinces; and (5) cooperation with foreign economic organizations overseas, including those in Hong Kong and the SEZs in South China. For example, in Kunshan county, there were 303 economic cooperative projects in 1986. Among them, 91 projects (about 30 percent) belonged to the first type of cooperation; 10 projects (about 3.3 percent) belonged to the second type; 187 projects (about 61.7) belonged to the third; 12 projects (about 4 percent) belonged to the fourth; and 3 projects (about 1 percent) belonged to the fifth (*ibid.*: 99).

As discussed earlier, in 1983, the provincial government proposed a new administration system — "*shi guan xian*" (the city management of the county) — to the central government. After the proposal was approved, the provincial government implemented this new system province-wide. A major goal of this system was to promote horizontal economic cooperation with a given area. Each city government was granted the authority to coordinate economic activities in the counties attached to it, especially between urban and rural areas. The new system created a dynamism for the rise of economic cooperation. For example, the Suzhou area developed 844 economic cooperatives between 1985–1987, and 1,328 enterprises joined these cooperatives. Among them, 62.6 percent were rural enterprises, 8 percent were county enterprises, and 29.4 percent were city enterprises (*ibid.*: 100).

The integration into a provincial market was very successful. Two economic communities in south Jiangsu, i.e., (1) Nanjing, Zhenjiang and Nantong; and (2) Suzhou, Wuxi and Changzhou, were noted for their joint economic activities. The provincial government also attempted to integrate the south Jiangsu and north Jiangsu markets.

A strategy for South-North economic cooperation was proposed and various measures were implemented to achieve such a goal (The Government of Jiangsu, 1986g).

Cooperation between economic organizations in Jiangsu and Shanghai was most important for rural enterprises. Geography, tradition, personal networks and many other factors determined the high reliability of cooperation between these two adjoining administrative territories. According to an investigation, more than 60 percent of the economic cooperation in South Jiangsu occurred with Shanghai. In the Wuxi area, of 1,233 cooperative projects in 1985, about 60 percent of the total, occurred between Wuxi and Shanghai. In Suzhou, 63.2 percent of the total cooperative projects (11,320) occurred with Shanghai in the same year. In three counties — Changshu, Kunshan and Taicang — cooperative projects between them and Shanghai were 67.6 percent, 72.8 percent and 76.8 percent of their total, respectively (Tao, 1988: 100).

Cooperation with other provinces, especially with inland provinces, was important because from it, enterprises in Jiangsu gained numerous raw materials. For example, up to the mid-1980s, the city of Wuxi had established 350 raw material and energy bases in inland China. From 1983–1985, the city gained about 2.3 billion *yuan* of raw materials from the inland provinces (*ibid.*). Finally, various cooperatives were also established between Jiangsu and SEZs or overseas economic organizations. A major goal of this sort of cooperation was to seek a profitable market for Jiangsu products. Increasing numbers of Jiangsu products now were sold in international markets through economic cooperation.

The provincial government also established trade centers through which the province acquired and sold its products in bulk. For example, the Center of Material Trade of Suzhou was established in 1985. The center had various advanced modern facilities and became an important place where rural enterprises could exhibit and sell their products on the one hand, and obtain materials they needed on the other. For instance, from January to August 1986, the center initiated 66 trade fairs that attracted numerous businesses from other provinces (*ibid.*: 120).

Further, local governments in Jiangsu established special government organizations such as "coordination offices" — the economic commissions and bureaus of rural industry management that were in charge of obtaining raw materials for rural enterprises. These organizations devoted themselves to establishing relations with areas rich in energy and raw materials. From 1983 to 1985, the Suzhou area gained 1 billion *yuan* of raw materials through government effort, and the Wuxi area gained 1.1 billion. Through government channels, 14 rural enterprises in Kunshan county acquired 77 percent of their steel, 69 percent of their cement, and 62 percent of their brick — items they could not get in the market during this period (*ibid.*: 121).

Local governments also attempted to establish networks similar to alumni associations and following a long tradition in China of *tongxiang* (common place of origin) associations. Such associations frequently became an important source of raw material supplies for rural enterprises. A local chronicle recorded,

> After 1973, every commune and brigade cadre, enterprise worker and other community member was asked to provide information about people who were working in other areas such as their relatives, friends, colleagues, classmates, and any other persons they knew. Then commune and brigade officials, enterprise party secretaries, managers, and salesmen went to visit them and asked them to support rural enterprises [in Jiangsu]. Since 1978, local cadres invited them to visit the places where they were born, and held tea parties and discuss with them during holiday seasons. Local cadres also write letters, expressing the local people's appreciation and asking them to support rural enterprises. In 1986 and 1987, all townships undertook a survey and identified the places where most of these people were working and held townsmen association conferences (*tongxiang hui*). Daxin, Nansha and three other township governments held their townsmen association conferences in Shanghai and Beijing. In the conferences, they discussed how to develop production projects, how to acquire capital and raw materials and so forth for Jiangsu (The Office of Local Chronicles of Changjiagang City, 1990: 77–78).

The absence of a nationwide market also made the flow of rural enterprise products difficult. The rural industry was not subject to state planning; so most rural enterprise products had to be sold in the "marketplace," as had been the case since the very beginning of the reform in the rural industry. Table 4.9 shows the rural enterprises' overall marketing structure in Changjiagang area, one of the developed areas in Jiangsu province. Most rural products in this area have been sold in the marketplace.

Before 1978, marketing was not a major problem facing the rural industry in the province. Due to the small size of the rural industry, rural products were not too many to be consumed in the area. Also, at that time, a major goal of the rural industry was to provide services for agriculture. Relatively-developed agriculture in this area created a great demand for rural enterprise products. Consequently, the market then was rather regional. Such a situation no longer existed after the reform. At the early stages of the reform, the rural industry in Jiangsu developed rapidly. An essential portion of rural products flowed to outside places. However, with the nationwide rapid development of the rural industry and the beginning of urban reforms, which led to a dramatic increase in production, the rural industry in Jiangsu faced serious challenges. Many rural enterprises were not able to arrange their production in accordance with demand due to the lack of marketing information.

With the absence of a true marketplace, the interference of local governments became important. Various measures were taken to create a marketplace for the products of rural enterprises within

Table 4.9 The Marketing Structure of Ten Townships in Changjiagang in Selected Years (percentage)

	1962	1970	1978	1985	1988
Commerce department purchase	20.02	14.5	8.1	3.6	2.7
Foreign trade purchase	n.a	0.1	2.1	3.3	11.0
Contractor purchase	25.1	34.7	36.0	27.0	33.5
Cooperative sale	n.a	n.a	0.3	6.7	4.8
Sale in the market	54.7	50.7	53.3	59.4	48.0

Source: The Office of Local Chronicles of Changjiagang City, The Rural Industrial Bureau of Changjiagang City, *Changjiagang Shi Xiangzhen Gongye Zhi* (A Chronicle of The Rural Industry in Changjiagang City), Shanghai: Shanghai Renmin Chubanshe, 1990, p. 80.

their home domains. The establishment of horizontal economic cooperation and trade centers, as just mentioned, provided rural enterprises with a market not only for acquiring raw materials and energy, but also for selling their products. Local governments also encouraged enterprises to establish various information networks around the country. Industrial information was collected by numerous marketplaces set up by rural enterprises themselves or directly by local governments. Local governments then adjusted their industrial policies for rural enterprises according to marketing information. For example, the rural industry in Wuxi originally produced mainly agricultural machines. In 1982, the local government, based on the information it collected, saw that the textile industry would be more profitable. It thus "rectified" 105 major rural enterprises within the areas through mandatory orders. As a result, 330 new products were created. This adjustment in effect increased rural enterprises' profitability and economic efficiency (Tao, 1988: 123).

The fiscal policy also became an important means by which local governments provided strong incentives for enterprise managers to create a market. Financial organizations such as local banks and rural financial cooperatives were active in encouraging rural enterprises to adjust their production by making loans to those enterprises whose products were popular in the market. Local governments also frequently issued regulations for overstocked products.

Local officials in Jiangsu were not only market organizers, but often became salesmen themselves. Local governments frequently organized various trade groups traveling around the country. According to a local chronicle,

> In 1981, the marketing for rural products became difficult.... The county government (Shazhou county, later renamed Changjiagang city) organized commerce, industry, material, rural cooperatives and other departments to sell rural enterprise products. In 1983, the sales rate of rural enterprise products reached 80.7 percent.... In May 1986, County magistrate Shen Shudong and the director of the Commerce Bureau organized the Horizontal Economic Trip Group of Shazhou County, a truck group, traveling around 10 cities and 32 counties in 4 provinces of South China, covering 5,000 km.... The group exhibited 684 rural enterprise products in these places and sold 11.65 million yuan of products.

Under the leadership of the county magistrate, township and village cadres soon followed. The whole county thus created a product-sales campaign (The Office of Local Chronicles of Changjiagang City, 1990: 82).

Based on 1,376 reports of rural enterprises of Jiangsu in 1989, Table 4.10 shows the distribution of answers when enterprise managers were asked the question, "What led to .your enterprise's success?" We can see that most enterprises put the emphasis on improving product quality, creating a marketplace, the contract system, and qualified leaders. Plan-making, property rights within

Table 4.10 Categorization of Management Experiences of Rural Enterprises in Jiangsu (1989)

	Management Category	No.
1	Developing the marketplace	73
2	Emphasizing promotion strategy	178
3	Managing industrial information	58
4	Correct decision-making	57
5	Planning management	3
6	Managing product process	63
7	Managing product quality	263
8	Managing costs & capital flows	61
9	Managing labor division	90
10	Technological progress	124
11	Clarifying property rights	8
12	Implementing contract systems	107
13	Making use of foreign capital	6
14	Horizontal cooperation	126
15	Economic regulations	3
16	Public relations	11
17	Relations among workers	47
18	Leadership quality and skill	46
19	The use of talented workers	35
20	Others	17

Source: Categorized from Wu Xiangjun, ed., *Jiangsu Xiangzhen Qiye Guanli Jingnian Qianli Xuan* (1376 Cases of Management Experience of Rural Industry in Jiangsu), Beijing: Zhonggong Zhongyang Dangxiao Chubanshe, 1990.

an enterprise and economic regulations were not seen as playing an important role in their successes.

CONCLUSION

The provincial government gained greater autonomy in a *de facto* federal structure. How the provincial leadership in Jiangsu responded to economic decentralization became a test to see whether the province was able to cooperate with the central government. As discussed in this chapter, the provincial leadership in Jiangsu did not use their autonomy to deviate from central policies greatly. Cooperation was achieved between the center and the province. Nevertheless, it did not mean that the province had to rigidly follow central policies. Indeed, the very aim of *de facto* federalism was to give leeway to the province to implement central policies flexibly, on the one hand, and to formulate local policies in accordance with local conditions, on the other.

As a matter of fact, how the provincial leadership could cooperate with the center was seriously constrained by local conditions. For the center, the market-oriented reform, by its very nature, required the withdrawal of government from businesses to let individual enterprises compete in the marketplace. But due to the absence of an integrated market, the government's interference, in fact, became necessary to create a marketplace. Certainly, the government's interference in economic affairs was affected by existing economic institutions. In Jiangsu, the government played an important role in both promoting economic development and creating a marketplace for the products of Jiangsu. Since the governments at different levels could benefit greatly from local economic growth, they acted like entrepreneurs: acquiring raw materials and energy for enterprises; providing the financial resources enterprises needed; and creating markets for enterprise products.

In order to make and implement policies effectively, decision-making by the provincial leadership was characterized by pragmatism. In Jiangsu, the collective ownership system was still in a dominant position in the 1980s, and the system was very effective in providing incentives for local officials and promoting economic growth. With inter-governmental decentralization, property rights were defined rather clearly among government organizations at different levels. Each level of government organization had relations with a higher-level government through some relatively institutionalized contract systems. Within a given contract system, contractors (government officials and enterprise managers) had the greatest autonomy in decision-making. Compared to most other provinces, the Jiangsu province had a heavier fiscal burden that was repeatedly regarded as a hindrance to provincial economic growth because the fiscal burden had led to a shortage of investment capital (The Investigation Group of Industrial Efficiency, 1990). But with inter-governmental decentralization, the central government no longer had mandatory power in the economic affairs of the province. The provincial government further decentralized economic power to lower-level government organizations. Due to the small size of governance, the provincial government was quite successful in coordinating economic development within its domain.

The provincial government also cooperated with the central government in adjusting its industrial policy toward international trade. The difficulties of adjusting international trade policies came from the fact that the province's products were still quite profitable on the domestic market because of a relatively solid industrial infrastructure. The provincial government had to be able to provide lower-level government organizations or enterprises with greater incentives to develop international trade. Production for international trade had to be more profitable than production for domestic use. The provincial government's efforts in mobilizing productions for international trade had to be judged to be quite successful. After the mid-1980s, Jiangsu's international trade boomed. Further, learning from other provinces with a developed international trade, such as Guangdong and Fujian, the provincial government of Jiangsu made great efforts to create favorable circumstances for foreign businessmen. Numerous privileges were granted to foreign businesses or joint ventures within the province. These efforts were effective in attracting capital from foreign businessmen and overseas Chinese.

The first decade of development shows that the provincial government's development strategy was very effective and that government officials were very pragmatic toward different types of ownership. The private economy was also encouraged, as the north Jiangsu case shows. Governments at different levels frequently assigned local officials and enterprise managers to visit other provinces such as Zhejiang and Guangdong, where the private economy tended to be dominant. In the mid-1980s, after governor Gu Xiulian led a group to visit Wenzhou's private economy, she called for the Jiangsu province to learn from Wenzhou how to develop a private economy. According to her, a private economy had many advantages in promoting economic growth; it provided individuals with greater incentives than the collective did; individual initiatives were also greater in the private sector than in the collective (Gu, 1986). But it was not an easy task for the provincial leadership to introduce changes into the collective ownership system. Once an institution came into existence, it was able to struggle for its own survival. The role of the Jiangsu leadership in the 1980s was not to carry out any radical reform, but to implement pragmatic policies to promote local development. Nonetheless, when the collective ownership system became less efficient in promoting local growth, it was necessary to introduce changes into this system. In the next decade, the provincial government successfully transformed the province into a manufacturing center in China. Again, such a transformation took place without much intervention from the central government.

Chapter

5

The Center, Local State and Local Community: Zhejiang under Inter-governmental Decentralization

The last chapter showed that the government of Jiangsu played the role of entrepreneur in formulating and implementing local reform policies to promote economic growth. Entrepreneurship did not mean that the provincial leadership had to strictly follow central policies; instead, it meant that the local leadership could take a pragmatic approach to local development strategies. China's *de facto* federal structure provided an institutional setting for local entrepreneurship. In such a structure, reciprocity existed since the center allowed the province to deviate from central policies to a certain degree, and the province did not deviate far from central policies. Both actors were able to cooperate implicitly and explicitly to achieve the goal of economic growth — a goal that both actors identified with and could benefit from.

This chapter continues to examine how the government of Zhejiang played the role of entrepreneur to promote local growth by adjusting development strategies, especially through an export-led policy, and by protecting a private sector. Similar to Jiangsu province, throughout the era of inter-governmental decentralization, the government of Zhejiang continued to adjust its development policies in order to meet changing circumstances. But Zhejiang encountered a rather different situation from Jiangsu. This chapter shows how the provincial government formulated and implemented its reform policies in accordance with specific local conditions; and how the province and the center interacted in a reciprocal way by legitimating these local policies.

Zhejiang has been regarded as an unique model in China in promoting the development of the private sector. Compared to any other province, Zhejiang has been very successful in developing the private sector. But the development of the private sector was not an easy task in the early stages of the reform when this sector was not legitimate. Through examining how the Wenzhou model survived, we can see how the center and the local community interacted in a reciprocal manner. Wenzhou had a deep tradition of favoring private ownership. This tradition largely determined the local government's choice of its development policy. This fact, however, did not mean that local governments did not play an important role in developing such a strategy. Nor did it mean that a locally-formulated model of the private economy would be accepted by the center. Also, the government's preference for the private sector did not mean that the government no longer interfered in local economic activities and let a laissez-faire system function. Instead, local governments were involved in economic growth and imposed their own priorities on private behavior through various measures. So, the Wenzhou case provides us with an example of how the local government was involved in the local economic development in an area with a strong private sector without deviating greatly from central policies.

COMMERCIAL TRADITION AND ITS IMPACT ON MODERN ZHEJIANG

Zhejiang has been a rich place since the early years of China. Before the establishment of a unified Qin China (221–206 BC), Zhejiang was ruled by several dukedoms. Even then, Zhejiang's agriculture and industries such as iron-making and textiles were among the most advanced in the whole nation. The Qin unification war had a negative impact on the province's agriculture and industry. The province's economy did not recover until the "six dynasties period" (222–580 AD). Numerous wars during this period in north China brought a large population of migrants to Zhejiang where order had been less problematic. An increase in the population and advanced agricultural and industrial techniques brought by migrants from the north became strong dynamics for economic development in Zhejiang. The Grand Canal was opened in the Sui dynasty (589–681) and became a main transportation system connecting south and north China. A ship-building industry was developed that, in turn, led to the fast development of overseas commercial trade. Under the Tang and Song dynasties, Zhejiang became the richest area in China. Major cities such as Ningbo, Wenzhou and Hangzhou became trade centers for businessmen from Japan, Korea, Southeast Asia and Arabic countries. Meanwhile, these cities also exported numerous agricultural and industrial products to neighboring countries.

The border of Zhejiang was largely stabilized in the Ming (1368–1644) and Qing dynasties (1644–1912). During these two dynasties, disturbances caused by pirates in south China often led to orders by the emperors to close overseas commercial trade, but economic growth still gained momentum. Farmers began to specialize in commerce and various handicraft industries. Many early modern factories were built and a labor market also emerged. In the early Qing dynasty, Zhejiang had many large-sized factories that employed 3,000 to 4,000 workers (Zhou, 1989).

The capitalist expansion into China created a strong dynamic for economic development in Zhejiang. An entrepreneur class came into being. Most entrepreneurs combined comprador and domestic backgrounds (Wang, 1989). Due to the area's commercial tradition, foreign businessmen liked to recruit compradors from among Zhejiang residents. The rise of an entrepreneur class led to the birth of modern industry in Zhejiang, and also in other provinces. From 1887–1913, businessmen of Zhejiang established 32 modern enterprises in

Zhejiang and another 45 in other provinces. More specifically, 27 of these enterprises were established by government businessmen, 20 by private businessmen, and 19 by those who had comprador backgrounds (cited in Zhou, 1989: 37). Modern enterprises developed quickly from then onwards. As of 1921, there were 128 modern enterprises in five major cities in Zhejiang, — Hangzhou, Ningbo, Wenzhou, Huzhou and Shaoxing (Zhou, 1989: 36). Zhejiang businessmen also established many private financial institutions in Zhejiang and Shanghai. These financial institutions were then very efficient and highly competitive.

At the same time, numerous Zhejiang residents emigrated to foreign countries, especially European countries, for commercial reasons. According to one estimate in 1935, there were more than 38,000 Chinese businessmen in Europe and most of them came from Zhejiang. In 1933, there were more than 20,000 businessmen in Europe from Qingtian county (in Wenzhou) alone (Zhang, 1989: 36–37). Emigration was important for the economic growth of Zhejiang because after emigrants earned money in foreign countries, they frequently came back to their hometowns to open businesses. Unlike other provinces, finance never seemed problematic in opening new businesses. More importantly, a deep tradition was established: that is, people in Zhejiang were very confident about their capacity to develop their own businesses (Fei, 1988).

After its establishment in 1949, the PRC government initiated a series of movements, both political and economic, to strengthen the state's dominant position over society. The private economy became the most important target. But in the Zhejiang province, the PRC government met serious resistance in implementing its policies. In 1949, state enterprises (former government enterprises confiscated by the PRC) created only 5.4 percent of the total industrial output, compared to 94.1 percent from the private sector. The private sector also generated 99.7 percent of the total commercial sales value (Shang *et al.*, 1989: 31). After a strong political structure was built, the PRC government implemented various effective measures to change the ownership structure. Table 5.1 shows the dramatic changes in the ownership structure. Total grain purchases controlled

Table 5.1 Ownership Structure in Terms of Grain Purchases and Sales
in Zhejiang (1950–1952)

Year	Percentage of Grain Purchases				Percentage of Grain Sales		
	State	Collective	Private	Others	State	Collective	Private
1950	19.08	2.06	78.40	0.46	37.63	1.49	60.88
1951	54.96	3.87	39.74	1.43	63.70	7.85	28.45
1952	77.15	5.57	18.18	1.10	82.23	5.60	12.17

Source: Shang Jingcai *et al.*, eds., *Dangdai Zhongguo de Zhejiang* (Contemporary Zhejiang), Beijing: Zhongguo Shehui Kexue Chubanshe, 1989, p. 33.

by the state increased from 19 percent in 1950 to 77 percent in 1952, while the total grain sales by the state increased from 38 percent to 82 percent in the same period. The private sector declined rapidly. The number of state enterprises increased from 83 in 1949 to 736 in 1952; employees in this sector increased from 7,710 to 50,265; and the percentage of industrial output created by state enterprises increased from 5 percent to 17 percent in the same time period. The state also controlled the banking system and foreign trade in the province by 1952.

But, due to the solid foundation in the private economy, the private sector continued to play an important part in the province's overall economy. At the end of 1952, the private sector produced 41 percent of the total industrial output of the province. In rural areas the private sector was dominant and it produced 99.8 percent of the total agricultural output (Shang *et al.*, 1989: 40–41).

In the early 1950s, the PRC initiated the agricultural collectivization movement. The pace of collectivization in Zhejiang was rather slow. By 1955, only 30 percent of all households had joined the agricultural cooperatives. Due to the resistance from individual households, local governments frequently employed coercive political measures to implement central policies. But these measures often became ineffective because of peasants' effective resistance (*ibid.*: 45). Facing strong resistance, the provincial government of Zhejiang made various concessions in mid-1955. Agricultural cooperatives decreased from 53,114 to 37,507, and households that had joined such cooperatives decreased from 30 percent of the total to 17.8 percent of the total in one year's time (*ibid.*: 46).

The resistance against collectivization in Zhejiang and some other places led to a serious debate among top leaders in Beijing. Those who were in charge of agricultural affairs such as Deng Zihui argued that such a reversal was necessary. But Mao criticized the retrogression of the provincial government of Zhejiang and proposed to implement a more radical policy toward collectivization (He *et al.*, 1989: 100–101). By the end of 1956, it was reported that about 99 percent of rural households nationwide joined agricultural cooperatives (Shang *et al.*, 1989: 47). Yet, resistance in Zhejiang continued to be strong. In mid-1956, under the protection of vice-county Party Secretary Li Yunhe, Yongjia county implemented the household responsibility system in more than 200 agricultural cooperatives. This system immediately spread to 1,000 agricultural cooperatives in Yongjia's neighboring counties. Li wrote a report entitled "The individual responsibility system and household contract system are a good method to resolve conflicts within cooperatives" and sent it to the county, prefecture and central government. The provincial government gave clear and strong support to Li, and his report was published in *Zhejiang Daily* (27 January 1957). In another important area, Ningbo, where the pace of collectivization had been very slow, 5 percent of all households that had joined agricultural cooperatives earlier already withdrew from these organizations by 1956. In early 1957, another 20 percent of all households wanted to withdraw. Among those who left, roughly half were rich peasants (He *et al.*, 1989: 151). Li's report clearly provoked major leaders in Beijing. In July 1957, the household responsibility system was forcibly stopped and was replaced in rural areas in the province (*ibid.*: 47–48). The system and Li himself were seriously attacked.

From then onward, the provincial government leadership implemented very radical policies, especially during the Great Leap Forward and the Cultural Revolution. Although local state officials sometimes proposed or allowed the household responsibility system, these officials cracked under extreme political pressure from above. During the Great Leap Forward, following the top leadership's priorities, the provincial government initiated various mass movements to speed up the development pace of industrialization and agricultural communization. From 1958 to 1960, the total investment in capital construction reached 2.2 billion *yuan* — about five times that of the First Five-Year Plan period. Meanwhile, heavy industry was given the highest priority. More than 59 percent of the total investment went to heavy industry during the Second Five-Year Plan period (Shang *et al.*, 1989: 76–77). This development strategy did not lead to positive economic results for the province. In 1961, the total agricultural output decreased by 11.4 percent from that of the prior year, and the total industrial output decreased by 36.1 percent (The Statistical Bureau of Zhejiang, 1989: 22).

In February 1961, Mao visited Hangzhou, the capital of Zhejiang province, where First Provincial Party Secretary, Jiang Hua, and other major leaders discussed the serious consequences of previous radical policies. Mao agreed to implement moderate policies in Zhejiang. A new wave of the individual responsibility system was thus initiated. As of 1962, about 3 percent of all households in the province implemented such a system. But this action was soon regarded as an effort to revive capitalism. In Xinchang county, a local state official, Chen Xinyu, wrote six letters to the central government and *People's Daily*, defending the household responsibility system and proposing new policies that he thought were practical in the rural areas and could promote agricultural growth. Predictably, both Chen and his proposal fell under serious attack from above.

During the Cultural Revolution, the provincial leadership continued its radical policies. Political conflicts among top provincial leaders reached a peak during the 1967–1968 period and further extended into lower-level state organizations. Although different political factions frequently initiated mass movements to promote economic development, a major goal of these movements was political. Real incentives could not be provided to both local state officials and the province's residents. The total industrial and agricultural output decreased by 4.2 percent and 2.4 percent from that of prior years in

1967 and 1968, respectively (*ibid.*). Economic development was unstable throughout the whole period of the Cultural Revolution. From 1966–1976, the annual growth rate of national income in Zhejiang was 3.4 percent, compared to the national average of 6.1 percent (The Center of Economic Studies of Zhejiang, 1986). During the Cultural Revolution, it was reported that the province had to ask the central government to "import" grain from other provinces to aid famine, especially in 1975 (*ibid.*: 113).

It is worth noting two aspects of development during the Cultural Revolution. First, numerous rural enterprises were established. As in Jiangsu province, these enterprises had a great impact on the development of the rural industry after the post-Mao reform began. Second, unlike in Jiangsu, the collective ownership system did not achieve great success in Zhejiang. Even under great political pressure, underground economic activities, including modified forms of the household responsibility system, illegal trade with overseas Chinese and small private businesses still existed, especially in the Wenzhou area (Sun, 1989). With inter-governmental decentralization, all these economic activities came to surface.

POLICY ADJUSTMENT UNDER INTER-GOVERNMENTAL DECENTRALIZATION

Ironically, Zhejiang, where local state governments and peasants had attempted to implement the household responsibility system and other forms of economic activities even during the Great Leap Forward and the Cultural Revolution, did not lead the reform in China. A major reason was that the provincial leadership was divided into several factions during the Cultural Revolution.[1] After the Deng regime was established, leadership adjustment was very gradual in the province. Although many top radical leaders were expelled from provincial and lower-level state organizations, power struggles among different factions were still serious. At an early stage, a compromise or a balance of power among them seemed to

---

[1] On factionalism in Zhejiang during the Cultural Revolution, see Forster (1990).

be reached. Nevertheless, a consensus on economic reforms was hardly achieved among major leaders. No faction wanted to take reform initiatives. Only after 1980 were more reform-oriented and younger leaders recruited into the leadership. By that time, economic reforms, especially rural reforms, had developed rapidly in other provinces such as Anhui and Sichuan. In Zhejiang, an official report stated,

> To implement the household responsibility system is a fundamental revolution of production relations in rural areas. Peasants have been very enthusiastic about it because they have suffered seriously from the old system. By contrast, many of our cadres have not realized the deep shortcomings of the rural collective economy and they are influenced deeply by the "leftist" ideology. As a result, they cannot lead the reforms and open their mind. They have thus been in a very negative position since the reform began (Shang *et al.*, 1989: 130).

From 1978 to 1980, some local state organizations carried out the group contract system. Brigades or production teams were divided into many small groups, with each group as a production unit. The system was rather effective in providing incentives for peasants. In September 1980, the central government issued a regulation about the reform in rural areas, which required that the household responsibility system be implemented in poor areas. Top provincial leaders, however, were not able to reach a consensus on whether or not the province should implement the reform. Many seemed to argue that since the collective ownership system had been well-developed in Zhejiang, the province did not need to implement the individual contract system. In January 1981, the provincial government drafted a regulation about the individual contract system, criticizing the contract system *per se* and those local state officials who had supported such a system. Although the regulation was circulated among top provincial leaders and was not allowed to spread among local state organizations, many local state officials still felt great political pressure from above. Their incentives in promoting reforms were consequently constrained (*ibid.*: 131).

In the spring of 1981, provincial resistance to reform was under attack by the reformist regime in Beijing. Deng Xiaoping himself called for local officials to "open their minds" further and keep themselves in line with the reform (Deng, 1983: 275–276). What happened in Beijing encouraged the reformist faction in the government of Zhejiang. In April 1981, the provincial government held a working conference attended by prefecture and city officials. Conservatives were attacked and many of them were forced to criticize themselves in the conference. The conference, however, did not reach a consensus on whether or not the individual contract system should be implemented in affluent areas. Encouraged by the rise of reform forces in the provincial government, leaders in local state organizations, especially prefecture and county officials, now provided very strong support to implement such a system. The reform spread rapidly in the province. By the end of 1983, more than 90 percent of all brigades had carried out the contract system in various forms (Shang et al., 1989: 132).

The contract system per se was diversified by the reform leadership's pragmatic attitude. Different policies were implemented in different areas within the province. Similar to south Jiangsu, some important areas in Zhejiang such as Hangzhou and Ningbo had a solid foundation of collective ownership. But in the Wenzhou area, collective ownership did not work at all. It was difficult for the provincial government to implement any unified reform policy. Consequently, municipal governments were granted great power to initiate and implement policies that were appropriate to their own particular circumstances. Indeed, local policy diversity became effective in promoting agricultural growth.

In urban areas, based on various experiments, the reform began in 1984. One of the major goals of China's economic reform was to deal with fiscal crisis. The central government had to bargain with the provincial governments, especially those in rich provinces such as Zhejiang and Jiangsu, and impose increasing fiscal burdens on the provinces. The provincial governments further needed to set up various fiscal goals for lower-level government organizations and enterprises in order to achieve Beijing's mandates. Like its neighbor Jiangsu, Zhejiang had a heavy fiscal burden. In 1965, the province contributed 63.3 percent of its total budgetary revenue to the central government, and the province retained 36.7 percent. Up to 1980, the province continued to contribute about half of its revenue to Beijing (The Economic Institute of Zhejiang Academy of Social Sciences, 1990). Given the fact that most provincial revenue came from the urban sector, the provincial government felt great pressure, both political and economic, to start urban reform before the nationwide reform began.

The provincial government implemented a decentralization policy in 74 state enterprises and 109 collectives in 1979. Decentralization was extended in 1980 to 211 state enterprises and 337 collectives. Meanwhile, collective and private commerce were allowed to grow. Small urban markets and trade companies were established. Decentralization experiments were very effective. Those state enterprises that carried out experiments reached a 32 percent annual growth rate for production output, 52.3 percent for profits and 46.6 percent for revenue contribution in 1980, much higher than other state enterprises (Shang *et al.*, 1989: 138).

In 1980, influenced by the student movement in Beijing, "illegal" political activities, it was reported, also emerged in some major cities in Zhejiang. Many underground associations were established (*ibid.*: 125). Meanwhile, serious corruption among government officials was exposed. Following Beijing, the provincial leadership called for a halt to reform, and political stability, rather than economic reform, was given the highest priority. But economic reforms never stopped at the local level. Many successful reforms such as that in the Haiyan Shirt Factory encouraged reform leaders in the province. In January 1983, the CCP Provincial Committee held a conference that focused on how to bring economic reforms onto the government's agenda. The conference reached the conclusion that reform was the only means to economic development and political stability. In April 1984, the provincial government issued two important regulations about further reforms in urban collectives and decentralization in state enterprises. The regulations summarized previous experiences of reforms and proposed further reform measures (*ibid.*: 141). In effect, Zhejiang's reform also encouraged the reform leadership in Beijing. In October 1984, the central government issued *The Decision on Economic System Reforms of the CCP* that legitimated various local reforms and declared the start of nationwide urban economic reform.

Many measures had been implemented by 1985. First, small collectives were given priority again and the private sector was restored. In contrast, the importance of the state sector declined. From 1980 to 1985, enterprises and their employees in the state sector increased by 67 percent and 65 percent, respectively; those in the collective sector increased by 166 percent and 130 percent; those in the private sector, by 19 times and 24 times; and those in cooperatives, by 29 times and 22 times. In 1978, the state sector created 65 percent of the total industrial output, and the collective sector created 35 percent. But in 1985, the proportion of the industrial output by the state sector decreased to 36 percent, and that by the collective increased to 59 percent. The remaining 5 percent was created by the private sector and cooperatives.[2]

Second, the provincial government decentralized decision-making powers to the individual enterprise by a large extent. The provincial mandatory planning scale was reduced. In 1984, the provincial government issued a regulation under which the mandatory plans for industrial products were reduced from 149 to 65, and the provincial budgetary appropriation was turned into a bank loan. In 1985, provincial planning only covered about 10 percent of the total industrial output. Further, the provincial government implemented preferential financial policies for enterprises and encouraged them to put much emphasis on technological innovations and long-term investments. Changes were also introduced into the ownership system. Many small-scale state enterprises came under collective ownership. Meanwhile, the management of the contract system was implemented in enterprises, and large enterprises were divided into many small units of production, each of which had the authority to formulate and carry out different measures.

The provincial government also made great efforts to expand horizontal economic cooperation. Historically, Zhejiang had close economic relations with other provinces because of its shortage of

---

[2] Calculated from *Zhejiang Tongji Nianjian* (The Statistical Yearbook of Zhejiang 1981, 1986).

raw materials and energy. During the Maoist era, all provinces were prevented from developing economic cooperation with one another. After the reform began, the tension between supply and demand in raw materials and energy increased. In 1979, the provincial government established two crucial organizations, The Leading Small Group of Zhejiang Economic Coordination (*Zhejiang Sheng Jingji Xiezuo Lingdao Xiaozu*) and The Office of Zhejiang Economic Coordination (*Zhejiang Sheng Jingsi Xiezuo Lingdao Bangongshi*). In 1982, these two organizations were merged into the Office of Economic Coordination of Zhejiang Province, and in 1985, the office was again changed to the Office of Zhejiang Economic and Technological Coordination. The office was responsible for internal and external economic cooperation. By 1985, Zhejiang had established extensive economic relations with 28 provinces through the coordination office. The province "imported" numerous raw materials through such horizontal cooperation. The tension between supply and demand in raw materials was thus relaxed to a great degree. For example, by the early 1980s, Zhejiang needed about 10 million tons of coal for local industry, but could only get 6 million through state planning. Through close economic relations with Shanxi province, Zhejiang was able to "import" about 3 million tons of coal in three years and many other raw materials. Meanwhile, the province also "exported" its products and technology by establishing many "joint ventures" in Shanxi, Anhui, Henan and many other provinces. Usually, Zhejiang provided these provinces with financial resources and technologies and they provided Zhejiang with raw materials and energy in return.[3]

FISCAL DECENTRALIZATION AND CHANGES IN INVESTMENT PATTERNS

In 1980, the central government implemented a new fiscal system — "cooking in separate kitchens." The provincial government of Zhejiang soon implemented such a system in its relations with

---

[3] On horizontal economic cooperation, see The Center of Economic Studies of Zhejiang (1986: 673–677).

municipal and county governments. Roughly speaking, there were three variants of this system. First, a method called "fixed contribution" was carried out in 29 municipal and county governments in affluent areas. Under this measure, except for the Production Tax, the Value Added Tax and the Sales Tax, other income was assigned to municipal and county governments as their fixed revenue. With the ratio between revenue and expenditure as the base, the low-level state organizations could retain 70 percent of the above expenditure-base revenue and contribute the remaining 30 percent to the provincial government. But the lower-level state organizations had to achieve the contracted revenue contribution goal that was decided through bargaining between them and the provincial government. If they could not achieve that goal, they needed to use their own revenue to reach the figure targeted by the provincial government. In addition, because the three taxes (Production, Value Added and Sales) were largely collected by municipal and county governments, the provincial government allowed them to retain 5–15 percent above the quota in revenues in order to provide them with an incentive.

A second method called "coordinated sharing" was implemented in 34 municipal and county governments in relatively poor areas. According to this measure, municipal and county governments could share the revenue from the three taxes mentioned above with the provincial government if their total revenue was below the expenditure quota. These governments could also retain 5–15 percent above the quota in revenues they collected from the three taxes.

A third measure was called "fixed subsidy," in which the provincial government subsidized municipal and county governments, if the total of the three tax revenues and all other revenues could not match their expenditures. The amount of subsidy increased by an annual rate of 5–10 percent. This method was implemented in the 16 poorest municipal and county governments.

Furthermore, many grassroots financial institutions were established in order to guarantee that revenues in society could be generated. As of the end of 1985, 1,507 townships — about 46 percent of the total in the province — had established their own financial institutions.

Between 1983 and 1985, the province and its lower-level state organizations implemented the *li gai shui* (tax for profit) system in state enterprises. This system was expected to increase enterprises' incentives in improving economic efficiency by allowing them to retain more profit than before. In 1985, state enterprises retained 33 percent of their total profit compared to 14 percent in 1980.

The fiscal reform became effective in stimulating economic development in the province. From 1978 to 1988, the province's GDP doubled, reaching a 11.65 percent annual growth rate; the total agricultural and industrial output increased by 18.3 percent annually; provincial exports increased by 41 percent annually. See Table 5.2 for details. So, how did the fiscal reform affect investment patterns?

From the establishment of the PRC to the end of the 1970s, the province's highest investment priority was given to heavy industry. Investment in heavy industry increased from 40 percent of the total investment for capital construction between 1949 and 1952 to 86 percent of the total between 1971 and 1975. In contrast, investment in

Table 5.2 Selected Indices of Economic Growth in Zhejiang

	1978 (billion *yuan*)	1988 (billion *yuan*)	Annual Growth Rate %
1. GDP (billion *yuan*)	12.25	71.54	11.65
2. Total agricultural & industrial outputs	19.78	142.37	18.30
Total agricultural output	6.57	28.26	5.4
Total industrial output	13.2	114.10	22.2
3. Total retail sales	7.11	37.70	12.6
4. Fiscal revenue	2.75	8.56	12.1
5. Provincial exports (million US dollar)	52.4	1,620	40.9

Source: Adapted from The Economic Institute of Zhejiang Academy of Social Sciences, "*Zhejiang Jin Shinian* (1979–1988) *Jingji Fazhan De Xitong Fenxi*" ("A Systematic Analysis of Economic Development in Zhejiang 1979–1988"), in *Zhejiang Xuekan*, 63: 4 (1990), p. 17.

light industry decreased from 60 percent to 14 percent in the same period (Shang *et al.*, 1989: 138). This investment pattern did not bring about high industrial growth for the province. From 1953 to 1976, the annual rate of industrial growth in Zhejiang was 9.43 percent, lower than the national average of 11.12 percent (Zhu, 1990: 27).

After 1979, high priority was given to light industry. In 1981, the provincial government issued a document entitled, "*The Report on Problems of the Economic Situation and Economic Development*," which stated that Zhejiang should develop light industry rather than heavy industry. The old heavy industry-oriented development strategy was criticized and a new one was proposed. The provincial government called for reemphasizing light industry, especially those sectors that could gain a return in a short period. Adjustment had to be carried out within heavy industry and heavy industry had to provide services for light industry and agriculture (The CCP Provincial Committee of Zhejiang, the Government of Zhejiang, 1981). This report was approved by the central government. The total investment in light industry increased gradually, while that in heavy industry declined. Further, more investment was channeled to the non-state sector. The investment in fixed assets in state enterprises decreased from 53 percent of the total in 1978 to 34 percent in 1988, and that in collectives decreased from 37 percent to 23 percent, while that in the private sector increased from 10 percent to 43 percent in the same period (The Economic Institute of Zhejiang Academy of Social Sciences, 1990: 22). Changes in investment patterns resulted in changes in the structure of "national income" in Zhejiang. From 1979 to 1988, the average annual growth rate of agriculture was 5.4 percent, while that of industry was 22.2 percent (*ibid.*: 21). The annual growth rate of agriculture was only one-fourth that of industry. The investment in agriculture decreased from 5.7 percent of the total investment in capital construction in 1982 to 3.2 percent in 1988. Although investments in the energy sector and the transportation and communications sector also increased, their growth rates were far below that of industry (Shang *et al.*, 1989: 21).

The banking system reform in 1987 further reinforced the provincial government's priorities. After the reform, the banking system was required to be an independent enterprise and its decision-making was not supposed to be influenced heavily by government officials. In reality, the separation of the banking system from the local government was impossible. In Zhejiang, the banking system's priority coincided with that of the provincial government. The banks preferred to invest in the projects from which they could gain profits in a short time. Bank loans were channeled to light industry and agricultural raw material sectors. More importantly, with the decline of financial aid from the state budget, self-raised funds increased drastically. In 1979, self-raised funds were about 48 percent of the total fixed-asset investments of the province. But the figure increased to 66 percent of the total in 1988 (*ibid.*). Most self-raised funds went to projects that were profitable in a short time, because they were not subject to the control of state organizations at different levels.

Adjustment in the industrial structure led to adjustment in the agricultural structure because of the province's shortage of raw materials. Incentives were provided to peasants to produce raw materials for light industry, and prices for agricultural raw materials were raised. Priorities such as energy supply, budgetary investments and talented people were assigned to raw material sectors (Zhu, 1990: 27). The agricultural policy based on material incentives resulted in great changes in the agricultural sector. Farming production declined from 74 percent of the total agricultural output in 1978 to 46 percent in 1988, while sideline production increased dramatically from 3 percent to 28 percent of the total in the same period (Shang *et al.*, 1989: 16). As a result, the level of rural industrialization was raised. The percentage of the total industrial output by state enterprises declined from 61.33 percent in 1978 to 31.25 percent in 1988, while that by rural enterprises increased from 16 percent to 45.77 percent in this period. The average annual industrial growth rate was 22.2 percent in the state sector and 35.7 percent in rural enterprises from 1979 to 1988 (The Economic Institute of Zhejiang Academy of Social Sciences, 1990: 20).

There was little change in the industrial structure despite the provincial government's great efforts. Growth within the industrial sector increased quite evenly. Little change occurred in five major industries in Zhejiang, i.e., machinery, textiles, chemicals, catering services and construction materials (*ibid.*: 21–22).

Nevertheless, the fiscal reform and changes in investment priority brought about new developments to the structure of the ownership system. The percentage of the total industrial output by the state sector decreased from 61.34 percent in 1978 to 31.25 percent in 1988, while that by collectives increased from 38.66 percent to 66.6 percent in this period. From 1979 to 1988, the average annual industrial growth rate in the state sector was 16 percent, while that in the collective sector was 26.9 percent, and that of rural industry was 37.7 percent. In the same period, the average annual growth rate of industrial profits in collectives was 21.2 percent, compared to 17 percent in the state sector (*ibid.*: 23).

The impact of the fiscal reform on provincial investment behavior was rather complex. The fiscal reform provided provincial officials with a strong incentive to expand the amount of investment. There was a close link between revenue growth and local economic development. Fast growth in Zhejiang was mainly due to the large input of productive elements, especially investment. From 1978 to 1987, the revenue from the industrial sector reached 18.7 percent of the annual growth rate. According to one estimate, of this growth rate, 57 percent was from capital investment (*ibid.*: 19). Under fiscal decentralization, increasing revenue became a major goal, economic, as well as political, for local state organizations. For local officials, more revenue meant both economic and political achievement. After the reform, revenue in Zhejiang increased dramatically. The provincial revenue increased from 2.75 billion *yuan* in 1978 to 8.56 billion in 1988, reaching a 12 percent annual growth rate. As of 1988, there were only five municipalities and counties whose annual revenue was below 10 million *yuan*, and there were 14 municipalities and counties whose annual revenue was above 100 million (*ibid.*: 24). An official report stated,

> Increasing revenues are an important source of economic development. But, [the new fiscal system] "cooking in separate kitchens" constrains economic growth. Because the new system is a fiscal contract system of

"set membership" type, it creates a great passion for local governments and bureaucracies to seek their interests by expanding economic size infinitely. This has led to a symptom of hunger for investment, which in turn led to duplicate and blind construction, and it is impossible for the government to control an expanding investment scale. Meanwhile, every locality employs its own policies, appears as an independent organization, isolating itself from the outside world and avoiding competition with other localities in order to prevent its resources from flowing out of its territory and thus decreasing its fiscal revenue (*ibid.*).

The fiscal decentralization led to a rapid industrial expansion that reinforced the tension between the demand for and supply of raw materials in Zhejiang, as in many other places in China. This tension, in turn, constrained further industrial growth and thus forced the provincial government to channel more financial sources to the raw material and energy sectors and infrastructure construction. During the Sixth Five-Year Plan period (1981–1985), 39 percent of the total provincial budgetary investment was channeled to power, transportation and raw materials production (The Commission of Economic Planning of Zhejiang, 1988: 241). In 1986, investment in the energy sector reached an annual growth rate of 28 percent, and that in transportation and communications reached 54 percent. Indeed, investment by the provincial budget in these sectors have not continued to increase in the following years.[4]

A major source of investment expansion was the fast development of the non-state sector, especially the private sector. In Zhejiang, the state budget generally did not cover the collective sector. For example, only 1 percent of the total investment in fixed-assets in the collective sector came from the state budget. Fully 35 percent of the total came from domestic loans and nearly 49 percent of the total from self-raised funds (The Statistical Bureau of Zhejiang, 1989: 189). According to an official report, although the provincial government could use measures such as controlling bank loans to collectives, the collective sector became increasingly beyond state control due to a rapid increase in its self-generated

---

[4] Calculated from *Zhejiang Jingji Nianjian* (Yearbook of Zhejiang Economy), various issues.

funds (The Economic Institute of Zhejiang Academy of Social Sciences, 1990: 22). With the reform, more and more non-state budgetary financial resources became available to individuals or households. Considering that fixed-asset investment in the private sector increased dramatically and became the largest part of the total, the contribution of this sector to an expanding scale of investment was obvious. An official report warned that "self-raised funds and private investment have become a main resource of fixed-asset investment, the [old] system which only deals with investment by the state budget is no longer suitable to cope with new situations with multiple investment actors" (*ibid.*).

THE DEVELOPMENT OF AN EXPORT-LED STRATEGY

An ambitious goal of the provincial government of Zhejiang in the 1980s was to achieve a growth rate higher than that of the national average. The expansion of international trade was one of the links in this overall strategy. In 1986, the government issued a document on development strategy, which stated, "The strategic goals of the province's modernization between 1986 and 2000 are to achieve three major objectives: (1) to develop productivity and to promote coordinated development between the economy and society and to achieve a growth rate of economic power and people's living standards higher than that of the national average; (2) to develop international trade … and to build the province as a center of international trade and a culturally advanced place; (3) to lay the foundation for high growth in the twenty-first century" (The Government of Zhejiang, 1986a: 54).

More specifically, an export-led development strategy was about how to turn Zhejiang as a province poor in resources into one with a big economy. In 1987, the Director of the Institute of Economic Research under the Provincial Economic Planning Commission, Zhu Jialiang, proposed a strategy to the provincial government. According to Zhu, if the province still continued its past strategy of development, i.e., domestic market-oriented development, it would not be able to keep a fast growth rate, while an export-led strategy would be able to promote the technological level of processing industries and thus provide products from the province, which are highly competitive in the market (Zhu, 1987).

This proposal was received with strong appreciation from top leaders in the provincial government, including then Governor Xue Ji and Vice Governor Sun Zulun. In his lecture at a conference, based on Zhu's proposal, Sun formulated the province's export-led development strategy that he called "rejuvenating the province through 'export-led' international trade" (*chukou daoxiang maoyi xingsheng*). Sun criticized the past development strategy that put emphasis only on the domestic market and thus ignored the international market. Because of the fast development of the domestic industry, especially light industry, the province's products would be facing serious challenges in domestic markets in the near future. So, the province needed to develop an export-led development strategy. Further, such a strategy would promote labor-intensive industries in the province and thus would reduce the government's burden in coping with population growth and the tension between the supply and demand of raw materials. Also, to develop such a strategy, the provincial government and lower-level government organizations had to give high priority to promoting technological progress, thus lifting the technological level for processing industries and industrial management. Equally important was the need to implement preferential policies toward foreign businesses in order to absorb advanced foreign capital and technologies (Sun, 1987).

What drove the provincial government to adapt such a strategy and to what extent was the provincial government successful in implementing this strategy? An examination of the development of such a strategy enables us to see how the provincial government responded to the initiative from Beijing.

Zhejiang had a long tradition of international trade. But under the Maoist development policy that emphasized local self-sufficiency, international trade performance in the province became very poor. In 1955, the province established a bureau of international trade. But this bureau was soon turned into an office that was subordinated to the central bureaucracy. Although the bureau of international trade was reestablished in 1973, it continued to rely heavily on the central bureaucracy and its main task was to achieve goals set forth by the central bureaucracy — mainly collecting products for international trade.

After 1979, the provincial government was assigned autonomy in foreign trade. In December 1979, the central government allowed it to open the Ningbo harbor and Hangzhou as tourist centers. In May 1984, Ningbo and Wenzhou cities were on the list of open cities. In February 1985, the central government allowed the opening of Jiaxing and Huzhou cities as a part of the Changjiang delta open area. In March 1988, the State Council agreed to the provincial government's proposal to open 37 municipalities and counties in the coastal area. By 1988, 44 percent of the total area of the province had become an open zone (The Office of Coordination of International Economy of Zhejiang, 1989). Many organizations engaging in international trade were established by the provincial government and local state organizations. But international trade performance was regarded as unsuccessful. As of 1986, the province's exports only comprised 10 percent of its total GNP (Sun, 1988).

A major constraint in foreign trade development was the tension between the demand for and supply of products in the domestic market. The Maoist heavy industry-oriented development strategy led to an undersupply of commodities. Although high priority was given to light industry since the reform, demand was still far above the supply of products. The reform created great demand for products by increasing people's living standards. With fast local economic development, Zhejiang residents' bank savings and cash deposits increased dramatically, from 2.51 billion *yuan* in 1980 to 7.37 billion in 1984 to 17.49 billion in 1987 (The Statistical Bureau of Zhejiang, 1989: 72). Table 5.3 revealed the tension between the people's purchasing power and the supply of commodities in Zhejiang. Fast growth of savings was mainly due to the undersupply of products in the province. The potential of this purchasing power led to a fear on the part of the government that undersupply would lead to political instability. The government's use of non-economic measures to limit people's purchasing power in turn often led to discontent.

Table 5.3 The Tension between Residents' Purchasing Power and Supply of Commodities in Zhejiang (billion *yuan*)

Year	Total Social Purchasing Power	Total Retail Sources	% of Total Retail Sources Over Total Purchasing Power
1980	9.95	9.50	95.5
1981	10.95	10.95	100
1982	12.27	12.03	98.0
1983	13.37	12.76	95.4
1984	17.10	15.40	90.1
1985	22.31	20.41	91.6
1986	26.99	24.24	89.8
1987	31.83	28.60	89.9

Source: The Statistical Bureau of Zhejiang Province, *"Zai 'Jie' De Guonei Xuqiu Yali Xia Fazhan Zhejiang Sheng Waixiangxing Jingji de Duice Sikao"* ("Considerations on Strategy to Develop an Export-Oriented Economy in Zhejiang under a 'Hungry' Domestic Demand Pressure"), in The State Statistical Bureau, (ed.), *Yanhai Jingji Kaifangqu Jingji He Tongji Ziliao* (Economic Studies and Statistical Data of Coastal "Open" Economic Areas), Beijing: Zhongguo Tongji Chubanshe, 1989, p. 72.

Further, the export structure also worsened the circumstances for the government's exports policy. In Zhejiang, farming and sidelines had been major export items. After the reform began, industrial products increased in the total of exports, but grain products and sidelines were still an essential portion of the total exports. As a result, the increase in grain product exports necessarily meant constraints on domestic demand for those products. Also, peasants now increasingly turned to the rural industry and other non-agricultural industries such as commerce, construction and catering, which were more profitable than grain production, and grain production in rural areas actually declined drastically in the province. This fact made it more difficult for the government to purchase grain products for export.

Consequently, an export-led development strategy necessarily had political significance. An increase in the purchase of export commodities meant a decrease in domestic supply, which, in turn, led to a rise in retail prices for domestic products. Further, local state organizations competed with one another for export products in order to achieve their export goals. Intensive competition among them also led to an increase in prices. As an official report described, "a decrease in products in the domestic market leads prices to rise. Because of undersupply in the domestic market, an increase in export products will lead to a further shortage in domestic supply.... Devaluation will occur and prices will go up. Raising prices again will lead to residents' scrambling for commodities and their fear will worsen" (*ibid.*: 79). Political considerations thus became important. The implementation of the export-led development strategy should not endanger political stability. As the report emphasized, this important aspect had to be considered seriously when governments implemented this strategy. Domestic supply had to be given higher priority because if residents in the province could not be satisfied, discontent would rise and political stability would become problematic. The political situation in effect would have a major impact on international trade. Without political stability, international trade could not be developed smoothly (*ibid.*: 78).

An undersupply of products for the domestic market resulted in great difficulty in implementing the export-led development strategy. The same report stated,

> The domestic market still has great demand for many kinds of commodities, especially for grain products and light industrial products; domestic production is not able to meet residents' consumption demands. Because of oversized demands, commodities are undersupplied. As a result, commodity producers and enterprise managers can gain profits from the domestic market much higher than in the international market. High profitability in the domestic market, plus consumers' low demand for commodity's diversity, category and quality, tempts strongly commodity producers and enterprise managers to put an emphasis on the domestic market. Meanwhile, enterprises have no great interest in developing international trade. So, theoretically, there would be great difficulties in implementing the export-led development strategy when the domestic market is undersupplied (*ibid.*: 70–71).

Nevertheless, an export-led approach was imperative, because for the government, this strategy would be more effective in the long run. Zhao Ziyang, the then General Secretary of the CCP, visited Zhejiang and Jiangsu twice at the end of 1987 and early 1988, and called for provincial cooperation in implementing the central government's grand strategy of international trade. Since the mid-1980s, the central government had implemented a contract system regarding foreign trade with the provincial government of Zhejiang. Under this contract system, the province could gain greater benefits from increased exports so that a strong incentive was expected to be provided to provincial officials. As a response to the reform leadership in Beijing, the provincial government proposed the policy of "rejuvenating the province through export-led international trade." Many think-tank persons and intellectual circles argued for such a strategy after the mid-1980s (Zhu, 1988; Jiang, 1988). For them, Zhejiang's success in developing the local economy had been mainly due to the province's open-door policy. Mao's self-sufficiency strategy did not bring the province fast development. From 1949 to 1978, the average annual growth rate of the total agricultural and industrial output was 8.2 percent, lower than the national average (9.51 percent). Since the reform, Zhejiang had turned its emphasis to light industry and opened its door to the rest of country. The province had thus established almost a nationwide market for its products. This policy led to fast economic development in the province. But now again it was time for the province to transform its development strategy so that fast growth could be sustained.

Zhejiang was poor in resources. With fast economic development in the whole country, Zhejiang would be facing great difficulties in gaining raw materials from other provinces and the province's processing industry would be thus less competitive in the domestic market. The province had to turn to open international markets for both the raw materials it needed and the products it produced. Further, an export-led approach was very helpful for the government to cope with an increasing surplus of agricultural laborers generated by the implementation of the household responsibility system. If these surplus laborers could not be absorbed, social stability would be endangered (Zhu, 1988).

In mid-1985, the provincial government began to make great efforts to implement economic, as well as political, measures to promote the province's exports. In 1985, the Office of Agricultural Policy Studies investigated ten export bases of grain products and sidelines, and reached the conclusion that production for international trade was too centralized. Local firms could not engage in direct foreign trade, and all that they could do was to achieve the goals set forth by higher-level government organizations. So, effective incentives could not be provided. The Office called for further reforms in foreign trade system, especially further decentralization (The Investigation Group of the Office for Agricultural Policy Studies, 1985).

In 1986, the provincial government developed the Seventh Five-Year Plan in which foreign trade was given high priority. According to this plan, up to 1990, the total export had to reach US$1.4 billion, achieving an 11.7 percent average annual growth rate from the previous year (The Government of Zhejiang, 1986b). *The Strategy of Economic and Social Development* that was issued in the same year also emphasized the need to speed up international trade development. Some general guidelines were established for local state organizations' reference when they made their own development policies. They included:

1. To adjust the export structure, i.e., increasing exports of manufactured goods and reducing those of raw materials and preliminarily processed products.
2. To adjust the market structure, i.e., expanding international markets from mainly Hong Kong and Japan to many other countries such as the United States, Western Europe, Russia, Eastern Europe and other Third World countries. Local governments had also to develop various channels of foreign trade through overseas Chinese.
3. To further reform the system of international trade in the provinces by various measures. First, the provincial government should

discuss with the central government and gain greater autonomy in foreign trade than before. Second, the governments at different levels had to implement favorable policies for those enterprises that were producing goods for export and provide them with greater incentives. Third, local state organizations had to make great efforts to establish a foreign trade network in foreign countries.

The provincial government also stressed the strategy of attracting more foreign investment in the province. Governments at different levels were called to provide very favorable investment circumstances for foreign businessmen. In dividing profits between the province and foreign businessmen, the governments had to use measures to transfer more profits to the foreign side because only profitability could attract more foreign capital. By doing so, the province would gain more profits in the long run (The Government of Zhejiang, 1986a).

More detailed measures had to be implemented to promote foreign trade development. On 2 January 1986, the provincial government approved the *Report on Expanding Exports and Increasing Foreign Exchange* by the Provincial Bureau of Foreign Trade, which emphasized decentralizing decision-making power to lower-level state organizations and enterprises. It also stressed that local governments had to cooperate with one another to achieve both mandatory and directory targets of international trade set up by the provincial government. A contractual relation between the provincial government and municipal and county governments, between government organizations and enterprises had to be established. Those who failed to fulfill the contract had to be fined in financial terms. The report also set up a new reward system for foreign trade. An enterprise could gain fifteen cents for each US$10 of export within the quota and could gain 30 cents for each additional 10 dollars of export. Enterprise managers had full autonomy in spending those retained profits. Further, those enterprises that could gain a high profit rate of foreign exchange could retain more profits, and tax rates for those enterprises would also be reduced (The Government of Zhejiang, 1986c).

After 1988, a new contract system was implemented. Through the negotiations between the central government and the provincial government, a base of foreign trade was established for the latter. The provincial government then divided this base into many pieces and distributed them among municipal and county governments and foreign trade companies, which further set forth plans for individual enterprises. The contracts between the provincial government and the municipal and county governments, between governments and enterprises, once set up, was valid at least for three years. Local governments and enterprises could retain 80 percent of above-quota profits and remit the remaining 20 percent to the central government. More importantly, any enterprises or corporations, if they satisfied certain conditions, could engage directly in foreign trade and made decisions independently (The Government of Zhejiang, 1988b).

Meanwhile, many favorable policies were carried out toward foreign businesses. According to a regulation issued in 1985, foreign enterprises would not be taxed locally for five years, and they could apply to continue not to be taxed when the five-year term expired, if they satisfied one of the following conditions: (1) their products were for export; (2) they were knowledge-intensive and highly technology-oriented; (3) foreign capital was above US$30 million and they needed a long time to gain profits; (4) they focused on energy production, transportation, harbor and other infrastructure construction; (5) they focused on agriculture, forestry, animal husbandry, or fisheries; or (6) they were in poor areas. Foreign businesses or joint ventures did not need to pay rent for land use for five years and needed to pay only half of the standard rent set up by the central government for another five years. Foreign businesses or joint ventures could also be given higher priority, in terms of the supply of raw materials, energy and financial sources. Further, local state organizations could not impose illegal levies on foreign enterprises as they often did toward domestic enterprises (The Government of Zhejiang, 1988a). Another regulation stressed that foreign business managers had personnel power much greater than domestic managers had. These managers had to a great extent the freedom to recruit, train and fire employees, and local governments could not block talented workers from moving into foreign businesses or joint ventures (The Standing Committee of the Seventh Congress of Zhejiang, 1988).

All these measures proved to be effective in promoting foreign trade in the province in the 1980s. For instance, the total exports and imports increased from US$7.93 million in 1984 to 20.0 million in 1988, and the total purchase of commodities for export increased from 2.35 billion *yuan* to 6.1 billion in the same period.[5]

STATE SPONSORSHIP AND THE GROWTH OF THE NON-STATE SECTOR

The non-state sector in Zhejiang developed even during the Cultural Revolution as a result of Mao's mandate for a self-sufficient industrial system. The numbers of rural enterprises increased from 35,000 in 1974 to 45,700 in 1975 and 51,000 in 1976. Such development conflicted seriously with the Maoist ideology. The provincial government implemented numerous policies to constrain the development of the rural industry. Even more than a decade later, people still remembered the so-called "red typhoon movement" that was initiated by radical provincial leaders to eliminate rural enterprises in the province. Many enterprises were closed, others went "underground" and not a few managers were put into prison. Ironically, such movements did not stop the further development of rural enterprises. By the end of 1978, the number of rural enterprises increased to 74,000, which employed 1.9 million workers and produced 2.17 billion *yuan* in industrial output (Shang *et al.*, 1989: 269–270).

The reform legitimated these underground enterprises and their "illegal" commercial activities. After the central government repeatedly called for faster development of the rural industry between 1979 and 1983, the provincial government began to see the rural industry as an important agenda in the province. Preferential policies were implemented toward rural enterprises. Newly-opened rural enterprises were exempted from taxation for one or two years; production teams or villages were allowed to process grain products and other agricultural raw materials and sell the new products in the marketplace; banks

---

[5] On exports (1981–1985), see The Bureau of Foreign Trade of Zhejiang (1987); on exports & imports (1986–1988), see annual reports, various issues in *Zhejiang Jingji Nianjian*; on the total purchases, see The Statistical Bureau of Zhejiang (1988: 253).

were requested to issue loans at low interest rates to rural enterprises and lower-level state organizations were asked to reduce the peasants' burden so that capital for rural enterprises could be accumulated. These measures laid a solid foundation for the rapid growth of rural enterprises later. In 1985, rural industrial output was above that of agriculture, and was one-third of the combined agricultural and industrial output in the province. The rural industry also contributed to one-fifth of the total provincial revenue. From then on, the provincial government and lower-level state organizations would have to give high priority to rural enterprises in their policy-making.

In the mid-1980s, fast economic growth and an increasing deficit led the central government to fear that an overheated economy would lead to serious inflation and thus social instability. This fear led the central government to call for rural industrial development to halt. The provincial government was asked to implement four major aspects of policy for rural industry, i.e., controlling the pace of development, reducing bank loans, controlling the scale of construction, and limiting the size of consumption funds. The provincial government of Zhejiang did, to some extent, implement these policies. But it also used many other measures to promote the further development of the rural industry. Further "decentralization" was encouraged within the rural industry, and enterprise managers were given greater autonomy in their decision-making about profit distribution, organizational establishment, labor recruitment, retirement and so forth. The provincial government also repeatedly emphasized that peasant cooperatives and individual enterprises could receive the same preferential conditions as collectives. Banks were required to give rural enterprises low-interest loans (The Government of Zhejiang, 1985). Facing a shortage of financial resources for rural enterprises, the provincial government held a conference in the city of Shaoxing, where the municipal government had been successful in establishing various non-state financial institutions and collecting financial resources for rural enterprises. The conference called on local governments to follow the model of Shaoxing and promote the establishment of various non-state financial organizations so that rural enterprises in the province could achieve a sustained development when financial support from above was reduced (The Bureau of Rural Industry of Zhejiang, 1986: 146).

At the beginning of 1986, the rural industry felt intense political pressure because government organizations at different levels called for a political campaign to attack corruption among local officials and enterprise leaders, especially those who committed economic crimes. Grassroots party leaders were again assigned greater power in economic affairs. Many enterprise managers were criticized. Statistics showed that the growth rate of rural industry declined dramatically in the first two months by 41.5 percent and 17.9 percent, respectively. The provincial government discovered that such a movement resulted in serious consequences for the overall economic performance of the province, and thus issued two regulations about policies toward the rural industry to protect enterprises from negative political impacts. Enterprise managers were encouraged to open their minds further (The Bureau of Rural Industry of Zhejiang, 1987: 165). Given the circumstances in China then, these measures were important and offered symbolic support for enterprise managers, especially those in the private sector.

In 1987, Chinese senior leader Deng Xiaoping showed strong support for the fast development of the rural industry in Zhejiang when he met his Italian guests. Zhao Ziyang also showed strong support by visiting Zhejiang and investigating the rural industry there. These two events were regarded by the local governments as important messages of support for a high growth rate in the rural industry. At the end of that year, rural industrial output reached more than half of the total industrial output in the province, and created about one-third of the total provincial revenue (The Bureau of Rural Industry of Zhejiang, 1988: 167–168).

Also important was that the private sector developed at a fast pace in the province. In 1984, the central government called for local state organizations to treat different forms of ownership of rural enterprises equally. The private sector gained strong development momentum in Zhejiang in the 1980s, as shown in Table 5.4. Also, according to a 1986 investigation of private enterprises in 18 counties, of 230 private enterprises, 8.7 percent opened in 1983, 29 percent in 1984, 37 percent in 1985 and 25 percent in 1986 (He & Li, 1988: 29). The private sector grew faster than both the state and collective sectors because of its capacity to adjust priorities in

Table 5.4 The Development of Private Enterprises in Zhejiang in the 1980s

Year	1980	1984	1985	1986	1987	1988
Private enterprises (1,000)	33	47	637	715	821	944
Employees (1,000)	34	592	864	988	1,165	1,395
Registered capital (million *yuan*)	–	–	869	1,044	–	2,297
Total retail (million *yuan*)	–	–	2,743	3,292	–	6,587

Sources: Adapted from the annual report of the Bureau of Industrial and Commercial Administration of Zhejiang province, *Zhejiang Chengxiang Geti Gongshangye* (Urban and Rural Private Enterprises in Zhejiang), in *Zhejiang Jingji Nianjian*, various issues (1980–1989).

facing changing circumstances, while both the state and collective sectors had difficulties in doing so due to administrative interference from the "political side." In 1985, peasant cooperatives and individual enterprises represented about 71 percent of the total rural enterprises, 20 percent of the total employees, and 12 percent of the total rural industrial output (*ibid.*: 277). In 1986, the numbers of peasant cooperatives and individual enterprises reached 330,000, producing 4.9 billion *yuan* of industrial output and reaching an annual growth rate of 56 percent (The Bureau of Rural Industry of Zhejiang, 1987: 165). The private sector also developed faster than the collective sector in the province. For example, in 1987, the total number of rural collective enterprises declined by 4.8 percent, while in the private sector, it increased by 17 percent; employees in the collectives increased by 1.4 percent, while in the private sector, they increased by 12 percent. In 1988, the annual growth rate of rural collective enterprises was 1.22 percent, while it was 6 percent for the private sector; that of employees in the collectives was negative, while it reached 8 percent for the private sector; that of the total number of products for the collective sector was 30 percent, while it was 52 percent for the private sector; that of the industrial output for the collective sector was 31 percent, while it was 55 percent for the private sector. At the end of 1988, the private sector in rural areas produced about 20 percent of the total rural industrial output of the province (The Bureau of Rural Industry of Zhejiang, 1988).

The provincial government also stressed the role of entrepreneurs in local economic development. Those managers who had been criticized for their "illegal" economic activities during the Cultural Revolution were allowed to return to their enterprises soon after the reform began. Realizing that fast economic growth needed an entrepreneurial class, the provincial government called for the implementation of various policies favorable to talented people. In 1985, Wang Fang, then the First Provincial Party Secretary of Zhejiang, emphasized in a conference on rural development that local governments should recruit more talented people into local leadership. According to Wang, old leaders were no longer able to meet changing circumstances even though they performed well before, arguing:

> We have to be brave enough to recruit those who ... are younger, have wide economic knowledge and are able to lead people to get rich into our leadership. [They can] substitute for older and little educated cadres and can be dominant in local leadership. There are many talented people in those villages in which rural enterprises have developed well, among special households, among demobilized soldiers and those who have just finished their high school education. Many of them now are not cadres, but they are actual organizers of local economic activities and are *de facto* leaders in people's minds. We should first recruit such people into our leadership and let them play an important role. Some of them can be party or government leaders and some of them can be leaders or managers in factories, companies, associations and many other non-state organizations (Wang, 1985).

Many measures were implemented to foster an entrepreneurial class. First, the provincial government established various connections with colleges, universities or research institutes and sent enterprise managers there to receive training. For example, in 1985, the province sent 796 rural enterprise managers to universities and another 1,120 to colleges for full-time training. It was reported that those who received special training were playing an important part in the development of the rural industry (Shang, 1989: 288). Second, the provincial government itself established the Center of Education and Technological Training in the mid-1980s. It also called for local governments to establish such training centers for rural enterprises. According to a statistic in 1985, the Yuyao municipal city government established 96 special training colleges that enrolled 3,778 students. In Ning county, 14 township governments had their own training centers. In 1985, about 60,000 rural enterprise managers or supervisors accepted training of some sort (*ibid.*). As of the end of 1987, the province had seven training centers at the municipal level, two colleges, 45 educational and technological training centers at the county level and 148 special training centers. About 145,000 managers and rural workers received such training in this single year (The Bureau of Rural Industry of Zhejiang, 1988: 169).

Third, many talented people were recruited into the managerial class. Many local government organizations had occupational

Table 5.5 Entrepreneurs in Rural Collectives in Zhejiang

	Total	Percentage (%)
Age		
Below 35	4	11
35–45	21	57
46 and above	12	32
Total	37	
Schooling		
Primary school	5	16
Middle school	12	39
High school	9	29
College	5	16
Total	31	
Prior Career		
Technicians	10	29
Managers	12	35
Local leaders	9	26
Salespersons	3	9
Total	34	

Source: Adapted from Sun Gengfa, (ed.), *Zhejiang Sheng Xiangzhen Qiyejia Zhuanlue* (A Biography of Entrepreneurs in Zhejiang), Hangzhou: Zhejiang Daxue Chubanshe, 1989.

surveys and compiled special files for those who had the potential for management. For example, Shaoxing County established files for 15,971 talented people through several surveys. This figure was about 3.4 percent of the total number of rural laborers there. Of 15,971 talented people, 39.6 percent had special skills, 13 percent were good at enterprise management, 13 percent were good at commercial work, and 4.5 percent had skill in many respects. It was reported that many of them were appointed as enterprise managers (Shang *et al.*, 1989: 287–291).

An investigation of entrepreneurs in rural collectives reveals that many younger and educated people with special career experience were recruited into enterprise leadership. See Table 5.5 for details. The same situation was also found in the private sector as an investigation of 40 private enterprises (see Table 5.6).

Table 5.6 Entrepreneurs in 40 Rural Private Enterprises

	Total	Percentage (%)
Age		
Below 25	1	2.5
26–35	9	22.5
36–45	16	40
46–55	9	22.5
56 and above	5	12.5
Schooling		
No education	1	2.55
Primary school	15	37.5
Middle & high school	20	50
University & college	4	10
Prior career		
Managers who quitted from		
state & collective enterprises	7	17.5
Technicians	12	30
Demobilized soldiers & unemployed	8	20

Source: Adapted from He Tohong and Li Jianxin, "*Zhejiang Nongcun Siren Qiye Fazhan Gaikuang Ji Duice*" ("Private Enterprise Development in Rural Zhejiang and Strategies"), in *Zhejiang Xuekan* (The Journal of Zhejiang), 50: 3 (1988), pp. 29–32.

THE WENZHOU MODEL: THE STATE
AND THE PRIVATE ECONOMY

Wenzhou has been well-known for its booming private economy, but the establishment and recognition of the Wenzhou model has its own bitter story. An examination of the development of the Wenzhou model in the 1980s enables us to see how local community, local state organizations and the center interacted; how the local state protected the nascent private sector; and how the state organized private economic activities to bring them in line with state priorities.

As elsewhere in China, the private sector continued to exist in Wenzhou after the establishment of the PRC. Employees in this sector increased from 19,500 in 1949 to 25,500 in 1956. The total output increased from 9 million *yuan* to 32.2 million in the same period (Shang *et al.*, 1989: 308). The Great Leap Forward and the communization movement in 1958 brought great damages to the private sector. The household economy was regarded as illegal and small rural markets were closed. Many private businesses were forced to integrate into the state-owned enterprises.

After 1962, due to the implementation of moderate policies, private economic activities reemerged in this area and small special markets were allowed. But new developments did not last longer. The beginning of the Cultural Revolution almost eliminated a newly-rising "capitalist force." However, in the late period of the Cultural Revolution, the private sector and also the small collectives again gained a development momentum in Wenzhou. An economy of shortage created an opportunity for the private sector to seek fast development. Numerous private economic activities revived. Interestingly, because large-scale enterprises were more vulnerable to attack by radical policies, many state enterprises turned themselves into collective ownership, and big collectives were split into small ones, while small ones were privatized in Wenzhou. A small boom in the rural industry thus occurred in this period. In 1977, commune collectives created 40 million *yuan* of industrial output, increasing by 81.3 percent from that of 1971. Industrial output from small collectives more than doubled in this period (*ibid.*: 309).

The end of the Cultural Revolution in 1976 did not lead right away to dynamism in the private sector in Wenzhou. According to an official report in May 1977, the municipal government initiated a massive movement aimed at destroying rising "capitalist forces," closing local markets, and preventing peasants from entering cities to do business. More than 6,000 government employees were authorized to patrol local markets in the area daily. This anti-capitalist force campaign lasted only for several months; it failed because more and more private economic activities went underground (The Municipal Government of Wenzhou, 1984). Until 1978, higher authorities continued to regard Wenzhou as a model of the restoration of capitalism and private economic activities were still illegal. But this "underground" capitalism seemed irreversible because local communities and local leaderships, as organized forces, provided very strong support for it. Although Wenzhou was viewed as a bad model by the official ideology and conservative leaders in Beijing, capitalistic development was not interrupted in Wenzhou. After the reform leadership in Beijing took power, the policies toward the private sector continued to be controversial among Beijing leaders, but became moderate (Kraus, 1991).

In the early 1980s, the Wenzhou municipal government wrote an official report on the private economy in Wenzhou. The report mildly criticized state ownership and pointed out that state ownership failed to provide the satisfactory services needed and was thus inappropriate to this locality. In contrast, the private sector, although it was still "illegal" and underground, could provide various services for both local communities and local governments. Since private businesses were profit-oriented, they could provide higher quality services than both collectives and state firms. If the private sector was allowed to compete with state and collective firms, the latter would be pressured to improve their performance. Furthermore, the private sector absorbed numerous rural and urban surplus laborers, reduced greatly the burden on the government, and created favorable conditions of social stability. The report called for local government officials not to use the old ideology to judge the role of the private sector, but to handle it properly (The Municipal Government of

Wenzhou, 1984). The report gained strong public support when it was published. A commentator argued that the state could no longer use coercion to eliminate the private sector because past experience showed that a unified ownership system was extremely harmful for economic development and social stability. As long as the private sector could provide good services, the state should promote its fast development, rather than constrain it. Further, the state should encourage competition among enterprises with different forms of ownership. If collectives were not competitive, they should be transformed to private firms (Li, 1985).

Controversies over the private sector in Wenzhou extended into the late 1980s because the Wenzhou model totally departed from both the old ideology and other models such as the south Jiangsu and the Zhujiang models (Guangdong province).[6] The rise of the private sector put the state sector in a weaker position in competition in Wenzhou. During the Sixth Five-Year Plan period (1981–1985), the average annual industrial growth rate was 8.9 percent for the state sector, 32 percent for the rural industry and 51 percent for village or street level enterprises. By the mid-1980s, the state sector produced only 18 percent of the total product; the collectives and private cooperatives produced 52 percent; and the private individual enterprises generated 30 percent (Chen *et al.*, 1987: 82). More seriously, the state sector declined at a fast pace. Economic efficiency was much lower in the state sector than in both collectives and the private sector. The industrial products of the state sector piled up because product quality was better in the non-state sector. Compared to other sectors, workers in the state sector had no strong incentives to improve their performance. Many of them left the state sector and were employed by the non-state sector or opened their own businesses. Nearly 20 percent of state firm workers had a second job outside their firms (*ibid.*).

A major source of the decline of the state sector was the state ownership system itself. The rise of the private sector was charged with causing the state sector to decline due to various reasons. First,

---

[6] For debates about the Wenzhou model, see articles in Pan Shangen (1988).

numerous raw materials and energy resources that were originally assigned to state-enterprises were now taken by the private sector. Second, by paying them much higher wages, the private sector attracted most talented people away from the state sector. Third, the local state implemented favorable policies toward the private and collective sectors, while policies toward the state sector remained rigid and the state sector could not be provided with incentives. Actually, local state officials had no interest in improving the economic performance of the state sector because of its lower economic efficiency. Finally, as of 1988, 55–80 percent of state-enterprise workers had a second job. Since they could earn more money from their second job, they had no motivation in the state sector. Many state workers even paid a certain amount of money to their state firms in return for a permit to be transferred to the non-state sector (Yan, 1988).

The central government was not able to give strong support to the Wenzhou model as it did to other models because the Wenzhou model was the furthest of all the models from socialism. For a long period after the reform began, ideological conflicts among top leaders in Beijing were very intense. Both the conservative or moderate political factions among leaders disliked radical reforms, both in economic and political terms. The Wenzhou model was attacked in almost all political campaigns such as the "rectification campaign" in early 1985 and the "anti-bourgeois" campaign at the end of 1986. It was frequently charged that the Wenzhou model was the way of capitalism, and that Wenzhou's private economy was the economic foundation of "bourgeois liberalism."[7] But new developments here deeply impressed many reformist leaders in Beijing. While controversies existed, the Wenzhou model received strong support from the reformist faction. After 1980, many central leaders paid visits to Wenzhou, including Wan Li (who led a successful rural reform in Anhui and had close personal connections with China's senior leader, Deng Xiaoping), Tian Jiyun (Political Bureau member and then Vice Premier), Du Runsheng (Director of the Rural Policy

---

[7] For ideological debate on the Wenzhou model, see Liu Qing and Tang Hai (1987), and Mi Shuzu (1986).

Research Center under the Secretariat of the Central Committee), Wu Xiang (Deputy Director of the Rural Policy Research Center under the State Council), Fei Xiaotong (sociologist and a close personal acquaintance of former General Secretary of the CCP, Hu Yaobang), and many others. In early 1985, Wan Li visited Wenzhou and promised local leaders that he would show Deng Xiaoping a videotape describing Wenzhou's achievements. Later that year, Zhao Ziyang led an investigation group to the area. Many leading official economists and scholars also showed strong support for the model. Fei Xiaotong called for according a high prestige to the Wenzhou model in the national economic reforms (Fei, 1986).

The Wenzhou model also gained special support from Shanghai, an industrial center of China. The *Liberation Daily,* the organ of the CCP Shanghai Committee, frequently released information about new facts in Wenzhou's development. On 12 May 1985, the newspaper first referred to Wenzhou as a "model" in a front-page report. The report attracted nationwide attention. From the time the report was published to October 1986, according to a second report on Wenzhou, many central leaders visited Wenzhou. Many policy study institutes came to Wenzhou and examined its great achievements, including the Policy Research Center under the Secretariat of the Central Committee, the Rural Policy Research Center under the State Council, the Shanghai Academy of Social Sciences, the Zhejiang Academy of Social Sciences and Fudan University. The intellectuals' enthusiasm led to an ideological turnaround on the Wenzhou model. More than 15,000 Party cadres and government officials at the provincial level and below, and grassroots cadres visited Wenzhou during this period (*Liberation Daily,* 18 October 1986). Leaders in many rich areas such as Jiangsu, Guangdong and other provinces sent their investigation groups to Wenzhou. These visitors had different opinions about the Wenzhou model. An investigating group sent by the Wuxi Municipal Government of Jiangsu praised the fast development of the marketplace in Wenzhou, but reached the conclusion and argued,

> Although the south Jiangsu model is more advanced than the Wenzhou model in terms of both economic development level and ownership forms,

the south Jiangsu model needs two basic prerequisites, i.e., a relatively huge capital accumulation by a collective economy, and a well-developed city group. Because most areas in this country do not have these two conditions, the Wenzhou model has general application in poor areas (The Center of Economic Research of Wuxi Municipal Government, 1988).

Most visitors responded very positively. Many argued that it was difficult to judge whether the collective ownership was more developed than the private ownership or not in terms of abstract ideology. Both should be judged by whether they were appropriate to local communities and whether they could promote local economic growth (Pan, 1988: 95–128). Many visitors saw greater potential for the private economy to increase economic efficiency than for either the state or collective sector. After her examination of Wenzhou's market, Jiangsu's then Governor Gu Xiulian called for Jiangsu leaders to learn from Wenzhou and to put more emphasis on fostering the market (Gu, 1987).

More importantly, the local leadership played an important role in legitimating the Wenzhou model and protecting the model from outside attacks. After the reform began, the Wenzhou municipal government regarded the development of the private sector as the most reliable way of promoting local economic growth. At the beginning of the reform, the government initiated many discussions regarding the private sector and issued a government regulation every year, supporting and encouraging fast development of the private sector. In the early 1980s, when the Wenzhou municipal government was criticized for its emphasis on small collectives and the private sector, Yuan Liefang, the Secretary of the Municipal Party Committee offered this rebuttal:

[They] say that we put emphasis only on the small economy rather than economies of scale, only on the private economy rather than the state sector. This is because they do not understand the reality in Wenzhou. We once wanted to develop an economy of scale, but failed. The state had no money [to invest in Wenzhou], and Wenzhou had no foundation to develop such an economy of scale. [So] we could only depend on ourselves and mobilize local people and their initiative to develop an economy appropriate to our local communities. We were not able to develop an economy of scale, and if we were not allowed to engage in small economies, there would be no hope for Wenzhou's economy and the people could not have a good life (cited in Zeng & Jiang, 1987: 7).

Between 1986 and 1987, Wenzhou faced a serious attack from above, and was viewed as a model of bourgeois liberalization in the economic field. But this political campaign was resisted by the local leadership. In a conference attended by most local government officials and grassroots cadres in mid-1987, Dong Zhaocai, the Secretary of the Wenzhou Municipal Party Committee, called for local cadres to focus on economic development and asked them not to turn their attention away from their economic work. The municipal government issued many regulations and aimed at promoting further development in the private sector (Dong, 1988). Meanwhile, the municipal government also called for local state bureaucracies to provide various services for the private sector. The local government's protection and the great enthusiasm aroused among local leadership in other places and intellectual circles created a favorable condition for Wenzhou. In 1986, Hu Qiaomu, one of the Communist Party's top ideologues and not a supporter of the private economy, visited Wenzhou, which meant that Hu began to accept the Wenzhou model. In 1987, relevant authorities in Beijing claimed Wenzhou as one of 14 reform experimental zones (*People's Daily*, 12 September 1987). The official legitimacy of the Wenzhou model was thus firmly established.

Local Communities and the Development of a Private Sector

When we turn to local governments and local communities, we see a rather different picture of Wenzhou's fast development. In the pre-reform period, the local community was very vulnerable to attacks from above. The local leadership did resist, to an extent, inappropriate policies from above, but Maoist anti-bureaucratism and the mass-mobilization development strategy made the local leadership itself vulnerable to attack. From 1949 to 1984, the position of First

Secretary of the CCP Wenzhou Committee changed hands 17 times, an average two-year tenure for each secretary (Liu, 1992: 705). Under the reformist regime, the local government gained great autonomy in decision-making for its own territory. It now became a strong protector of the local community by protecting it from outside attack or criticism. Because the local community did not need to face pressure from above directly, its economy followed its own track.

Economic development in Wenzhou before the Great Leap Forward reached about the same level as other major areas in Zhejiang, such as Ningbo. But from 1957 onwards, Wenzhou suddenly became a poor area. From 1966 to 1976, Wenzhou had only 0.1 percent annual industrial growth rate and fell to one-third of industrial output of the Ningbo area. One major cause of such slow development was a shortage of investment. During Mao's time, Wenzhou was regarded as a frontline area because of its proximity to Taiwan and thus could not gain any advantage from the state investment system. Within 35 years after the establishment of the PRC, Wenzhou had only 0.7 billion *yuan* of fixed-asset investment — about 3.24 percent of the total fixed-asset investment of the province and one-fourth of the total investment in Ningbo (Yuan, 1987: 6). Furthermore, a household-centered private sector was not permitted before the reform and the public ownership system failed to provide individuals with strong incentives.

The reform did not enable Wenzhou to attract more investment from the state. But local communities gained *de facto* legitimacy of their own ways of developing the economy. A major characteristic of Wenzhou, which distinguished it from the south Jiangsu model, was its booming household-centered private sector. Tables 5.7 and 5.8 show the rapid development of the private sector in Wenzhou. The industrial output of the private sector reached a 26 percent average annual growth rate during the Sixth Five-Year Plan period (1986–1990), compared to 6 percent and 16 percent in the state and collective sectors, respectively. In 1990, the private sector produced 40 percent of the total industrial output in Wenzhou, compared to 16 percent and 42 percent by the state and collective sectors, respectively.

Table 5.7 Annual Growth Rate of Industrial Outputs in Wenzhou (in percentage)

Year	State	Collectives	Private	Cooperative & Joint Venture
1984	0.03	12.30	–	–
1985	9.30	7.70	–	–
1986	5.93	15.15	22.41	41.41
1987	5.38	28.28	47.17	–7.89
1988	13.20	26.50	30.43	–12.25
1989	–4.30	7.89	7.40	81.77
1990	10.0	4.02	20.88	66.10

Sources: The Statistical Bureau of the Wenzhou Municipal Government, *Wenzhou Tongji Nianjian* (Wenzhou Statistical Yearbook, 1985, 1991), Wenzhou: The Wenzhou Municipal Government, 1986, 1992, p. 125, 155.

Table 5.8 Changes in the Structure of Industrial Output by Ownership in Wenzhou (in percentage*)

Year	State	Collective	Private**	Others***
1980	37.05	62.81	–	0.14
1983	35.03	64.37	–	0.6
1984	29.93	69.55	–	0.52
1985	18.23	51.18	29.76	0.7
1986	18.26	48.03	32.72	0.97
1987	16.26	45.19	37.6	0.91
1988	16.68	54.22	28.5	0.62
1989	16.98	42.74	39.11	1.16
1990	16.48	41.57	40.33	1.65

* Percentages do not add up to 100 due to rounding.
** Before 1985, official statistics yearbooks did not have the category of the private sector. In this table, the category of "the private sector" includes: (1) individual and household enterprises, (2) enterprises below village level, (3) urban and rural cooperatives.
*** The category of "others" includes: (1) joint ventures, (2) collectives and state jointly invested enterprises, and (3) collectives and individuals jointly invested enterprises.
Sources: Calculated from *Wenzhou Tongji Nianjian* (Wenzhou Statistical Yearbook), various issues.

Although the fast development pace in the private sector could partially be ascribed to external forces such as the central government's rural policies and outside support, the most important dynamism in development originated from local communities themselves. Various characteristics of local communities determined that their residents would find their own ways of handling the economy. The urban area in Wenzhou was about 4 percent of the municipality's 11,500 square kilometers and housed one-fourth of the population that stood at 6.4 million in 1989. About 78 percent of the territory was mountainous. In rural areas, there were 2.9 million *mu* of arable land. As of the early 1980s, there were 1.9 million rural laborers, and each laborer had only 1.54 *mu* of arable land, about one-third the national average. The implementation of a rural household responsibility system again created numerous surplus rural laborers. According to one estimate, there were 880,000 surplus rural laborers soon after the beginning of the reform (Yuan, 1987: 18).

In south Jiangsu, the collective sector achieved fast development after the late Cultural Revolution and thus accumulated massive capital for further development. Rural areas in south Jiangsu were also organized around several major cities and various townships. These conditions made it possible to absorb a massive surplus of rural laborers there. But Wenzhou did not share these advantages with south Jiangsu. In Wenzhou, industry, both in the state and collective sectors, was far less developed and it was not able to absorb a big surplus of rural labor. The level of urbanization was also much lower than in south Jiangsu and was not able to get the surplus labor organized. Also, after the reform, many enterprises in the collective sector were decollectivized and privatized. A household-centered private economy became a major alternative for local communities.

After 1980, household enterprises gained a strong development momentum. According to official statistics, from 1980 to 1985, the total number of individual enterprises increased from 1,844 to 130,407, and their employees increased from 1,844 to 156,726. Capital owned by these enterprises increased from nearly 3 million *yuan* in 1981 to 116 million in 1985, and the total retail sales by the private

Table 5.9 Managers in the Private Sector in Wenzhou

	Percentage (%)		Percentage (%)
Age		Previous career	
Below 29	15	Farming	15
30–39	35	Industrial worker	20
40–49	35	Local cadres	2.5
50 & above	15	State enterprise worker	5
Schooling		Salesperson	27.5
College & above	2.5	Government official	17.5
High school	32.5	Unemployed	12.5
Middle school	37.5	Financial sources	
Primary school	27.5	Cooperative*	36.7
Technical background		Private investment	41.7
Industrial technique	19.5	Bank loan	13.3
Agricultural technique	2.4	Others**	11.7
Management	14.6		
Special skills	24.4		
No technical background	39.1		

* Cooperatives refers to joint investment by several households or individuals.
** Others include investments by companies or unites, and individual lending.
Source: Adapted from The Research Office of the Central Committee of China's Democratic Construction Association, "*Wenzhou Siren Jingji Mianmian Guan*" ("A Comprehensive Look at Wenzhou's Private Economy"), in The Research Group of China's Private Economy during the Seventh Five-Year Plan, (ed.), *Zhongguo de Siying Jingji: Xianzhuan, Wenti, Qianjing* (China's Private Economy: Current Situations, Problems, and Prospects), Beijing: Zhongguo Shehui Kexue Chubanshe, 1989, p. 144.

sector increased from 14 million *yuan* to 857 million in the period (*ibid.*: 227).[8] Table 5.9 shows the results of a survey of 50 managers in the private sector in Wenzhou. Most of these managers were 30 to 40 years old and had middle and high school education, and also had some sort of special skill. The development of the private sector also brought in numerous talented people who were good at business. As

---

[8] The statistics refer to enterprises registered by the government and do not include those unregistered. The actual figures are thus much bigger than the stated ones in the table.

of the end of 1987, Wenzhou had about 100,000 salesmen, 20,000 technicians and 20,000 managers. In Liushi, a major township in Wenzhou, about 29 percent of the total population had skills of different kinds (The Research Office of the Central Committee, 1989: 148).

The fast development of the private sector changed the ownership system as well as the industrial structure, as shown in Table 5.8. More importantly, the private sector absorbed numerous surplus rural and urban laborers and reduced the burdens for the government. From 1979 to 1985, the private sector absorbed 880 laborers, about 40 percent of the total of rural laborers (The Research Group of China's Private Economy, 1989: 9). In many townships, there was even a labor shortage. A booming private sector also speeded up overall industrial growth in the area. In 1976, the area had 0.5 billion *yuan* of the total industrial output, about 100 *yuan* per capita. But as of 1985, the total industrial output reached 4.2 billion *yuan*, increasing by 534 percent, compared to that of 1976 (*ibid.*: 8). Again, the private sector also contributed to the fast growth of government revenues and peasant income. In 1976, the municipal government had revenue of less than 30 million *yuan*. But from 1976 to 1985, revenue growth reached a 17 percent annual rate. The average peasant income increased from 165 *yuan* in 1980 to 924 in 1989 (Yuan, 1987: 10; The State Statistical Bureau, 1990: 75).

Local Communities and Market Building

As of the mid-1980s, there were 130,000 household enterprises and 417 special marketplaces in Wenzhou. The successful development of the private sector mainly rested on the creation of marketplaces by local communities. The market became the center of enterprise operations. As discussed in the last chapter, government officials in south Jiangsu frequently became organizers of the marketplaces. But in Wenzhou, major market organizers were individuals.

One of the most important things for private businesses was a sales market. In Wenzhou, such a market was built by numerous *gongxiaoyuan* (those who are in charge of the supply and marketing of enterprises). There were about 100,000 such salespersons in the area. Every special market had about 1,000 such salespersons. Table 5.10 shows the results of a survey of 147 salespersons. We can see that most of them were young and had a middle school or above educational background. Salespersons' incentives were provided mainly by their high income. Another study in 1984 revealed that out of 7,000 "ten thousand *yuan* households" (those at the time who were regarded as wealthiest with a minimum 10,000 *yuan* in income), 50 percent had at least one salesperson (Ma, 1989).

A labor market also came into being. To develop a private sector, a labor market seemed necessary. In Wenzhou, such a market was developed almost spontaneously. Although serious criticisms over free labor markets existed, the local leadership's pragmatic attitude toward them formed a valuable buffer zone and protected these

Table 5.10 Salesperson and Marketing in Wenzhou

	Total	%		Total	%
Age			Marketing contract (*yuan*)		
21–30	31	21.1	10,000–20,000	4	2.7
31–40	73	49.7	30,000–100,000	48	33
41–50	34	9	110,000–200,000	31	21
50–60	9	6.1	210,000–300,000	20	14
Schooling			310,000–400,000	12	8
Primary school	43	29.3	410,000–500,000	11	7
Middle school	80	54.4	510,000–600,000	5	3.4
High school	22	15	610,000–900,000	11	7
College and above	2	1.4	1,000,000 & above	3	2
Income Structure (*yuan*)					
1,000–2,000	32	21.9			
2,500–5,000	31	21.3			
11,000–20,000	18	12.2			
21,000–50,000	25	17.12			
51,000–100,000	2	1.3			

* Sales contracts refer to the contract between salesmen and enterprises.
Source: Adapted from Yuan Enzhen, (ed.), *Wenzhou Moshi Yu Fuyu Zhilu* (The Wenzhou Model of Economy and the Road to Affluence), Shanghai: Shanghai Shehui Kexueyuan Chubanshe, 1987, pp. 70–71.

markets from direct attacks. The rural reform produced about 880,000 surplus rural laborers in the Wenzhou area by the mid-1980s. The absorption of these laborers into the private sector was through market mechanisms, rather than administrative allocation. Many forms of labor market were built. First, there was a labor market based on personal connections. Most private businessmen recruited employees using various personal networks. In Wenzhou, it was increasingly difficult to recruit employees who had special training or skills because a nationwide labor market did not exist. The private sector attracted many technicians from the state and collective sector in the area. To recruit talented people from outside, personal networks became important. According to a study of 31 private enterprises, out of 1,560 employees, nearly 90 percent were recruited through personal networks (Yuan, 1987: 126). Second, there were fixed labor markets in some locations, usually in economically developed areas. Employees from both Wenzhou and outside met their employers there and the contracts were established among them through bargaining. Third, grassroots public service organizations also established various labor service offices. In addition, many private businessmen also used the media to recruit employees.

The hiring of labor, which was prohibited and almost eliminated during the Mao era, now became usual and *de facto* legal. As of the mid-1980s, there were 42,000 workers employed by 13,100 enterprises in the private sector. Out of these workers 12 percent were employed by 120 enterprises, i.e., 120 enterprises had a minimum of 30 workers each. But most private enterprises were small and employed fewer than ten workers, as shown in Table 5.11.

Another important fact in the development of the private sector in Wenzhou was the financial market. More correctly, access to financial resources was an initial condition for the development of small businesses. This was true both for the private and the collective sectors as the south Jiangsu case showed. But again, collective enterprises in south Jiangsu gained financial resources through joint effects by local collectives and local state organizations. In Wenzhou,

Table 5.11 Employment in the Private Sector in Jingxiang Township (1985)

No. of Employees that an Enterprise Hired	Number of Enterprises		Number of Employees	
	Total	Percentage (%)	Total	Percentage (%)
1–2	290	58.6	470	34.2
3–7	191	28.6	751	54.6
8–10	14	2.8	155	11.3
Total	495	100	1,376	100

Source: Adapted from Yuan Enzhen, (ed.), *Wenzhou Moshi Yu Fuyu Zhilu* (The Wenzhou Model of Economy and the Road to Affluence), Shanghai: Shanghai Shehui Kexueyuan Chubanshe, 1987, p. 129.

private enterprises gained financial resources through creating a financial market by local individuals or communities. Numerous forms of financial activities emerged in the area. Roughly, they could be organized into the following categories. First, lending activities occurred among individual businessmen and enterprises, and between individuals and enterprises. This activity usually happened among individuals who knew one another and had mutual trust. Second, two different associations, i.e., the *yinbei* (financial trust) and the *hui* (financial associations) were developed in the area. Lending was difficult among individuals who did not know each other. Prestigious individuals established such associations, using their personal networks to collect and lend financial resources. In effect, this form of lending activity occurred among different personal networks and was very effective in collecting and distributing surplus financial resources in the area.

Third, private banks (*qianzhuang*) were also developed. They originated from the *yinbei* institutes. Most *yinbei* were actually illegal banks that went underground. Under the tacit encouragement of the local government, there was a boom of private banks between 1984 and 1985. Within two years, more than 20 entrepreneurs submitted applications for opening private banks to local state organizations. But private banks had a very difficult time in their development. In late 1985, a regulation issued from higher authorities stated that the establishment of private banks had to be approved by higher-level financial institutions. Many private banks again went underground. Interestingly, numerous non-financial organizations began to engage in financial activities and became quasi-banks after the mid-1980s. These organizations performed the functions of the private bank, while avoiding the pressures from above.

The development of private financial institutions occured mainly for the following reasons. First, the old state financial system could not meet great demands from the private sector. Overly low interest rates in state financial institutions made private businessmen reluctant to open accounts. Second, the overly complicated approval process by state financial institutions for lending, especially to the private sector, led to a low efficiency of operation. Third, private businesses did not trust state policies because of the state's reluctance to legitimate the private sector over a long period. As of 1984, out of 720 private enterprises in Oianku township, only 95 had an account in a state financial organ, about 13 percent of all enterprises, and with 13.7 percent of the total income (Yuan, 1987: 112). Most financial resources of state banks and rural financial cooperatives went to the collective sector. As a result, private financial institutions, whether they were legal or illegal, public or underground, played an increasing role in local economic development. Generally, about four-fifths of the total financial resources were provided by private financial institutions, compared to one-fifth by state organizations. In one area, state financial institutions only provided 0.8 percent and 1.3 percent of the total loans in the private sector in 1983 and 1984, respectively (Xie, 1988: 103). High efficiency and greater flexibility of private financial institutions also attracted collective enterprises. A survey in Pingyang county of Wenzhou showed that 97 percent of all rural collectives, 84 percent of cooperatives and 47 percent of household enterprises preferred dealing with and had financial relations with private financial institutions (Yuan, 1987: 110).

Also important was a market for information. Local governments played an important role in creating such a market. The municipal government of Wenzhou established an office of Wenzhou Information in the early 1980s, which was in charge of information collection and distribution in the area. As of the mid-1980s, the municipal government had established 31 information centers. These centers had close relationships with more than 50 organizations in coastal areas and Special Economic Zones, research institutes, colleges and universities. Later, their relations extended to 15 information centers abroad including the United States and Japan. *Wenzhou Daily*, the organ of the Wenzhou Municipal Party Committee, also became a major collector of information nationwide. An organization called the "Marketing and Supply Research Association" collected most major newspapers around the country and exchanged information with more than 200 major cities.

Every county government had its own information center that was frequently assigned special tasks. Often, enterprises in a county were organized under major information centers. For example, in Ruian county, the government's Economic Information Research Office, up to 1985, had established close relations with more than 6,000 organizations in other provinces, and had organs in every township and some major villages (Yuan, 1987: 157). Also important were many grassroots information service organs. Most townships in Wenzhou had their own information service centers. Many organs such as Jingxiang Township Information Association (JTIA) and Dongfeng Information Service Association (DISA) gained national prestige. The JTIA was established in 1984 and had 70 members. As of 1985, members increased to 120. The JTIA had its own newspaper, *Jingxiang Information*, circulating around the country. In October 1985, the association initiated a national conference and invited 550 partners from 28 provinces. The DISA was established by 12 unemployed persons in 1984. The association collected 240 major newspapers around the country and published a journal, *240 Materials*. After the mid-1980s, the association, cooperating with a university, initiated a program aimed at collecting and spreading nationwide information. The program was joined by 4,000 members from 29 provinces.

Private Sector and State Priority

An interesting question was whether the development of the private sector conflicted with state priorities. Wenzhou was criticized by both conservatives and moderate reformers. The former attacked Wenzhou because the Wenzhou model departed too far from the traditional ideology. A growing private sector led to a fear by the conservative faction in both the central and local governments that the Wenzhou model would undermine the foundation of the CCP's rule and destabilize both the economy and the political order. The influence of this criticism declined dramatically with the gradual development of the Wenzhou model and also with the consolidation of reform coalitions between the center and the province (Liu & Tang, 1987; Mi, 1986).

The moderate reformers criticized the Wenzhou model because they feared that the private economy would be far beyond state control and would seriously conflict with the state's overall modernization goals. For example, criticisms were raised concerning Wenzhou's investment patterns. Oversized private investment, it was said, weakened the state capacity of coordinating the development of all aspects there (*ibid.*). But a careful reading of Wenzhou's development shows that the interaction between private preferences and state priority was rather complicated; that the local leadership, cooperating with local communities, was able to coordinate overall developments. Unlike south Jiangsu where local governments were able to penetrate into enterprises because of the dominance of the collective sector, in Wenzhou, such a penetration became impossible because of the dominance of the private sector. Local governments, however, developed different ways to relate themselves to the private sector.

As mentioned earlier, the state did not put much money into Wenzhou. Thirty-five years after the establishment of PRC, there were only 0.7 billion *yuan* of investment here. Also, the private sector was prohibited before the reform. Given the fact that there were close correlations between investment and growth, slow economic development in Wenzhou was understandable. Slow economic development in turn led to a low level of people's living standards. In 1978, per capita peasant annual income was only 55 *yuan*, much lower than the provincial average. Furthermore, the local government also did not have many revenue resources. For example, in 1979, the municipal government had revenue of less than 30 million *yuan*.

Economic reforms brought about a high growth rate for government revenue (see Table 5.12). The government revenue increased from 171 million *yuan* in 1980 to 889 million in 1990, reaching a 24 percent annual growth rate in the 1983–1990 period. Basically, there are two major revenues for the government, i.e., state enterprise profit contribution and tax revenue. The profit contribution by state enterprises declined dramatically from 15.5 percent in the total revenue in 1980 to 0.04 percent in 1984. After the mid-1980s, most state enterprises lost money. In contrast, tax revenue increased drastically from 155 million *yuan* in 1980 to 853 million in 1990. The private sector contributed an essential portion of tax revenue due to the overwhelming dominance of the private sector in Wenzhou industry and commerce. According to one estimate, as of the

Table 5.12 Revenue Structure and Expenditure in Wenzhou (million *yuan*)*

	1980	1983	1984	1985	1986	1987	1988	1989	1990
Total revenue	171	229	272	406	503	609	754	877	889
Annual growth rate %	–	34.4	18.8	49.1	23.9	21.1	23.8	16.3	1.37
Enterprise submission	26.5	26.0	16.9	15	22	27	–14	–51	–79
Percentage %	15.5	11.3	6.2	0.04	0.04	0.04	–	–	–
Tax revenue	144	201	252	363	444	542	718	848	853
Percentage %	84.2	87.7	92.6	89.4	88.3	89.0	95.2	96.6	96.0
Expenditure	122	172	253	322	474	47.0	609	758	873
Annual growth rate %	n.a	40.9	46.6	27.5	47.2	–0.1	29.6	24.5	15.2
Research, education & health care	51	73	92	115	148	161	203	248	279
Annual growth rate %	–	45.1	25.5	25.2	28.7	8.8	26.1	22.2	12.5

* This table does not include the revenue of the category "others," because of its tiny percentage in the total.

Sources: Adapted and calculated from The Statistical Bureau of the Wenzhou Municipal Government, (ed.), *Wenzhou Tongji Nianjian* (Wenzhou Statistical Yearbook, 1985, 1987, 1988, 1989, 1990, 1991).

mid-1980s, the private sector already produced about 20 percent of the total government revenue and it kept a 10 percent annual growth rate afterwards.

Economic growth also led to fast growth in investment. The total investment increased from 512 million *yuan* in 1984 to 1,723 million in 1990 (see Table 5.13). The total investment in three sectors, i.e., the state, the collective and the private, increased rapidly between 1984 to 1990 from 144 to 491 million, from 74 to 306 million, and from 294 to 866 million, respectively. But the percentages of investment in these three sectors in total did not change much in the same period. The state sector dropped from 28.2 percent in 1984 to 27.9 percent in 1990. The private sector maintained about half of the total investment throughout the 1980s. Most investment in the private sector went to house-building. Also, an essential portion was channeled, through government levy or voluntary contribution, into various public enterprises such as city or township construction. For example, in 1985, 60 million *yuan* were invested in township

Table 5.13 Changes in Investment Structure in Wenzhou (million *yuan*)

	1984	1985	1986	1987	1988	1989	1990
Total investment	512	768	1,059	1,273	1,730	1,682	1,732
Annual growth rate %	31.3	49.8	38.0	20.2	35.9	−2.7	4.8
The state sector							
Subtotal	144	226	317	344	474	457	491
Annual growth rate %	–	56.49	40.49	8.30	37.89	−3.6	7.58
Percentage of total %	28.18	29.43	9.96	27.0	27.40	27.14	27.86
The collective sector							
Subtotal	74	125	151	205	294	298	306
Annual growth rate %	–	68.20	22.06	35.02	43.33	1.25	2.8
Percentage of total %	14.45	16.22	14.35	16.12	16.99	17.69	17.36
The private sector							
Subtotal	294	417	590	724	962	928	866
Annual growth rate %	–	42.02	41.33	22.76	32.83	3.5	6.7
Percentage of total %	57.35	54.37	55.69	56.88	55.60	55.16	49.11

Sources: Adapted and calculated from *Wenzhou Tongji Nianjian* (Wenzhou Statistical Yearbook), various issues.

construction in Wenzhou. This figure was equal to the total investment by the state in the past 30 years. Out of the 60 million investment, the state contributed only about 5 percent and the private sector contributed the rest. The private sector also provided financial resources to state priority sectors such as communications and transportation, and school construction (Yuan, 1987: 227). A study concluded that without financial resources from the private sector, Wenzhou could not have made great achievements in its infrastructure construction. Nevertheless, local state organizations did not develop any effective mechanisms to institutionalize their relations with the private sector (*ibid.*).

Compared to their incapacity to cope with private investment, local governments were able to keep investment in the state sector, even the collective sector, in line with state priorities. A substantial portion of the budgetary expenditure went to the category of research, education and health care. The expenditures in this sector increased from 51 million *yuan* in 1980 to 279 million in 1990 (see Table 5.12). Systematic data about investment patterns in the state sector were not available, but information in Table 5.14 revealed the Wenzhou municipal government's efforts in bringing the investment pattern in line with state priorities. Three priority sectors, i.e.,

Table 5.14 Investments in State Priority Sectors in Wenzhou (million *yuan*)

	1984	1987	1988	1989	1990
Total fixed-asset investment	127	344	474	457	591
Annual growth rate %	−8.4	8.3	37.8	−3.7	29.3
Total investment in capital construction	78	251	353	342	376
Annual growth rate % in which	−15.9	30.8	40.6	−3.1	10.0
Transportation & communications	−	71	99	−	94
Annual growth rate %	5.6	15.3	37.8	−	−
Research, education & health care	−	44	−	45	−
Annual growth rate %	30.8	39.2	−	22.6	−
Power	−	8	57	85	142
Annual growth rate %	−	200	1,140	49.6	67.1

Sources: Adapted and calculated from *Wenzhou Tongji Nianjian* (Wenzhou Statistical Yearbook), various issues.

(1) communications and transportation, (2) power, and (3) research, education and health care, had a high growth rate in investment and absorbed most of it in the total investment in fixed assets.

CONCLUSION

The development of Zhejiang's export-led growth strategy showed that decision-making by both the central and provincial governments was oriented to problem-solving. Conflicts did exist between the two levels of government, but to resolve conflicts, the central government did not take back power from the province. Instead, the central government made efforts to solicit provincial cooperation by providing local officials with incentives. On the other hand, once incentives were provided, the provincial government was able to cooperate with the central government to achieve the central government's priority goals. Moreover, the central government no longer provided detailed development policies for the provincial government, but only suggested general principles regarding its overall export policy. It was the provincial government that made detailed development policies that promoted export growth. Facing great difficulties in developing an export-led policy due to great demand in domestic markets, the provincial government decentralized its decision-making power on exports further to lower-level state organizations, even enterprises. Benefits from exports were also distributed among them. So, incentives were created, and local state organizations were able to implement effective policies in promoting export growth because they had *natural* advantages in accessing local resources and were able to make policies appropriate to their territories.

When we turn to examine the fast growth of the private sector in Wenzhou, the role of both local state organizations and local communities becomes clear. The establishment of the private sector had been closely related to local leaderships. Although there were serious debates about the private sector, external forces hardly had actual influence on the development of the private sector because local leaderships became a buffer between the outside world and local communities. The reformist regime in Beijing granted the local government legitimacy to protect local activities. The development of the private sector in Wenzhou had a significant political dimension. A report concluded (Xie, 1988: 97–98),

> [Since the reform began], numerous rural economic policies of [the central government] have provided very favorable circumstances for the development of the rural industry in Wenzhou. Local governments at different levels in Wenzhou have had tolerance toward new facts which are favorable for the development of a commodity economy which is very controversial. Many cadres have had great courage to explore new policies and give strong support to people's initiatives.... A liberal policy environment and strong support from local governments, plus people's initiatives, created a great dynamic of local development.

Local communities were able to use their own power to develop the local economy, but local leaderships did matter. Obviously, the central policy could not have a strong and direct influence on local communities. Indeed, without cooperation from local leaderships, the central policy could only be a dead letter. Because of intergovernmental decentralization, local state organizations were given great autonomy in governing their territories, and they could have their own policies toward local development. Another study described how local leaderships dealt with local development, which conflicted with the old system (Yuan, 1987: 331):

> There was a close correlation between the local leadership's attitudes toward reform and the pace of reform development. An important condition that led to the success of the Wenzhou model was strong support by local party and government leaderships. Local leadership's protection for people's initiatives provided a great dynamic for the local economy. Many ways by which a commodity economy in Wenzhou developed, such as household industry, special markets, private financial activities, labor markets, were in conflict with state policies and regulations under the old system. Generally speaking, local leaderships had two ways to cope with very controversial things emerging during the development of a commodity economy. First, local leaderships always provided strong and unambiguous support for the things about which they were able to reach a clear conclusion.... Second, local leaderships frequently held "no attitude" toward the things about which they were not quite sure. That meant they

just watched things happen and did not use any measure against them. The "no attitude" position of local leaderships in effect provided a favorable condition for local economic development.

Local communities had their own power bases or resources originating from numerous local factors such as the cultural tradition, customs, the way local people handle their own lives, personal networks, and access to local resources. These resources were often used to develop local economy as the Wenzhou case shows. The state could constrain the influences of these factors on local economic development as occurred during Mao's time. But they were hardly eliminated so long as local communities existed as an entity. Inter-governmental decentralization created favorable institutional circumstances for local communities to flourish. Local communities were regarded as autonomous entities and had their own ways of doing business. Nevertheless, inter-governmental decentralization did not mean that local state organizations withdrew completely from local economic businesses. Instead, it meant that local state organizations changed their way of handling local affairs. Local communities were granted autonomy because state organizations could benefit greatly from local economic development.

Chapter

6

Coercion and Policy Enforcement: Guangdong under Inter-governmental Recentralization

In April 1999, a Hong Kong author wrote, "After Jiang Zemin and Zhu Rongji crumbled the Chen Xitong group in Beijing (in 1995), it became necessary to cope with the deep-rooted Guangdong group which had ganged together for clandestine and illegal activities… What Zhu wanted was to change the (existing) development model in South China, and he made many surprising decisions in order to achieve that goal" (He, 1999: 68). As a matter of fact, after the new administration was formed in March 1998, the central government initiated a forceful campaign against "illegal" activities committed by party cadres and government officials in Guangdong. The campaign caught worldwide attention, and caused many deep concerns at home and abroad, especially in Guangdong's neighbor, Hong Kong. One main worry was whether the new generation of leadership wanted to reverse the decentralization trend that was set forth by Deng Xiaoping and reestablish a highly centralized regime.

The messages in the above-cited paragraph are twofold. First, Jiang Zemin and Zhu Rongji wanted to change the way in which

Guangdong had developed and to establish a new development model for Guangdong. Second, to establish such a new development model, Zhu had to crumble the old (corruptive) power networks, implying that administrative means or coercive forces had to be used to cope with local strong men.

The campaign against Guangdong is significant enough for us to examine China's *de facto* federalism in the post-Deng era from two perspectives. On the part of Guangdong, many questions can be asked: What is the so-called localism there? How has it developed and been reinforced in the Deng Xiaoping era? What is the boundary of localism? Or to put it differently, to what extent can localism be regarded as legitimate by Beijing, and to what extent does localism become intolerable? On the part of the central government, we can ask: What is the reach of central power in a *de facto* federal power structure? What does it mean that the central government uses the campaign against localism? What new form of central-local relations does the central government want to establish? What is the rationale behind the center's efforts in doing so? An examination of Guangdong's relations with the central government will enable us to see what changes happened to central-local relations in the 1990s, compared to development in Jiangsu and Zhejiang under inter-governmental decentralization in the 1980s, and bring us to examine the nature of *de facto* federalism and its impact on central-local relations in China.

This chapter first examines the formation of so-called localism in Guangdong. The term "localism" has been widely used to describe the negative side of central-local relations in China. Scholars, however, often tend to avoid giving "localism" a meaningful definition. This chapter attempts to define "localism" in the Guangdong context and to explore the nature of localism against which the central government initiated the campaign. The second part provides an analysis of how Guangdong localism became excessive and went beyond the boundary. The third part describes the central government's campaign against Guangdong and analyzes the rationale behind the campaign. The last part discusses the limit of central power and explores the making of a new relationship between the center and the province.

THE FORMATION OF LOCALISM IN GUANGDONG

Among China scholars, Guangdong has been widely cited as an example of the rise of localism in post-Mao China. "Localism" has also been used by the Chinese government as a discourse against Guangdong. Whenever central officials are dissatisfied with Guangdong, they accuse the latter of being localistic. The term "localism," however, is very vague. The vagueness of the term often prevents us from reaching a better understanding of Guangdong's relations with the central government. To understand the nature of Guangdong-Beijing relations, it is important to "deconstruct" localism in Guangdong.

Localism is often defined both as an interest and an identity. For example, *The Oxford English Dictionary* (1987: 1468) defines "localism" as an "attachment to a locality, especially to the place in which one lives," and "limitation of ideas, sympathies, and interests growing of such attachment," or as a "disposition to favor of a particular locality."

Therefore, localism is, first of all, an attachment and an identity to where one lives, and second, an interest growing from such an attachment. Individuals pursue local interests because of their emotional attachments to where they live. Localism is neutral here. It is a natural tendency for individuals to pursue their (local) interests. "Localism" as a local identity and interest exists everywhere and cannot be eliminated. Apparently, it is not in this sense that Guangdong is often cited as an example of "localism." What China's central government strongly opposed is a relational form of localism, i.e., localism in the context of central-local relations. As Mao Zedong argued, some forms of local independence (read as localism) are necessary and should be encouraged, while other forms of localism cannot be tolerated (see discussions in Chapter 3). In other words, within a certain boundary, localism is "positive," but it becomes "negative" beyond this boundary. "Negative" implies that local interests are in conflict with central interests.

The campaign by the Zhu Rongji administration against Guangdong was not because the Guangdong leadership had pursued their local identity-based interests, but because the way that the Guangdong leadership had pursued local interests was not in accordance with central lines. In other words, there are two categories of factors that had led to the rise of localism in Guangdong: objective (natural) factors and subjective factors. There is not much that the central government can do to cope with localism caused by natural factors. What the central government wanted was to constrain subjective-factor-based localism. When provincial officials pursue these interests that are seriously in conflict with central interests or they ignore central mandates in so doing, it becomes intolerable. Therefore, it is important to distinguish between natural localism and a subjective one in order to understand the rationale behind the campaign against Guangdong and the limitations of such a campaign.

Historical Origins of Guangdong Localism

From the above brief discussion, we can see that localism as pursuing local interests can be viewed as a legitimate action, while localism, as rejecting central mandates, can be viewed as unjustified and illegitimate. The two, however, are closely linked. Pursuing local interests can lead to the strengthening of local power, which in turn tends to reinforce local officials' will and capability to resist central mandates and thus to be in a position that is conflicting with central interests. To understand how localism in Guangdong was formed and why the central government initiated a campaign against it, we have to examine the uniqueness of localism in Guangdong to see the real rationale behind the center's decision to do so. This in turn requires us to see, first of all, whether Guangdong has unique natural factors (not shared with other provinces) that lead to localism, and second, whether the Guangdong leadership pursues local interests in a way different from other provinces.

Many factors have contributed to the inevitable rise of localism in Guangdong. Geographically, Guangdong is far away from the capital, or the center of power. Anywhere in the world, peripheral areas are often less integrated into a given state's formal political structure.[1] So is Guangdong. This is not the place to describe how Guangdong has been gradually integrated into China proper.[2] For a long time, throughout traditional China, until the Song dynasty, "Guangdong was viewed as nothing but a semicivilized frontier, to which disgraced officials were exiled as punishment" (Yeung, 1994: 3). Less integrated means less important politically. Traditionally, China's national space was divided into several main echelons that were organized into a hierarchy from the core area through the intensive ecumenical area, the extensive ecumenical area to the contact zone and the outer zone (Whitney, 1970). Within this hierarchy, the political significance of different echelons varies, with Guangdong located in a lower echelon (*ibid.*).

After the Chinese Communist Party (CCP) came into power in 1949, the central government made great efforts to integrate Guangdong into its highly-centralized regime via the means of political campaign, tight personnel control and others (Vogel, 1969). Nevertheless, the intensive use of such political means only implies that the central government had difficulties in bringing this southern periphery into control. As a matter of fact, because Guangdong was less integrated, it was able to initiate a far-reaching reform movement in the late 1970s.

That Guangdong has been less integrated is also a consequence of another important geographical factor. It was among a few maritime provinces in China enjoying a long coastline. It is adjacent to Hong Kong, a British colony until 1997. As a coastal province, Guangdong has been a commercial center throughout the long Chinese history. As early as the Han dynasty, trade routes to as far as Malacca were opened, and trade became an important component of local economic activities. The situation remained during the Song and Yuan dynasties. During the Ming dynasty, the central government imposed tight restrictions on maritime travel and trade, and the province's link with the outside world was consequently

---

[1] For a study of center-periphery relations, see Sidney Tarrow (1977).
[2] For a brief discussion of Guangdong's integration into China proper, see Lau (1994), and Yeung and Chang (1974).

weakened. Nevertheless, during the Qing dynasty, the center loosened its tight control over maritime trade and Guangdong became one of the four foreign trade centers. In 1757, the center closed the other three trade centers, i.e., Xiamen, Ningbo and Shanghai, and from then on until the end of the Opium War (1839–1842), Guangdong was the only trading port of the country for about a century. This led Guangdong to become the most commercialized province in China.

The fact that the province is less integrated is also politically significant for the province's relationship with the center. First of all, being remote from the center of power, local residents in Guangdong have had difficulties in developing a strong identity towards the center. Traditionally, emperors in Beijing often practiced a "do-nothing" policy and left local people to manage local affairs. In other words, the presence of central power in Guangdong was very weak. A weak central presence not only prevented a central identity from developing, but also encouraged a local identity to be strengthened. One important aspect of the local identity is the political indifference of Guangdong people. Locals did not feel that they needed to pay attention to what happened in Beijing. For centuries, the province was more a commercial center than a political one. The local identity was further reinforced by the province's unique culture, manifested in its physiography, climate, language, folklore and products.

Nevertheless, people in Guangdong do have a strong interest in Chinese politics. One may argue that their political indifference led them to be apolitical. This is true only in the sense that central policies did not have a major impact on Guangdong. To say that Guangdong people are interested in Chinese politics means that they want to use their ideas to reform China. The contrast between indifference to central politics and strong interests in reforming China highlights the "seriousness" of Guangdong localism from the center's point of view. As emphasized earlier, localism does not mean that provincial government officials pursue their local interests. Instead, it implies that they resist and/or challenge central authority.

Guangdong played an important role in the shaping of modern China. Why was Guangdong more capable of posing political challenges to the central government than other provinces? One author highlighted three important features of Guangdong that are related to the province's geographical location (Dai, 1986). First, the province was among the earliest exposed to Western influence through the port of Guangzhou and its overseas emigrants. Early contacts with the West always triggered political challenges for the central government. Second, the province produced illustrious personages who led both reform and revolution. Third and consequently, the province emerged as a fertile ground for endeavors aimed at bringing about changes to the *status quo.*

Since the mid-19th century, Western powers intensified their intrusion into Guangdong, while the imperial regime was unable to cope with increasingly intensive challenges from the outside. In 1850, Hong Xiuquan (1816–1864) of the Hua county near Guangzhou and his followers such as Feng Yunshan (1815–1852) initiated the Taiping Rebellion that almost toppled the Qing dynasty. Hong Xiuquan was presumably influenced by Western ideas. During one of his many attempts at the civil service examination held in Guangzhou, Hong received a Christian tract entitled *Quanshi Liangyan* (Good Words Exhorting the Age) by a Chinese Protestant pastor. The Taiping movement failed, but it unveiled a legacy for future revolutionaries.

In the following years, two Guangdong natives, Kang Youwei (1858–1927) and his student Liang Qichao (1873–1929) initiated a far-reaching reform movement to rejuvenate the country. In 1895, when China was defeated during the Sino-Japanese War (1894–1895), Kang and Liang led a joint petition in Beijing by the metropolitan examination candidates. A few years later (1898), they even gained political support from Emperor Guangxu (1875–1908) who endorsed Kang and Liang's proposal to streamline the imperial bureaucracy by clearly defining and institutionalizing responsibilities for each government office and its officials. Nevertheless, for political conservatives, especially Empress Dowager Cixi (1835–1908), the reform was suspicious since it could undermine the traditional

Manchu system. This deep fear prompted the conservatives to crush the reform movement in September 1898.

The failure of the reform did not frustrate the attempts of Guangdong elites to influence Beijing politics. Dr. Sun Yat-sen (1866–1925) soon came into China's political scene by initiating a revolutionary movement against the Qing system. Sun and many of his early followers came from Guangdong or were overseas Chinese originally from the province. Hu Hanmin (1879–1936), Liao Zhongkai (1877–1925), Zhu Zhixin (1885–1920) and Wang Jingwei (1883–1944) were some examples. Indeed, without the manpower and financial support from Guangdong, Sun would not have been able to initiate such a radical movement. After years of revolutionary efforts, Sun and his followers succeeded in overthrowing the Qing dynasty in 1911 and establishing a new regime in Guangzhou for the country, i.e., the Republic of China.

After the revolution, Guangdong continued to play an important role in consolidating the new regime and unifying the country. The province became a stronghold for Chinese revolutionaries. After 1917, Sun Yat-sen led another revolution aimed at toppling the warlord-controlled regime in Beijing. In 1924, the Nationalist Party under Sun's leadership formed a political coalition with the newly-established CCP to bring China out of the chaos associated with Western imperialism and domestic warlordism. Chiang Kai-shek served as commander at the Huangpu Military Academy on the outskirts of Guangzhou and built his early base of power around the academy's graduates. From 1926 onward, the revolutionary troops led by Chiang Kai-shek charged north from Guangzhou and Guangdong in the heroic expedition against the warlords' armies. The Northern Expedition defeated powerful warlord forces along the Yangzi and Yellow River valleys. In two years, the Nationalist force swept the way into Beijing and unified China.[3]

The unique role of Guangdong in unifying China did not continue after the CCP came into power in 1949. After the People's

---

[3] For a discussion of the rise of Chinese nationalism before the Northern Expedition, see Waldron (1995).

Republic was established, China was almost isolated from the capitalist world. Mao and his fellow leaders started to build the country into a self-sufficient system. Guangdong's advantages in bringing the unity to the country now became its disadvantages. As Vogel (1989:5) observed,

> People who were too Westernized or too capitalistic, or who had overseas relatives and other contacts, were suspects and on the defensive. No province was better suited as a target for criticism than Guangdong, and no province was more completely wrenched by China's closing to the outside world.

The unique role that Guangdong played in shaping modern China has had very contradictory consequences for the province's relations with the central government. Guangdong has been the most important province to provide the rest of the country with new ideas and institutions. For political leaders in Guangdong, by doing so, they are not pursuing local interests; instead, they want to lead the country in modernization and economic development. However, from Beijing's point of view, in doing so, Guangdong often deviates from central policies and poses challenges to the central government. The leading role that Guangdong has played is often read and interpreted by the central government and other provinces as a symbol of localism.

In other words, when interpreting localism in Guangdong, two factors need to be identified. The first is geographical elements-related localism, and the second is perceptions-related localism. Objective geographical factors have led Guangdong to play the role it did in the past, while subjective perceptual factors tend to give political meanings to Guangdong's unique development.

GUANGDONG "LOCALISM" IN THE POST-MAO ERA

The story of the rise of the so-called Guangdong localism in the post-Mao era is similar to what happened to the province in its modern history. After the fall of the Gang of Four and Deng Xiaoping came back to power, the central leadership initiated what Deng later called a "Second Revolution," that is, the reform and open-door policy (Harding, 1987). To initiate a new revolution, the leadership desperately needed new ideas and institutions, which were not easily found after many years of communist rule. Throughout modern history, Guangdong's advantage has been its plentiful new ideas and revolutionary experiences. When a "Second Revolution" came, Guangdong was again at the frontline. It was natural because of the province's various advantages (Kuang *et al.*, 1991: 145–146).

The first factor can be called the peripheral advantage. For any established political system, it is always risky to introduce radical new ideas, but it will also be wise to practice such ideas in peripheral areas first, so that the central leadership can limit the impact of these new ideas on the rest of the country. Guangdong, without doubt, has this peripheral advantage. Located far from Beijing in China's southeast corner, the province could experiment with little worry that the impact of political and economic disruptions would threaten the power center of the nation.

Second, the post-Mao reform was to fulfill an old dream of generations of Chinese, that is, to meet the foreign challenge and enrich the nation.[4] To do so, the central leadership had to study Western management and technology. Again, Guangdong became unique. Located next to Hong Kong, a rising economic star (one of the four little dragons) in Asia, the province had the best access in the country to world developments and was most able to test the usefulness of foreign technology and management. Also important was that Guangdong cadres and officials were more receptive than others to new ideas, and had access to world technology and management systems through Hong Kong. These two factors allowed the province to experiment with new systems and became engines of growth for China. This role was especially highlighted by Gu Mu, then Vice Premier of the State Council. In May 1979, Gu led a central working group to Guangdong. After the group's investigation, Gu reached the conclusion that compared to Hong Kong and Macao, "we lagged far

---

[4] For a discussion of this point, see Wang (1995).

behind. For many years, we were sunk in sleep, now it is time for us to wake up. We (Guangdong) need to fight for a way out and to create experience" (Kuang *et al.*, 1991: 145). The role of Guangdong was to "sift out what was useful from a plethora of foreign practices" (Vogel, 1989: 5).

A third advantage is related to the provincial leadership. The leadership regarded the reform and the open-door policy as great opportunities for Guangdong to lead the development of the country. Although Guangdong's new role had a historical basis, reopening was a totally new experience. Leaders feared to make political mistakes in complex new situations, but they became determined to bring a closed province of poor and poorly-educated people into the modern world.

An additional advantage that strengthened Guangdong's uniqueness was that the issue of national unification became the highest priority on the political agenda for the post-Mao leadership. After Deng came to power, the central leadership began to claim sovereignty over three territories, i.e., Hong Kong, Macao and Taiwan. The national unification issue had a major impact on Guangdong's relations with the central government. The decision of Hong Kong's return to China created enormous worries among people in Hong Kong. From the center's point of view, Guangdong had to be built as a second "Hong Kong" to prove that the socialist China could not only accommodate capitalistic Hong Kong, but also create another "Hong Kong." Furthermore, Guangdong's prosperity and wealth could reduce the worries of Hong Kong residents about the return and thus smooth Hong Kong's return to China. To achieve these goals, the central leadership had to take preferential policies that could lead Guangdong to fulfill these goals.

What happened to Guangdong before Zhu Rongji's campaign was indeed a result of the coalition between central reformist leaders and the provincial leadership. Without such a coalition, Guangdong's take-off would not have been possible. In January 1978, during a central working conference held by the central leadership, Xi Zhongxun, then the Provincial Party Secretary in Guangdong, proposed that the central government give the province more autonomy to facilitate economic growth. Xi even suggested that the central government apply the model of American states for Guangdong (Vogel, 1989: 85). Though a federal type of the relationship between Guangdong and the center was declined by top leaders in Beijing, Xi's idea was welcomed by Deng, who was then considering new strategies for the country's development. In April 1979, with strong support from Deng, the central government decided to establish some special economic zones in Guangdong and Fujian, implement preferential central policies there, and further allow the two provinces to implement their own flexible local policies. On 15 July 1979, the central government formally issued the decision to implement preferential policies in the two provinces. The policy package was rather comprehensive, covering six major policy areas:

- The national planning system was no longer applied to the province. Instead of the central planning bureaucracy, the provincial leadership became the main actor in making provincial economic plans.
- The province was given more freedom to manage foreign trade. Many Guangdong branches of national trading companies were allowed to split and become autonomous. The provincial government could decide prices for locally-manufactured export goods. The province also could set up its own organizations in Hong Kong and Macao for trade promotion.
- The province was given more autonomy in a wide range of management in order to respond to its own needs including agriculture, industry, transport, commerce, education, culture, technology and public health.
- The province was given new fiscal autonomy. A special fiscal arrangement was reached between the center and Guangdong, under which, instead of contributing to the center a certain percentage of taxes collected, Guangdong would pass on, in addition to customs fees and fees directly collected by the center, a fixed sum for a term of five years. On the financial side, banks in Guangdong were given more leeway to make their own investment decisions.

- The province was given greater authority to determine the distribution and supply of materials and resources within the province.
- The province was allowed to establish three special economic zones in the province, i.e., Shenzhen, Zhuhai and Shantou (Kuang *et al.*, 1991: 147).

All aspects of progress in the province indeed were related to these preferential measures endorsed by the reformist central leadership. To a great degree, all those measures tended to promote "localistic" development. Although for the central government, all these policy changes were only measures of economic decentralization, the implementation of these policies certainly had great political significance and thus affected the province's political relations with the center. The reason seemed very simple, that is, they were preferential. If "localism" is defined as pursuing local interests, there is nothing wrong with the Guangdong leadership. By granting all these preferential measures to Guangdong, the central leadership expected that the province would be able to search for a new model. Therefore, for the reformist central leadership, it is in accordance with national interests for Guangdong to use all these measures to pursue local interests.

Moreover, high expectations towards Guangdong on the part of the central government in turn strengthened the perception of the provincial leadership that Guangdong had to play an important role not only in leading the country's development, but also in facilitating its unification with Hong Kong first and Macao later. To do so, provincial leaders needed not only to make full use of all preferential policies granted by the central government. More importantly, they had to explore all possible new policies and methods to promote local developments. Many of these new local policies and methods were not "illegitimate," since they were not defined and practiced previously. But for better or worse, they were definitely new. For the provincial leadership, they had to behave so since local interests here could be identified as national interests. In other words, national interests were embedded in local interests. To fulfill the mandates from the center, the provincial leadership needed to pursue Guangdong's interests.

The Guangdong leadership understood what they should do to play again a leading role in the country's development. It is important to mention that Guangdong now was playing a much more difficult role than it did in modern times. What Guangdong did throughout the modern era was to lead revolutions to overthrow the old regime and build a new one. Though Guangdong was expected to lead the reform and the open-door policy or a "Second Revolution," the provincial leadership had to do so in a totally new context. As Vogel (1989: 5) pointed out, "China was by then a strong, independent nation, and leadership was firmly in the hands of the Communist Party. Guangdong's role was not to push China to stand strong against foreigners but to lead the modification of the socialist system." In other words, the "Second Revolution" had to take place within the existing system. This put Guangdong in a very difficult position. The province was vulnerable to being regarded as an example of localism. Whatever the province did in leading the reform and the open-door policy was not only just a deviation from the existing system, but also frequently a challenge to it.

What the Guangdong leadership did to minimize its vulnerability was to search for more leeway among defined and undefined policy areas. At the Fifth Provincial Party Congress of Guangdong in 1983, Ren Zhongyi, the then Provincial Party Secretary, summarized the policy package granted by the central government as follows: "To the outside, more open; to the inside, looser; to those below, more leeway" (Kuang *et al.*, 1991: 147). These guidelines were undoubtedly aimed at soliciting and facilitating every possible new initiative to promote development in the province. According to Ren, the province had to take a "flexible tactic" (*bian tong*) to central policies. More concretely, the meanings of a flexible tactic are threefold. First of all, there had been many central policies and regulations. What Guangdong should do was to find those that were favorable for the province's development policies, instead of finding unfavorable policies to block local initiatives and policies. Second, flexibility was embedded in many central policies. What Guangdong should do was to figure out to what extent the province could implement central policies flexibly. Third, if existing central policies and regulations did not support the province, experiments should be carried out, and efforts should be made to break through these existing policies and regulations (*ibid.*: 149). Put simply, if something is not explicitly prohibited, then go ahead; if something is allowed, then use it to the hilt.

What the Guangdong provincial leadership did was certainly "localistic." However, this was what the reformist central leadership expected. To reform the old system was to deviate from it. In this sense, nothing was wrong with the strategy that the provincial leaders had taken to practice new ideas and institutions, since only by doing so, could they achieve the mission that the central government assigned to them, i.e., setting up a new model for the country. The questions are: if Guangdong's localistic developments were in accordance with national interests, why did the central government initiate a campaign against the province? Was it because Guangdong localism became excessive and uncontrollable? Or, was that because there was a major shift in the development strategy on the part of the central government? The answer is "both."

GUANGDONG LOCALISM: BEYOND THE BOUNDARY

The rise of Guangdong localism has to be understood in the context of decentralization. An immediate question is: What does decentralization mean? The term "decentralization" has been continuously used to describe China's reform in the post-Mao era, but not many scholars have clearly defined decentralization in the Chinese context.[5] Commonly, "decentralization" was defined as the central government's decentralization of central power to local governments at different levels. "Central power" was defined as the power that originally belonged to the central government. In this sense, all preferential policies that the central government assigned to Guangdong were measures of decentralization.

---

[5] For example, Roy (1995); The World Bank (1990); and Perry and Wong (1985).

Nevertheless, decentralization defined as the delegation of central power to local governments is not sufficiently clear. In terms of such a definition, everything that the center did could be regarded as decentralization, since in the Communist system, everything theoretically belonged to the central government. Even though the Communist system also frequently emphasized local autonomy, the responsibilities for governance were not clearly distributed between levels of government. For the central government, all levels of government only served as its local branches, it did not need to distribute the responsibilities for governance clearly, and local governments governed local territories only on behalf of central mandates. The fact that there was no institutionalized power distribution between the center and the provinces *per se,* indeed, tended to lead to the rise of localism. Local government officials could easily legitimate their localistic behavior because they were not sure what their power and responsibilities were and whatever they did was only on behalf of the central government.

Why did decentralization result in excessive localism? A better way to understand decentralization is to look at how decentralization occurred and was actually practiced. The path of China's decentralization under Deng has been characterized by, first, from the periphery (locality) to the center, and second, the institutional withdrawal of central power from local areas.[6] Why did the reform process go from the periphery to the center? This was the only choice that the reformist central leadership could take. The reasons are threefold. First, as discussed earlier, the periphery was less integrated into the Communist system than the center, and thus more permeable to reform initiative. Second, it would be very difficult for the leadership to begin the reform from the center, since to do so would provoke vested political interests in the central areas and meet great political resistance. Third, it would be safer to implement the reform in the peripheral areas first. Whatever occurred in the peripheral areas would not affect the central areas greatly.

---

[6] For a discussion of this point, see Zheng Yongnian (1999, Chapter 2).

Furthermore, decentralization means withdrawing national institutions from and reducing the presence of national power in local areas. Two main factors explain the withdrawal. First, the role of the provincial government changed. In the old highly-centralized system, the provincial governments were often viewed only as branches of the central government and behaved on behalf of the latter. But with the implementation of decentralization, the provincial governments tended to be relatively independent government units with their own power sources. In other words, the provincial governments now represent more provincial interests than central interests. Therefore, compared to the old days, the central government now lacked effective organizational means to present its power in local areas. Second, to decentralize central power to local governments was to provide the latter with the means to practice new ideas and establish new institutions. In order to create more leeway for new institutions, the reformist leadership had to constrain the old institutions in some cases or simply lift (old) institutional control in others.

The peripheral priority of the reform and the withdrawal of central power from the periphery are significant for relations between the center and the provinces. Decentralization led to the rise and expansion of local institutions. In order to promote local development, local governments had to create various local institutions and mechanisms, which were beyond the control of the central government. Given the fact that these local institutions and mechanisms effectively facilitated local development, the central government became less relevant to local economic life. Without decentralization by the central government, local development would not be possible. But newly-created local economic wealth was less relevant to the center. Compared to the rise of local institutions, national institutions were greatly weakened.

This was the context of why Guangdong localism became excessive and uncontrollable. It was out of control because national institutions were increasingly weakened. It became excessive because locally-developed institutions and mechanisms tended to be increasingly efficient to pursue local interests. What was worse, localism even went beyond the control of the provincial government, since within the province, power was also decentralized. The provincial government delegated much of its power to lower levels of government. This aspect of decentralization is even more important than that from the center to the provinces for two reasons. First, within-province-decentralization means that developments below the provincial level are often out of the control of the provincial government. Second, even if the central government is capable of executing political control over the provincial leadership through the Party's nomenklatura system, it does not have the effective mechanisms to execute control over local government officials below the provincial level. Without any institutionalized measures to deal with its relations with local governments below the provincial level, the campaign became an effective, and probably the only, means against excessive localism.

Bureaucratic Enterprises and Dynamism of Excessive Localism

What the central government wanted to attack was the excessiveness of localism, which affected the national economy and national power. It is important to note that the dynamics of Guangdong localism not only came from within the province, but also from outside. When the province was given all the above-mentioned preferential policies, outsiders also came in to make full use of these policies and pushed Guangdong localism to an extreme. Without the dynamics from outside, Guangdong localism could not have gone so far beyond the boundary. Similarly, by initiating a campaign against Guangdong, Zhu Rongji was not only aiming at Guangdong *per se*, but at the country as a whole. Both inside and outside forces that we exemplified by the rise of bureaucratic enterprises in the province, together promoted localism in Guangdong.[7]

Bureaucratic enterprises (BEs) refer to companies and enterprises founded, managed and controlled by Party cadres, government

---

[7] As a matter of fact, the rise of bureaucratic enterprises was a national phenomenon during the reform period. See Gore (1998).

officials and their family members, and followers both inside and outside the province. Various types of bureaucratic businesses in Guangdong can be identified.[8]

1. BEs directly managed and controlled by officials of the various ministries and commissions of the State Council. Almost every central ministry or commission had one or several enterprises under its direct control. Leading management positions were filled by former officials of the department, bureau or division level in the ministries and commissions. Even Party departments such as the Central Organization Department and International Liaison Department established their companies in Shenzhen. Some ministries had so many companies in Guangdong that they had to set up group companies headed by retired vice-ministers to coordinate their activities. The funds of such companies came from the allocations of the ministries and commissions, and their operations were connected with the official business of the ministries and commissions concerned. By investing and doing business in Guangdong, these companies added to the funds and material resources from outside the state plans available to Guangdong.

2. BEs founded by local officials of different levels in Guangdong, or jointly founded by local cadres and cadres from central ministries and commissions. It was found that party, government and military officials of all levels within the province organized companies with impunity. In spite of the often-repeated ban imposed by the Central Committee and the State Council on incumbent officials and retired high cadres assuming leading positions in such companies, there were many cadres of the provincial level holding such positions. Generally speaking, provincial officials who exercised control over one or several BEs were autonomous in deciding how to make use of the funds and personnel of such companies. A few examples serve the purpose: The Guangdong

---

[8] This description is based on a field report by a retired government official who ran a bureaucratic business in Guangdong in the 1990s (Special Correspondent, 1994).

Development Bank was founded by Guangdong provincial-level officials and was aimed to increase the financial income of the province. The Zhujiang Landed Property Development Corporation, the largest company of its kind in Guangzhou, whose chairman was the former Vice Mayor of Guangzhou and the Chairman of the Standing Committee of the Provincial People's Congress of Guangzhou, was founded by officials of Guangzhou Municipal Government.

3. BEs that were founded, managed and controlled by children of leading cadres at the Center (including elders and incumbent officials), such as China Risk Entrepreneurial Investment Company Ltd. with Chen Weili (Chen Yun's daughter) as president, and Zhongzhan Enterprise Ltd. with Chen Fang (Chen Yun's son) as Chairman, usually established their headquarters in Hong Kong, but conducted business operations in Guangdong through their branches and obtained a major share of their profits there.

4. BEs founded and managed by children of local high government officials. The companies run respectively by Ye Yuanping's five children serve as examples. In scope of operation and financial strength, such companies were at a disadvantageous position, compared to those in the last category, but in a privileged position in Guangdong.

5. BEs founded by the PLA (People's Liberation Army), the Public Security Department, the Armed Police, and the intelligence organizations on the pretext of meeting special needs, but, in fact, to obtain economic benefits for themselves. For example, the general department of the Central Military Commission had branches of their directly affiliated companies in the main cities of Guangdong.

6. One special type of BE deserves special attention. These companies were originally founded by local cadres, but had since built up close economic connections with companies run by the central ministries and commissions or children of high cadres of the central level. They might form "relationship of affiliation" with the latter.

7. BEs founded by cadres of other provinces, whose sources of capital came from the financial expenditures of the provinces concerned.

The rise of BEs under decentralization had a very mixed impact on the economic development of Guangdong. At early stages, they provided a dynamic for economic growth in the province. Since these enterprises had close connections with the government sector, it was easy for them to obtain capital and funds for take-off. Furthermore, these enterprises usually had powerful backing and enjoyed certain privileges such as buying commodities in great demand like steel, coal and fuel oil at planned prices, obtaining low-interest loans and benefitting from tax exemption for several years. These economic privileges enabled the companies to amass profits and increase their capital rapidly.

BEs also affected Guangdong's relations with the central government. BEs harmonized the economic interests of the central and those of local governments. By making profits directly in Guangdong, BEs enabled central leaders (or their children), and leading cadres of the ministries and commissions to share directly all preferential policies that the center granted to Guangdong. This reduced greatly the contradictions between the center and the province. After the reform began, there was no lack of criticisms against the Guangdong model of development, but cadres in Guangdong were not afraid of the severe criticisms of individual central leaders because in due course, there would always be some other central leaders or influential children of high cadres to intercede on behalf of Guangdong. In other words, BEs in Guangdong became an important channel in which local officials could influence central policies.

Nonetheless, given the fact that all BEs were closely connected to the government sector, they also provided a dynamic for localism to be excessive, as exemplified by excessive corruption and smuggling. Although the central leadership attempted to constrain excessive localism, the situation tended to worsen. As of the mid-1990s, corruption and smuggling had been institutionalized and were increasingly out of control. From the center's point of view, excessive localism had seriously undermined China's national interests.

Take smuggling as an example. The smuggling of goods such as drugs, weapons and counterfeits, raw industrial materials (e.g., cement, steel, petroleum, etc.), consumer goods and articles for daily use increased greatly after the early 1990s. The availability of smuggled goods brought down the prices of the commodities for which customs were paid. Smuggling benefited consumers, but cut down government revenues, and also brought harm to the development of the domestic industry that was normally protected by tariffs.

Moreover, smuggling tended to be corporatized, meaning that business enterprises were directly involved in smuggling, or commissioned the activity, or fiddled with the paperwork associated with the illegal importers. Smugglers were organized professionals. Methods used included false customs declarations, fake certificates of approval, or seals. Even if smugglers were caught, they managed to obtain authentic documents, intimidate or obstruct investigations, as reported by *China Daily*.[9] Smuggling posed such a great threat to the national economy that Zhu Rongji argued in early 1998 that China's economic performance was dependent on the success of anti-smuggling campaign (Yang, 1998).

Corruption was rife in almost every major sector in Guangdong. Although no systematic statistics are available, cases in the Appendix show how serious corruption was in the province. Indeed, both corruption and smuggling were not new in Guangdong. Since the reform began, central leaders had attempted to take measures against various forms of corruption. But no measure was successfully implemented. From the center's point of view, many local economic institutions and practices *per se* were corruptive and needed to be taken under control. Nevertheless, it was local institutions and practices that had effectively promoted Guangdong's economic growth. The central leadership had to choose between promoting local economic growth and constraining localism. When economic growth was given

---

[9] Statistics showed that 93 percent of the value seized in major smuggling cases during January–August 1998 was associated with enterprises (Yang, 1998).

the highest priority, it was hard for the central leadership to implement effective measures against corruption.

However, once both corruption and smuggling became increasingly serious, they endangered national interests as a whole and thus went beyond the boundary. Zhu Rongji warned that the campaign against corruption and smuggling was an issue of life and death, arguing that "whether the Party (CCP) will change its color and lose its power depends on whether smuggling can be cracked down" (Zhu, 1998: 1). Why did Zhu Rongji perceive smuggling to be so serious? Again, according to him, massive smuggling had disabled the central government's ability to implement its policies. It also had resulted in economic corruption and political degeneration. Zhu argued, "if smuggling cannot be stopped, it will not only have an impact on the reform and open-door policy, but also undermine our economy, our political power and our Party. Therefore, anti-smuggling is not only an important economic struggle, but also a serious political struggle" (ibid.).

SHIFTING PERCEPTIONS ON GUANGDONG LOCALISM

I have argued that the central government initiated a campaign against Guangdong because localism there had gone beyond the boundary. The definition of that boundary, however, is rather subjective. To understand the campaign against the province thus requires examining how perceptions towards Guangdong localism shifted after the formation of the new leadership in the mid-1990s.

As discussed earlier, the implementation of preferential policies in Guangdong was a result of the political coalition between the reformist central leaders and the provincial leadership. Among top leaders, a consensus on the Guangdong model of development was never reached. Throughout the 1980s, disagreements remained over Guangdong between the Deng Xiaoping faction and the Chen Yun faction.[10] The major difference between the two top leaders was

---

[10] For a general discussion of different ideas on the reform among major leaders in the 1980s, see Bachman (1986). Also see Vogel (1989: 77–78).

whether or not to practice the new systems. Chen Yun, one of the fathers of China's planned economic system, believed that China's failure of development during the Mao era did not come from the system *per se,* but from mistakes, inadequate controls and the poor implementation of central policies.[11] Based on his perceptions of the Chinese economic system, Chen Yun argued against the introduction of new models of the reform, especially the Guangdong model, which put an emphasis on opening up the domestic market to foreigners and thus subjected China's national sovereignty to foreign influence. On the contrary, according to Deng, China's slow progress was not only due to the mismanagement of the old system; more fundamentally, it was because of the old system *per se.* Therefore, the country's modernization would have to heavily rely on whether new institutions could be established. It was in this context that Deng strongly supported the Guangdong model of development since it, to a great degree, deviated from the old system.

As the Guangdong model deviated from the old system, the province's development was always controversial. Moreover, since the province experimented with new institutions under decentralization, these new institutions were beyond the control of the central government and often became quite corrupt. Leaders in Beijing were not certain whether highly-decentralized development would lead the province to a full deviation from the old system. While reformist leaders in Beijing attempted to protect newly-established institutions in Guangdong by emphasizing the "positive" aspects of the Guangdong model, the conservatives tried to limit the impact of the Guangdong model on the rest of the country by highlighting the "negative" aspects of the model.[12] This can be exemplified by the following two examples.

Example one: The implementation of preferential policies in Guangdong in the late 1970s led to the rise of criminal economic activities, especially smuggling. Many party cadres and government

---

[11] For a discussion of Chen Yun's ideas, see Bachman (1985).

[12] For a discussion of different attitudes towards the Special Economic Zones, see Crane (1990, 1996).

officials were involved in different kinds of criminal activities. On 22 December 1981, at a national conference attended by all provincial first Party secretaries, Chen Yun asked for the reconsideration of the policy of establishing Special Economic Zones (SEZs), since it had resulted in very serious consequences. On 1 March 1982, based on Chen's talk, the central government issued a document, requesting that Guangdong and Fujian draw lessons from the previous practice of preferential policies.

Example two: In January 1984, Deng Xiaoping made a high profile visit to the two SEZs in Guangdong, i.e., Shenzhen and Zhuhai, to show his strong political support for the Guangdong model. Deng emphasized that the central government's policy to establish SEZs was correct. Regarding the view that centralization was needed to correct "negative" consequences of decentralization, Deng argued that "we need to be clear about our guideline that we are not going to reverse, but to push the policies of SEZs and open-door" (Kuang *et al.*, 1991: 53). In May, the central government decided to establish Guangzhou and Zhanjiang as "Open Economic Zones." In December, the Zhujiang (Pearl River) Delta became another "Open Economic Zone."

In the 1980s, though Guangdong was often accused of localism and independence, decentralization was not reversed. Three main factors explain the course of decentralization in this decade.[13] First of all, the dominant reform paradigm of the 1980s was decentralization. Once a new paradigm was set up, it gained a momentum of development. Within a period of time, decentralization created a great dynamic for the country's development and the benefits it generated were above the cost it incurred. Therefore, even though controversies arose frequently, decentralization was irreversible. Second, during this period, the Deng faction that set up the paradigm of decentralization was in a dominant position in China's power politics. When the paradigm was under attack from political conservatives, the Deng faction came out to show its strong political support. Third and more importantly, the Guangdong model provided a "demonstration

---

[13] This analysis is based on Zheng (1999), Chapter 2.

effect" for the rest of the country. Though local leaders in other provinces were quite dissatisfied with the fact that the central government granted preferential policies only to Guangdong and Fujian, they certainly learned from Guangdong how rapid local economic growth could be achieved by using different development strategies. As *The Economist* (1992: 7) asserted in the early 1990s,

> Every Chinese province has been transfixed by the success of Guangdong, whose real GDP has grown by an amazing 13 percent a year for the past 14 years. All realize that Guangdong has had the incomparable advantage of being next to Hong Kong. But most now realize as well that Hong Kong, would not have knocked on Guangdong's door had it not been for the province's pro-business government and the small share of state-owned firms there. The result is that provinces are striving for carrying out models of reform.

This important role that Guangdong played in the process of reform and open-door enabled the province to elicit quite strong support from many other provinces. The positive "demonstration effects" of Guangdong on the rest of the country and strong political support from the reformist central leadership indeed reinforced the momentum of decentralization in the 1980s.

A major shift of perceptions on the Guangdong model began after Deng's southern tour in early 1992. During the tour, Deng made an extremely important talk that ultimately ended the long debate between the reformist and conservative factions about whether China should go along with capitalism.[14] A new wave of decentralization was initiated and various new economic institutions came into existence. For instance, in August 1992, the Shenzhen Stock Exchange was opened and a fever of stock-buying immediately followed. It was reported that within one day about one million people rushed to buy stock application forms (Yang, 1992). Rapid decentralization soon led to high inflation. In 1993, Zhu Rongji, who was summoned to Beijing earlier, was appointed to be

---

[14] For the text of Deng's talk, see Deng (1993); for analyses of the impact of the talk, see Zhao (1993) and Zou (1992).

in charge of bringing high inflation rate down and establishing the mechanisms for the country's macro-economic control.

Within this context, a debate was raised on whether the central government needed to abolish preferential policies towards Guangdong and some other provinces. It was widely believed that it was radical decentralization that had resulted in economic instability. Among others, preferential policies played an important role in undermining macro-economic control. These provinces that had practiced preferential policies were often out of central control and their policies were independent from the center. Though preferential treatments promoted local growth there, they affected the national economy badly and were thus not in accordance with national interests. In other words, decentralization as a reform paradigm should be ended, and a new paradigm that would enable the center to exercise its control over localities should be established.[15]

The debate on the SEZ policy reached its peak during the Beidaihe Meeting in August 1995. The conference discussed the Ninth Five-Year Plan (1996–2000). Much of the discussion involved the controversial issues concerning the regional distribution of central government investment and the future of the preferential policies, especially the SEZ policy. Why did the SEZ policy become so controversial?

The major concern among government officials and elite groups was about regional disparities that were continuously enlarged since the reform began in the late 1970s. To a great degree, the Guangdong model was a result of the policy of "letting some regions get rich first" initiated by Deng, a policy that led the central government to grant coastal provinces many preferential treatments. Initially, inland provinces were patient and expected that they would get rich after the coastal areas. Nonetheless, after more than a decade of waiting for the center to modify its pro-coast policies, they lost their patience and began to step up their demand for regional policy change in anticipation of the drafting of the Ninth Five-Year Plan.

---

[15] For a discussion of the shift from the old paradigm to the new one, see Zheng (1999).

Because previous five-year plans had indicated that the geographic focus of China's development would gradually shift to the interior by the 1990s, government officials in inland provinces believed that their opportunities were coming. Since the early 1990s, they continuously demanded to establish SEZs in the interior.

The calls for interior SEZs gained essential support from the government and social groups as well. It was reported that delegates to the National People's Congress, especially those from interior regions, showed the central government's grievances about the SEZs' special privileges and called for a readjustment in Spring 1995 (Zhong, 1996). Serious arguments were raised against the SEZ policy (Yang, 1996; Tang, 1995). First of all, while the preferential policies had played a positive role in promoting China's economic take-off, they also distorted economic incentives and produced various negative consequences. Different organizations, be it government departments or enterprises, attempted to seek preferential policies and treatments, rather than make efforts to improve technology and management. This greatly hindered the country in improving its economic efficiency.

Second, by encouraging local authorities to offer special treatments such as tax reductions and exemptions, preferential policies undermined the integrity of state laws and stipulations. Third, preferential policies for foreign investors weakened the competitiveness of domestic enterprises, rather than fostered fair competition.

Fourth and more important, the SEZ policy was a major factor leading to an increase in income disparities among regions. According to Hu Angang, a researcher at the Chinese Academy of Sciences, the preferential policies that the central government granted to the coastal areas not only undermined the fiscal strength of the central state; more seriously, they also increased regional inequality that had increasingly become a source of social and political instability, and thus had a very negative impact on China's national integration and unity. Hu called for the end of the privileges enjoyed by SEZs, arguing that the "SEZs should no longer possess a 'special status,' that is, no longer be 'special' in terms of preferential policies" (Hu, 1995: C6).

Naturally, these criticisms against the SEZ policy provoked government officials in the SEZs to fight back. As usual, they overwhelmingly stressed various positive aspects of the preferential policy (Yang, 1996). In order to gain political support from the center, SEZ officials especially argued that it was Deng who set up the SEZ model. During the Beidaihe Meeting in August 1995, Li Youwei, Mayor of Shenzhen, in an interview with a Shenzhen newspaper, fiercely argued against abolishing the SEZs, saying that such a view would be against the "thought of Deng Xiaoping" (*Ming Pao*, 9 August 1995).

For the Jiang Zemin-centered new leadership, it was indeed a dilemma to deal with issues concerning SEZs. Choice was limited for the central leadership. Practically, the SEZ policy and other preferential policies had resulted in various negative consequences for the country and new measures had to be introduced to cope with these consequences. Nevertheless, it would be politically incorrect to end the SEZ policy simply because it was the model that Deng established. Since to abolish SEZs could be read as ending the reform and the open-door policy, it would be irrational for the new leadership to do so.

What the central leadership did was to please both coastal and interior areas. In June 1994, President Jiang Zemin argued that it was erroneous to consider that the role and function of the SEZs would weaken and gradually disappear with China's comprehensive opening up. Jiang stressed that the center did not change and would not change its determination to develop the SEZs and its basic policies toward the zones. According to Jiang, the SEZs were to retain their roles and functions in China's reform and opening up (*People's Daily*, 23 June 1994: 1). In September 1995, regarding the rise of various arguments against the SEZ policy, *People's Daily* (16 September 1995: 1, 3) praised Shenzhen for laying a solid foundation for the new edifice of socialism and for having played a powerful role in setting an example for and bringing along the inland provinces. With the approval of the National People's Congress, the central government issued a regulation to grant law-making powers to the Shantou and Zhuhai SEZs in Guangdong in early 1996. Following this decision, all SEZs acquired a province-level legislative power that allowed them to enact local laws and regulations.

On the other hand, the central government decided to extend the SEZ policy and other preferential treatments to other areas, especially interior provinces. Though the center decided not to allow the interior to set up SEZs, it allowed the opening of more interior cities to foreign investors as "open cities." In mid-1996, interior provinces were also given the same authority to approve investment projects, just as the coastal provinces and SEZs (Yang, 1996).

Without doubt, the shift of perceptions on the Guangdong model of development had a major impact on the center's policies toward Guangdong. As discussed earlier, the campaign initiated by Zhu Rongji was aimed at attacking "negative" consequences of the preferential policies or excessive localism. Nevertheless, as I have already mentioned, it would be irrational for the central leadership to attack preferential policies *per se* since these policies were already highly politicized. To cope with excessive localism, the center needed a more effective and feasible strategy. Only after Zhu became China's new Premier in 1998 was such a strategy gradually formed.

THE CAMPAIGN AGAINST GUANGDONG LOCALISM

The campaign against Guangdong localism began in mid-1998 after Zhu formally became the new Premier in March. Nevertheless, the campaign was a plan that was gradually formulated by the new leadership in the previous years. Even during the years as a Vice Premier, Zhu already saw the negative impact of excessive localism on the national economy. Since 1993, Zhu had been responsible for China's overall economic plan. With the appointment of Zhu, the central leadership gradually became determined to cope with excessive localism that was widely believed to have been one of main factors that had undermined the country's macro-economic stability. Why did the leadership not implement the campaign earlier? There are several reasons to explain this.

First of all, there was a transitional period from 1993 when Zhu started to be in charge of economic affairs, to 1998 when the new government was formed — a transition from the reform paradigm of decentralization to that of "selective centralization."[16] The process from initial ideas to the formulation of a new paradigm took time. Second, given the fact that the old paradigm of decentralization was established by Deng, it was difficult for the new leadership to totally deviate from the old one when Deng Xiaoping was still alive. The new leadership had to handle the issue of preferential policies cautiously. Third and practically, Zhu lacked effective institutions to implement measures against excessive localism. Though he was responsible for the country's overall economic affairs, he worked under Li Peng and was not capable of building his own organizational instruments for policy implementation.

A new political context was ready for the new paradigm to come out when the CCP held its 15th Congress in September 1997. Deng died in February 1997 and the ultimate power of the CCP was now in the hands of Jiang Zemin. During the congress, Zhu was internally appointed by the CCP to be China's next Premier in charge of another wave of administrative restructuring. The new leadership formed a new package of economic reforms, which emphasized the separation of the government from the enterprises.[17] From then onward, several major personnel changes made by the central government indicated that a campaign against Guangdong localism was coming.

* Towards the end of 1997, Wang Qishan, President of China Construction Bank, was transferred to Guangdong and became a member of the Standing Committee of the Provincial Party Committee. In January 1998, Wang was appointed as Vice Governor of the province.

---

[16] For a discussion of the concept "selective recentralization," see Zheng Yongnian (1999).

[17] For an analysis of the agenda set up by the 15th Party Congress, see Wong *et al.* (1997).

- In February 1998, Li Changchun was appointed to replace Xie Fei as the Party Secretary of Guangdong.
- At the same time, Xie Fei was transferred to Beijing to be one of the Deputy Chairmen of the Ninth National People's Congress (NPC). Xie was forced to criticize himself at the Beidaihe Conference in 1995 for failing to follow the central government's line on reducing preferential policies for coastal regions.

In March 1998, the Ninth NPC formally elected Zhu as the new Premier. The Zhu administration initiated a new policy package to further China's economic reform. Central to the new policy was how government units could be separated from enterprises.[18] The new policy package indeed provided the central government with a legitimate base to crack down on excessive localism that was widely believed to be the result of close connections between the government and enterprises. As discussed in the last section, close connections between the government and enterprises, especially BEs, had provided the dynamics for smuggling and other related illegal economic activities. Although preferential policies resulted in enormous negative consequences, it was almost impossible to bring them to an end since doing so would be politically unacceptable. Nevertheless, the central leadership had sound reasons to end commercial links between the government and enterprises. It was Deng who defined the goal of China's economic reform as separating the government from enterprises. Furthermore, what the central government wanted to crack down was not really preferential policies, but excessive localism resulting from these preferential policies. More importantly, to initiate a crackdown on excessive localism in Guangdong in the context of separating the government from enterprises would not provoke local resistance since measures against Guangdong were not specially for Guangdong, but only a part of the center's overall plan of economic reforms. Indeed, as shown in the smooth process of the campaign, this strategy was

---

[18] For a discussion of Zhu Rongji's plan to carry on economic reforms, see Zheng and Li (1998).

quite successful. The development of the campaign can be briefly summarized as follows:

- In mid-1998, the campaign against smuggling and corruption was formally initiated. On 15 July 1998, a national conference was held in Beijing, and Zhu made an important speech on the campaign and highlighted guidelines for the implementation (*People's Daily*, 1 September 1998).
- It was reported by *People's Daily* (9 August 1998) that within ten days in mid-1998, President Jiang Zemin delivered two important speeches on anti-smuggling and anti-corruption campaigns to show his strong political support. All major top leaders also expressed their strong support to the campaign.
- On 21 July 1998, President Jiang talked to heads from different departments of People's Liberation Army (PLA), and asked the military's support to unlink the military from businesses (*ibid.*).
- On 28 July 1998, the Central Discipline Inspection Commission and the Central Political and Legal Commission held a joint national TV conference on initiating the campaign to separate PLA, People's Armed Police, and other law enforcement organizations from businesses (*ibid.*).
- In October 1998, Wu Yi, then an Alternate Member of the Standing Committee of the Political Bureau, was sent to Guangdong to supervise the campaign. Wu took part in the whole process of the campaign.
- From 10–25 October 1998, Zhu made a high-profile tour to Guangdong and Guangxi and made investigations about smuggling and corruption in many cities in the two provinces (*People's Daily*, 26 October 1998).
- On 25 October 1998, the State Council held a national conference attended by provincial officials from eight provinces, and Zhu drew lessons from the campaign so far and gave further instructions to promote the campaign (*ibid.*).
- On 1 December 1998, the central government set up the deadlines for the separation of government institutions, military and armed forces from businesses. Sheng Huaren, Minister of

the State Economic and Trade Commission, declared that the separation would be achieved at the end of 1998.

- On 12 December 1998, Guangdong province declared that the regional military command had formally relinquished their control of commercial enterprises two days in advance of the schedule (*Ming Pao*, 12 December 1998).

- From 18–22 December 1998, Zhu made a trip to Hainan province and confirmed that the central government would not change preferential policies in the SEZs (*People's Daily*, 25 December 1998).

The campaign was rather successful. It went on smoothly without strong local resistance. Major cases of smuggling were disclosed and corrupt Party cadres and government officials were punished (as described in the Appendix). According to the statistics provided by the Guangdong provincial government, from January to October 1998, more than 3,410 cases of corruption among officials were disclosed, and about 2,500 high-level Party cadres were punished (*People's Daily*, 4 December 1998). The smooth process of the campaign was largely due to two major factors.

First, as explained earlier, what the central government aimed to achieve was a crack-down on excessive localism, not localism defined as pursuing local interests, implying that the campaign had a perceived boundary. The central government was constrained in using the campaign against localism, since it resulted from many factors such as preferential policies and newly-established local institutions. It was these factors that promoted rapid economic development in the province. Certainly, it would be irrational and politically unfeasible for the central government to eliminate all these local institutions. Without a certain degree of central control, local economic development would be chaotic. But without local economic development, social and political instability would also come to the surface. What the center did was to achieve a relatively balanced development between central control and local initiative. Therefore, when the campaign reached the perceived boundary, it came to an end.

Second, the campaign did not meet strong local resistance because provincial officials perceived that there should be a boundary for localism. Local officials developed various local institutions to maximize their interests, and decentralization meant their behavior was unconstrained by any external factors. Although provincial officials realized Guangdong's localism, as expressed in smuggling and corruption, was beyond its boundary, they did not have any incentive to crack down on it because it greatly benefited the province's economy. Now that the central government initiated such a campaign against excessive localism, provincial officials regarded it as legitimate.

The rise of localism in post-Mao Guangdong was due to various reasons. Many factors such as geographical location and local officials' efforts to maximize their local interests were far beyond the control of the central government. Preferential policies granted by the central government undoubtedly strengthened Guangdong localism. Since decentralization meant an institutional withdrawal of central power from the province, localism met no constraint, and campaigning became an effective means for the center to crack down on excessive localism. The question is: What will happen after the campaign? One can argue that a campaign can only constrain localism for a period, and once it is over, localism comes back since various factors leading to the rise of localism still exist. Indeed, this was the major challenge facing the Zhu government. Whether Zhu's campaign succeeded should not be judged by whether localism was constrained for the time being. Instead, it should be judged by whether the new government was able to plant new national institutions that were capable of constraining localism or keeping localism within the boundary. Therefore, it is important to see what new institutions have been created by the central government to adjust its relations with the province.

THE LIMITATIONS OF THE NOMENKLATURA SYSTEM

It is commonly argued that the nomenklatura system is the most effective organizational tool for the central government to exercise control over the provinces. Thus, so long as the nomenklatura system remains intact, localism cannot become excessive; even if localism becomes excessive, the central government does not need to worry about its control over the provinces. From this perspective, the decision by the central government to send Li Changchun to Guangdong as Provincial Party Secretary was aimed at exercising central control over the province. We do not cast any doubt that the move was to strengthen the center's control over Guangdong. But it is not certain whether the nomenklatura system was capable of bringing localism under control. It is thus worthwhile to examine whether the central government was successful in exercising control over Guangdong through its nomenklatura system. Particular attention needs to be paid to the issues regarding locals vs. outsiders.

A common perception has been that locals tend to represent more local interests, while outsiders represent more central interests. Indeed, the ratio of natives to outsiders has been used as an indicator of localism. The rise of localism in the post-Mao era was because the proportion of the natives in a given local leadership was rising (for instance, Li & Bachman, 1989; Zang, 1991). So, Guangdong's localism often became a matter of whether top positions in the provincial leadership were filled by locals or outsiders. The following discussion attempts to show the complicated nature of locals vs. outsiders in understanding Guangdong's localism.

Table 6.1 shows the changes in the provincial leadership (both the Party and the government) from 1949 to 1998. In order to highlight how locals vs. outsiders affected the province's relations with the central government, our analysis will focus on three periods: Tao Zhu (1955–1965), Ren Zhongyi (1980–1985), and Li Changchun (since 1998).

After 1949, Ye Jianying took over the power of Guangdong. Ye was born to a wealthy merchant belonging to the Hakka minority in Meixian, Guangdong province. He was a graduate of the 12th Course of Yunnan Military Academy, served as instructor at Huangpu Military Academy and commanded the 21st Division during the Northern Expedition. After the rift between the Nationalist Party and Communist Party in 1927, he joined the Communist Party

Table 6.1 Party Secretaries and Governors in Guangdong (1949–1998)

Name	Tenure	Previous Position	Education	Place of Birth
		Provincial Party Secretaries		
Ye Jianying	1949–55	Mayor of Beijing	Military school	Guangdong
Tao Zhu	1955–65	Vice Provincial Party Secretary	Military school	Hunan
Zhao Ziyang	1965–70	Director of Rural Working Bureau, CC	Party school	Henan
Liu Xingyuan	1970–72	2nd Political Commissar, Guangdong Military Region	Unknown	Shandong
Ding Sheng	1972–73	Unknown	Unknown	Unknown
Zhao Ziyang	1974–75	Provincial Party Secretary, Sichuan	As above	As above
Wei Guoqing	1975–78	Director, Guangxi Revolutionary Committee	Military school	Guangxi
Xi Zhongxun	1978–80	Vice Premier Minister	Primary school	Shaanxi
Ren Zhongyi	1980–85	First Party Secretary, Liaoning	University	Hebei
Lin Ruo	1985–91	Party Secretary of Zhanjiang Committee	Zhongshan Univ.	Guangdong
Xie Fei	1991–98	Vice Party Secretary, Guangdong	Central Party school	Guangdong
Li Changchun	1998–	Governor of Henan	Ha'erbin Indu. Univ.	Liaoning
		Governors		
Ye Jianying	1949–53	Mayor of Beijing	Military school	Guangdong
Tao Zhu	1953–57	Vice Provincial Party Secretary	Military school	Hunan
Chen Yu	1957–68	Minister of Coal Industry	Moscow State Univ.	Guangdong
Huang Yongsheng	1968–69	Commander of Guangzhou Military Region	Unknown	Hubei
Liu Xingyuan	1969–72	2nd Political Commissar, Guangdong military region	Unknown	Shandong

(Continued)

Table 6.1 (*Continued*)

Name	Tenure	Previous Position	Education	Place of Birth
		Governors		
Ding Sheng	1972–73	Unknown	Unknown	Unknown
Zhao Ziyang	1974–75	Provincial Party Secretary, Sichuan	Party school	Henan
Wei Guoqing	1975–78	Director, Guangxi Revolutionary Committee	Military school	Guangxi
Xi Zhongxun	1978–81	Vice Premier Minister	Primary school	Shaanxi
Liu Tianfu	1981–83	Secretary of Guangdong Party committee	Unknown	Sichuan
Liang Lingguang	1983–85	Vice Governor of Fujian	Unknown	Fujian
Ye Xuanping	1985–91	Mayor of Guangzhou	Ha'erbin Indu. Univ/Qinghua Univ.	Guangdong
Zhu Senlin	1991–96	Mayor of Guangzhou	Studied at Qinghua Univ.	Shanghai
Lui Ruihua	1996–	Vice Governor	Zhongshan Univ.	Guangdong

Sources: Liao Gailong, Zhao Baoxun, Du Qinglin (eds.), *Dangdai Zhongguo Zhengzhi Dashidian* (Dictionary of Major Political Events in Contemporary China), *Changchun: Jilin Wenshi Chubanshe*, 1991, pp. 105, 265; Ting Wang, Li Changchun yu Guangdong Zhengtan (Li Changchun and the Guangdong Political Scene), Hong Kong: Celebrities Press, 1998, pp. 102–103.

and in December of that year, took part in the Guangzhou uprising. Ye played a decisive role in the planning of the Long March. During the Anti-Japanese War, Ye was the Chief of Staff of the Eighth Route Army. During the Civil War, he held the post of Deputy Chief of General Staff of the Communist Armed Forces. In the last phase of the Civil War, he was appointed First Secretary of South China Bureau, Central-South China Bureau of the CCP Central Committee, as well as Chairman of Guangdong People's Government and Mayor of Guangzhou, Commander of Guangdong Military Region and Chairman of Guangzhou Military Control Commission.

Under Ye, the provincial leadership was largely composed of Guangdong natives, who were responsible for the local guerrilla forces during World War II and the war against the Nationalist regime. All these local appointments indeed enabled the CCP to exercise tight control over the province right after the People's Republic was established since they were familiar with local conditions and capable of initiating and implementing suitable policies. Nevertheless, this contradicted the intention of the central government. Mao wanted to implement radical policies, especially land reform policies, in the province in the early 1950s, but local Guangdong leaders opposed such policies. Therefore, Mao Zedong believed that these Guangdong locals were forming a local power network that prevented the penetration of central power into the province. In 1952, Mao sent Tao Zhu and a group called the Southbound Work Team to Guangdong to work with Ye. Just a year later, Ye was transferred to the central military system, and Tao became the most powerful figure in the province.

Tao Zhu (1908–1969) was born in Hunan. In 1926, Tao became a student at Huangpu Military Academy. As a regimental staff officer, Tao participated in the Guangdong uprising of December 1927, and after the Communist units were badly mauled in the uprising, he was appointed as Chief of Staff of a reorganized Red Army regiment. After 1929, Tao worked as a Party official in Fujian. During the Anti-Japanese War, Tao served as a Party official and military commander in the New Fourth Army. After the Japanese surrendered in 1945, Tao was sent to northeast China and held various important positions in the military. Tao's working experience in different locations gave him a unique advantage within the Party leadership when anti-localism became important later. Since he was frequently transferred, Tao did not belong to any local power network and was able to represent central interests more than local ones. So, when Mao felt that Guangdong localism became excessive, he sent Tao there to cope with the issue.

When Tao Zhu and the Southbound Work Team took over the leadership of Guangdong, they were accompanied by thousands of officials outside of Guangdong. Backed by Mao Zedong, Tao initiated an anti-localism movement between 1952 and 1953. All major sections of the government, which were previously occupied by locals, were now filled by outsiders. In 1957, Tao became the first Provincial Party Secretary. A year later, he initiated a second wave of anti-localism movement, and almost all major local political elites became the victims of the movement between 1957 and 1958. After Tao consolidated his power network that was composed by outsiders, the provincial leadership implemented Maoist radical policies. As a Maoist follower, Tao was promoted to be a Vice Premier and also a member of the Standing Committee of the Political Bureau from 1965–1966. Tao was succeeded by Zhao Ziyang, a close Tao associate. Zhao spent most of his career in Guangdong, and fell from the position of power during the Cultural Revolution.[19]

The two movements of anti-localism strengthened the control of outsiders over the province, but created a deep split between locals and outsiders. Until 1985, all provincial party secretaries were outsiders (see Table 6.1). During the Cultural Revolution (1966–1976), political struggles in the province were no longer between locals and outsiders, but between solely outsiders, since locals were all out of power.

The split between locals and outsiders was gradually bridged after Deng came into power and Guangdong became important in experimenting with reform policies. Xi Zhongxun and Yang Shangkun were sent to Guangdong to be responsible for taking reform initiatives. Xi, a Shaanxi native, was a former political commissar of the First Field Army and held many important positions in the central government before his purge by Mao in 1962. Yang, a Sichuan native, was the director of the General Office of the Party's Central Committee, until he became Mao's victim during the Cultural Revolution. Both Xi and Yang were Deng's closest political allies in the reform era.

Since Xi himself was also a victim of Maoist radical policies of anti-localism,[20] he was very sympathetic to the victims of the two

---

[19] Vogel, *Canton under Communism.*

[20] Xi Zhongxun fell from his power position for his alleged localistic behavior when he was the Second Secretary of the Northwest Bureau of the Party (1952–1954).

anti-localism movements in Guangdong, and, together with Yang, Xi played an important role in rehabilitating Maoist victims. Meanwhile, Xi was very cautiously building his own power network. When he came to the province, he only brought one personal secretary. Both Xi and Yang largely used the established political structure in the province, and there was no power struggle between locals and outsiders. Unfortunately, because of their lack of experience in economic business, they did not live up to the mission that Deng assigned to them, i.e., to promote economic growth in the province and set up a model for the rest of the country. Both Xi and Yang were summoned to the central government later.

Dramatic changes in the province occurred after Ren Zhongyi came into power in 1980. Ren, a Hebei native, was born in 1913. He experienced both the Anti-Japanese War and the Civil War. As a young university student, Ren took part in the December 9th Movement and fled from the Japanese-occupied areas to the Communist-led border areas in Yanan in 1935, where he joined the CCP. Ren certainly benefited greatly from his revolutionary experience. In 1951, Ren was appointed as secretary of the Democratic Youth League of Lushun-Dalian Municipality. In 1956, he was appointed as the First Party Secretary in Harbin. In 1961, he was elected as the First Party Secretary of Heilongjiang province and kept that position until the Cultural Revolution. In 1973, Ren was reinstated after the Cultural Revolution to his previous position as Party Secretary of Heilongjiang. In 1977, he was appointed as the First Vice Chairman of the Revolutionary Committee and as a second secretary of the Communist Party of Liaoning Province. In the same year, he was elected as a member of the CCP Central Committee by the 11th Party Congress. In 1978, Ren was appointed as the First Secretary of the Communist Party and Chairman of the Revolutionary Committee of Liaoning province, as well as the First Political Commissar of Liaoning Military District.

During the Liaoning period, Ren showed his capability in dealing with complicated political and economic issues. Liaoning was a troublesome province in the Cultural Revolution. Mao Yuanxin, Mao Zedong's nephew, was the head of the province, and implemented

Maoist leftist policies there. Due to his satisfactory performance in Heilongjiang (1973–1977), Ren was transferred to Liaoning right after the Cultural Revolution. In Liaoning, Ren skillfully used his capability for management and won the wide support of provincial cadres and government officials. With such strong political support, Ren advocated an export-processing zone and economic reform in Liaoning. Indeed, he was among the earliest provincial leaders who implemented flexible economic policies. His policy initiatives received strong political support from Deng Xiaoping and Hu Yaobang, and he was thus transferred to Guangdong to be in charge of promoting the province's economic reform.

Like his predecessor Xi, Ren brought no team of his own fellows with him when he came to Guangdong. Without building up his own power network, Ren turned to rely on already-established organizations and personnel. Though, then, Guangdong provincial bureaucracy was over-staffed with incompetent cadres, Ren did not intend to reform the old bureaucracy before the implementation of new economic policies. Instead, Ren regarded local cadres as his allies and relied on those who showed good political initiative. It seemed to Ren that nothing was more important in promoting local initiatives and searching for a new model of development than gaining the loyalty of local cadres. Ren's priority was really on the province's economic development, rather than the redistribution of political power. This strategy was effective and local cadres became loyal followers of Ren.

Ren was an outsider, but this did not prevent him from pursuing local interests. Probably, Ren was among the few who pushed for local interests vigorously. Without doubt, most allegedly so-called localistic policies were formed during the Ren period such as "pushing policy to the limits" (*yongzu zhengce*) and "implementing policy flexibly" (*biantong zhengce*). Thanks to his connections with senior leaders in Beijing, especially Deng, Ren himself created a buffer zone between the center and the province. Under his protection, local cadres were able to take a pragmatic approach to local development without paying much attention to the pressure from the center. For example, in 1982, when Guangdong was criticized for the rise of smuggling, and in 1984 when it was again under fire in the Hainan car-smuggling scandal, Ren was summoned to Beijing to be criticized. Ren personally accepted the blame and defended local cadres who had pursued the province's development. For Ren, it was difficult to distinguish between pursuing local interests and central (national) interests since what Guangdong local cadres had done was to set up a new model for the rest of the country. With such strong leadership, the province was able to fend off severe criticisms from the conservatives in Beijing and maintained rapid development throughout the reform era.

As shown in Table 6.1, after Ren, locals increasingly filled leading positions in the province. But it can be confidently argued that all these local leaders followed, more or less, what Ren had set up before them. Before Zhu Rongji, the reform in the province was dominated overwhelmingly by decentralization that was closely associated with Ren. It is important to note that Guangdong was increasingly regarded as localistic in the 1990s, not because the Guangdong provincial leaders became more localistic than before, but because of many other factors. First, as discussed in the last section, in the 1990s, the perception of the central leadership over the reform paradigm of decentralization began to change. The decentralization paradigm was no longer regarded as an effective means to promote economic reform further. Second, various local institutions that were established under decentralization began to become an effective means for the province to promote further decentralization. The gap between central perception and provincial behavior was thus enlarged. Third, various vested interests that benefited from these local institutions tended to show their resistance to new policy initiatives from the center. All these factors, plus an increase in corruption, led the central government to believe that Guangdong localism had gone beyond its boundary.

Li Changchun and Guangdong

As usual, when the central government wanted to introduce major policy initiatives into Guangdong, a new wave of personnel reshuffling took place first. In February 1998, Li Changchun was transferred from Henan to Guangdong to replace Xie Fei as the Provincial Party Secretary, while the latter was summoned to Beijing as the Vice Chairman of the National People's Congress. Soon after Li came to Guangdong, a major personnel reshuffling was initiated and a new provincial leadership (both the party and the government) was put in place, as shown in Tables 6.2 and 6.3.

Li Changchun was born in 1944 in Jilin province. After his graduation from Harbin Industrial University, Li worked in various state-owned enterprises in north China and occupied different positions such as Company Manager and Party Secretary. In 1983, Li was elected as mayor of the Shenyang Municipal City of Liaoning province at age 39, making him the youngest mayor in China then. In 1985, Li became an alternate member of the 12th Central Committee. The next year, Li was elected as the Governor of Liaoning province at age 42, making him the youngest governor in the country then. In 1987, Li became a full member of the 13th Central Committee. In 1992, Li was transferred to Henan province to be the Provincial Party Secretary. Thanks to his impressive performance in both Liaoning and Henan, Li was welcomed among central and provincial leaders. At the 15th Congress of the CCP in 1997, Li was elected as a full member of the Political Bureau of the Central Committee — the youngest member in the Bureau.

The central leadership appointed Li as the Provincial Party Secretary in order to promote a new model of reform in Guangdong. The personnel reshuffling that occurred under Li was aimed at providing political support to the transition from the old decentralization paradigm to the new paradigm of "selective recentralization." As shown in Tables 6.2 and 6.3, the most visible change over the provincial leadership was that the percentage of outsiders increased drastically. In the provincial Party leadership, outsiders were increased from zero to three (43 percent), while in the provincial government, outsiders were increased from five (33 percent) to seven (47 percent).

Should this personnel change be regarded as a measure against Guangdong localism by the central government, as commonly

Table 6.2 Changes in the Provincial Leadership (Party)

Name	Place of Birth	Education	Previous Position
	Party Leadership of the Seventh Party Committee		
Secretary			
Xie Fei	Guangdong	Central Party school	Vice Secretary of Guangdong Party Committee
Vice Secretary			
Zhang Jinying	Guangdong	Secondary school	Vice Director of China Women's Federation
Huang Huahua	Guangdong	Zhongshan Univ./ Central Party school	Secretary General of Guangzhou Party Committee
Lu Ruihua	Guangdong	Zhongshen Univ.	Mayor of Fushan/Vice Governor of Guangdong
	Party Leadership of the Eighth Party Committee (since 1998)		
Secretary			
Li Changchun	Liaoning	Ha'erbin Indu. Univ.	Secretary of Henan Party Committee
Vice Secretary			
Lu Ruihuan	Guangdong	Zhongshan Univ.	Vice Governor
Huang Huahua	Guangdong	Zhongshan Univ./ Central Party school	Secretary General of Guangdong Party Committee
Gao Qiren	Shandong	Hefei Indu. Univ./ Central Party school	Secretary of Guangzhou Party Committee
Zhang Gaoli	Fujian	Xiamen Univ.	Vice Governor of Guangdong
Huang Liman	Liaoning	Ha'erbin Military Eng. College	Vice Secretary of Shenzhen Party Committee
Chen Shaoji	Guangdong	Zhongshan Univ.	Director of Guangdong Security Bureau

Source: Author's database.

Table 6.3 Changes in the Provincial Leadership (Government)

Name	Place of Birth	Education	Previous Position
		Before 1998 Reshuffling	
Governor			
Lu Ruihua	Guangdong	Zhongshan Univ.	Mayor of Fushan
Vice Governor			
Ou Guangyuan	Guangdong	Primary school	Secretary of Fushan Party Committee
Liu Weiming	Hunan	Central Party school	Standing Committee of Guangdong Party Committee
Zhang Gaoli	Fujian	Xiamen Univ.	Chairman of Guangdong Academy of Social Sciences
Lu Zhonghe	Guangdong	Shanghai Organic Chemistry Institution	Chairman of Guangdong Academy of Social Sciences
Li Lanfang	Guangdong	Huanan Agri. College	Vice Mayor of Guangzhou
Zhong Qiquan	Guangdong	College	Secretary-General of Zhongshan Party Committee
Tang Binquan	Guangdong	High school	Secretary of Zhongshan Party Committee
		After 1998 Reshuffling	
Governor			
Lu Ruihua	Guangdong	Zhongshan Univ.	Governor
Vice Governor			
Wang Qishan	Shanxi	Northwest Univ.	President of China Construction Bank
Lu Zhonghe	Guangdong	Shanghai Organic Chemistry Institute	Chairman of Guangdong Academy of Social Sciences
Ou Guangyuan	Guangdong	Primary school	Secretary of Fushan Party Committee
Li Lanfang	Guangdong	Huanan Agri. College	Vice Mayor of Guangzhou

(Continued)

Table 6.3 (*Continued*)

Name	Place of Birth	Education	Previous Position
		After 1998 Reshuffling	
Zhong Qiquan	Guangdong	College	Secretary-General of Zhongshan Party Committee
Tang Binquan	Guangdong	High school	Secretary of Zhongshan Party Committee
Xu Deli	Guangdong	Huanan Normal College	Secretary of Shantou Party Committee
You Ningfeng	Fujian	University	Deputy Secretary-General of Guangdong provincial government

Source: Author's database.

assumed (Ting, 1998: 105)? This seemingly reasonable assumption needs to be examined closely. If the central government was aiming to crack down on localism, Guangdong natives could be ousted from the provincial leadership, as Tao Zhu did before. This did not happen, in fact. The number of outsiders increased in the provincial leadership, but all outsiders had served Guangdong previously, except Li Changchun and Wang Qishan. Although the number of outsiders increased, the number of locals was not reduced. Instead, the provincial leadership was expanded. We can see that the numbers of deputy provincial party secretaries were increased from three to six, while the number of vice governors increased from eight to nine (see Tables 6.2 and 6.3).

It can be reasonably argued that though the personnel change was to provide political support to the campaign against excessive localism in Guangdong, using the nomenklatura system to contain localism was not the only instrument that was available to the central government. As a matter of fact, since the reform began, the central government has learnt from past experience that positioning too many outsiders in the provincial leadership would cause political conflicts between locals and outsiders, and thus would have a very negative impact on political stability in the province. This, in turn, would seriously constrain the capability of the provincial leadership to promote local development. This is especially true in Guangdong. In the early 1980s, the central government recognized that the two campaigns initiated by Tao Zhu in the 1950s were incorrect, and local cadres who were accused of localism were rehabilitated (Bo, 1997).[21] In 1997, Bo Yibo, one of the few senior leaders alive then, argued that the leadership should learn from the two anti-localism campaigns in Guangdong. According to Bo, it would be difficult to regard appointing locals to important positions in the provincial leadership as localism, and since local cadres were familiar with their localities, the central government needed such local cadres to deal with complicated local situations. Bo also implicitly argued that it would be normal for the center and the provinces to have different opinions on certain issues and such differences should not be regarded as evidence of localism (*ibid.*).

For Zhu Rongji, cracking down on excessive localism was only part of the overall plan of the new administration. What the new government really wanted to do was to build new and centrally-managed institutions to penetrate central power into the province and thus restrain localism from going beyond its boundary. Therefore, what the central government did to Guangdong can be regarded as a step towards restructuring central-local relations, a step ahead of the rest of the country.

ONE STEP AHEAD IN ADJUSTING CENTRAL-LOCAL RELATIONS

Even though Zhu Rongji utilized coercive administrative means to crack down on Guangdong's localism, he was aware of the limitations of such a centrally-initiated campaign in constraining localism. The campaign enabled central power to penetrate into the province

---

[21] Gu Dacun was a leading cadre of the Guangdong provincial leadership in the early 1950s and was purged by the second wave of anti-localism between 1957 and 1958.

effectively in a short period of time. The question is: What comes next after the campaign?

Decentralization led to the withdrawal of central power from the province. In order to extend the reach of central power again, recentralization becomes imperative. Nevertheless, recentralization cannot be achieved by dismantling all localistic institutions since it is these institutions that have promoted local development. Therefore, the strategy Zhu took was to implement "selective recentralization," that is, selectively planting central institutions in the locality. In doing so, the central government has to crack down on excessive localism since the latter prevents the central government from planting new institutions. The question thus becomes: What new centrally-managed institutions should the new administration attempt to plant?

It is important to note that the responsibilities of Zhu are in the areas of economics and administration.[22] So, in discussing Zhu's efforts in restructuring central-local relations, I refer to central-local economic and administrative relations, rather than political relations. In this context, the new administration attempted to build a more efficient government by separating all government units from the enterprises, and building new institutions that would enable the center to exercise macro-economic control over the province.

In the context of central-local relations, building a more efficient government meant increasing the capacity of the central government to penetrate into and efficiently manage local societies — a capacity that had been reduced drastically by decentralization in the past two decades. Decentralization changed the way the central government dealt with the province. The center withdrew its power from localities, while local government organizations that were supposed to behave on behalf of the central government gained greater autonomy. Motivated by their desire for economic interests, local government organizations were deeply involved in local economic

---

[22] For a discussion of the division of labor among top leaders and the responsibilities of Zhu Rongji in economic and administrative reforms, see Zheng Yongnian (1999).

activities. More seriously, these local government organizations often formed coalitions with newly-established local economic organizations to strengthen their capacity to pursue economic interests. All these factors had effectively corrupted local government organizations.

This was especially true in Guangdong. As discussed earlier, the rise of bureaucratic enterprises became phenomenal in the province, and almost all government units, especially the People's Liberation Army (PLA), the People's Armed Police (PAP), and the Judiciary, were engaged in various types of economic activities. While their economic activities benefited themselves and local societies as well, the system of governance became very corrupted. Central power was thus seriously constrained and even blocked by such a corrupt system. Indeed, the local government organizations became entrenched vested interests and began to resist central policies if these policies were against their interests. With their resistance, the reach of central power was greatly shortened. In order to strengthen the presence of central power in the province, such excessive local interests had to be crumbled.

As discussed earlier, the new reform agenda that was set up by the new leadership aimed to separate the government from the enterprises. This overall agenda gave the Zhu administration a legitimate basis to crack down on excessive localism. Ideally, the separation was an effective strategy to constrain localism and to make the system of governance more accountable. To a great degree, the 1998 campaign was rather successful. By early 1999, all government organizations announced that they had delinked themselves from economic affairs and met the deadlines set by the central government.[23] This did not mean in any sense that these government organizations were really separated from businesses. Nevertheless, with the birth of central regulations separating the government from the enterprises, it became illegal for government organizations to engage in economic activities.

---

[23] For a discussion of the 1998 campaign, see Zheng and Zou (1999).

A second goal of the 1998 campaign in Guangdong was to plant new economic institutions to strengthen central control over provincial economic affairs. Rapid economic development in Guangdong had been promoted by newly-established local institutions. Local development was less relevant to the central government. Consequently, it was increasingly difficult for the central government to exercise macro-control over provincial economic situations.

The efforts to build centrally-controlled economic institutions could be exemplified by the appointment of Wang Qishan as Vice Governor of Guangdong. Wang Qishan, a Shanxi native, graduated from Northwest Industrial University during the Cultural Revolution. In the early 1980s, Wang became son-in-law of Yao Yilin, the then Vice Premier and a member of the Secretariat of the Party's Central Committee. From 1982 to 1988, Wang served in the Research Center of the Secretariat of the Central Committee of the CCP and the Research Center of Agricultural Development of the State Council respectively. In 1988, Wang was appointed as the President of China Agricultural Trust and Investment Corporation, a newly-established company under the State Council. A year later, Wang was appointed as Vice President of the China Construction Bank. In 1993, Zhu Rongji was appointed as Vice Premier and came to be in charge of China's overall economic affairs. As a technocrat, Zhu preferred to work with many technocrat-oriented economists and solicit their views on tackling high inflation, a serious issue facing the country then. Among others, Wang became a close associate to Zhu. In 1994, Wang was appointed as the President of China Construction Bank. Wang's performance during his presidency in the Construction Bank seemed to be highly appreciated by Zhu Rongji. Due to his experience in the banking sector, Wang was transferred to Guangdong in 1997 to be in charge of the province's overall financial affairs.

The appointment of Wang Qishan can be better read as an effort to build new institutions than as a measure by the central government to crack down on excessive localism there. In November 1997, the central government held a national financial conference and attempted to set forth guidelines to prevent the rising Asian financial crisis from spreading in China. The conference, attended by all governors and other important local officials, discussed some main concrete institutional measures to strengthen central control over the local financial situation. The most important measure was to establish a federal-style central banking system.

This was certainly a reconstruction of China's financial system. To achieve this goal, the central leadership had to practice the new system in some regions first. Guangdong was among the first few experimental regions. Because of his experience in the banking sector, Wang was sent to Guangdong to implement this new system. In November 1998, the Guangzhou branch of the central bank was established. Naturally, it was not easy for such a new institution to function. In doing so, Wang had to cope with various old institutions, especially those that were characterized by excessive localism. The clash between the old and new institutions became inevitable. On 6 October 1998, the central bank announced the closure of Gitic (Guangdong International Trust and Investment Corporation), and on 11 January 1999, it announced the bankruptcy of Gitic for its failure to pay foreign debts worth US$2.5 billion. Since Gitic had been a "window" company — a symbol of China's open-door policy — to close it down indeed was quite risky politically. As a matter of fact, the announcement of the closure and bankruptcy of Gitic shocked the country, as well as the outside world, especially Guangdong's neighbor, Hong Kong. Many wondered whether China's financial system was reliable and whether the central government would change its open-door policy (Concepcion, 1999; Pun & Reuters, 1999). Nevertheless, for the central government, it had no choice but to close Gitic. As Wang explained in an interview with *Nanfang Daily* (12 March 1999: 3), the closure of Gitic was aimed not only at preventing the spread of the Asian financial crisis into the country; more importantly, it was part of the overall plan of the central government to reconstruct the country's financial system.

CONCLUSION

It is important to reiterate two main points this chapter has discussed. First of all, the campaign by the Zhu Rongji administration against

Guangdong was aimed at constraining excessive localism in the province. Second, the campaign was not targeted exclusively against Guangdong. Instead, it was part of the overall plan of the Zhu government to restructure central-local relations.

The rise of localism in Guangdong was closely linked with the reform paradigm of decentralization that granted the province preferential policies. Localism, defined as pursuing local interests, played an important role in promoting rapid development in the province. Without a strong incentive for local interests, it would be hard for Guangdong to achieve great economic success in the past two decades. More importantly, for the provincial leadership, since its mission was to set up a new model for the rest of the country, to pursue local interests was to pursue national interests. The identity between local and national interests strengthened the forces towards localistic development.

When localism became excessive, it came to have a negative impact on the national economy. Nevertheless, it was decentralization that had led localism in Guangdong to be excessive. Indeed, decentralization meant the withdrawal of central power from the province. Without a strong presence of central power, development in Guangdong became irrelevant to the central government. In other words, local leaders rather than central leaders became the main actors in promoting local development. The greater role of local leaders enabled them to resist central mandates, while the weakening of central power in the province prevented the central government from using institutional means to constrain the development of localism. Campaigning became the only effective measure for the center to cope with excessive localism.

In the face of rising localism, the central government encounters a dilemma. Excessive localism often destabilizes the national economy, but without strong incentives for local interests, local development will become difficult. Therefore, for the central government, what should be done is to achieve a balance between localism and national stability. It is impossible for the center to eliminate any localistic development in a *de facto* federal structure of central-local relations. So far, the central government has attempted to constrain localism by employing the rather traditional nomenklatura system. However, the role of the nomenklatura system is also limited, and provincial leaders appointed by the central government only have very limited choices. Without cooperation from local party cadres and government officials, it will be hard for the provincial leadership to implement policies effectively. Thus, a better strategy for provincial leaders is to strike a balance between local and national interests.

A more effective way for the center to constrain localism is to reintroduce central power into the province. In other words, national institutions have to be planted and national power has to be present in the province. To plant new institutions, excessive localism has to be cracked down on first. This was the rationale behind the campaign against Guangdong. As emphasized earlier, what Zhu really wanted was to shift the reform paradigm from decentralization to "selective recentralization." Recentralization did not mean dismantling all local institutions that had grown out of decentralization. Instead, it implied planting national institutions in selective areas that would enable the center to resume its control over the province without affecting local initiatives badly.

The campaign against corruption and smuggling was rather successful. The issue is what will happen after the campaign. The Zhu Rongji government made enormous efforts to reintroduce central power into localities. Nevertheless, to plant new national institutions among well-developed local institutions was not an easy task. Can these new institutions be firmly established? Will they be able to match the center's expectation to constrain localism effectively? Will they be able to contend with or coexist with local institutions? All these questions take time to answer.

APPENDIX: SELECTED CASES OF CORRUPTION IN GUANGDONG

Party and Government

1. The Yu Fei case. Yu Fei was former Vice Governor and Vice Chairman of the Standing Committee of the People's Congress of Guangdong. When the reform began, Yu was in charge of the

financial sector and foreign trade department; this enabled him to travel between Hong Kong and the mainland and establish wide connections with millionaires in Hong Kong. Nobody knew how much benefit he got by using his position of power and connections. But the case leading to Yu's fall was a land-trading scandal, the biggest illegal scandal of this type since PRC was established in 1949. Yu used his power to negotiate and buy land from the Management Committee of the Daya Bay Development Zone (MCDBDZ) for his daughter's company in Hong Kong under the name of Guangdong Provincial Economic and Technology Co-Operation Office. He managed to buy a piece of land at 180 *yuan* per square meter, and authorized the Huizhou Municipal Government and the MCDBDZ to transfer the right of land to the company in Hong Kong. His daughter resold the land at 380 *yuan* per square meter, making a profit of about 28 million *yuan* (*Xin Bao*, 10 December 1998).

2. The Chen Tongqing case. Chen, former Party Secretary of the Zhanjiang Municipal Party Committee, was sentenced to death for accepting bribes of about 1.1 million *yuan* during the period between 1994 and 1998. Chen was charged for the following five crimes he committed: selling government positions; taking bribe from contractors; interfering in the investigations to his crimes; issuing illegal single entry visas to Hong Kong;[24] and using his authority to get jobs for his followers. The case involved 31 Party cadres and government officials, implying that the Zhanjiang Municipal Party Committee as a whole became a Mafia-style organization (*Ming Pao*, 14 May 1999).

3. The Shao Rucai case. Shao served the Guangzhou Municipal Government for many years and held various important positions consecutively, including Director of the Bureau of Finance, Director of the Tax Bureau and Director of the State-Owned Asset Management Bureau. Shao was arrested for bribery and embezzlement of funds of about 10 million *yuan* (*Ming Pao*, 4 February 1999).

---

[24] The single-entry visa means that one is eligible for a permanent residence status.

4. The Zheng Rong case. Zheng, former Vice Mayor of Enping Municipal Government (Guangdong), was sentenced to 20 years in jail for bribery, and dereliction of duty in the embezzlement of public funds of about 10 million *yuan* (*Ta Kung Pao*, 12 December 1998).

5. The Wu Shihua case. Wu, former Director of the Bureau of Justice (Jiangmen city, Guangdong), was arrested for corruption and embezzlement of public funds of about 2 million *yuan*. In 1994, Wu put the money that belonged to the Bureau of Justice into a hotel construction project that was also under the Bureau of Justice. Later, he paid the first installment of 1.1 million *yuan* for decoration. In early 1996, in order to balance the account, he used fake receipts of purchasing construction materials to claim the amount. Wu also used public funds to buy the house and car for private use and conducted illegal businesses (*Sing Tao Daily*, 18 December 1998).

6. The Zeng Linghong case. Zeng, former Director of the Grain Bureau of Meizhou Municipal Government (Guangdong), was sentenced to death. From 1994 to 1996, Zeng took about 2 million *yuan* in bribe from a contractor (*Ming Pao*, 26 July 1998).

7. The Cai Long Case. Cai, former Director of the Propaganda Department and member of the Standing Committee of the Yangjian Municipal Party Committee, was arrested for his involvement in the loss of public funds. During his tenure, he was cheated by a Beijing company and lost about 27 million *yuan*. He accepted bribes of 40,000 *yuan* (*Ming Pao*, 9 July 1998).

8. The Ma Liumei Case. Ma, Vice Mayor of the Shanwei Municipal Government, was sentenced to eight years for accepting bribes worth 110,000 *yuan* (*ibid.*).

9. The Chen Guoquan case. Chen, former Director of the Guangdong Bureau of Public Security, fell from his position for abusing his power. He asked a Hong Kong businessman to buy the single-entry visa for his wife in Hong Kong at 550,000 Hong Kong dollars (*ibid.*).

10. The Yang Qizhou and Lin Qiju case. Yang, former Vice Mayor of the Yangchun Municipal Government, and Lin, former Deputy

Director of Finance and Trading Office, were arrested for attempting to assassinate the mayor, accepting bribes from a Hong Kong businessman and misappropriating public funds (*ibid.*).

11. The Chen Peilin and Zhou Yongliang case. Chen, Political Commissar of the Huangpu Bureau of Public Security, and Zhou, Vice Director of the same bureau, were expelled from the Party for misusing their offices, accepting bribery, illegally borrowing fines collected for their personal use, etc. (*ibid.*).

12. The Qiu Qihai case. Qiu, former Director of the Shenzhen Social Insurance Bureau, was sentenced to jail for 12 years for accepting bribes of 800,000 *yuan*. From 1993 to 1996, Qiu used his influence to deposit the insurance principal into his friends' private accounts. His relatives earned big marginal interest profits from the deposit and Qiu himself also profited from it by about 700,000 *yuan* and 20,000 Hong Kong dollars. In 1995, Qiu accepted 100,000 *yuan* in bribe from a contractor who wanted to win the bid for the construction of an office building for the Shenzhen Social Insurance Bureau (*Ming Pao*, 3 September 1998).

13. The Wang Zhaocai case. Wang, former Director of the Anti-Smuggling office of the Dongguan Municipal Government, was arrested and dismissed from the Party for releasing smugglers and accepting bribes during his tenure. It was reported that Wang asked for 500,000 *yuan* from the owner of smuggled cars. Wang was a Dongguang local and served as the director for many years. Some two-thirds of municipal government officials were involved in this case (*Ming Pao*, 1 October 1998).

Police and Law Enforcement

1. The Jin Tianbao case. Jin, former Director of the Sea Safety Inspection Bureau, was sentenced to 15 years' imprisonment. Jin abused his power by taking bribes for the approval of the right of land use, approving contracts for projects and selling government positions (*Hua Sheng Pao*, 22 May 1998).

2. The Zheng Guoqiang case. Zheng, Director of the Bureau of Public Security, was taken to Beijing before the 1998 Chinese

New Year. Zheng was involved in the car smuggling case involving former Deputy Minister of State Security, Li Jizhou, who was arrested for corruption and became the most senior police officer to be detained since the Communist Party came to power in 1949. Zheng was the subordinate of Li between 1991 and 1992, when Li was the Deputy Director of the Bureau of Public Security (*Lianhe Zaobao*, 25 February 1998).

Finance

1. The Li Guoqing case. Li, former Director of the Zhuhai State Asset Management Bureau, was arrested for bribery of 200,000 *yuan* and embezzlement of public funds amounting to 70 million *yuan*. Li was Deputy Director of the Finance Bureau from 1991 to 1996. During his tenure, he gave the fiscal turnover fund, agriculture enterprises' turnover funds and agriculture tax funds, etc., to private companies. In 1996, even after he was expelled from his position, Li still managed to embezzle public funds worth 3 million from the Zhuhai Investment Management Co. At the end of 1997, as Director of the Zhuhai State Assets Management Bureau, Li illegally lent 1 million to a private company again. From all these transactions, Li took bribes of about 170,000 *yuan* and 50,000 HK dollars (*Sing Tao Daily*, 26 July 1998).
2. The Huang Yantian case. Huang, former General Manager of Gitic (Guangdong International Trust & Investment Corporation), was reported to have accepted a bribe from one Shenzhen real estate developing company by instructing the company to deposit remitted money to his relatives' account in the US. He also conducted a similar under-table business with another US beverage company (*Hong Kong Standard*, 2 February 1999).
3. The Dong Hucheng case. Dong, former President of the Guangdong Branch of the Construction Bank of China, was found guilty of causing the loss of about 100 million HK dollars.

During his tenure, Dong signed a contract with a Hong Kong company to develop a property site in Hong Kong without the approval from higher authorities. The Construction Bank of China paid the first payment of about 160 million HK dollars to a partner company, in which Dong's wife had a stake. In the end, the project did not succeed and the down payment could not be withdrawn. Dong was found to have accepted bribes of 300,000 y*uan* (*Ming Pao*, 25 July 1998).

4. The Zhang Guoqing case. Zhang, former President of J&A Securities, was arrested for conducting enormous under-table transactions (*Ming Pao*, 16 July 1998).

Customs

1. The Cao Xiukang case. Cao was former Director of the Zhangjiang Customs Office, Guangdong. Together with the former Vice Director of that office, Cao was charged for involvement in the smuggling of steel, oil and automobiles worth about 10 billion *yuan*. The case was handled by Premier Zhu Rongji himself since it involved border security forces, smugglers, and a former head of the Investigation Department (*Yazhou Zhoukan*, 16–22 November 1998).

2. The Shantou Customs Office *et al.* case. Directors of the Shantou Customs Office and the Nan Ao Customs Office, together with a bank governor and several economic and trade officials, were arrested for a 60 billion *yuan* worth of cigarette smuggling scandal. The case was handled by Premier Zhu because it involved many senior government officials (*Lianhe Zaobao*, 23 October 1998).

3. The Shenzhen Futian Customs case. Deputy Director of the Shenzhen Futian Duty-Free Zone Customs Office and over 20 other customs officers were arrested for smuggling and bribe-taking. They formed the biggest corruption and smuggling group that accepted bribery and allowed cargoes to enter China without paying tariffs (*Ming Pao*, 24 September 1998).

Others

1. The Luo Rong case. Luo, former Vice CEO and General Manager of Hong Lian Information Industry Co. Ltd. in Guangdong (a state-owned company), was sued for corruption and misappropriation of public funds amounting to 32 million *yuan*. Luo diverted 10 million *yuan* from his own company to Guangdong Guoao Communication Co. Ltd., a company under the name of Luo himself (*Ming Pao*, 4 February 1998).
2. The Ma Guohua case. Ma, former Deputy Manager of Guangdong Supply, Sale, Infrastructure Material Company, was sentenced to life imprisonment for taking money 11 times from a company, amounting to 360,000 *yuan* (*Ming Pao*, 30 September 1998).

Chapter 7

Collective Bargaining and Central-Local Reciprocity: Inter-provincial Coalition in *De Facto* Federalism

Inter-governmental decentralization resulted in great changes in relations between the levels of government. Decision-making power was devolved to lower and more manageable levels, and power bases became increasingly lodged in local units, rather than the central government. The central government found it increasingly difficult to exercise direct hierarchical control over lower-level governments in order to resolve differences among them. While inter-governmental decentralization allowed individual provinces flexibility in responding to the needs and demands of multiple con-stituencies, it also posed problems for the coordination of policies that cut across two or more provinces.

The growing demands for regionalization and decentralization in the reform era can be interpreted as both political and economic reactions to the central planning system. Various negative effects of central planning led China's central leadership to realize the necessity to decentralize the economic system and the creation of regional forms of problem-solving. Inter-governmental decentralization refers to the empowering of regional and local levels of government to react to particular substantive differences in their regions. It necessarily means endowing the decentralized levels of government with greater autonomy. Inter-governmental decentralization and regionalization can also be interpreted as expanded participation of regional and local governments in the process of national policymaking. Although decentralization is often perceived in the sense of the transfer of functions and resources to autonomous units, in effect, decentralization as participation from below may be even more important for analyzing *de facto* federalism in reform China.

In examining the dynamics of *de facto* federalism in the reform era, one needs to look at not only how individual provinces have responded to decentralization, but also how provinces have collectively responded to it. Decentralization has been characterized by regionalization and the "region" has become an analytical unit among China scholars (Yang, 1997; Wang & Hu, 1999). In the early 1990s when the power of the central government was perceived to have been weakened due to continuous decentralization and the rise of regional powers, scholars addressed a most daring question regarding China's central-local relations, that is: Will China's provinces or regions form coalitions to collectively challenge the power of the central government, as happened in the 1920s when local warlords initiated the so-called *liansheng zizhi* (the federalist) movement (for example, Waldron, 1990)?

Although regionalization has become a main form of economic activity, virtually no research has been done to see the political impact of regionalization on central-local relations. Many legitimate questions can be raised regarding economic regionalization. Why did the central government allow, even encourage, it? How did the provinces collectively respond to it? What does it imply politically? Will economic cooperation among China's provinces become political?

The previous chapters have examined how the provinces individually responded to inter-governmental decentralization, as in the cases of Jiangsu and Zhejiang, or to recentralization, as in the case of Guangdong. This chapter shifts our focus to how China's provinces collectively bargain with the central government through a case study of the Economic Coordination Association of Southwest China (ECASC). The ECASC was undoubtedly *the* most successful across-provincial economic association in the 1980s and 1990s. The ECASC was significant for China's central-local relations for several reasons. First, it shows how the central government employed institutional methods to influence relations among different provinces in a decentralized setting. Second, the case demonstrates how provinces collectively bargained with the central government and sought the decentralization of power from the center. And third, the case reveals the complicated nature of regional economic associations and their impact on central-local relations in China.

INSTITUTIONAL ROOTS FOR THE FORMATION OF THE INTER-PROVINCIAL COALITION

In Mao's China, the provinces were relatively independent and self-sufficient units, and there was no institutional horizontal link between them (Donnithorne, 1972; Lyons, 1987, 1990). After the reform began in the late 1970s, the vertical control by the central government over the provinces was greatly reduced, and horizontal links between them grew gradually. Even though the provinces played a crucial role in developing such links, it was the reformist leadership that had provided provinces with incentives and created the institutional conditions for them to develop inter-provincial relations to improve provincial economic performance.

Zhao Ziyang played an essential role in initiating horizontal cooperation among the provinces in the 1980s. Based on his local experiences in Guangdong, Sichuan and Tibet, Zhao realized that local horizontal relations were crucial in developing a nationwide market system. According to Zhao, three aspects of horizontal relations needed to be emphasized. First, there should be economic coordination among the provinces. In 1981, Zhao, then Premier, stressed that economic coordination among coastal areas and inland provinces had to be developed so that every region's comparative advantage could be employed to promote growth. Shanghai,

Tianjin, Guangzhou and other major cities in the coastal areas needed to "export" their technologies and skilled personnel to inland provinces, and to make use of their relatively advanced technologies to participate in international trade (Zhao, 1988). In 1983, Zhao clearly claimed that, without the development of inter-local economic cooperation, China would not be able to improve its economic performance. The central government had to reduce its vertical interference into local economic affairs and decentralize decision-making power to the localities. To make local economic cooperation feasible and profitable, the central government had to create various institutional conditions. Zhao stressed,

> I think, in economic areas, a crucial task is to make regional plans well, that is, inter-provincial and inter-municipal economic cooperation. [T]he lines between regions and ministries have to be eliminated. Regions and ministries have to be in line with unified regional plans and cannot have plans independent from each other. The aim of regional economic plans and cooperation is to develop productivity and increase economic efficiency. It will be easy to deal with how to distribute interests equally as long as economic efficiency increases.... The central government cannot rely on its regional plan committees alone to develop regional economic cooperation. Instead, every locality should be encouraged to participate in engaging in such programs and local support has to be solicited (*Shijie Jingji Daobao*, 8 August 1983).

The central government implemented various favorable policies towards regional economic cooperation in order to create incentives for provinces to initiate or participate in inter-provincial projects. Investment priority was given to projects that involved several local-ities. Preferential tax policies were carried out toward the profits that resulted from inter-local projects. Formal institutions were also cre-ated from above to coordinate inter-local economic cooperation, such as the Shanghai Economic Zone Planning Office, the Shanxi Energy Base Planning Office and the Northeast Economic Zone Planning Office. Many institutions created from below were also legitimated such as the North China Economic and Technological Association, the Northeast Economic and Technological Association, the Economic Coordination Association of Southwest China, and the Bohai Region Mayors Associations.

Second, the reform leadership emphasized that major municipal cities had to become economic centers and play an important role in building economic links among regions (Solinger, 1993). In 1980, a conference of the directors of commercial bureaus at different levels was held in Wuhan. Participants reached a consensus that major cities had to transform themselves as centers of political control to those of economic activities (*People's Daily*, 27 November 1980). Well-known economists such as Gao Shangquan, Ma Hong, Tong Dalin and Jiang Yiwei justified the role of major cities in integrating China's entire economy, while reducing the center's vertical administrative management.[1] In 1985, Zhao Ziyang formally stated his plans for the role of major cities in China's entire urban reform, emphasizing that a main theme of urban reforms was to transform the role of major cities in the Chinese economy, so rural and urban areas could be integrated through major cities.[2]

With strong endorsement from the top leadership, many reform measures were implemented in transforming urban cities' functions. From 1983 to 1989, nine major cities were granted authority as "*jihua danlie shi*," which enjoyed the provincial-level economic power, including Chongqing, Wuhan, Shenyang, Dalian, Guangzhou, Xian, Harbin, Qingdao, Ningbo, Xiamen, Shenzhen, Nanjing, Chengdu and Changchun. According to the reform leadership, great financial and fiscal power should be transferred to these cities from both the central and provincial governments.[3] Below the major municipal level, a new administrative system, *Shiguanxian* (city-directed county), was established. In pre-reform China, rural areas were mainly managed by county governments, while urban areas were managed by municipal governments. This system was regarded by the reform leadership as harmful for economic integration. The *Shiguanxian* system brought counties under the

---

[1] See, Gao Shangquan (1983), Ma Hong (1982), Tong Dalin *et al.* (1985), and Jiang Yiwei (1983).

[2] Zhao Ziyang talked about how to make full use of major cities' functions to facilitate overall reforms of economic system (*People's Daily*, 29 April 1985).

[3] In reality, these cities' financial and fiscal power was still very limited. See Schroeder (1992).

direction of municipal governments; so there was no longer a division of labor between county and municipal governments. Rural and urban economies were thus expected to integrate.

The third aspect of horizontal cooperation was to establish a variety of enterprise groups. Major leaders, including Zhao Ziyang, were very interested in the development of enterprise groups. It seemed to Zhao that without enterprise groups, both regional economic cooperation and horizontal links among major cities could not effectively integrate China's economy since, ultimately, a market economy required cooperation among individual enterprises. According to Zhao,

> Horizontal cooperation is one of the fundamental conditions of the existence and development of a market economy. Horizontal links are required to open every domestic production entity. Under the old system, the economy was managed by "*tiaotiao*" (ministries) and "*kuaikuai*" (provinces) separately. There was no link between *tiao* and *tiao*, between *kuai* and *kuai*, as well as between *tiao* and *kuai*. This system has to be eliminated if a market economy is to grow. The reform is to achieve this goal.... Enterprise groups will change greatly the structure of China's industrial organization (*People's Daily*, 17 March 1986).

Zhao argued that the development of enterprise groups would bring changes to China's ownership structure and the internal organizational structure of enterprises. Under the old system, enterprises of "whole people ownership" became *de facto* ministerial ownership and local ownership. Enterprises relied heavily on ministries and regional governments and became self-sufficient systems. Economic efficiency was thus very poor due to the absence of competition among enterprises. Enterprise groups would produce an interest-control mechanism because an enterprise group would consist of many different interests. Even if competition were limited, economic efficiency could be expected to increase because actors would seek to maximize their interests (*ibid.*).

The ECASC grew out of this grand goal of economic reform by the reformist leadership. For the central government, the initial goal of building horizontal economic links was to provide an institutional condition for the development of a nationwide market and reduce administrative interference into economic affairs. But local officials were also political actors and they always sought to maximize their interests. Regional economic cooperation was frequently used by local governments as an opportunity to bargain with the central government to maximize their territorial interests. The ECASC case shows: (1) how the provincial governments in southwest China cooperated with the central government, making great efforts to integrate economic activities within their regions to promote local development; (2) how they behave *in coalition,* bargaining with the central government and its bureaucracies, seeking favorable policies for the region and facilitating decentralization of the power of the center; and (3) how the central government responded to the provinces as a group in a reciprocal way.

THE ECONOMIC COOPERATION ASSOCIATION OF SOUTHWEST CHINA (ECASC)

Southwest China usually refers to four provinces, namely, Guizhou, Yunnan, Sichuan and Tibet. These provinces border seven countries in South and Southeast Asia. After the establishment of the People's Republic in 1949, China's industrial policies over this area underwent several major changes (Table 7.1). In early days, as a peripheral area, the southwest region was not given investment priority. Only 11 out of the 156 major projects were located in this area during the First Five-Year Plan (FYP) period — about 7.3 percent of the total (Lu, 1990: 23). In 1958, the central government decided to divide the nation into seven economic coordination regions and each region was required to establish itself as a relatively independent economy.[4]

During the Second FYP, investment in the southwest region increased drastically. For example, Sichuan, Guizhou and Yunnan doubled their investments during this period. In 1964, Mao Zedong further emphasized that the concentration of China's industry in

---

[4] Solinger and Goodman discussed regional administration in the southwest in different periods. See Solinger (1977) and Goodman (1980).

Table 7.1 Changes in Investment Distribution among Regions (percentage of the total)

	1st FYP (1953–1957)	2nd FYP & Adjustment Period (1958–1965)	3rd FYP (1966–1970)	4th FYP (1971–1975)	5th FYP (1976–1980)	6th FYP (1981–1985)
Southwest	6.18	10.58	16.20	11.71	10.23	8.4
Northwest	12.33	10.44	13.03	11.15	10.53	8.5
Central China	11.35	14.46	15.53	15.84	15.80	11.9
Eastern China	7.78	11.85	8.08	10.22	12.69	15.5
North China	11.66	21.59	16.85	19.84	24.43	22.2
Northeast	22.49	15.52	10.25	13.29	14.16	12.6
South China	5.53	7.62	6.40	7.39	8.46	11.7

Source: Lu Dadao *et al.*, *Zhongguo Gongye Buju De Lilun Yu Shijian* (Theory and Practice of China's Industrial Distribution), Beijing: Kexue Chubanshe, 1990, p. 23.

coastal areas was unfavorable for the national defense. Ministries and provinces were required to move their industries into inland areas, or establish their own industrial bases there. China entered a period of the "Third Front Construction." Investment in the southwest region skyrocketed. In 1972, with the improvement of Sino-American relations, the central government changed its investment patterns and began to move the investment priority to the coastal areas. After the end of the 1970s, the leadership implemented pragmatic investment policies and most financial sources flowed to coastal areas. Investment in the southwest region dropped to about 8 percent of the total during the 6th FYP (1981–1985) — the lowest in all regions.

In effect, the region was experiencing a serious shortage of financial resources when the post-Mao reform began. Due to the decline of central fiscal power, the region was not able to acquire financial sources from the center. Also, although the region adjoins several foreign countries, the central government did not give it a favorable foreign trade policy as Guangdong and Fujian had acquired. How to accumulate financial resources to revive the region's economy became a major agenda for all provincial governments within this region. The new preferential policies by the reformist leadership for developing horizontal links among provinces provided governments there with an opportunity to seek mutual cooperation to resolve problems they faced.

In early 1984, Hu Yaobang, the then General Secretary of the CCP, visited southwest China and discussed various issues regarding the region's situation with local leaders. Aware of Hu's liberal mindset, local leaders complained to him about the central government's investment policy. Hu stressed that the central government was encountering a serious fiscal crisis and was not able to give the region strong financial resources, but could implement some other preferential policies towards the region. Hu suggested that local leaders take policy initiatives since they understood local situations better than the central government. After talking with government officials from different provinces, Hu proposed that the region establish an economic coordination association. Hu's proposal was immediately supported by two other major leaders, Deng Xiaoping and Zhao Ziyang (Tang, 1986: 1). With strong support from major leaders in Beijing, the provincial governments decided to establish a cross-provincial economic association, as suggested by Hu. Because of Tibet's political importance and its special economic conditions, it was excluded from the association and maintained an independent economic area. But, in 1986, Tibet applied to join the association, and that request was approved at the third association conference in 1986. Because Sichuan, Yunnan and Guizhou provinces are inland, the central government allowed Guangxi to join the association, providing, at last, access to the sea.[5]

In April 1984, the first conference of the Economic Coordination Association of Southwest China was held in Guiyang, the capital city of Guizhou province. Major leaders from Sichuan, Yunnan, Guangxi, Guizhou and Chongqing (Sichuan) attended the conference as representatives of association members.[6] The conference announced that the ECASC was formally established and passed the association's "constitution" — "Principles of the Economic Cooperation Association of Southwest China" (hereafter "Principles").

The Organization and its Principles

The "constitution" is composed of four major parts. It describes the nature of the association, its organizational principles, the functions of the presidency, and the association's liaison structure.

The nature of the association and its task. The association was defined as a "cross-provincial (*kua shengqu*), open (*kaifang xing*), loose (*songsang xing*) and regional (*quyu xing*) economic coordination organization, not an administrative one." After 1990,

---

[5] Interviews with provincial officials (Nanning Guangxi, 25 June 1993).

[6] Chongqing was an independent member in the association at the very beginning because of its position as a "*jihua danlie shi*." In 1997, Chongqing joined three other cities (Beijing, Shanghai and Tianjin) and became a city managed directly by the central government. Chengdu joined the association later after it gained the position as "*jihua danlie shi*."

the term "loose" was deleted from the "constitution," and the association was defined as a "cross-provincial, open and regional high-level organization." The association defined its major functions as follows:

1. *Research.* In order to promote economic cooperation within the region, the association is to organize information exchanges, policy studies of common interests in reforms, "open door," and economic construction.
2. *Policy coordination.* The association promotes and initiates cooperation within the region on major policy issues including development planning, agricultural growth, transportation, energy, raw materials and tourism.
3. *Multilateral industrial cooperation.* The association promotes and initiates bilateral, multilateral and multiform economic and technological activities among provinces. It organizes cooperation programs among enterprises, industries and provinces.
4. *Market integration.* The association organizes and fosters regional market systems, eliminating local protectionism, and promoting the free flow of commodities among provinces.
5. *Horizontal integration.* The association creates and improves institutional conditions and circumstances for cooperation by (a) making full use of major cities to integrate industries in the region, as well as between rural and urban areas; and (b) organizing major enterprises as inter-regional and inter-provincial enterprise groups.
6. *Policy implementation.* The association makes its policies according to the guidelines set forth by the central government and local conditions. It also coordinates individual provinces' efforts in implementing central policies.

These goals underwent considerable changes after they were established in 1984. Initially, the association did not highlight the issues of minority groups in the regions. After Tibet became a member, the association turned to put much emphasis on the importance of economic development in minority areas. Indeed, as I will show later, minority issues became a forceful instrument for the association to bargain for preferential policies for the region from the central government.

Another main change was about the role of the association in promoting the region's foreign economy. What role the association should play in promoting the region's foreign economic activities was very controversial among provinces in the 1980s due to several factors. First, the central government did not grant the region independent authority in developing foreign trade. Second, developing the region's foreign trade with its neighboring countries such as Vietnam was far beyond a merely economic matter. Only after Beijing adjusted its overall foreign policy towards the South and Southeast Asia was it possible for the region to establish economic ties with its neighbors. Third, benefits from foreign trade could hardly be equally distributed among the provinces in the region because most members of the association are inland provinces. Considerations about the distribution of interest had a negative impact on the provincial and municipal leaderships' decision-making about foreign trade.[7] Nevertheless, in 1992, after Deng called for more rapid development during his southern tour, the association formally decided to make joint efforts to develop foreign trade, which was eventually defined as a major function of the association at its ninth conference.

An even more important change is the association's relations with the central government. Initially, the association was to coordinate internal economic activities among the provinces in the regions and implement central policies through internal cooperation. After 1989, the association began to emphasize its *guanxi* (linkage) with the central government. The "Principles" revised at the sixth conference (1989) stated that the association should report its proposals to the central government (The Secretariat of ECASC, 1989: 12). Nevertheless, all proposals made by the association appeared in the form of "opinions" (*yijian*) and were for the reference of the central government only, when the latter made decisions relevant to the region. After 1996, the association redefined the proposals it sent to

---

[7] Fieldwork (Nanning, Guangxi, 1993).

the central government as "requests for approval" (*qingshi baogao*) (The Secretariat of ECASC, 1996: 2).

The conference and its institutional arrangements. The association decided on Chongqing as its headquarters. Later, it also decided to establish a newspaper as its organ. With the development of the association, many communication networks were developed in order to strengthen links among the provinces. Before 1990, the association published a newspaper, *Xietiao Dongtai* (Current Affairs of Coordination) as its organ. In 1991, the association improved its organ by establishing *Xinan Xinxi Bao* (Southwest News). In 1992, the newspaper was expanded and changed to *Xinan Jingji Ribao* (Southwest Economic Daily).

According to the "constitution," the summit conference would be annual and attended by leaders at the highest level from all members of the association. Every association member had equal rights, chairing the conference in turn and having independent rights to a veto (The Secretariat of ECASC, 1984). The president of the annual conference makes decisions on inviting government officials from the central government and other relevant provinces. More concretely, the responsibilities of the presidency include:

- Overseeing the daily operation of the liaison office of the association; organizing economic cooperation activities among the association members; and coordinating efforts by the association members to report to the central government.
- Communicating with members of the association; initiating liaison working meetings; and supervising the implementation of the policies that were made during the summit conference.
- Reporting to the association in the next summit conference.
- Discussing with members of the association; setting up agendas; and making plans for the next summit conference.
- Supervising the association organ, *Southwest Economic Daily*, and being responsible for its daily operation.

The Liaison Office. The association established a liaison office with each member appointing three representatives. The position of the directorship is filled by the side that chairs the annual conference. Summarily, the responsibilities of the liaison office include:

- Managing the daily activities of coordination among members of the association; initiating and organizing cross-provincial economic activities; and supervising the implementation of cooperation projects that were reached among the members.
- Investigating the implementation of plans and decisions made during the summit conference by each member and reporting to the president.
- Overseeing the preparation of the summit conference, a task assigned by the president.
- Communicating with members of the association, relevant ministries in Beijing and counterparts in other provinces; and supervising the newsletter, *Current Affairs of Coordination*, to improve coordination among the members.

The conference was highly institutionalized after its establishment in 1984. Up to 1998, the association had held 14 annual conferences (Table 7.2).

Internal Cooperation

The major function of the association was to make joint efforts to coordinate activities among its members in order to promote horizontal economic cooperation. Provincial officials were highly motivated by both economic and political factors to make great efforts to develop the ECASC into an efficient organization.

Generally speaking, four major factors explained why provincial leaders were motivated to establish such an association without much interference from the central government. First of all, creating the association was worthwhile. Almost all other associations were established based on the initiatives from the central government. An organization that was voluntarily organized could become a model for the rest of the nation. By doing so, certain local leaders could establish their political prestige. Second, individually, the provinces in the southwest region were rather weak. The association made it

Table 7.2 Annual Summit Conferences of the ECASC (1984–1998)

	Date	Place	Chair
1	15–19 April 1984	Guiyang	Chi Biqin, PS* of Guizhou Provincial PC**
2	23–28 April 1985	Chongqing	Liao Bokang, PS of Chongqing Municipal PC
3	20–24 May 1986	Kunming	Pu Chaozhu, PS of Yunnan Provincial PC
4	25–29 May 1987	Chengdu	Yang Rudai, PS of Sichuan Provincial PC
5	18–20 April 1988	Nanning	Chen Huiguang, PS of Guangxi Autonomous Region PC
6	30 June–7 July 1989	Lhasa	Hu Jintao, PS of Tibet Autonomous Region PC
7	8–12 August 1990	Guiyang	Liu Zhengwei, PS of Guizhou Provincial PC
8	5–9 September 1991	Chongqing	Xiao Yang, PS of Chongqing Municipal PC
9	27–29 October 1992	Kunming	Pu Chaozhu, PS of Yunnan Provincial PC
10	6–8 October 1993	Chengdu	Xiao Yang, Governor of Sichuan
11	9–11 May 1995	Nanning	Zhao Fulin, PS of Guangxi Autonomous Region PC
12	2–9 August 1996	Lhasa	Raidi, Vice PS of Tibet Autonomous Region PC
13	18–22 October 1997	Chengdu	Huang Yinkui, PS of Chengdu Municipal PC
14	26–28 August 1998	Guiyang	Liu Fangren, PS of Guizhou Provincial PC

*PS: Party Secretary.
**PC: Party Committee.
Source: Fieldwork, Nanning, 1999, information was provided by the Secretariat of the ECASC.

possible for the provinces to make joint efforts. Provincial officials could behave in coalition to show the central government the importance of certain problems the region encountered and to persuade it to implement preferential policies towards it or give more investment sources to the region. Third, with the implementation of decentralization, local governments had the autonomy to create favorable circumstances for their regions. Intense competition occurred among regions. Individually, the provinces in the southwest region were not able to compete with others such as Guangdong, Zhejiang and Jiangsu. By forming an economic association, the region would become more competitive. Finally and practically, the association members together could resolve many problems that provinces were not able to cope with individually.[8]

Intense bargaining occurred among the members of the association at every conference. It was frequently difficult to make joint decisions due to each member's independent consideration of their own interests. But because of interdependence among the provinces and each member's comparative advantage, leaders usually were able to reach compromises that led to the preparation of documents. Once a joint policy was made, each member of the association would follow it because, first, leaders expected to gain prestige among their colleagues; second, deviating from the agreements that were reached during the conference would make further cooperation impossible and other members could possibly impose "sanction" or "punishment" on the deviators in other fields; and third, the central government sometimes persuaded possible deviators to be cooperative.[9]

The association undoubtedly promoted horizontal economic cooperation among its members. At the very beginning, the association expected to build a unified market and achieve a rational distribution of industrial production within the region through cooperative projects. Such joint projects usually could be implemented because the association's conference actually was a summit among highest provincial leaders. From 1984 to 1998, the association members established 57 cross-provincial enterprise groups within the region and 20 enterprise groups with adjacent provinces (The Secretariat of ECASC, 1999: 4). The association achieved 9,161 major cooperative projects among the members of the association. The distribution of these cooperative projects among provinces is

[8] Interview with a provincial official of Guangxi (Nanning, Guangxi, 25 June 1993).
[9] Fieldwork and interviews with provincial officials (Nanning, Guangxi, 26 June 1993).

shown in Table 7.3. Table 7.4 shows the main agendas and policy issues of the annual summit between 1984–1998. Some important aspects of the association's internal horizontal economic coordination and cooperation can be summarized as follows.

Joint development of transportation, post and telecommunications systems. Through collective bargaining with the central government, the association gained enormous central financial and fiscal support that enabled the association to engage in infrastructure building for the transportation, post and telecommunications systems. Some 64 roads (about 1,500 km) and four bridges were constructed, connecting the provinces in the region. The China Southwest Airlines and many other local airlines were established, connecting the region with other parts of the country through 159 airlines. Furthermore, a telecommunications network among Chengdu, Chongqing, Kunming and other major cities was developed (*ibid.*).

Table 7.3 Cooperation Projects among Members
of the ECASC (1984–1998)

Year	Number of Achieved Cooperative Projects	Contracted Capital (100 million *yuan*)
1984	103	
1985	1,006	
1986	1,056	
1987	592	
1988	1,109	
1989	724	
1990	380	
1991	633	2.2
1992	997	10.9
1993	569	29.7
1995	530	13.9
1996	460	30.4
1997	480	25.5
1998	522	26.7

Source: Fieldwork, Nanning, 1998. The information was provided by the Secretariat of ECASC.

Table 7.4 Main Agendas and Policy Proposals of the ECASC (1984–1998)

Year	Main Agendas and Policy Proposals
1984	• Summary of the forum on developing steel and coal bases in the region • Summary of the forum on power development in the region • Summary of the forum on transportation development in the region • Agreement on developing commercial cooperation among association members • Some principles of the ECASC
1985	• Interim procedures on economic and technological cooperation of mutual benefit • Jointly developing transportation and post and telecommunications systems • Jointly developing priority industries • Developing economic relations and cooperation among major cities • Developing technological and talent cooperation • Building techno-economic cooperation with the coast regions
1986	• Implementing a comprehensive investigation of national resources in the region • Making great efforts to develop horizontal economic coordination and cooperation • Policy proposal for the Central Government to build the Nanning-Kunming railway • Jointly exploiting subtropical national resources in the region • Jointly developing tourist industry in the region
1987	• Building economic and technological cooperation in agriculture, animal husbandry and fishery • Developing a horizontal cooperation net among financial organizations • Jointly developing coordination and cooperation in chemistry industry • Jointly developing light industry • Agreement on developing coordination and cooperation in engineering industry • Making further efforts to develop post and telecommunications system • Jointly developing cooperation in construction industry
1988	• Promoting economic development in poor areas • Jointly developing foreign economy

(Continued)

Table 7.4 (*Continued*)

Year	Main Agendas and Policy Proposals
1989	• Building technological market cooperation • Developing relations among fiscal departments in the region • Promoting economic development in minority areas • Building agricultural cooperation • Developing techno-economic cooperation between adjacent areas • Jointly developing joint-ventures among association members • Some supplementary agreements on developing foreign economy
1990	• Building horizontal agricultural coordination • Jointly developing energy industry • Jointly promoting economic development in minority areas • Managing horizontal cooperation network among financial organizations • Coordinating construction organizations in the region • Measures for measurement of horizontal fiscal cooperation • Speeding up economic development in the region
1991	• Jointly exploiting national resources • Reforming traditional industries and developing enterprises groups • Building regional technological markets • Developing internal and external markets in the region
1992	• Policy request for the central government to open the region to South and Southeast Asia • Jointly pushing the open-door policy and developing techno-economic cooperation • Jointly exploiting markets in South and Southeast Asia
1993	• Jointly developing infrastructure for transportation and communications • Jointly strengthening an integrated market in the region • Jointly developing a tourism net in the region • Jointly preparing the establishment of the Southwest Development Bank
1995	• Jointly speeding up infrastructure construction for transportation and communications • Jointly exploiting markets in South and Southeast Asia • Speeding up the construction of an integrated market system in the region • Jointly building a tourism network in the region • Strengthening techno-economic cooperation and coordination

(*Continued*)

Table 7.4 (*Continued*)

Year	Main Agendas and Policy Proposals
1996	• Speeding up infrastructure construction for transportation and communications • Jointly exploiting markets in South and Southeast Asia • Jointly building a tourism network in the region • Strengthening techno-economic cooperation and coordination • Speeding up economic development in minority areas
1997	• Speeding up infrastructure construction for transportation and communications • Strengthening an integrated market system in the region • Speeding up jointly tourism industry • Pushing the industrialization of agricultural products
1998	• Pushing forwards infrastructure construction for transportation and communications • Integrating tourism network in the region • Making further efforts to build an integrated market system in the region • Promoting cooperation between the southwest region and coastal provinces

Source: Adapted from the ECASC, *Lianhe Xiezuo Chengguo Zhanshi* (Exhibition of Achievements of Cooperation and Coordination of the ECASC), Kunming: Government Print, 1999, pp. 5–6.

Jointly developing energy industry and exploiting natural resources. In the 14 years (1984–1998), the association members developed some 170 major projects for developing energy industry and exploiting natural resources, amounting to 9.3 billion *yuan* in total investment. The provinces jointly established the Southwest Power Company. Many other bilateral and multilateral projects were also developed (*ibid.*).

Building an integrated market system in the region. According to various agreements at annual conferences, provincial governments in the region used administrative means to remove local protectionist barriers to promote an integrated market system. From 1985 to 1988, every year the association organized a trade fair to promote commercial flows among the provinces. In 1992, the provinces jointly held the Southwest China Trade Fair for international customers. Since 1993, the Kunming Fair is organized annually.

Promoting economic development in minority areas. It has been among the highest priorities of the association. Provincial leaders brought the issues of economic development in minority areas to the central government and required the latter to have preferential policies towards these areas. (This point will be discussed in detail later.)

After the reform began in the late 1970s, the reformist leadership consistently called for the development of cross-provincial economic cooperation and the establishment of relevant organizations. Many provinces indeed reacted positively and there were several waves of economic regionalization. Nevertheless, most great efforts of economic regionalization failed due to various reasons. By contrast, the ECASC became the most successful cross-provincial economic organization from various perspectives. In 1991, Huang Tianhua and Gao Lianqing, officials from the State Planning Commission, reviewed the development of all major cross-provincial associations and reached the conclusion that the ECASC had performed much better than any other such associations in the country.

What led to the success of the association? According to Gao, there had been several factors. First of all, the association members (provincial governments) were able to take into full account the central government's development priority when they made decisions for the region. Second, most cross-provincial organizations in other regions did not have standing executive organs to implement and supervise decisions made by the associations, and their decisions were not effective. By contrast, the ECASC established a standing organ and had been institutionalized. Third, an information network connecting all members was well-developed, with a newspaper as the association's organ. Gao emphasized that these institutional factors had distinguished the ECASC from other such organizations (The Secretariat of ECASC, 1991: 108–110).

Zou Jiahua, Vice Premier (1991–1998), was a strong supporter of the ECASC. According to Zou, the success of the ECASC lay in the fact that the association utilized market forces, not administrative or political means, to solve problems of development within the region (The Secretariat of ECASC, 1997: 105–106). Between 1997 and 1998, Zou formally instructed twice that other provinces should learn from the ECASC (The Secretariat of ECASC, 1998: 15). By the mid-1990s, the ECASC had become a national model for cross-provincial economic cooperation.

ASSOCIATION AS COALITION: COLLECTIVE BARGAINING WITH THE CENTER

During the Mao regime, ideology and party loyalty were the most important standards used to evaluate local leaders' political perform-ance. Mao often used ideological and other political means to elicit local leaders' initiatives for economic development. Although local leaders had some degree of autonomy in implementing policies made in Beijing (Goodman, 1984), their capacity to bargain with the central government, to a large extent, depended on what kind of patron-client connection existed between the two, as Solinger (1982) suggested in her study of Yunnan's relations with the central government.

Decentralization under Deng greatly differentiated the provinces' capacity in bargaining with the central government. Economic performance became the most important standard for the center to judge local leaders' political achievement. Given the fact that China's economic growth was extremely uneven among regions, the provinces with more developed economies were more powerful than the poor ones in bargaining with Beijing. For instance, the provinces such as Zhejiang, Jiangsu, Guangdong and Shandong were in a very favorable position in their relations with Beijing because of their actual or potential revenue contribution to the center.

Thus, many poor provinces made efforts to form various cross-provincial coalitions to bargain with the central government collectively. The initial goal of the central government to encourage local governments to form horizontal economic coordination was to build a nationwide market system. Nevertheless, the provinces often used this policy to further their own interests. They formed coalitions and engaged in collective bargaining with the central government in all aspects of economic activities such as fiscal policy, investment and locations of major projects. Generally speaking, coalitions among poor provinces were more stable than in rich areas. The Shanghai Economic Coordination Association was less successful than the ECASC because the former consisted of rich provinces such as Zhejiang and Jiangsu, which had greater capacity to bargain with the center individually, while in the ECASC, all the provinces were poor and an individual province did not have many resources to bargain with the center.[10]

As discussed earlier, after the reform began, the central government's investment priority shifted from inland provinces to coastal ones, and investment in inland areas was reduced dramatically. As shown in Table 7.1, the southwest region only received 8.4 percent of the total investment in the nation from 1981 to 1985 — the lowest in all regions, compared to 16 percent in the Third FYP period and 12 percent in the Fourth FYP period. The southwest area, especially Guizhou and Sichuan provinces, once were the center of the Third Front Construction. The Third Front Construction, as part of China's defense industry, absorbed about two-thirds of the government's industrial investment then (Naughton, 1988). The industrial reform in post-Mao China left many facilities of the Third Front unused because of, first, their slow economic returns, and second, the decline of the central government's fiscal power. In fact, the shift of the central government's investment priority had a very negative impact on the region's economy. How to accumulate the capital to revive the region's economy became a major concern of provincial officials in this area.

The central government granted great power for the association to make economic decisions relevant to the region's economy, but this did not mean that provincial officials as a coalition could make decisions completely autonomously. The degree of autonomy in

---

[10] Interview with an official of the Development Research Center of the State Council of PRC (Beijing, 3 July 1993).

decision-making depended on policy areas. For the policy areas that only dealt with the association's internal relations, provincial officials could have a final say without central interference. In most cases, the association's autonomy was rather limited. This was because, first of all, for these decisions that related to the central government or whose impact went beyond the association members, they would be effective only after they were legitimated by the center. Second, because the goal of the association was to bargain with the central government to obtain various forms of support, provincial officials had to take the central government into consideration. The bid could not be too high, otherwise the central government would not accept it. Provincial officials had to restrain themselves from deviating far away from central policies.

Thus, to a great degree, what the association could gain from the central government depended on how the association presented its problems and how it legitimated its demands for support. This section examines how the association used its unique power resources to bargain with the central government.

The Political Use of Minority Issues

The most powerful resource that the association could invoke was the minority population.[11] There are more than 40 million in the minority population in the region — about 60 percent of the total minority population in China. Seventy percent of the total area of the region is inhabited by the minority population. After the establishment of the PRC, Guangxi and Tibet were designated autonomous regions because of their dense ethnic population. Many sub-provincial autonomous areas were also established in Yunnan, Sichuan and Guizhou. Constitutionally, these autonomous regions were granted a great deal of autonomy. But the reality was that the CCP leadership, especially under Mao, exercised rather tight control over these areas. The localities were not able to avoid being dragged into political

---

[11] Major minority peoples living within the region include: *Zang, Dai, Jingpo, Benglong, Miao* and *Zhuang.*

movements initiated by leaders in Beijing. However, deep penetration did not enable the CCP to reduce the level of poverty there. An official report by the ECASC in 1989 stated (The Secretariat of ECASC, 1989: 30),

> The Central Committee of the CCP and the State Council have put much emphasis on economic development in minority areas, especially since the late 1970s. The government has implemented many preferential and flexible policies toward these areas and the situation is getting better due to the support from the central government.... Nevertheless, because of historical factors and the constraints of natural circumstances, and more importantly, because of the limits of China's system and great mistakes made in the past, the overall economic situation in these minority areas is still bad, and in effect, disparities between minority peoples in this region and those in Northwest China is being enlarged because China economic growth has been faster in Northwest China.

When Hu Yaobang came to the region in the early 1980s, he acknowledged that the CCP had made great "policy mistakes" towards the minority areas. Hu stated clearly that the CCP and the central government wanted not only to adopt a moderate cultural policy, but also to offer economic assistance to minority areas. But what Hu said was never put into practice. According to some provincial officials, the central government implemented a variety of moderate cultural policies in minority areas, but because of its fiscal burden, the central government was not able to increase financial support to the minority population. Therefore, "one of the major aims of the ECASC was to show the central government the political significance of minority areas and persuade it to increase financial aid to the region."[12]

As a matter of fact, the association has treated the minority population as an effective resource in bargaining with the central government. As early as 1985, the association issued a document — *A Report on How to Liberalize Policy Further Toward and Give Higher Priority to Support to Minority Areas in the Region* — and sent it to the State Council. At its fourth conference in 1987, the

---

[12] Interview with provincial officials of Guangxi (Nanning, Guangxi, 25 June 1993).

association again emphasized that the 1985 document expressed the basic expectations of the minority population and of local officials in the region, and requested that the central government implement and materialize the preferential policies towards minority areas (The Secretariat of ECASC, 1987: 2–3).

At its sixth conference, the association made a decision — *Agreement on Strengthening Horizontal Economic Cooperation and Promoting Economic Development in the Minority Areas.* According to that decision, about 10 million of minority people in the region did not have adequate food and clothing. The association almost warned (The Secretariat of ECASC, 1989: 30),

> Speeding up economic development in these [minority] areas is of great significance for strengthening the unification of nationalities, the unity of the nation and the national defense of Southwest China. It is also significant for the further development of joint reform, the open door policy and political stability in the region, on the one hand, and economic and political stability in the nation on the other.

In order to promote economic development in the minority areas, the association reached agreements to coordinate members' activities. The main themes of these agreements can be summarized as follows:

- The provinces in the region had to act collectively to explore and make use of rich natural resources in minority areas. Major municipal cities and developed areas within the association had to develop different sorts of processing industries which could use raw materials from minority areas. They had to provide support to minority areas such as technology, industrial instruments and financial resources. Entrepreneurs should be encouraged to open various industries in minority areas (The 1989, 1990 conferences).
- The major cities in the region had to play an important role in developing horizontal economic links between cities and minority areas. County governments should be responsible for improving poor conditions within their jurisdictions (The 1989 conference).

- The provincial governments in the region needed to implement various preferential policies to encourage the development of foreign trade between the minority areas and foreign countries, especially those in South and Southeast Asia. Borders had to be opened. Preferential tax policies had to be provided to both foreign and domestic businessmen if they opened businesses in border cities. The provincial governments also needed to request the central government to liberalize the licenses for imports and exports in the minority areas (The 1989, 1990 conferences).
- The association needed to coordinate individual provinces' policies for developing the tourist trade in the region. All association members should jointly plan tourist routes and organize the construction of tourist faculties (The 1989 conference).
- The transportation systems had to be improved in the minority areas. Railways, roads and waterways needed to be connected (The 1989 conference).
- The association was responsible for organizing labor training and promoting skilled laborers in the minority areas. Major cities needed to provide trainers and various facilities for trainees. Labor training had to be institutionalized (The 1989 conference).
- The provincial and county governments in the region had to change the way that the financial support from the central government was used. The financial support could not be used for regional expenditures. Instead, the governments had to use it to build an industrial and service infrastructure for the minority population (The 1989 conference).

Further, the association also argued that though the provincial governments in the region had to play an important role through their coordinated actions to improve economic situation, the support from the central government was also particularly important and necessary since not all of the major problems in the minority areas could be solved by the region alone. The association reached various agreements aimed at bargaining with the central government and demanding more support from the center. Major requests could be summarized as follows:

- Minority autonomy was a prerequisite for economic and political development in the minority areas. *The Minority Autonomy Bill* was passed by The National People's Congress long ago, but the central government was not able to implement it. The Bill granted minority population's a variety of rights, under which the central government had to provide more support such as financial resources and material supplies for the minority areas. The provinces in the association collectively requested that the central government consider fully the necessity of economic development in minority areas and implement the Bill (The 1989 and 1990 conferences).
- The central government had to give higher priority to economic development in minority areas in its Eighth FYP and Ninth FYP. Preferential policies and investment priority had to be given to the minority population. The association argued that in considering major projects and investment plans, "the State Council and its ministries should give priority to the construction of the infrastructure of energy, transportation, communications, raw material processing and technological education in Southwest China. Major processing industries had to be built in the region so that economic growth could be taken off" (The 1989 conference).
- The central government needed to implement various special "poverty-reducing" methods or set up special funds out of the central government's fiscal resources to develop economic projects to help the minority population, especially the 10 million who did not have adequate food and clothing (The 1989 conference).
- The central government needed to set up education funds for minorities or use special subsidiaries for minority education to develop vocational education, technical education and other basic education in the minority areas (The 1989 conference).
- The central government needed to attract major international support projects to promote resource exploration and economic development in minority areas (The 1989 conference).

• The central government needed to implement a preferential policy towards the minority areas in terms of the center's mandate planning: (1) those enterprises that had sufficient production capacity could retain all profits above the state quota; (2) the local governments in the region should be allowed to share profits with the central government from new enterprises in which the central government invested. If enterprises were founded by the central government and the local governments jointly, the central government should allow the local governments to share more of the profits; and if enterprises were founded by the local governments alone, the local governments should have complete freedom in dealing with profits; and (3) the central government should compensate the local governments for the export of raw materials in the minority areas in which the local governments had no license to engage (The 1989 conference).

• The central government needed to exempt energy and transportation taxes, and remove increments in agricultural and custom taxes in the minority areas. These taxes should all be retained by the local governments to develop local economies (The 1990 conference).

• The central government and its ministries needed to give loans at low interest rates to minority areas (The 1990 conference).

As a matter of fact, even without local demands, central financial support to minority areas tended to increase. For instance, the central government's fixed subsidy to Tibet, Guangxi, Guizhou and Yunnan increased from 4.5, 2.7, 4.8 and 3.0 billion *yuan* in 1979 to 7.5, 7.2, 7.4 and 6.4 billion in 1985 respectively (Cheng *et al.*, 1988: 387). But it was not certain how much benefit the minority population had actually received. The key was that the provincial governments wanted to utilize the minority population as an effective instrument not just to legitimate its demands for central support, but also to seek benefits from the central government. According to an economic official in Beijing, the central government knew that the local governments in minority areas attempted to get more resources from Beijing. Thus, while the central government encouraged the local governments to give support to minority populations, it also required them to realize revenue self-sufficiency, meaning that the central government would not be able to provide fiscal subsidies to the minority areas indefinitely since the center itself faced a fiscal crisis.[13] To a great degree, this was true. The degree of revenue self-sufficiency in Guangxi, Yunnan and Guizhou increased from 60 percent, 63 percent and 56 percent in 1986 to 70 percent, 81 percent and 73 percent in 1990, respectively (Ma & Sun, 1992: 157).

Exploring National Resources

Exploring natural resources is another important power resource of the ECASC to bargain with both the central government and its neighboring provinces. The region has 0.2 billion KW of exploitable water resources — about 54 percent of the total in the nation; 77.7 billion tons of coal — about 9 percent of the total in the nation; more than half of the natural gas and nuclear energy in the nation (Zhang, 1989). The region also has rich nonferrous metal resources. The reserves of bauxite, manganese, lead, zinc, tin, antimony and copper are about 38 percent, 43 percent, 27 percent, 39 percent, 48 percent, 44 percent and 17 percent, respectively, of the amount in the nation (Tang, 1986: 8).

In the early 1980s, several senior economic advisors to Deng Xiaoping such as Tong Dalin proposed a division of the country into seven economic zones including the Guangdong-Fujian Zone, the Changjiang Zone, the Longhai-Lanxin Zone, the Yellow River Zone, the Bohai Bay Zone, the Northeast China Zone and the Southwest Zone. The Southwest Zone was greatly emphasized as an area of greatest natural resources (Tong, 1990: 1). Before the establishment of the association, many measures were implemented to explore natural resources in the southwest region. In 1982, some central

---

[13] Interview with an economic official in the Development Research Center of the State Council (Beijing, 20 July 1993).

ministries, in cooperation with the four provinces in the region, established a company to be in charge of exploring for natural energy. But due to the declining fiscal capacity of the central government, the progress of policy implementation was rather slow.

After its birth in 1984, the association gave high priority to the exploration of natural resources in the region, because, first of all, the region could benefit greatly from it. Second, the association could treat it as another important means in demanding for financial, technological and other forms of support from the central government, and seeking investment and cooperation from its neighboring provinces and foreign countries. Upon the association's request, in 1985, the central government decided to finance a team of scientists from the Chinese Academy of Sciences and the State Planning Commission to engage in a large-scale survey of natural resources in the region. A decision was made at the third association conference in 1986 to speed up surveying natural resources and studying development strategies for the region. In 1986, Tibet joined the association. At its fourth conference, the association suggested that the central government also initiate a survey on natural resources in Tibet. A chief economic official in Sichuan explained the aim of this survey (Lin, 1986: 2):

> People have not understood the reality of southwest China. Different opinions were raised toward the construction of the Third Front in the 1960s. Now people disagreed on the position of the southwest region in terms of national defense; they also disagreed on development strategies for the region. More importantly, people never reached a consensus over the advantages and disadvantages of exploring the natural, economic and social resources in the region. So, a systematic analysis and evaluation of the region is significant for people to reach a consensus for rediscovering the region and promoting its modernization.

A provincial official in Guangxi stated more clearly that the association had to push the central government to realize the political and economic importance of the southwest region by showing the richness of its natural resources, and this survey would enable the region to make very constructive proposals for the central government. At any rate, it would be very effective to attract both the central government and the neighboring provinces to invest in the region.[14]

The investigation group consisted of 300 scientists and made a four-year survey of the natural resources in the region (1986–1990). The group wrote more than 200 reports covering 30 subjects. These reports provided very detailed information about the region's resources and provided very useful guidelines for both the central government and provincial governments in their policy-making.

At its seventh and eighth conferences, the association adopted two important decisions on taking collective action to explore the resources in the region. According to these two decisions, the provincial governments in the region should put great emphasis on developing horizontal cooperation in many priority areas including exploring the development of agricultural resources, water resources, the coal industry, the chemical industry, tourism, the transportation system (roads, railways and waterways) construction, financing and so on.

From 1986 to 1990, the association members approved 160 joint projects related to the exploration of natural resources. But most were short-term projects that could generate quick economic returns. Large projects were very problematic mainly because of the lack of financial resources. Agreements were difficult to reach among the provinces over some medium-sized projects because disagreements could not be solved over financial problems. Consequently, the association repeatedly requested financial and other forms of support from the central government.

In the association's reports to the central government, the exploration of resources was linked tightly to economic development that in turn was linked to political stability. A report to the central government passed at the seventh conference stated that, due to various reasons, the region's economic development level was still very low and was the largest poor area in China, and warned, if this situation could not be changed, it would be very unfavorable not

---

[14] Interview with a provincial official of Guangxi (Nanning, 24 June 1993).

only for the rational distribution of productivity and the adjustment of industrial structure in the nation;[15] more importantly, it would produce a very negative impact on the nation's political stability, national unification and defense strengthening, and on the stable and coordinated development of the whole national economy. Thus, speeding up economic development was not only a major concern of the people in the region, but also a great problem for the whole nation (The Secretariat of ECASC, 1990: 2). Further, economic development in the region relied heavily on the exploration and development of resources as the key to economic take-off input. Because inputs in the reform era had been reduced and state investments declined, local governments were not able to change the situation. Therefore, the association requested that the state still needed to give more financial support to the region and increase fixed investment, that the State Council and the ministries concerned fully consider the actual problems in the region, giving priority to infrastructure construction projects, agricultural, energy, and raw material exploration projects, and technological updating projects in the eighth and ninth FYP periods (*ibid.*: 3).

The association also proposed how the central government could help the region. The central government should: (1) assign more priority projects to the minority areas in the region; (2) exempt a portion of taxes that the region paid to the center as the funds for the region's construction; (3) allow the region to establish the Southwest Development Bank to accumulate capital by issuing stocks and absorbing both domestic and foreign investments, and to grant the bank great authority; and (4) allow the enterprises within the region to retain more profits in order to increase the enterprises' capacity for self-development (*ibid.*: 50–51).

---

[15] In 1989, per capita GNP, per capita national income, per capita agricultural and industrial income, and per capita revenue in southwest China were 62 percent, 63 percent, 54 percent and 43 percent of the national average. From 1980 to 1989, the difference in per capita GNP between the region and the national average increased from 164 *yuan* to 541; per capita national income increased from 127 *yuan* to 415. See The Secretariat of ECASC (1990: 2).

Linking the Association to the Central Government

I have so far discussed how the association presented its problems to the central government, as in the cases of the issues of promoting economic development in the minority areas and exploring natural resources. Another important issue in understanding the relations between the center and the provinces was how the association linked itself to the central government and central bureaucracies. One major aim of the association was to bargain collectively with and gain support from the central government. Without central support such as financial aid and material supplies, the association would not be able to realize joint cross-provincial projects. On the other hand, the central government also needed cooperation from the provinces in order to promote local development effectively. Provincial officials played an essential role in providing information for decision-making in Beijing on the one hand, and implementing central policies on the other hand. Although the association was not an administrative unit, it still held rather great power since it was a summit in the region. In other words, the association mattered for both the association members and the central government. According to one provincial official,

> Before the establishment of the association, the central government had to deal with the provinces in the region one by one. Though the center probably had to use information provided by the provincial governments in decision-making, it was doubtful whether the provinces had a real say in the process of decision-making. The central government could simply impose its decisions upon the provincial government. After the establishment of the association, individual provincial activities were coordinated. The association now almost has all information that the center needed for new policy initiatives. As a matter of fact, the association attempted to "impose" its decisions upon the central government. Major decisions by the association needed to be approved by the center, but the process could be formalistic.[16]

In effect, one major task of the association was to establish connections with the central government. From its establishment in 1984 to 1998, it was done mainly through four forms of activities

---

[16] Interview with provincial officials of Guangxi (Nanning, 24 June 1993).

including providing information for decision-making in Beijing; submitting the association's decisions to Beijing for approval; reporting the association's annual conferences and major themes; and seeking direct support from central bureaucracies.

Nonetheless, the center often found that it was difficult to agree with all decisions made by the association without any reservations. Great differences existed frequently between the two levels. The association also felt that without central support, it could not implement major cross-provincial projects. Therefore, a dilemma was raised. One provincial official argued that "the association could make decisions without interference from the central government and its ministries, but central bureaucracies would probably never pay attention to policy proposals or requests raised by the association."[17]

After 1989, the association developed new links between itself and the central bureaucracies by making major decisions jointly with officials from Beijing. Before 1989, the association also invited officials to attend its annual conference mainly as "a symbol of the support of central ministries."[18] Since 1990, many major figures in Beijing have become involved directly in the association's decision-making.

Table 7.5 shows an incomplete list of the major officials and central bureaucracies involved in the process of decision-making at the association's summits. By so doing, the bargaining between the provinces and the center became an internal part of the whole decision-making process. It mattered for both the center and the provinces. For the center, this process meant that its policy intentions could be expressed in the association's decision-making process, a process which, to a degree, enabled the center to constrain local independent behavior. For the association, the process enabled it to legitimate its behavior and thus gain immediate support from the center. Given the fact that the center participated in the process of decision-making of the association, it was easy for the association to

---

[17] Interview with provincial officials of Guangxi (Nanning, 24 June 1993).
[18] *Ibid.*

Table 7.5 Major Central Ministries and Leaders Involved in the ECASC Conferences (1984–1998)

Date	Central Ministries and Leaders Involved
1984	• Liu Shinian (Deputy Director of State Planning Commission) • Wang Zhanyi (Vice Minister of Communications) • Jiang Yiwei (economist, Advisor to the State Council) • State Economic Commission, State Commission of Science and Technology, Ministry of Posts and Telecommunications, Ministry of Coal Industry, Ministry of Water and Power, Ministry of Chemical Industry, Ministry of Nonferrous Metals
1985	• Wang Guangying (Vice Chairman of the Chinese People's Consultative Conference) • Tong Dalin (economist, Advisor to Deng Xiaoping) • State Planning Commission, State Economic Commission, State Commission of Science and Technology, State Commission of Economic Reforms, Office for Third Front Construction
1986	• Research Bureau of the Secretariat of the Central Committee of the CCP, Research Office of the State Council, State Planning Commission, State Economic Commission, State Commission of Science and Technology, State Commission of Economic Reforms, Office for Third Front Construction
1988	• Wang Zhanyi (Vice Minister of Communications) • State Commission on Nationalities, Ministry of Petroleum Industry, Ministry of Economy and Trade, Ministry of Mechanical Engineering, Ministry of Materials, Office for Third Front Construction
1990	• Tian Jiyun (member of the Political Bureau of the Central Committee, Vice Premier Minister of the State Council) • Zhao Yannian (Deputy Director of State Commission on Nationalities) • Tu Yourui (Vice Minister of Railways) • Wan Baorui (Vice Director of Planning Bureau of Ministry of Agriculture) • State Commission on Nationalities, Ministry of Agriculture, Ministry of Economy and Trade, Ministry of Communications, Ministry of Energy, Ministry of Construction, Ministry of Railways, Ministry of Nonferrous Metals, Office for Third Front Construction
1991	• Liao Hansheng (Vice Chairman of the Standing Committee of NPC) • Wang Hanbin (Vice Chairman of the Standing Committee of NPC)

(Continued)

Table 7.5 (*Continued*)

Date	Central Ministries and Leaders Involved
	• Liu Zhongyi (Minister of Agriculture) • Zhou Ping (Deputy Director of State Commission of Science and Technology) • Gao Lianqing (Director of Bureau of Land Planning of the State Planning Commission) • Huan Tianhua (Director of Bureau of Long-Term Planning of the State Planning Commission)
1992	• Tian Jiyun (member of the Political Bureau of the Central Committee, Vice Prime Minister of the State Council) • Li Lanqing (Minister of Economy and Trade) • Gu Xiulian (Minister of Chemical Industry) • Wu Jinghua (Deputy Director of State Commission on Nationalities) • Zheng Guandi (Vice Minister of Communications) • Ke Deming (Deputy Director of General Bureau of China's Civil Aviation) • Zhang Pan (Deputy Director of Development Research Center of the State Council) • Zhou Changqing (Deputy Director of Office for Third Front Construction)
1993	• Zheng Guandi (Vice Minister of Communications) • Zhang Pan (Deputy Director of Development Research Center of the State Council) • Lu Dadong (Director of Office for Third Front Construction) • Shen Longhai (Director of Bureau of Land Planning of State Planning Commission) • Li Tienjun (Deputy Director of Planning Bureau of State Planning Commission) • Ministry of Internal Trade, Office for Special Economic Zones of the State Council
1995	• Chen Yaobang (Deputy Director of State Planning Commission) • Yu Xiaosong (Deputy Director of State Commission of Economy and Trade) • Cha Keming (Vice Minister of Power) • Liu Pingyuan (Vice Minister of Posts and Telecommunications) • Zhao Yundong (Deputy Director of Office for Special Economic Zones of the State Council)

(*Continued*)

Table 7.5 (*Continued*)

Date	Central Ministries and Leaders Involved
	• Zhang Pan (Deputy Director of Development Research Center of the State Council) • Wang Lulin (Vice President of Chinese Academy of Social Sciences) • Deng Hongxun (Deputy Director of Development Research Center of the State Council)
1996	• Pagbalha Geleg Namgyai (Vice Chairman of the Standing Committee of NPC) • Lu Zhiqiang (Deputy Director of Development Research Center of the State Council) • Liu E (Vice Minister of Communications) • Yao Zhongmin (Vice President of State Development Bank) • Zhao Haipei (Vice President of Economic Planning Institute of Ministry of Railways) • Ministry of Finance, Ministry of Communications, State Development Bank, General Bureau of Civil Aviation, Ministry of Foreign Trade, Ministry of Power, Ministry of Posts and Telecommunications, Ministry of Civil Affairs
1997	• Zou Jiahua (Vice Premier Minister) • Yang Rudai (Vice Chairman of the Chinese People's Political Consultative Conference) • Hu Xijie (Vice Minister of Communications) • Cheng Wendong (Deputy Director of the State Tourist Bureau) • Ministry of Economy and Trade, Ministry of Railways, Ministry of Internal Trade, Ministry of Civil Affairs, General Bureau of Civil Aviation, China People's Bank, Ministry of Posts and Telecommunications, Ministry of Communications
1998	• Yang Rudai (Vice Chairman of the Chinese People's Political Consultative Conference) • Xiao Wanjun (Deputy of the Office of Central Policy Studies of the Central Committee) • Chen Shineng (Director of the Bureau of Light Industry) • Lu Jiwei (Vice Minister of Finance) • Lu Zhiqiang (Deputy Director of Development Research Center of the State Council) • Shang Fulin (Vice President of China People's Bank) • Sun Gang (Deputy Director of the State Tourism Bureau)

(*Continued*)

Table 7.5 (*Continued*)

Date	Central Ministries and Leaders Involved
	• Ministry of Finance, Ministry of Railways, Ministry of Economy and Trade, Ministry of Communications, Ministry of State Development Planning Commission, State Development Bank, Development Research Center of the State Council, Ministry of Civil Affairs

Sources: The Secretariat of the ECASC, collected documents of the ECASC annual conferences; fieldworks.

have its decisions endorsed by the center and thus to have them implemented effectively. More importantly, officials from Beijing often helped the association in terms of the presentation of problems. Frequently, the association did not know how a given issue or problem should be presented to the center even though it was able to identify important issues or problems. Since officials from Beijing are familiar with the process of decision-making, they knew how a given issue could be put on the agenda of the central government. As a matter of fact, officials from the central government contributed to the association greatly in the process of issue-formation at the association's annual conferences. A few major examples show how central officials helped the association to formulate its agendas.

At the association's seventh conference in 1990, Zhao Yannian, Vice Director of the State Commission on Nationalities, suggested that issues related to minority affairs should be put on the association's agenda. According to Zhao, the association could establish itself as a model in dealing with minority affairs and should provide the central government with important information about the region's minority affairs, as well as policy proposals. Zhao argued that the association needed to make use of the advantages of the minority areas in the region to develop border trade. It seemed to Zhao, since the minority issues were becoming increasingly an important agenda for the central government, the association's request to develop border trade should not meet with great difficulty for central approval (The Secretariat of ECASC, 1990: 143–146).

Wan Baorui, Vice Director of the Planning Bureau of the Ministry of Agriculture, also argued that minority issues should become an agenda for the association and be brought to the central government. Wan presented the problems of minority affairs from the perspective of agricultural development. According to Wan, many minority peoples were living in the southwest region that had rather poor infrastructures in agriculture and communications. Since the reform, the disparities between the region and other regions, especially coastal areas, had been continuously enlarged. The Ministry of Agriculture was also worried about whether the region's agriculture could be developed. The region needed to depend mainly on itself to achieve agricultural growth, but the central government also needed to provide various forms of support.

As mentioned, many policy proposals raised by the association were indeed accepted by the central leadership. In 1988, the center provided the region with several special agricultural funds that played an important role in promoting the region's agricultural development. After Tibet became a member of the association, the center also gave greater priority to agricultural growth there and many agricultural programs had been implemented. Without policy input by the association, the central government could not have implemented such preferential agricultural policies towards the region.

Indeed, the Ministry of Agriculture very much appreciated the policy proposals raised by the association since these proposals brought the issues of agricultural development to the central leadership. To a great degree, the Ministry of Agriculture and the association had a common goal, i.e., to promote the region's agricultural development. The ministry needed provincial cooperation in formulating central agricultural policies towards the region. According to Wan, the ministry would continue to provide the association with various forms of support because of this common goal (*ibid.*: 150–151).

The significance of the involvement of central officials was also shown in the formulation of policies of infrastructure construction. Also at the seventh conference, Tu Yourui, Vice Minister of Railways, stated that his ministry had put priority on railway construction in the region because of its rich resources. But overall, infrastructure construction had been rather slow. Tao suggested that the association make further efforts to assign the highest priority to railway construction and plan major construction projects in the region. Tao promised the association that his ministry would certainly cooperate with the association to gain central support to build a systematic communications network in the region. Also the ministry would give priority to connecting the region's railway system to those in other regions such as the northwest, central China and the southeast since such a communications system could lay down a foundation for the region's economic take-off. Tu also proposed that the association and his ministry could take joint action for this purpose (*ibid.*: 147–149).

At the eighth conference in 1991, Huang Tianhua and Gao Lianqing, two high-level officials from the State Planning Commission, sent the association a signal that the central government would put its emphasis on developing agriculture, energy, communications, telecommunications and the raw materials industry based on its Eighth FYP and the 10-Year Plan. According to them, the association needed to give high priority to these fields so that it could gain financial aid and other forms of support from the center. Further, the association had to make full use of preferential policies that the center already gave to the region (The Secretariat of ECASC, 1991: 107–113). Huang indicated that the central government was planning to promote economic cooperation between the southwest and south regions. Hainan province was to become the greatest special economic zone, but the province itself had very limited resources and had to rely heavily on the southwest region. The State Council was planning on how the southwest and south areas could be integrated. Therefore, if the association could take initiatives in leading cooperation between the two regions, it would certainly gain strong central support (*ibid.*: 114–115).

The cooperation between the association and central officials was undoubtedly effective in formulating central policies towards the region. In 1993, the State Council formally issued an important central policy towards the southwest and southeast regions. The policy, entitled *Essentials of Regional Planning for Some Provinces and Autonomous Regions in Southwest and Southeast,* was largely based on various proposals raised by the ECASC and other provinces in the southeast region (The State Council, 1993). The central government indicated that it would give development priority to the two regions, especially in minority areas. The document marked a major priority shift of the center's regional development policy from the coastal areas to inland regions.

ESTABLISHING PROVINCIAL DYNAMISM IN CHINA'S FOREIGN TRADE

At the ninth conference in 1992, Vice Premier Tian Jiyun, Economic and Trade Minister Li Lanqing, and other high-level central officials, were involved in the process of one of the association's major decisions, i.e., opening up the region to foreign countries. It is worthwhile examining how the center and the association jointly made this decision since it will enable us to see how far the association can go in influencing foreign trade policies.

Background

Before the post-Mao reform, China's foreign trade was highly centralized. As one Chinese scholar described it, "foreign trade was centralized in a few foreign trade companies managed directly by the central government, foreign exchange was under unified controls by the state banks, all export and import businesses were planned by the state, and all costs and profits were only linked to state finances" (Chong, 1988: 135). After the reform began, the central government implemented various reform measures toward foreign trade. In July 1979, the center carried out a special policy for foreign trade in Guangdong and Fujian provinces, a policy that enabled the two provinces to engage in direct foreign trade. In August that year, the center decided to decentralize foreign trade. Those regions that had customs offices could directly engage in exports and use foreign exchange revenues that occurred to them. In 1980, the central government also decentralized a portion of authority over imports to the localities. Companies managed by local governments could undertake direct import businesses.

In 1982, the central government decided to expand the power of foreign trade for coastal provinces. Foreign trade in the coastal areas was to be managed by both the center and the provinces. Provincial governments were granted greater autonomy and were responsible for deficits or profits in foreign trade, but they had to achieve the quota for foreign exchange earnings that the central government assigned to them. In 1984, the central government decided that the state's special companies should not monopolize all foreign trade businesses; so many other small and medium companies were allowed to engage in foreign trade. Competition was introduced among foreign trade companies.

Meanwhile, foreign exchange management was decentralized. In order to provide local governments with incentives in promoting foreign trade, the central government in 1980 allowed the provinces to retain a portion of foreign exchange earnings from their foreign trade. Guangdong and Fujian provinces could retain 70 percent of their total foreign exchange over five years (1980–1985). In other regions, two main policies were implemented. The first policy concerned the export of commodities that were under the control of the central government. Within this category, the provinces could retain 20 percent of foreign exchange earnings, which had to be distributed between the provincial governments and the enterprises. The second policy concerned the commodities that were under the control of the provincial government, and provinces could retain 40 percent of foreign exchange earnings, which had to be distributed among provincial governments, county governments and enterprises. Later, the central government modified those policies, mainly adjusting the shares of foreign exchange between the center and the provinces, but no dramatic change occurred. In 1988, the central government implemented two other major policies, i.e., to increase the provinces' retention portion of foreign exchange, and to open the foreign exchange market nationwide. The state's mandate plans for foreign exchange were abandoned, and local governments at different levels and enterprises were allowed to purchase and sell foreign exchange in the market.

Decentralization changed the relationship between the center and the provinces, and enabled the provinces to make full use of the decentralization strategy as an effective means to seek benefits for themselves. According to one economic official in Beijing, the decentralization of decision-making power for foreign trade was to promote China's foreign trade, but it had become an effective means for local governments to seek benefits from the central government. The provinces had used various means to get the central government's financial support for their foreign trade business. Because the central government subsidized local exports, local governments were encouraged to develop their exports as fast as possible. Therefore, the more exports local governments achieved, the more benefits they could get from the central government, and the more subsidies the central government had to provide (*ibid.*: 145–146).

The ECASC and Foreign Trade

For many years after its establishment, the ECASC gave its priority to internal economic cooperation, and foreign trade did not become an important agenda. But at its ninth conference in 1992, the association formed a systematic policy program for foreign trade. This program consisted of a package of policies that were based on the region's comparative advantages in developing foreign trade. Importantly, this package of policies received immediate support from the central government. The program also gained popularity among minority peoples in the region.[19] How could this policy be effectively made?

The ECASC never mentioned how to take collective action to develop the region's foreign trade until its sixth conference held in Lhasa, the capital city of the Tibet Autonomous Region, from 30 June to 7 July 1989, immediately after the crackdown on the 1989 pro-democracy movement in Beijing. Indeed, the major theme of the conference was still on how to promote internal economic cooperation within the region. Nonetheless, the conference issued

---

[19] Fieldwork (Nanning, Guangxi, 27 June 1993).

two supplementary documents regarding the region's "open door" policy, entitled *Four Supplementary Recommendations on How to Speed Up the Region's Open Door Policy* (hereafter *Four Recommendations*), and *Some Problems that the Association's Members Need to Consider Jointly in Implementing the Central Government's Economic Development Strategy in the Coastal Areas* (hereafter *Some Problems*). In the *Four Recommendations*, the association argued,

> Peace and dialogues have become a major trend in international relations, and this trend has led to new changes in China's relations with its neighboring countries and regions. Many of our neighboring countries have taken initiatives in developing relations, especially economic relations, with China. Southwest China has more than 1,600 kilometers of coastline and more than 8,000 kilometers of land-line and adjoins seven countries in Southeast and South Asia. Therefore, the association believes that the region has to not only use the region's customs to develop its economy and foreign trade, but also explore markets in neighboring countries and promote border trade so that an overall development of the region's international economy can be achieved (The Secretariat of ECASC, 1989: 54).

The *Four Recommendations* presented the central government with the rationale and feasibility for developing foreign trade. Why should the development of foreign trade become the association's priority? According to the association, the region was short of foreign exchange and could export only primary products, and thus its trade with developed areas such as North America, Europe and Japan was very limited. The region also was not able to compete with China's coastal areas for foreign investment because the coastal areas had a better environment. The region, however, had advantages in terms of natural resources and relatively strong technologies. So, the association had not only to develop trade relations with developed countries through its customs, more importantly, it had to promote trade relations with neighboring countries. Most countries in Southeast and South Asia were still developing and they needed primary products. Engaging in such trade did not require highly advanced technologies and the region could use existing technologies to produce the commodities that Southeast and South Asian countries needed (*ibid*.: 55).

How could the policy of developing foreign trade be implemented? According to the association, in order to realize this plan, it would establish a research group which aimed to achieve the following goals: (1) working out the alternatives of foreign trade, which were feasible in the region, based on the region's geographical conditions and economic development levels; (2) laying out plans for exploring markets in Southeast and South Asia based on extensive studies of these regions; and (3) studying what kinds of flexible policies would be welcomed by neighboring countries. Further, the ECASC needed to take collective action to: (a) coordinate individual provinces' approaches to open border trade; and (b) coordinate individual provinces' industrial policy to act collectively in order to speed up resource exploration and infrastructure construction to lay down a solid basis for foreign trade.

Also, central preferential policies were essential. The central government assigned preferential foreign trade policies to the provinces in northwest China, which had been very effective in promoting the region's foreign trade with Russia and East European countries. The ECASC also needed to be granted such policies to compete with other regions. Moreover, the central government needed to allow the region to become an inland experimental open zone so that the region could build a model of the "open door" for inland areas. Three kinds of experimental zones could be built, i.e., economic exploration zones, processing zones for exports and free trade zones (*ibid.*: 57–58).

The *Some Problems* were mainly about the association's requests to the central government for various forms of special support to the region's foreign trade. According to the association, the conditions in the region for economic development and the "open door" were rather different from those in the advanced coastal areas, and the region needed central support in order to implement central development policies in the region (The Secretariat of ECASC, 1989: 61). The association's requests included:

1. In reforming the state's planning system, the central government should reduce state-mandated quotas for energy and raw materials, which the region originally had to turn over to the center.

2. In reforming its fiscal system, the central government should subsidize the region as an underdeveloped area.

3. In reforming its price system, the central government should increase prices for energy and raw material products so that local governments in the region could benefit from their exploration.

4. In reforming its credit and loan policies, the central government should lessen controls over the scale of loan and investments for the region because, by doing so, it would be very favorable for local governments to make full use of local resources and to absorb foreign investment.

5. In adjusting its investment arrangements, the central government should assign more major projects to the region in order to stimulate the region's development.

6. The central government should consider giving priority to the conversion of military enterprises of the Third Front to civilian production in the region.

7. The central government should implement special policies for border trade as it did for open zones in coastal areas (*ibid.*: 61–63).

The 1989 proposals did not become a part of the association's agenda at its seventh and eighth conferences in 1990 and 1991, even though the two conferences still suggested that the central government consider the 1989 proposals and allow the region to make full use of its advantages in developing foreign trade. Overall, the 1989 proposals laid down a general framework for the region's foreign trade strategy.

After the crackdown on the pro-democracy movement in Beijing, the association again proposed its new foreign trade policy to the central government. After the crackdown, the West immediately imposed serious economic and political sanctions on China. Due to this dramatic change in China's international environment, the conservatives attempted to modify China's foreign policy set forth by Deng Xiaoping.

According to conservative leaders in Beijing, China's international economic activities had to be limited because capitalism was penetrating into China and influencing its political system via economic activities. The ECASC's proposal to promote foreign trade was rather timely and provided strong support to the reform faction in Beijing. According to one government official, "local governments did not follow the central government's retrogressive policy. The ECASC and many other provinces' behavior effectively constrained the rise of conservatives in Beijing. China's economic policy did not retreat dramatically after the Beijing incident in 1989 mainly because localities persisted in progress."[20]

Promoting foreign trade became the most important theme at the association's ninth conference mainly due to three factors. First, Deng's southern tour talks revived the central government's reform policy and reforms regained their momentum. Second, the fact that Deng relied heavily on provincial governments to initiate a new wave of reform implied that provincial officials could gain politically through cooperative attitudes toward the center. Third, the rapid development of foreign trade in the northwest and northeast regions made the ECASC realize that "a new wave of economic competition is taking place and the southwest region had to seize this new opportunity to promote foreign economy."[21] Through intensive communications, provincial leaders decided that the theme of the ninth conference would be the development of the international economy. Provincial leaders in Yunnan and the secretary of the Sichuan Provincial Party Committee, Yang Rudai, played an important role in decision-making (The Secretariat of ECASC, 1992: 43).

The association's ninth conference was held in Kunming from 27 July to 29 July 1993. It was attended by major provincial leaders and those from 28 ministries in Beijing. Vice Prime Minister Tian Jiyun and Economic and Trade Minister Li Lanqing made major speeches on behalf of the central government about the region's foreign trade. The conference focused on how the provinces in the

---

[20] Interview with an economic official in the Development Research Center of the State Council (Beijing, 25 July 1993).

[21] Interview with a provincial economic official of Guangxi (Nanning, Guangxi, 24 June 1993).

region could develop horizontal cooperation to promote the region's foreign economy and to explore markets in Southeast and South Asia. The conference issued three major documents on the region's foreign trade, i.e., *The Association's Request For Speeding Up the Open Door Policy Toward Southeast and South Asia, The Association's Proposal on How to Speed Up the Implementation of the Open Door Policy and the Development of Economic and Technological Cooperation*, and *The Association's Proposal on How to Take Collective Action to Implement the Region's Policy on Opening Markets in Southeast and South Asia*. These documents indicated the establishment of the association's overall strategy for foreign trade. A major prerequisite of the formulation of these policies was that both local and central leaders were involved in decision-making. Table 7.6 shows the involvement of major leaders in the 1992 conference.

Provincial Initiatives in Policy-Making

It was the association that took the initiative in making the foreign trade policy for the region. As discussed earlier, two decisions passed at its sixth conference laid down the general framework of the region's strategy for foreign trade. At the next two conferences, the association persuaded the central government to approve those two decisions. In preparing its ninth conference, the association invited major figures in Beijing to take part in the formulation of the agenda of the conference. Actually, before leaders in Beijing came to the conference, they had already discussed the association's requests (The Secretariat of ECASC, 1992: 33). As one provincial official said, "We had flexible policy plans. Bargaining was necessary. We surely needed further efforts to persuade leaders from Beijing to give us preferential policies."[22]

All major provincial leaders in the region expressed their views at the conference. Yang Rudai, the Secretary of the Sichuan Provincial Party Committee and also a member of the Political

---

[22] Interview with a provincial official of Guangxi (Nanning, Guangxi, 24 June 1993).

Table 7.6 Major Leaders and Government Officials Involved in the ECASC's Ninth Conference (1992)

Name	Position
Tian Jiyun	Member of the Political Bureau, Vice Prime Minister
Li Lanqing	Minister of Economy and Trade
Gu Xiulian	Minister of Chemical industry
Wu Jinghua	Deputy Director of State Commission on Nationalities
Zheng Guangdi	Vice Minister of Communications
Ke Deming	Vice Director of General Bureau of China Civil Aviation
Zhang Pan	Deputy Director of Development Research Center of the State Council
Zhou Changqing	Deputy Director of Office for Third Front Construction of the State Council
Xun Xinghua	President of General Cigarette Corporation
Li Jianzhi	Deputy Director of State Bureau of Construction Materials
Zhang Jian	Vice President of General Corporation of Nonferrous Metals
Yu Yian	Vice President of General Corporation of Trust and Investment
Sheng Zhijie	Engineer-General of Ministry of Railways
Zhu Zhuanheng	Manager-General in Planning, Ministry of Construction
Yang Rudai	Member of the Political Bureau, Secretary of Sichuan Provincial Party Committee
Diao Jinxiang	Vice Governor of Sichuan Province
Zhu Rongyi	Director of Economic Coordination Bureau of Sichuan
Pu Chaozhu	Secretary of Yunnan Provincial Party Committee
He Zhiqiang	Governor of Yunnan Province
Yi Jun	Vice Secretary of Yunnan Provincial Party Committee
Bao Yongkang	Vice Governor of Yunnan Province
Li Shuji	Vice Governor of Yunnan Province
Liu Zhengwei	Secretary of Guizhou Provincial Party Committee
Wang Chaowen	Governor of Guizhou Province
Liu Yulin	Vice Governor of Guizhou Province
Zhao Fulin	Secretary of Guangxi Autonomous Region Party Committee
Cheng Kejie	Governor of Guangxi
Chen Ren	Vice Governor of Guangxi
Lin Chaoqun	Member of Standing Committee of Guangxi Party Committee
Zhang Xuezhong	Vice Secretary of Tibet Autonomous Region Party Committee
Pu Qiong	Vice Governor of Tibet
Xiao Yang	Secretary of Chongqing Municipal Party Committee

(Continued)

Table 7.6 (*Continued*)

Name	Position
Shang Tongchuan	Mayor of Chongqing
Wang Tingdian	Director of Economic Coordination Bureau of Chongqing
Wu Xihai	Secretary of Chengdu Municipal Party Committee
Huang Yinkui	Mayor of Chengdu

Source: Fieldwork, Nanning, Guangxi, June 1993.

Bureau of the Central Committee, emphasized that whether the association could be successful in developing its foreign trade depended on two prerequisites, i.e., effective internal cooperation and external support from the center. According to Yang, because a market economy in the country had developed so fast, competition in domestic markets was becoming very intense. At the same time, the world economy, including Southeast Asia, tended to be regionalized. Yang argued that "we have to take collective action to develop our international economy. Sichuan and Guizhou are inland provinces and we have no coastline and cannot get direct access to the markets in Southeast Asia. We therefore need the help from Guangxi and Yunnan which have long borders and coastlines. On the other hand, Guangxi and Yunnan can benefit from cooperation with Sichuan and Guizhou, which have more advanced industrial infrastructure and technologies" (The Secretariat of ECASC, 1992: 32–33).

Nevertheless, the region still needed central support to develop foreign trade. The region had been a poor area in the country, and the war against Vietnam had a negative impact on the region, especially Yunnan and Guangxi. Yang stressed that it was very important to make full use of current opportunities to speed up the open-door policy toward Southeast and South Asia, and the region needed the central government's special and preferential policy to support our foreign trade. According to Yang, top leaders in Beijing already began to pay special attention to the region's development when the Political Bureau discussed the country's reform and open-door policy. As a matter of fact, the center already met some of the association's requests, and many cities along borders, coastlines and in the provincial capitals were opened. But that was not enough. Yang expressed his hope, saying that "many leaders from Beijing are attending this conference, and we believe that they will give us further support" (*ibid.*: 33).

Pu Chaozhu, the Secretary of the Yunnan Provincial Party Committee, linked the association's foreign trade strategy to Deng's southern tour talks and pointed out,

> Many countries have given priority to economic development in order to gain a favorable position in a new world order. Southeast Asia is becoming significant economically, politics in this region has been stable, and the region is becoming a "hot spot" for investment. Domestically, China is engaging a new wave of reform and its international economy is expanding rapidly. We need to explore new world markets continuously. Otherwise, we will have great difficulty in sustaining economic growth. So, we have to open our southern door to integrate our economy with those in Southeast and South Asia. In other words, developing the region's international economy is significant for both the region and the nation as a whole (*ibid.*: 38–39).

Zhang Xuezhong, Vice Secretary of the Tibet Autonomous Region Party Committee, emphasized the importance of the establishment of trade relations between the Tibet region and south Asian countries, mainly Nepal, Burma and India. According to him, developing foreign trade could not only promote economic growth in the region, but also increase connections between different minority peoples and the Han majority. Zhang argued that the central government needed to invest in infrastructure construction in the region since poor infrastructure had "constrained seriously the region's economic as well as social development" (*ibid.*: 83). Zhang also argued that other association members had to cooperate with Tibet to develop foreign trade since Tibet had many advantages in doing so, given the fact that the central government had granted Tibet greater autonomy in developing its international economy.

Zhao Fulin, Secretary of the Guangxi Autonomous Region Party Committee, argued that the central government should provide various forms of support to Guangxi: (1) allowing the Beihai (a major coastal city in the association) Open Economic Zone to enjoy the policies that the central government had granted to the other coastal economic zones such as those in Guangdong and Hainan so that the association could make joint efforts to build the Beihai zone; (2) allowing the association to build a *baoshuiqu* (tax exemption zone)[23] in Beihai, where all association members could enjoy its privileges; (3) implementing policies in Qinzhou (a major port in Guangxi) that other open cities in the country had enjoyed; (4) allowing the association to establish a development bank that would be managed collectively by all association members; and (5) assigning major construction projects to the region (The Secretariat of ECASC, 1992: 72–80).

Other major leaders also reported their plans to establish a foreign trade development strategy and demanded strong central support. Those leaders included Diao Jinxiang (Vice Governor of Sichuan), He Zhiqiang (Governor of Yunnan), Liu Zhengwei (Secretary of the Guizhou Provincial Party Committee), Wang Chaowen (Governor of Guizhou), Xiao Yang (Secretary of the Chongqing Municipal Party Committee), Shang Tongchuan (Mayor of Chongqing) and Wu Xihai (Secretary of the Chengdu Municipal Party Committee). The association coordinated individual provinces' requests to the central government and submitted three decisions for central approval.

In *The Association's Proposal on How to Speed Up the Implementation of the Open Door Policy and the Development of Economic and Technological Cooperation*, the association defined how foreign trade could be promoted through internal cooperation among all association members. These measures (11 articles) can be briefly summarized as follows:

1. The association members would establish joint ventures or individual enterprises in major cities along the coastline and the border, and all such enterprises would enjoy preferential policies granted by both the central and local governments.

---

[23] The *baoshuiqu* is a special zone that extends the central government's special preferential taxation policy.

2. The provincial governments in the association would exempt those enterprises from some categories of taxes to increase their capacity for further development.

3. Individual provinces would support other association members to establish such enterprises in the above areas and grant the association the authority to coordinate their activities.

4. For those enterprises (in Article 1) that are in the areas of energy exploration, exports, advanced technologies and infrastructure construction, provincial governments would reduce their import custom duties.

5. Individual provinces had complete freedom to engage in border trade, except for those commodities that were prohibited by state regulations.

6. The association would encourage and support enterprises to act collectively to invest in Southeast and South Asia. Such enterprises could engage in technological exchanges with and export labor services to the countries there.

7. The association would establish companies or exchange centers for importing and exporting commodities. Profits would be distributed among the association members proportionally, based on their financial contributions. All provinces would follow the association's regulations when they conducted business with other countries.

8. The association members would have complete autonomy to decide the management styles, manager-labor relations and internal distribution for the enterprises in border, coastal and open cities.

9. The association members would be permitted to invest in other provinces of the association in the fields of port construction, communications, energy and telecommunications. Benefits would be distributed among provinces according to their contracts.

10. The association would organize an annual commodities fair in Kunming to attract foreign investors, especially those from Southeast and South Asia.

11. The association would establish coordination offices in Kunming and Nanning to coordinate provinces' business contacts with Southeast and South Asia.

The Association's Proposal on How to Take Collective Action to Implement the Region's Policy on Opening Markets in Southeast and South Asia contains some concrete plans on opening markets in neighboring countries. It consists of eight articles, briefly summarized as follows:

1. Guangxi and Yunnan needed to work together to establish concrete proposals, projects and methods on collective action for communicating among association members.
2. Guangxi and Chongqing were responsible for setting forth the proposals on port construction and maritime business.
3. Yunnan and Guangxi were responsible for proposing an international road transportation project and its concrete plans.
4. Yunnan was in charge of laying out the proposal for building a stock company for jewelry and gem production within the association.
5. Chongqing and Chengdu needed to work together to initiate proposals for foreign trade conferences, commodities fairs, and border trade conferences, mainly with Southeast and South Asia.
6. Guizhou and Tibet needed to work together, in cooperation with the association's tourism office, to form tourism plans for the association and to establish connections with countries in Southeast and South Asia.
7. Yunnan and Guangxi needed to make concrete plans to establish joint offices for coordination between Kunming and Nanning.
8. After receiving an approval from the State Council, Sichuan, Chongqing and Chengdu needed to work together to develop concrete plans for establishing the Southwest International Trust and Investment Company.

The Association's Request for Speeding Up the Open Door Policy Toward Southeast and South Asia contains the association members' joint requests and policy proposals for the central government, briefly summarized as follows:

1. Implementing policies that the central government had carried out in Special Economic Zones (SEZs) within state-designated border economic cooperation zones and economic and technological

exploration zones in the region, which if met the state's conditions, should be allowed to establish tax-exemption zones. implementing SEZ policy in the Beihai and Fangcheng areas (two major ports in Guangxi); allowing Chengdu and Guiyang and Tibet to enjoy the same policies as the coastal open cities did; granting Qinzhou (a major port in Guangxi) the open city status; establishing Jinghong (Yunnan) and Yandong (Tibet) as open-border counties and state customs points; resuming Guangxi's sea trade.

2. Allowing the association members to jointly establish the Beihai Economic Coordination Zone in Beihai and Processing Zones for Exports in Guangxi and Yunnan respectively.

3. Allowing each association member to establish a general foreign trade corporations in major ports and boundary cities, and granting those corporations central border trade policies.

4. Allowing open cities along the border and coastline to establish foreign trade corporations to engage in international trade, and international economic and technological cooperation; allowing each association member to establish a foreign trade company to engage in international trade.

5. Decentralizing trade quotas and trade licenses to Guangxi, Yunnan and Tibet; allowing these three provincial governments to share an essential portion of the trade quota and licenses.

6. Assigning major projects involving China, and Southeast and South Asian countries to the association; allowing the provinces to open businesses in those countries.

7. Allowing enterprises in the region to engage in technological exchange and the export of labor services with countries in Southeast and South Asia, and to retain all profits they made; lessening central limits on the import business.

8. Granting the association the power to approve joint ventures under US$50 million, and increasing central investment in the enterprises that were built through economic cooperation between the association and other provinces in open areas, and exempting them from taxes on investment adjustment, energy and communications construction.

9. Allowing the association to establish the Southwest International Trust and Investment Bank and granting the authority to issue stocks, both home and abroad; obtaining loans for the association from international organizations; and foreign governments; and allowing the association to open banks attracting investment from foreign business.

10. Allowing the association to retain more of its tax profits to accumulate financial sources to speed up the construction of a communications system; giving priority to the Nanning-Kunming railway when the center considered its investment plans; supporting the association to build or connect international roads and open international airlines to the countries in Southeast and South Asia.

Reaction from the Center

What were the options available to leaders and officials from Beijing toward the association's requests? Before they came to the conference, some of them actually participated in the formulation of these proposals, so they had prepared some flexible policy alternatives in answering the association's requests. In effect, they had to cooperate with the provincial governments. According to one official in Beijing, since the provincial government was an internal part of China's state organizations, the central government had to rely on the provincial government to get its job done. Now that the association had taken policy initiatives, it was not necessary for the central government to satisfy all of the association's requests. Bargaining was important between the center and the provinces, and compromises had to be reached; otherwise, cooperation could not be achieved. Without cooperation between the two, there would be disorder between the center and the provinces.[24]

At the conference, the association members brought up new requests. Leaders and officials from Beijing normally could not reject

---

[24] Interview with an official in the Development Research Center of the State Council (Beijing, 24 July 1993).

them. Neither could they accept them without any bargaining. Delayed decisions were acceptable for the provinces. As a matter of fact, provincial government officials did not expect immediate answers from the center. One provincial officials said, "Our aim is to make leaders from Beijing understand the significance of the major problems we raised and provincial leaders will do their best to persuade major leaders in Beijing to agree to our decisions."[25]

Regarding the association's requests and proposals, Tian Jiyun made a major speech. Indeed, Tian criticized the association that the region had developed its international economy rather slowly. For example, up to 1991, the total exports of the association's five provinces were only about 4 percent of the total of all provinces, and the region only absorbed about 2 percent of total foreign investment. Tian argued that the provincial leaders in the region needed to open their minds further in developing international economy. According to Tian, the central government had provided and would continue to provide different forms of support to the region. For instance, the Central Committee of the CCP and the State Council had decided to open cities in the southwest region, including Kunming and Nanning (two capital cities) and five border cities, i.e., Pingxiang, Dongxing, Ruili, Wanding and Hekou. Two inland cities, i.e., Guiyang and Chengdu, also could enjoy preferential policies as other open cities did. The central government did so in order to combine the coastal and inland areas and to promote fast economic development in inland regions. Nevertheless, the association's internal cooperation is also very important. Individual provinces would meet great difficulty in opening markets in Southeast and South Asia because the level of economic development in the region was still rather low. Without effective internal cooperation, the central government's support alone would not work. Tian emphasized that the central government surely supported some of the association's proposals and the disagreements between the center and the association at this conference would be taken to the central government. After further discussion, decisions would be made (The Secretariat of ECASC, 1992: 23–30).

---

[25] Interview with a provincial official of Guangxi (Nanning, Guangxi, 25 June 1993).

Li Lanqing replied to the association's concrete proposals on behalf of the central government and his Ministry. According to Li, the central government had agreed to most proposals that the association submitted, but there were still disagreements that the central government needed to give further consideration. The requests that the central government approved include: (1) allowing the association to establish foreign trade in import and export activities in open cities along the coastline and borderline in Guangxi, Yunnan and Tibet; (2) decentralizing the power of issuing licenses for foreign trade to provincial and municipal governments; (3) assigning the association China's major cooperation projects with the countries in Southeast and South Asia. But Li pointed out, since some proposals submitted by the association were far beyond the jurisdiction of his ministry, they would be discussed further by the central leadership (*ibid.*: 98–101).

It is worthwhile discussing Wu Jinghua's attitude toward the association's requests. As Deputy Director of the State Commission on Nationalities, Wu was in charge of minority affairs in Beijing. Every year, his Commission attempted to gain more financial resources and other preferential policies from the state budget by bargaining with major leaders and other ministries. To reduce the Commission's financial burden, the Commission indeed encouraged local governments in minority areas to seek more support from central bureaucracies. The commission's position was that it had to cooperate with the association in its bargaining with the central government and its bureaucracies.

At the conference, Wu first emphasized that the southwest region was a minority area. Based on this factor, Wu argued that "central ministries and provincial governments have to give priority to the minority population when they make any sort of decisions" (*ibid.*: 108–109). Wu quoted the General Secretary of the CCP Jiang Zemin to indicate the importance of the minority problem. Jiang once argued that China's minority problems were mainly about how to achieve rapid economic and cultural development.

Wu stressed that economic development in the region needed not only internal cooperation within the association, but also depended on strong support from the center. The center had to consider the special conditions of the region and grant it more preferential policies. Wu, on behalf of his Commission, expressed a total support of *Association's Request for Speeding Up the Open Door Policy Toward Southeast and South Asia.* Nevertheless, according to Wu, the association had to explain its difficulties fully and add further requests. For instance, the association should consider how to help the minority populations to speed up their economic and cultural construction. Wu argued that the minority areas along the region's borders should enjoy not only the preferential policies that *Association's Request* listed, but also special policies for minority autonomous areas, and the central government and ministries concerned should consider the region's minority population when they discuss *Association's Request.* Wu also suggested that "the provincial governments have to study how to make full use of preferential policies and how to combine central policies with the region's reality and to implement these policies flexibly" (*ibid.*: 111–112).

Many other officials of various ministries also expressed their support for the association's policy proposals. They emphasized the importance of cooperation between their ministries and the provinces in the association. Some ministries such as the Ministry of the Chemical Industry also showed its strong interest in establishing joint ventures with the association.

In mid-1993, the State Planning Commission issued (1993) document No. 387 and made a formal decision on the association's *Request* on promoting the region's foreign economy. According to this document,

1. The association members were allowed to open boundary trade companies in the state-designated open ports; each association member was allowed to open an international economic and technological cooperation corporation in the state-designated open cities along the borderlines and coastlines; the central government decentralized power of issuing licenses for a portion of export commodities to Guangxi, Yunnan, and Tibet; the central government gave priority to the association when it distributed

major economic and technological cooperation projects between China and countries in Southeast and South Asia.

2. Taxes on land for road construction could not be exempted, but the central government would lower the tax rate in poor areas in the region.

3. A Southwest Development Bank and a Southwest International Trust and Investment Bank were temporarily disallowed. Regarding the association proposals to establish a Southwest stock market, the provinces in the association were allowed to undertake experiments in joint stocks enterprises, and to issue stocks in Shanghai or other places.

4. Tax exemption zones were temporarily disallowed (*Keji Jingmao Bao*, 25 June 1993).

CONCLUSION

The provincial government is an internal part of the Chinese state and thus has to follow the central government's administrative mandates. From this perspective, the provincial government is an agent of policy implementation of the central government, as many have argued. Provincial officials, however, have their own interests and passions. They have *de facto* autonomy in understanding and implementing policies made in Beijing. Disagreements exist between the center and the provinces, and bargaining between the two is necessary to reach a compromise.

Given the fact that the provincial government has played an increasingly important role in promoting local development, it is no longer an agent of policy implementation for the central government. The provinces often take policy initiatives and make major policies for the central government. Although their *de jure* autonomy in policy-making has to be legitimated and their decisions approved by the central government, they have *de facto* autonomy in policy-making. Except those decisions over matters that are still under the control of the central government, the provinces have full freedom in deciding what they want to do, or what they want people in their jurisdictions to do.

Individual provinces in the southwest region are weak in bargaining with the central government simply because the central government cannot extract many resources from them. Because these provinces are poor, they need to bargain with the central government to gain strong central support. Realizing their common interests, the provinces formed a coalition and engaged in collective bargaining with the central government and its bureaucracies. Collective action has been very effective in extracting resources (financial support and preferential policies) from the center. But the association is not an interest group. The association has to be legitimated by the central government and acts within the boundary of the state, and it is the central government that forms the boundary in which the association acts. In other words, the relationship between the center and the province is interdependent. Bargaining between them is inevitable. Nevertheless, the two actors cannot be too selfish during the process and each side has to take the other party's interests into consideration. Without the other party's cooperation, bargaining will go nowhere.

The central government needs cooperation from the provincial governments. This is especially true in the post-Mao era because of the provincial government's policy initiatives. Decentralization means that the central government devolves decision-making power and responsibility to lower-level governments in order to reduce its burden. In doing so, the central government faces a dilemma. On the one hand, the central government has to decentralize its decision-making power and benefits in order to provide the local governments with incentives to help achieve its grand goal of economic development. On the other hand, decentralization often leads the local government to deviate from the central government's grand goal. To resolve this dilemma, bargaining between the central government and the local government has to be institutionalized, so that disagreements between the two are expected to be resolved through bargaining.

The provincial governments in the association also need cooperation from the central government. The association cannot work effectively without coordination by a higher and external organization, i.e., the central government. The provinces in the southwest region formed the association to strengthen their bargaining power with the central government, but great disagreements exist among the provinces, especially in the areas of financial contributions and distribution of benefits. Without external coordination, the association itself would have great difficulty in making decisions that effectively serve all the provinces. As one provincial official pointed out, "we need officials from Beijing to supervise and coordinate our activities, otherwise, the association cannot work well. Since all the provincial officials are at the same administrative level, no one has authority over anyone else. Only central officials have such authority."[26]

Without the central government's strong support, the association cannot engage in major cross-provincial projects such as the construction of communications and telecommunications systems and other infrastructure. The association members need the central government to support such projects. Bargaining with the central government has to be institutionalized to an extent so that the central government and the association can communicate regularly and reach effective decisions together.

---

[26] Interview with a provincial official of Guangxi (Nanning, Guangxi, 26 June 1993).

8

Whither China's *De Facto* Federalism?

To what end will central-local relations develop in China? Based on the major findings that are discussed in the previous chapters, this concluding chapter explores the possible direction of China's *de facto* federalism by placing it in a historical context.

My conclusions can be summarized as follows. Inter-governmental decentralization devolved economic power and a part of central political power to territorially-based lower-level governments. Local governments were granted great autonomy in dealing with local affairs and enabled to play an increasingly important role in promoting local economic development and managing local affairs. Rapid local development pushed an already decentralized system to decentralize further since it strengthened the power of the provinces. Given uneven economic development in China, inter-governmental decentralization, along with the uneven development policy, deepened regional diversities. It was increasingly hard for the central government to manage local affairs through unified policies, and local governments were granted the power to implement central policies flexibly on the one hand, and make their own policies to govern their territories with their intimate local knowledge on the other hand. Again, under inter-governmental decentralization, it became legitimate for local government officials

353

to participate in the formulation of national policies that were relevant to the provinces.

Acknowledging the rise of local power, the central government made continuous efforts to adjust its relations with the provinces and create new institutions to constrain local behavior through a movement of what can be called "selective recentralization," such as the new tax-division system and central banking system, to cope with unwanted consequences resulting from the current *de facto* federal structure. Consequently, great organizational changes have occurred to China's central-local relations.

Nevertheless, due to the absence of meaningful political reforms in terms of central-local relations, it is unlikely that China will institutionalize the *de facto* federal structure. China's provinces continue to be caught between decentralization and recentralization. While inter-governmental decentralization has resulted in enormous unwanted consequences, the central government has found that the provincial governments have to play an increasingly important role in managing local affairs. The *de jure* position of the provinces is still uncertain.

This chapter first reviews briefly the changing role of China's provinces in different historical periods. We will see that the perceived role of the provinces has changed considerably in different historical periods. The province is a deeply-rooted local unit with entrenched interests, and decentralization has been built in the structure of central-local relations, namely, *de facto* federalism. Over the years, while discourses on the role of the provinces change, this *de facto* federal structure has generated many implicit and explicit rules and norms, which actually regulate the interactions between the center and the provinces. This chapter then discusses how the central government has engaged in "selective recentralization" to institutionalize its own power. We will find that although the aim of "selective centralization" is to strengthen central power, it can indeed facilitate the process of the institutionalization of China's *de facto* federalism, namely, each level of government — the center and the provinces — now tends to have their institutionalized and independent powers. Finally, this chapter discusses why China is not ready for making the transition from a *de facto* to a *de jure* federal structure.

PROVINCE (*SHENG*): UNCERTAIN EXPECTATIONS

Sheng is equivalent to "province" in Western political systems. *The Oxford Encyclopedia English Dictionary* defines "province" as "a principal administrative division of a country" (Hawkins & Allen, 1991: 1164). Scholars have regarded the "province" as a level of administration that is subordinate to central authorities. This is also true in China. But China differentiates itself from other countries. Unlike many modern states in the West and elsewhere, the power and responsibilities between the center and the provinces in China are not clearly defined and institutionalized in legal terms. The lack of an institutionalized framework of central-local relations makes it difficult to evaluate the performance of the *sheng*. Conflicts arise between the center and the provinces, but we do not know which part should be responsible for what. To explore in what direction China's provinces are heading, it is useful to look at how their role has changed historically.

While the *sheng* in a modern sense refers to a local unit in traditional China, the concept of *sheng* has actually undergone complicated changes.[1] *Sheng* as a local administrative unit appeared in the Yuan dynasty (1277–1368). Before the Yuan, *sheng* indeed was not a local administrative unit, but a central one, meaning a central "department" or "office." During the Han dynasty (206 BC–AD 220), there was only one Chancellor, with whom the Emperor discussed important policy issues. In the Tang dynasty (618–907), three *shengs*, (*san-sheng*, i.e., three departments of administration) were established to share the functions and powers of the former Chancellor, i.e., *Zhong-shu Sheng* (the Imperial Secretariat), *Men-xia Sheng* (the imperial Chancellery), and *Shang-shu sheng* (the Executive Department).

---

[1] The following description of the traditional system of *sheng* is based on Ch'ien Mu (1982) and Diao Tianding *et al.* (1989).

During the Yuan dynasty, the Mongols introduced a rather drastic change to the *sheng* system. The central executive power was located in the Secretariat (*Zhong-shu sheng*), a position inherited from the Tang, but it was more popularly called *"Du Sheng"*, literally meaning "Office in the Capital." During that time, when a disturbance occurred in a local area, one to two officials would be sent out from the Secretariat to the locality to bring it under control. When away from the capital, these officials constituted a *Xing Sheng* (Itinerant Secretariat), or *Xing Zhong-shu Sheng*, and abbreviated to *Xing Sheng*. Thus the supreme organ of the central government was split into parts, each exercising the powers of the central government in different areas of the country. Clearly, though the *sheng* became a local unit during the Yuan, it was not institutionalized. There were about ten "Itinerant Secretariats," most of the time, during the Yuan. This did not mean, however, that the whole country was divided into ten administrative districts, because these central officials could be sent out or withdrawn at the Emperor's will, and the real purpose of the system of itinerant secretariat was to facilitate central control.

Until the late years of the Yuan, *Xing Sheng* became the highest local government organ. Central orders had to go through *Xing Sheng* in order to reach lower levels of government such as prefectures and counties. Similarly, the reports by prefectural and county governments to the central government had to go through *Xing Sheng*. *Xing Sheng* also had independent power from the central government to make decisions and issue policies over local affairs.

During the Ming dynasty (1368–1644), the *Xing Sheng* system was redefined. Threatened by the growing power of Itinerant Secretariats, the Emperor abolished the system in 1376 and changed the Chiefs of the Itinerant Secretariats into Provincial Administration Commissioners (PAC, or *Cheng-xuan Bu-zheng-si* in Chinese). The PACs were appointed to be in charge of 13 Provincial Administration offices (*Cheng-xuan Bu-zheng-si Si*) and became the highest officials in the provinces. Occasionally, the central government sent out Governors and Governors-General to the provinces to implement specific missions or to coordinate among PACs. Nevertheless, these central officials were not meant to be permanent since their appointments were canceled immediately upon the fulfillment of their missions.

The Qing dynasty (1644–1911) followed the Ming system of the PACs, but the posts of Governors and Governors-General were made permanent local supreme authorities and the PACs were largely in charge of military control over local areas. But for most of the Qing period, especially during war time, the Governors and Governors-General were not the supreme commanders. The central government often sent special envoys to localities to command the military forces directly, and Governors and Governors-General thus became merely liaison personnel receiving orders from these envoys and transmitting them to the PACs. Nevertheless, the *sheng* as a local administrative unit was firmly institutionalized during the Qing. From the Qing onward up to the People's Republic, there had been various debates on many aspects related to the *sheng*, and changes had occurred to the number and size of provinces, but the *sheng* as a local organizational unit had met no challenge.

What role the *sheng* should play, however, was always an issue throughout the last century. How the *sheng* was perceived depended on the changing political circumstances in different time periods. The 1911 revolution overthrew the imperial system, but did not produce a strong central government. After the revolution, the forces of decentralization became dominant in Chinese politics. Local elites at all levels benefited from the revolution simply because they had played a crucial role in initiating it. Provincial officials who had acted autonomously during the revolution sought to strengthen their autonomy and block the resurgence of an all-powerful and autocratic center.

Great political liberalization convinced Yuan Shikai, the most powerful military man in China then, that "the devolution of power from the center to the provinces and localities was inimical to the restoration of Chinese national strength" (Cohen, 1988: 522). Yuan believed that a constitutional monarchy was more appropriate to China's tradition than republicanism and became determined to reestablish the political dominance of the center. Yet, Yuan's various attempts to restore the monarchy failed because of political opposition from all sides. By early 1920, the Republican State began to disintegrate as a constitutional and parliamentary entity, and as a bureaucratic force. China entered a period of warlordism, and the whole country was governed by local warlords. As a matter of fact, with a weak central government, the role of *sheng* was indeed strengthened, and the internal structure of *sheng* was built up (Diao *et al.*, 1989: 82).

During the period of the Nationalist Government (1927–1949), the *sheng* as the highest local administrative unit was strengthened further by introducing changes to its internal structure (*ibid.*). Since the People's Republic was established in 1949, the system of *sheng* has undergone quite considerable changes. In the early 1950s, the *sheng* was not the highest local administrative unit. In order to strengthen Beijing's control over the provincial government, the CCP drew on its lineage of decentralized military base areas and set up six large regions, i.e., the Central-South, East China, the Northeast, the Southeast, North China and the Northwest (Inner Mongolia and Tibet were administrated separately). Meanwhile, for largely the same reasons, the Central Party Committee also established six central bureaus (*zhongyang ju*) in these regions. These regional party organs played a role in implementing the principle of the Party control of government. Regional leaders of both the party organs and governments were allowed considerable experimentation and soon gained much leeway in governing their territories.

The regional administrations were abolished in 1954 when central leaders perceived that some regional leaders were using their regional bases to further their personal political interests. Gao Gang of the Northeast and Rao Shushi of the East regions were purged partly for building "independent kingdoms" and using these to support their bids for more political power (Teiwes, 1993: 45–50). Since 1954, the *sheng* has become the highest local government. According to China's constitution, provincial governments are the executive bodies of the provincial organ of state power, as well as the provincial organs of state administration.[2]

While the *sheng* as the highest unit of local government is institutionalized, this is not the case in regards to what role the provincial government plays in China's political system. Perceptions toward the provincial government are still uncertain. In the early 1950s, following the model of the Soviet Union, China established a highly-centralized state structure, and the regime effectively eliminated local political forces through various political campaigns. Nevertheless, once centralization was achieved, it quickly became apparent that the highly-centralized regime carried its own burden of problems, that there were distinct advantages to decentralization and social initiatives. Since the mid-1950s, the Chinese leadership has begun to pursue a proper relationship between the center and the provinces.

Within the ideational framework of the CCP, the standardized guidelines on how the center and the provinces should deal with their mutual relations were presented by Mao Zedong's *On The Ten Great Relationships* (TGRs) in 1956, where Mao devoted a special chapter to discussing rules regulating central-local relations (Mao, 1977).[3]

---

[2] The provincial government is used in a broad sense to include the provincial Party committee, the provincial government, and the provincial people's congress.

[3] Mao wrote this article in 1956. The article has had several versions. When Mao finished it, it was widely circulated among very senior party cadres and government officials, i.e., ministry and provincial level and above. In 1965, upon Liu Shaoqi's suggestion, Mao allowed the circulation of this article as a party document among cadres and government officials at the county level and above. This version was different from the previous one. In 1975, Deng Xiaoping suggested that the article be reorganized. Mao responded as follows: the new version could be circulated among members of the Political Bureau, but not to be published; it could be circulated and discussed within the party, but could not be brought to the general public, until the selected works of Mao was published in the future. This background is based on Bo (1991: 485–486). It was formally published in 1977 as a part of the fifth volume of Mao's selected works after the death of Mao.

What Mao expressed was some general principles regarding central-local relations. Mao did not attempt to institutionalize the power distribution between the center and the provinces. Instead, he wanted to set up boundaries for both the center and the provinces. Beyond these boundaries, their behavior would be totally unacceptable.

The most important principle is to balance unity and particularity. The center needs to consolidate its unified leadership by centralizing the country's law-making power, while the provinces can have their own regulations, rules and policies in accordance with local conditions. According to Mao (1977: 271),

> We need unity, but we also need particularity. In order to build a strong socialist state, a strong unified central leadership is needed. We have to have national unified plans and disciplines. It will not be allowed to undermine such necessary unity. Meanwhile, we need to promote local initiatives fully, and every locality has to have its "particularity" suitable for its own conditions. Such "particularity" is needed for the interests and the unity of the entire country.

In order to balance unity and particularity, it was imperative to implement decentralization, given the fact that the system was already highly-centralized then. Mao argued that "we cannot follow the Soviet Union, centralizing everything and leaving no leeway for localities" (1977: 275). Indeed, this should always be the case, since "China is such a big country with a huge population and complicated situations, it will be much better to have two initiatives (central and local) than one initiative (central).... To promote socialist construction, it is necessary to promote local initiatives; to consolidate central power, it is necessary to pay attention to local interests" (*ibid.*).

Mao tried to define what he called "legitimate local independence" (*zhengdang de dulixing*) in terms of "particularity." That is, the central government needs to give the provinces independent power to deal with local issues. Local particularity-based local independence is not localism. That local officials seek independent power to deal with local issues should not be viewed as efforts to be independent from the central government (*ibid.*: 277). According to Mao, on the one hand, all local governments should have and should fight for their "legitimate independence," and on the other hand, the central government should "respect local independent power" (*ibid.*: 276).

How can the balance of power between the center and the provinces be achieved? According to Mao, to do so, the center should not arbitrarily impose its policies on the provinces; instead, it should consult with the provinces before policies were formulated. He argued that "we advocate consulting with the localities to deal with issues.... Central ministries should pay attention to this point: whenever they deal with issues that have something to do with the localities, they need to consult with the localities in advance" (Mao, 1977: 276).

Nevertheless, decentralization and independent local power did not mean that local governments could do everything at will. Mao warned, "[we] need to tell our local officials what matters should be dealt with in a unified way, and they cannot act recklessly" (*ibid.*: 277). Actions like Gao Gang and Rao Shushi had taken before, i.e., challenging the authority of the central government, could not be tolerated (*ibid.*: 276).

These principles undoubtedly were quite vague. Thus the question is: Why did Mao not attempt to institutionalize the power distribution between the center and the provinces? This is because, according to Mao, China did not have much experience in dealing with the issues, and it was thus important to adjust continuously central-local relations in accordance with practical changes and also by learning from other countries. Although it is necessary to set up a general institutional framework, central-local relations should be dynamic.

Mao's eagerness to learn from other countries in building central-local relations is also confirmed by Bo Yibo, who participated in making major decisions in the history of the PRC so far. According to Bo, what Mao Zedong did was to reform the Soviet model of central-local relations, which China had adopted, by learning from other models, especially the US model of relations between federal government and states. According to Mao (cited in Bo, 1991: 488),

> The Constitution regulates that local governments do not have the power to make laws, and law-making power is centralized in the National People's Congress. This is learnt from the Soviet Union. In drafting the Constitution, I once asked some comrades whether we should write this way. I heard that the Soviet Union did this way, some capitalist countries did this way too, but the United States did not do this way. States in the US can make laws, and state laws can be in conflict with federal laws.... The United States is very developed, it has done so only in a hundred years and so. This issue is worth noting. We hate American imperialism, which is not good. But the fact that the United States became so advanced has its reasons. Its political system is worth studying. It seems that we need to increase local power. Too limited local power is not favorable for socialist construction.

I discussed the TGRs in such detail because of their continuous great impact on China's central-local relations. The TGRs were published in 1977 after the death of Mao Zedong a year ago, but it was widely circulated among party cadres and government officials since Mao made that speech in 1956. Indeed, it has been required studying material for them since then. The significance of the text was not because it was written by Mao Zedong, but because it was a collective reflection of Chinese political elites. According to Bo Yibo (1991: 466–472), Mao's essay was based on enormous reports by 34 ministries and his own investigations in various provinces conducted in 1955 and 1956. The power of the text lay in the fact that this was a reflection of collective experience by both central and local leaders. Indeed, as Bo Yibo (1991: 470–472) argued, the TGRs were a collective reflection of the Chinese leaders, especially Mao Zedong himself, on the Soviet model and its impact on China. Since it is a collective reflection, it has served as an "ideational paradigm" for guiding both the center and the provinces in their relations.

The impact of Mao's TGRs can be seen in the consistent insistence by the Chinese top leadership on these principles. During the 13th Party Congress (1987), Zhao Ziyang, General Secretary of the CCP then, almost copied what Mao said before, regarding central-local relations. According to Zhao (1987: 437),

> Decisions and functions that can be properly handled at lower levels should be done so there. This is a general principle. In terms of central-local relations, it is essential to gradually distinguish between the duties of each, while ensuring that decrees of the central government are implemented across the country. Thus local matters will be handled by local authorities, while the central authorities determine major policies and exercise supervision.

Zhao reemphasized these principles in an era of great decentralization in the 1980s. But in his essay popularly known as *On Twelve Great Relationships*, Jiang Zemin expressed similar principles in 1995 when the decentralization of the 1980s was widely regarded as undermining central authorities and recentralization had been called for. According to Jiang (1995: 1472–1473),

> To make full use of both central and local initiatives is one of the most important principles in the country's political and economic lives, a principle relating directly to the unity of the country, the solidarity of nationalities, and the coordinated development of the national economy.... Our general principle is: we not only need unity which represents entire interests for the whole country, but also need flexibility which represents partial local interests; we not only need centralization which guarantees the state's macro-control, but also need to give localities necessary power.

Mao did not spell out exactly how power should be distributed between the center and the provinces; nor did Zhao Ziyang and Jiang Zemin. Such a situation is likely to continue. However, beneath these vague principles lies the fact that decentralization is inevitable in some areas, and so is centralization in some other areas. Indeed, this fact is the very basis of China's *de facto* federal structure. In practicing *de facto* federalism, China has developed some formal and informal institutions to regulate the interaction between the center and the provinces. As discussed in this book, among others, three main forms of institution include coercion, bargaining and reciprocity. These institutions have enabled both actors — the center and the provinces — to choose the "right" strategies in their interactions.

DYNAMICS OF *DE FACTO* FEDERALISM

The Rise of Local Power

As discussed in the previous chapters, inter-governmental decentralization was very successful by any measure. It resulted in rapid economic growth and dramatic improvement in people's living standards. The Chinese economy chalked up an average annual growth rate of 9.5 percent during the 1978–1992 period. According to the World Bank, China is to become the world's largest economy in 2010. Using purchasing-power parity calculations of gross domestic product (GDP), China already had the world's second largest economy by the early 1990s (*The Economist*, 1992; Garnaut & Ma, 1993). Indeed, without more than a decade of decentralization, the Chinese economy would not have developed so fast.

Nevertheless, excessive decentralization had its unwanted consequences. First of all, decentralization rendered the existing state structure problematic. Power shifted from the national state to local governments at different levels, but local-central relations were not institutionalized. Even though rapid decentralization did not lead to the breakup of the country, as it did with the Soviet Union, with no effective institutional constraints, localism or regionalism often became uncontrollable and posed a serious challenge to central power.

One sign of the crisis of central power was the decline of the fiscal and financial power of the central government. After the reform began in 1978, central revenue declined continuously until the 1993 taxation reform. Central revenue shrunk from 34 percent of gross national product (GDP) in 1978 to 6 percent in 1995 (Hu, 1996: 2). The provinces even began to resist new fiscal policies initiated by the central government. When the national government asked rich provinces to pay more taxes, resistance from them was increasingly strong. The rich provinces were able to challenge central authority because of their wealth generated by decentralization.

Further, economic decentralization widened income disparities among the provinces and regions. In coastal areas such as Guangdong, Zhejiang, Jiangsu and Shandong, local officials developed very strong non-state sectors including collectives, private economies and joint ventures, each of which was very profitable and beyond the control of the central government. In inland provinces, owing to the lack of financial resources and skilled personnel, local governments had difficulty pushing local growth, let alone adjusting the local industrial structure. Consequently, some provincial governments achieved a high capacity to lead local development and improve local residents' living standards, while others did not. Due to local diversity, the central government often failed to implement unified policies to lead and constrain local governments, and local officials could easily nullify central policies. The central government was thus unable to bring local governments in line with national interests.

By the mid-1990s, uneven development among regions had become a major issue on China's political agenda. Local officials in poor areas called for recentralization and asked the central government to pay more attention to their areas. Obviously, local officials felt great pressure from local residents concerning increasing diversities among regions. According to a survey among government officials at the provincial and prefectural levels in 1994, 84 percent of government officials believed that great regional income disparities would cause social instability, and 16 percent contended that they would lead to national disintegration, especially in minority areas. The same survey also showed that nearly 64 percent of local government officials believed that reducing regional disparities should be the most important political agenda for the national government (Hu, 1994: 88–90).

The decline of central power and authority gave rise to local protectionism and the national government was no longer able to coordinate local economic activities effectively. Rich provinces were reluctant to cooperate with one another when they could design local development independently. Even below the provincial level, coordination was very poor. One study (Taylor, 1990) suggested the fragmentation and lack of coordination in the well-developed Zhujiang Delta of the Guangdong province. Another study by Chinese scholars (Ding & Luo, 1993) indicated very poor coordination among the three richest areas within the Jiangsu province, i.e., Suzhou, Wuxi and Changzhou.

Poor and rich provinces were also reluctant to cooperate. Besides the presence of a similar industrial structure, the psychology of the local officials in poor provinces was important. For instance, local officials in the Anhui province did not cooperate with neighboring Shanghai because they believed that they had been victimized by Shanghai, and they regarded it as a "colonial center." Hunan was unwilling to cooperate with Guangdong because of a similar psychology of being victimized, and its leaders once blocked grain shipments to Guangdong. Local governments competed with one another for local development and used all possible administrative methods to protect local industries.

Economic decentralization also resulted in a relatively greater increase in interdependence between the Chinese provinces and the outside world, and a surprising decrease in inter-provincial interdependence. According to the World Bank, as of the early 1990s, internal trade as a percentage of the gross domestic product among the Chinese provinces was 22 percent, which was lower than the European Community's 28 percent and the 27 percent among the republics of the former Soviet Union before the union was dissolved. The World Bank thus warned that individual provinces had a tendency to behave like independent countries, with an increase in external (overseas) trade and a relative decline in trade flows with each other (Kumar, 1994).

Rapid decentralization indeed led to the provinces' relative independence from the central government on the one hand, and being independent from each other on the other hand. In the early 1990s, two well-known Chinese economists Shen Liren and Dai Yuanchen (1992: 12) argued that rapid local economic development was associated with the rise of various dukedoms:

> Economic circles describe the result of economic decentralization during the economic reform as a new economic phenomenon — "an economy of dukedom." That means, thirty provinces, autonomous regions and municipalities (Beijing, Tianjin and Shanghai) are big dukes, three hundred prefectures and cities are medium dukes, and two thousand counties are small dukes. These dukes have their own domains and political regimes, and seek to develop independently.

Inter-governmental decentralization, therefore, would inevitably introduce changes to the interaction patterns between the center and the provinces, since it empowered the provinces by promoting local economic development. The rise of local power led to a great power shift from the center to the provinces. Consequently, local governments began to pursue even greater power from the central government, and continuous decentralization became inevitable since local governments were not satisfied with the existing power distribution between the center and the provinces. Needless to say, the central government had to respond to increasingly high local demands.

By the mid-1990s, rapid globalization had generated new dynamics for China's *de facto* federalism. Globalization indeed has facilitated the transformation of China's *de facto* federalism. While economic decentralization in the 1980s led to the formation of *de facto* federalism, globalization since the 1990s has accelerated this process and generated increasingly high pressure on the Chinese leadership to institutionalize existing *de facto* federalism.

Like elsewhere, globalization has weakened the power of the national government over localities in many areas, while creating an opportunity for state transformation. Globalization has affected China's central-local relations with the creation of two opposite forces, i.e., decentralization and centralization. On one hand, globalization has decentralized economic activities further to local governments and other local organizations, making it increasingly difficult for the center to access local economic resources. On the other hand, globalization requires the center to regulate the national economy in order to accommodate external economic forces resulting from globalization. Centralization is thus a prerequisite for the national government to establish a national regulatory system. For China, the two opposite forces have created great political tension between the national government and local governments. In responding to globalization and its consequences, the Chinese leadership has implemented a strategy of what I called "selective recentralization" since the mid-1990s to reconcile the imperatives of decentralization and recentralization. With selective recentralization measures, *de facto* federalism is gradually being institutionalized.

Selective Economic Recentralization and Economic Federalism

The restructuring of the center-province relations has been taking place since the mid-1990s. The central government made enormous efforts to introduce central power into the provinces. Nevertheless, this did not mean that there was a whole-scale recentralization movement. The central government understood that it was economic decentralization that had provided local governments with enormous initiatives to promote local development; that due to increasing regional and local diversities, the provinces had to play a greater role in governing the provinces and maintaining national unity since the central government could hardly govern different localities directly. Like Mao Zedong before, Jiang Zemin (1995) also emphasized that China still needed two "initiatives" (e.g., central and local) in order to promote further development, while maintaining national unity. To achieve the two contradictory goals, i.e., greater local initiatives and central control, institutional innovations are needed. Based on the past 20 years of experience, what the center did was to build *selective* national institutions in the provinces. In other words, the central government attempted to restructure central-local relations and strengthen central power by penetrating localities in selective areas — a strategy that can be called "selective centralization."

Among others, selective centralization was concentrated on two major reforms, i.e., taxation reform and central banking system reform. In 1994, the central government began to implement a new taxation system, i.e., the tax-division system or a federal-style taxation system. Before this system, the center did not have its own institutions to collect taxes. All taxes from the provinces were collected by provincial governments first, and then were divided between the center and the provinces through bargaining between the two parties. The new taxation system changed the institutional base of the old system and thus the interaction between the center and the provinces.

First of all, under the new taxation system, taxes are divided into three categories, namely, central, local and shared. Central taxes would go into the central coffer; local taxes would go to local budgets; and shared taxes were to be divided between the center and the provinces according to previously established agreements.

Second, tax administration is centralized. Instead of authorizing local tax offices to collect virtually all taxes, the center now collects taxes by its own institutions independent of the provinces, meaning that the center has established its own revenue collection agency — the national tax service. Nevertheless, the new system also recognizes independent provincial power, that is, provincial authorities can collect several types of taxes without central interference. In other words, there are now two parallel and independent systems for tax administration — a national system for central taxes and a local one for local taxes. Shared taxes were collected by the central government first, and then divided between the center and the provinces.

These institutional changes have shifted fiscal power from the provinces to the center. Total government revenue has increased quite dramatically. The proportion of central collection has increased from less than 30 percent to around 50 percent. If the locally-collected revenues that local governments are obligated to remit to the central coffer are included, the central government's share will reach about two-thirds of total government revenue. Since most revenues are now collected and redistributed by the center, the fiscal dependence of the provinces on the central government has increased substantially. Before the new system, the central government tended to rely heavily on coastal provinces such as Shanghai, Shandong, Zhejiang, Jiangsu and Guangdong for revenue contribution. The new system has reversed this trend.[4]

Similar efforts have been made to reform China's central banking system. Before the reform, China's central banking system was highly decentralized. The central bank, People's Bank, established branches in every province and assumed that all provincial branches would take orders from the center, since they theoretically were a

---

[4] For assessments of the 1994 taxation reform, see Wang Shaoguang (1997) and Hu Angang (1996).

part or extension of the central bank. But, in reality, local branches were often exposed to the political influence of local government, since the personnel of local branches were arranged by local governments and their welfare was provided by local governments. This frequently led to local branches ignoring orders from the central bank and subordinating themselves to local influences. Indeed, local branches of the central bank often became an effective instrument for local governments to promote local economic growth. But rapid local growth was achieved at the expense of the stability of the national economy.[5]

As of the end of the 1980s, the central government introduced changes into the central banking system and decided that all directors of local branches should be appointed by the central bank, rather than by provincial governments. To do so, the central government expected that all local branches should act in accordance with the central directive and be independent from local political influence. However, the change did not lead to the expected results. Local branches had developed their own independent institutional interests, and preferred to use their resources to develop local economies since they could benefit greatly from local growth. This eventually led to a crisis of macro-economic management in the mid-1990s. After Zhu Rongji became China's new premier and a new government was established in March 1998, the central government declared a most daring measure to reform China's financial system: All provincial branches of the central bank were eliminated and nine cross-provincial or regional branches established (Bian, 1998).[6] The reform attempted to follow the American model of federal-state relations, aiming at getting rid of the institutional

---

[5] For discussions of the central banking system reform, see Bowles and White (1993) and Chen Yuan (1994).

[6] The locations of the headquarters of the nine regional branches include: Shanghai (Shanghai, Zhejiang and Fujian); Tianjin (Tianjin, Hebei, Shanxi and Inner Mongolia); Shenyang (Liaoning, Jilin and Heilongjiang); Nanjing (Jiangsu and Anhui); Ji'nan (Shandong and Henan); Wuhan (Jiangxi, Hubei and Hunan); Chengdu (Sichuan, Guizhou, Yunnan and Tibet); Xi'an (Shannxi, Gansu, Qinghai, Ningxia and Xinjiang); and Guangzhou (Guangdong, Guangxi and Hainan).

instruments of provincial governments to intervene into the central banking system.[7]

Strengthening the Nomenklatura System

I have argued that reciprocity has played an important role in mediating the interaction between the center and the provinces. Radical decentralization led to the rise of economic localism, and the provinces attempted to use their growing power to have some say in policy-making at the national level. As discussed in Chapter 3, interest representation occurred in terms of recruiting local political leaders into the central leadership. Even with their growing power, the provinces were still willing to cooperate with the central government, implying that they were constrained in pursuing political autonomy in decision-making. Nevertheless, reciprocity also made the central-local relationship fragile. Reciprocity appeared as a form of self-adjustment and deliberation or voluntary cooperation, and it produced only soft constraints on provincial behavior. Indeed, with the rise of local economic power, it became more difficult for reciprocity to mediate central-local relations. Therefore, the central government initiated selective economic recentralization by major institutional innovations, as exemplified by the taxation reform and the central banking system reform.

Nonetheless, compared with the economic side, no innovation has been made to institutionalize central-local political relations. Political recentralization took place, but it was done in the old ways. Certainly, the central government has not determined what a new central-local relationship should be and how it could be achieved. So far, the efforts of the central government have been on restrengthening the old nomenklatura system.

The central government has strengthened the cadre management (*ganbu guanli*) system. "Party management of cadres" (*dang guan ganbu*) has been one of the most important organizational

---

[7] Interviews in the Development Research Center, the State Council (6 May 1998); and Bian Ji (1998).

principles, and indeed this principle gives the central government a dominant say over personnel decisions (Burns, 1989). In 1995, the central government issued a document entitled "Temporary Regulations on Selection and Appointment of Party and Government Leading Cadres". The regulations reemphasized the cadre transfer system or the cadre exchange system (*ganbu jiaoliu zhidu*) that enabled the center to tighten its control over local cadres (*People's Daily*, 17 May 1995: 1).

The focus of the transfer is on leading members of Party committees and governments. According to the 1995 regulations, a leading member of a local Party committee or government should be transferred, if he/she has worked in the same position for 10 years. The Constitution of the CCP regulates that positions in Party committees of the county level and above have a term of five years. Therefore, a provincial-level cadre, by the end of his second term, if he has not reached retirement age, has to be transferred. Transfers may also result from the nature of his work, the need to broaden work experience and improve leadership, the requirement of the rule of avoidance, and other reasons. Whatever it is, the system of cadre transfer is an effective instrument for the center to constrain the rise of localism.

The cadre transfer system has been an effective means for the central government to control provincial leaders and solicit their compliance. Nevertheless, the system is becoming increasingly problematic over time. The transfer of local cadres has occurred in various ways. Among others, inter-provincial transfer, province-center transfer and center-province transfer are the most common. All these forms of transfer have met with difficulty.

The inter-provincial transfer is, in effect, a form of a more traditional control system — the system of avoidance — meaning that provincial leaders cannot serve their native provinces. From 1990 to early 1998 (the Ninth National People's Congress), there were 44 cases of inter-provincial exchanges.[8] For example, Wu Guanzheng of Jiangxi was transferred in April 1997 to Shandong to replace Zhao

---

[8] The author's database.

Zhihao and Li Changchun of Henan was transferred in March 1998 to Guangdong to replace Xie Fei.

This form of transfer system is contradictory to the central leaders' expectations of provincial officials. One major strength of the nomenklatura is that it enables the central government to recruit the "right" type of cadres into the leading bodies. Since the reform began in the late 1970s, the CCP's priority has been modernization and economic growth. Actually, the decentralization of the nomenklatura system was to give provincial leaders more political autonomy to promote local growth. To promote local development, provincial leaders have to collect adequate local information in order to make and implement policies suitable for local conditions. But the transfer system constrains, even undermines, provincial leaders' capability to access local information. When he/she begins to become familiar with local situations, he/she has to be transferred to another province. The frequent transfer of provincial leaders often makes it difficult for them to make and implement consistent policies.

The transfer from the center to provinces aims to enable the central government to exercise direct control over the provinces. From 1990 to early 1998, there were 19 such cases.[9] For instance, after the Chen Xitong case was disposed of in Beijing, Wei Jianxing was moved in to control the situation. Nevertheless, the utility of this type of transfer is also limited. When a central official is sent to hold a top position in the provincial leadership, he/she encounters a difficult choice: either to behave on behalf of the central government or to promote local interests. The first choice will make it difficult for him/her to solicit cooperation from local officials, and thus will stop him/her from achieving what the central government has expected, i.e., to promote local development. The second choice will certainly nullify the aim of central appointment *per se.*[10]

The transfer from provinces to the center is multi-functional. Also, from 1990 to early 1998, there were 50 such cases.[11] In some

---

[9] The author's database.

[10] For a discussion of this point, see Zheng (1998a).

[11] The author's database.

cases, the transfer was a promotion, but in other cases, transfers to the center meant only that they were deprived of the political power they enjoyed in their home provinces.[12] The transfer as a promotion has been used by top leaders to rejuvenate the central leadership, as in the case of Zhao Ziyang and Wan Li, who were promoted to the central leadership in the early 1980s because of their reform initiatives in their home provinces. Since the transfer also served to deprive power, provincial leaders tended not to be "promoted," as in the case of Ye Xuanping, Governor of the Guangdong province, who turned down attractive job offers in Beijing to stay in Guangdong in the late 1980s and early 1990s (Shirk, 1993: 189).

More importantly, the transfer system is incompatible with democracy, and has thus been undermined by newly-developed democratic factors in China. The strengthening of the People's Congress tends to weaken the cadre transfer system. Provincial congress-persons prefer to vote for native cadres, rather than outsiders. Furthermore, with the improvement of the provincial electoral system, provincial leaders are increasingly local interest-oriented. Regardless of whether they are natives or outsiders, they all have to pay attention to local interests. Otherwise, they will meet difficulty in winning local support. Therefore, leaders come and go, and local interests remain. Certainly, how central control and local interests should be reconciled is still an important political issue facing the Chinese leadership.

PROVINCIAL GOVERNMENTS AS SEMI-INDEPENDENT UNITS

Early studies defined the center and the province separately. Scholars of totalitarianism or authoritarianism defined the province merely as an organizational unit in the hierarchy of central-local relations, and regarded the provinces either as having no autonomy or very limited "operational autonomy." On the other hand, scholars of the cellular model and pluralism defined the province as an organizational unit

---

[12] For a discussion of this point, see Zheng (1998b).

with its own interests and preferences independently from the center. Most of these studies failed to provide us with a satisfactory explanation of central-local relations.

As discussed in Chapter 1, recent efforts have been made to define central-local relations in the context of the interaction between the two actors, as shown in the literature of the structural approach and the procedural approach. These studies examine how both the center and the provinces are constrained by the institution of central-local relations, and assume, implicitly or explicitly, that the center and the provinces are rational actors, with their primary goal being to maximize their interests. Though the constraints that were imposed upon the center and the provinces were taken into account in these studies, an important factor was underestimated, if not ignored totally, that is, their "rational goals" were already mediated by norms generated by China's *de facto* federal structure.

This is especially true in using the principal-agent model to explain China's central-local relations. The foundation of this model is the assumption of rationality, that is, both central and provincial officials behave strategically and opportunistically to maximize their preferences. According to this model, relations between the center and the provinces are similar to relations between stockholders (the principal) and managers (the agent), in which the principal delegates some control rights to the agent to perform tasks in the expectation that the agent will maximize the principal's utility. In this sense, "the Chinese central government possesses certain 'ownership' rights over provincial officials and delegates to or ... reclaims certain decision-making rights from the provinces" (Huang, 1996: 182). This is the case because of the fact that the provinces gain their decision-making rights from the central government and the central government makes personnel allocation decisions to the top level of a province. Moreover, because "ownership" rights belong to the center, provincial governments only have "operational autonomy" (*ibid.*).

This study shows that such an analogy of China's central-local relations is quite misleading. The rationality assumption is problematic, since unlike a firm, a bureaucracy is not profit-maximizing.[13] This is not only because of the differences between a firm and a political system, but also because "rational goals" of bureaucrats are mediated by norms and identities formed in the history of the interaction between the center and the provinces.

We can come to the conclusion that though provincial governments have to subordinate themselves to the central government, they are not merely agents of the center. The *sheng* is not merely a level of administration; instead, it is a level of government. In other words, a provincial government is not a local branch of the central government. In analyzing center-province relations in China, two layers of relationship can be distinguished: relations between the central government and provincial governments, and relations between provincial governments and their "provincial" (or internal) territories. Most studies, so far, have taken the center as an analytical unit. The province as an analytical unit makes a difference, however. Taking the center as an analytical unit is better suited to the analysis of the relations between the central government and provincial governments. But this type of analysis often underestimates relations between provincial governments and their territories. In other words, a top-down approach is less capable of highlighting the impact of relations between provincial governments and their territories in the central-provincial relations.

On the other hand, if the provincial government is taken as an analytical unit, we see a totally different game taking place. Generally speaking, it is something like a "two-level game" in world politics.[14] Provincial governments need to deal with the center and their own

---

[13] Huang (1996: 180–185) has applied this model to central-local relations in China. Nevertheless, he himself doubts the rational assumption by pointing out its limitation. For instance, corporate managers can control their subordinates through both administrative means and monetary remuneration, while bureaucrats rely more heavily on administrative means and do not use monetary ones for control purposes; the goal of corporate managers can be reduced to "profits," while bureaucrats are multi-task agents and have conflicting goals to pursue at the same time.

[14] For an analysis of "two-level games" in world politics, see Putnam (1988).

territories simultaneously. From this point of view, a provincial government is not an agent of the central government, and the latter also does not possess "ownership" rights over the former. Provincial government officials, though appointed by the center, have their own territory-based power resources. In other words, not all powers of local officials come from the center. As a level of government (not a level of administration), the power of the provincial government, to a great degree, is independent of the center.

Provincial officials are more like "generalists" than "functional specialists," using Lieberthal and Oksenberg's terms (1988: 36–37). A top-down approach tends to treat provincial governments as functional specialists who implement national policies on behalf of the center. But this is only one side of the story. A provincial government is not solely responsible for issues in specific functional spheres; it is a government that is responsible for a wide range of issues. Provincial officials are "generalists" not only responsible for implementing all central policies on behalf of the central government, be it political, economic, or social. More importantly, they have to govern their territories by initiating and implementing policies suitable for local conditions.

Nevertheless, like central power, the territory-based provincial power also cannot be exaggerated. Though provincial officials have substantial power resources to use in their dealings with the central government, their goals and strategies are constrained not only by the power structure, but also by the norms and identities of central-local relations.

INSTITUTIONALIZING *DE FACTO* FEDERALISM: A POLITICAL SOLUTION?

The difficulty of innovating the political relationship between the center and the provinces lies in the fact that the leadership is still uncertain whether *de facto* federalism should be institutionalized or formalized. Federalism has been accepted as an important political value because it is non-absolutist, and thus, to some degree, democratic. It is, as William S. Livingston (1976) argued, in the first instance, an organizational response to the pluralist nature and group structure of society, and thus a balance between individual and group liberties. Federalism is thus viewed as a better alternative to a unitary system. As Donald Smiley (1976: 72) pointed out.

> The justifications of federalism over a unitary system are political and the values furthered by federalism have nothing to do with rationalism in public policy. First, federalism is one of several possible devices for constraining political power, particularly executive power. Second, to the extent that within a nation attitudes and interests are not uniformly distributed on a territorial basis, federalism contributes to the responsiveness of government to the popular will.

This study has argued that the institutional arrangement of inter-governmental decentralization in China is characterized by *de facto* federalism. China has benefited from such an arrangement throughout the reform years. It not only granted local governments and society the power to pursue their own interests and created internal dynamics for rapid economic development; it also provided local officials with the power to make and implement policies in accordance with local diversities and thus enabled them to respond to local demands. More importantly, as has been argued, it prevented the central government from interfering into local economic affairs arbitrarily and thus created an institutional mechanism for a market system to grow out of the previous planned economy (Montinola, Qian & Weingast, 1995).

China's political elites seemed to have realized the value of federalism as early as the late 19th century.[15] What could China do in terms of central-local relations after the collapse of imperial hegemony? This was an important question that many revolutionary leaders, including Sun Yat-sen and Liang Qichao, considered. By the early years of this century, federal ideas were so strong that they played an important role in the constitutional reforms promulgated by the Qing between 1906 and 1911. The self-government movement revealed many leaders' belief that national strength would be based on local self-government (Fincher, 1981; Waldron, 1990). The

---

[15] For a brief survey of the origins and development of federal thought in China, see Yan Jiaqi (1992).

1911 revolution did not lead to the realization of the revolutionary leaders' federal ideal. In fact, the breakdown of the Qing dynasty led China to chaos and warlordism. During the period of warlordism, federalism was often used as a means for local officials to gain political power (Chesneaux, 1969; Schoppa, 1976, 1977).

The CCP employed the appeal of federalism and democracy in its struggle for state power. At the CCP's second national congress, the Party declared its intent to establish a federal republic of China, and to unify the main provinces with Mongolia, Tibet and Hui-Uighur regions on the basis of liberal federalism. The Party also recognized the right of minorities to complete self-determination (Yan, 1992). But the CCP did not bring a federal system to China. Instead, after the CCP took over political power, China became a centralized unitary country with the assignment of autonomy only to minority areas.

People are not ruled by abstract principles, however. Soon after the establishment of the PRC, Chinese leaders including Mao realized that a high degree of centralization carried its own burden of problems. In effect, even under Mao's regime, which was often regarded as totalitarian, localities enjoyed autonomy to some degree. Central to Deng's reform was inter-governmental decentralization. As discussed earlier, great efforts have been made to reconstruct the economic relationship between the center and the provinces, following federal systems elsewhere. Great demands for institutionalizing *de facto* political federalism also exist. This is because, in practice, federalism is often not a free choice, but a function of the political power of territorial leadership when open coercion is excluded as a possible option. The central government's dependence on localities has produced new seeds of political federalism. Indeed, after the mid-1980s, federalism became a popular topic within the reform leadership and its think-tanks. In 1986, initiated by Zhao Ziyang, the central leadership established the Group for Research on Political Institution Reforms. Seven subgroups were organized, with one assigned to focus on decentralization and institutional reforms. A major research theme of this subgroup was whether China could use federalism such as that in the United States and elsewhere to reform the existing power relations between the central and local government (Chen, 1990).

Inter-governmental decentralization has had great political significance for central-local relations. The rise of provincial economic power has created a great possibility for the formation of a system of checks and balances in terms of local-central relations, which is pushing China to political federalism. Since the early 1990s, Chinese scholars have called for the formalization of *de facto* federalism. While many have argued that only by institutionalizing *de facto* federalism can local autonomy be protected from arbitrary interference into local affairs by the central government and thus sustain the country's rapid development, many others believe that federalism can indeed strengthen central power, rather than weaken it.[16] Even for the proponents of centralization, federalism seems inevitable. For example, Wang Shaoguang and Hu Angang, two Chinese scholars who have been known for their calls for recentralization, argued that power has been too decentralized and the central government has to recentralize its power in order to maintain national unity. Nevertheless, they do not believe that the country should go back to the old style of central control, and called for political innovations to reconstruct central-local relations.[17] This view has gained popularity not only among Chinese scholars, but also among Chinese local officials. Local officials have strongly demanded the institutionalization of central-local relations. Take financial power as an example. Local officials regarded it as necessary for the central government to control central financial power, but they demanded their participation in decision-making at the national level, since they were afraid that the central government would abuse its great power. According to a survey conducted by Hu Angang in 1998, 55 percent of local officials argued that the power division between the center and the provinces should be institutionalized, and about 46 percent argued

---

[16] For the debates between the two views, see "A Symposium on Formalizing the Division of Power and Institutional Transition," *Dangdai Zhongguo Yanjiu* (Modern China Studies), special issues, Nos. 1–2, 1995.

[17] For a discussion of the views of Wang and Hu, see Zheng (1999), Chapter 2.

that the Financial and Economic Committee in the National People's Congress should consist of central and provincial representatives, and a system of "one province, one vote" should be implemented (Hu, 1999).

So, why is the central government reluctant to rebuild the political relationship between the center and the provinces according to federal principles? As mentioned above, it has been argued that federalism is the only way to institutionalize central-local relations (Yan, 1992; Jin, 1992). Nevertheless, without great political initiatives, central-local relations will remain in a state of *de facto* federalism, rather than federalism. To legitimate federalism would not be an easy task in China.

Ideologically, federalism is in a position that is contradictory to the ideology of the CCP. The last century's history of warlordism links chaos with federalism in people's minds (Fitzgerald, 1994; Waldron, 1990). For many, federalism will result in a divided China, or a divided China will go towards federalism. Given the fact that federalism has been discussed in the context of Hong Kong, Taiwan, Tibet, Xinjiang and other territorial issues, the ideological legitimacy of federalism becomes rather complicated. Although these territorial factors have pulled China toward federalism, the ideological barrier is not easy to overcome. Indeed, for many within the CCP, federalism has been seen as an ideology to divide China as a sovereign state. We have seen in the West that federalism has been a strong ideological foundation for federal political system, as liberalism supports democracy. As long as federalism cannot be legitimated ideologically, a transition from *de facto* to *de jure* federalism is unlikely to take place in China. Therefore, when Yan Jiaqi, the Director of the Institute of Political Science of the Chinese Academy of Social Sciences, proposed a Chinese federation with a democratic system as the best hope both for reforming China's internal politics and for resolving the problems of Hong Kong, Taiwan and Tibet, Yan was immediately denounced by his colleagues in the same institute (Xu, 1990).

Practically, it seems that timing is not "right" for the legitimation of federalism. Compared to *de facto* federalism, the advantages of federalism are obvious. The institutionalization of *de facto* federalism is favorable for political stability since it reduces the tension between the two actors, the central and the provincial governments. Nevertheless, institutionalization is also likely to render the system rigid. Given the fact that great diversities among the provinces exist, equal rights among them (implicit in federalism) are not likely. Rich provinces prefer a weak center, while poor provinces prefer a strong one. The recent call for recentralization by poor provinces is not without reason. Without doubt, top leaders fear that federalism will lead a China with great diversities to disintegration. Also, the leadership's priority is to promote economic development, rather than to divide power between the center and the provinces and among the provinces. To do so, it has to adjust continuously its relationship with the provinces and mediate the relations among the provinces in accordance with changing circumstances. The legitimation of federalism will render such continuous adjustments less likely. In contrast, *de facto* federalism has the advantage of flexibility. What the center needs is the creative ambiguity implicit in *de facto* federalism. In other words, the center needs, for the time being, not a clear-cut division between the center and the provinces, but ambiguity between them. As long as the center maintains its relative power over the provinces, it will be able to adjust central-local relations. Nevertheless, in the long run, various reform measures such as selective institutionalization will lay an institutional foundation for China's transition from *de facto* to *de jure* federalism.

References

Agarwala, Ramgopal, *China: Reforming Intergovernmental Fiscal Relations*, Washington, DC.: The World Bank, 1992.

Allison, Graham, *Essence of Decision*, Boston: Little, Brown, 1971.

Almond, Gabriel & Sidney Verba, *The Civic Culture: Political Attitudes and Democracy in Five Nations*, Princeton, NJ.: Princeton University Press, 1963.

Apter, David, *The Politics of Modernization*, Chicago: Chicago University Press, 1965.

Ashford, Douglas E. (ed.), *Financing Urban Government in the Welfare State*, London: Croom Helm, 1980.

Ashford, D. E., "Are Britain and France 'unitary'?" *Comparative Politics* 9: 4 (July 1977), pp. 483–499.

Bachman, David, "The Limits on Leadership in China," *Asian Survey* XXXII: 11 (November 1992), pp. 1046–1062.

Bachman, David, "Implementing Chinese Tax Reform," in Lampton (1987), pp. 119–153.

Bachman, David, "Differing Visions of China's Post-Mao Economy: The Ideas of Chen Yun, Deng Xiaoping, and Zhao Ziyang," *Asian Survey* XXVI:3 (March 1986), pp. 292–321.

Bachman, David, *Chen Yun and the Chinese Political System*, Center for Chinese Studies Research Monograph No. 29. Berkeley, CA.: Institute of East Asian Studies, 1985.

Bakvis, Herman & William M. Chandler (eds.), *Federalism and the Role of the State*, Toronto: University of Toronto Press, 1987.

383

Bardach, Eugene, *The Implementation Game*, Cambridge, MA.: MIT Press, 1979.

Barnett, Doak, *Cadres, Bureaucracy, and Political Power in China*, New York: Columbia University Press, 1967.

Barnett, Doak A. & Ralph N. Clough (eds.), *Modernizing China: Post-Mao Reform and Development*, Boulder, CO.: Westwive Press, 1986.

Baum, Richard, "Elite Behavior under Conditions of Stress," in Scalapino (1972), pp. 540–574.

Bennett, Robert J. (ed.), *Decentralization, Local Governments, and Markets: Towards a Post-Welfare Agenda*, New York: Clarendon Press, 1990.

Bennett, Robert J., "Decentralization, Intergovernmental Relations and Markets: Towards a Post-Welfare Agenda?" in Bennett (1990), pp. 1–26.

Benson, J. K., "Organizations: A Dialectical View," *Administrative Science Quarterly* 22:1 (1977), pp. 1–21.

Benz, Arthur, "Regionalization and Decentralization," in Bakvis & Chandler (1987), pp. 127–146.

Bian Ji, "31 Provincial Branches Replaced by Regional Ones," *China Daily*, 16 December 1998.

Binder, Leonard, *et al.*, *Crises and Sequences in Political Development*, Princeton, NJ.: Princeton University Press, 1971.

Blau, Peter, *Exchange and Power in Social Life*, New York: Wiley, 1964.

Blecher, Marc, "Development State, Entrepreneurial State: The Political Economy of Socialist Reform in Xinju Municipality and Guanghan County," in White (1991), pp. 265–291.

Bo Yibo, "Shenqie huainian Gu Dacun tongzhi" ("Deeply Cherishing the Memory of Comrade Gu Dacun"), *People's Daily*, 8 April 1997.

Bo Yibo, *Ruogan zhongda juece yu shijian de huigu* (A Review of Major Decision-making and Events), Beijing: Zhonggong zhongyang dangxiao chubanshe, 1991.

Bockman, Harald, "China Deconstructs? The Future of the Chinese Empire-State in a Historical Perspective," in Brodsgaard & Strand (1998), pp. 310–346.

Bowles, Paul & Gordon White, *The Political Economy of China's Financial Reforms: Finance in Late Development*, Boulder, CO.: Westview Press, 1993.

Breslin, Shaun, *China in the 1980s: Center-Province Relations in a Reforming Socialist State*, London: Macmillan Press, 1996.

Brodsgaard, Kjeld Erik & David Strand, *Reconstructing Twentieth-Century China: State Control, Civil Society, and National Identity*, Oxford: Clarendon Press, 1998.

The Bureau of Foreign Trade of Zhejiang, "Zhejiang dui wai jingji maoyi" ("Foreign Trade in Zhejiang"), annual report, 1987, in *Zhejiang jingji nianjian 1987* (Yearbook of Zhejiang Economy, 1987), Hangzhou: Zhejiang renmin chubanshe, 1988, pp. 293–294.

The Bureau of Rural Industry of Zhejiang, "Zhejiang xiangzhen qiye qiye" ("Rural Industry in Zhejiang"), annual report, 1988, in *Zhejiang jingji nianjian 1988* (Yearbook of Zhejiang Economy, 1988), Hangzhou: Zhejiang renmin chubanshe, 1988, pp. 167–170.

The Bureau of Rural Industry of Zhejiang, "Zhejiang xiangzhen qiye" ("Rural Industry in Zhejiang"), annual report, 1987, in *Zhejiang jingji nianjian 1987* (Yearbook of Zhejiang Economy, 1987), Hangzhou: Zhejiang renmin chubanshe, 1988, pp. 164–166.

The Bureau of Rural Industry of Zhejiang, "Zhejiang xiangzhen qiye" ("Rural Industry in Zhejiang"), annual report, 1986, in *Zhejiang jingji nianjian 1986* (Yearbook of Zhejiang Economy, 1986), Hangzhou: Zhejiang renmin chubanshe, 1988, pp. 145–147.

Burns, John P., "Strengthening Central CCP Control of Leadership Selection: The 1990 Nomenklatura," *The China Quarterly* 138 (1994), pp. 458–491.

Burns, John P. (ed.), *The Chinese Communist Party's Nomenklatura System*, Armonk, NY.: M. E. Sharpe, Inc., 1989.

Cao Zi (ed.), *Zhonghua renmin gongheguo renshi zhidu gaiyao* (A General Outline of China's Personnel System), Beijing: Beijing University Press, 1985.

Carnell, F. G., "Political Implications of Federalism in New States," in Hicks *et al.* (1961), pp. 16–59.

The CCP Provincial Committee of Jiangsu, the Government of Jiangsu, "Guanyu jiakuai wosheng duiwai kaifang bufa de yijian" ("On How to Speed Up Our Province's Pace in Implementing Open Door Policy," 20 July 1986a), in The Editorial Office of Jiangsu Yearbook (1987), Part I, pp. 49–55.

The CCP Provincial Committee of Jiangsu, the Government of Jiangsu, "Guanyu jiakuai kaifang chengshi he kaifang diqu jingji guanli tizhi gaige de yijian" ("On How to Speed Up Reforming the System of Economic Management in Open Cities and Areas," 20 July 1986b), in The Editorial Office of Jiangsu Yearbook (1987), Part I, pp. 59–61.

The CCP Provincial Committee of Jiangsu, "Jiakuai shehui zhuyi jianshe bufa de biyou zhilu" ("The Road That Must Be Taken in Accelerating the Pace of Socialist Development"), *Hong Qi* (Red Flag) 2 (1977), pp. 26–32.

The CCP Provincial Committee of Zhejiang, the Government of Zhejiang, "Guanyu jingji qingkuang he jingji fazhan wenti de baogao" ("A Report on Problems of Economic Situation and Economic Development"), 20 August 1981.

The Center of Economic Research of Wuxi Municipal Government, "Chenggong de tansuo, youyi de qishi" ("Successful Exploration and Valuable Implications"), in Pan Shangen (1988), pp. 77–78.

The Center of Economic Studies of Zhejiang, *Zhejiang shengqing gaiyao* (An Outline of Zhejiang Affairs), Hangzhou: Zhejiang renmin chubanshe, 1986.

The Central Committee of the CCP, "Dangzheng lingdao ganbu xuanba renyong gongzuo zhanxing tiaoli" ("Temporary Regulations on Selection and Appointment of Party and Government Leading Cadres," 9 February 1995), *People's Daily*, 17 May 1995, pp. 1–3.

Chang, Parris H., *Power and Policy in China*, Dubuque, Iowa: Kendall, Hunt, 1990.

Chang, Parris H., "Provincial Leaders' Strategies for Survival During the Cultural Revolution," in Scalapino (1972), pp. 502–539.

Chen Jiyuan & Xia Defang, *Xiangzhen qiye moshi yanjiu* (A Study of Models of Rural Enterprises Model), Beijing: Zhongguo shehui kexue chubanshe, 1988.

Chen Yan, *et al.*, "Wenzhou guoying gongye qiye kaocha yu suoyouzhi gaige de silu" ("An Investigation into Industrial Enterprises of the State Sector in Wenzhou and Thinking Line of Ownership System Reforms"), *Zhejiang xuekan* (Zhejiang Studies Monthly) 42:1 (1987), pp. 82–87.

Chen Yizi, *Zhongguo: shinian gaige yu bajiu minyun* (China: Ten Years of Reforms and the 1989 People's Movement), Taipei: Lianjing chuban gongsi, 1990.

Chen Yuan, *Zhongguo jinrong tizhi gaige* (Reforms in China's Financial System), Beijing: Zhongguo caizheng jingji chubanshe, 1994.

Chen Zhizhong & Wang Shalin, "Xiangzhen qiye de shijian jingyan yu lilun sikao" ("Practical Experiences and Theoretical Consideration for the Rural Industry"), in Wu Xiangjun (1990), pp. 5–16.

Cheng Rulong, *et al.* (eds.), *Dangdai Zhongguo caizheng* (Finance in Contemporary China), Vol. 1, Beijing: Zhongguo shehui kexue chubanshe, 1988.

Chesneaux, Jean, "The Federal Movement in China, 1920–1923," in Gray (1969), pp. 96–137.

Ch'ien Mu, *Traditional Government in Imperial China: A Critical Analysis*, translated by Chun-tu Hsueh & George O. Totten, Hong Kong: The Chinese University Press, 1982.

Chong Pengrong, *Shinian jingji gaige: licheng, xianzhuang, wenti, chulu* (Ten Years of Economic Reforms: Process, Situations, Problems and Outlets), Zhengzhou: Hunan renmin chubanshe, 1990.

Chong Shen & Xiang Xiyang (eds.), *Shinianlai: lilun, zhengce, shijian* (Past Ten Years: Theory, Policy and Practice), Vol. 3, Beijing: Qiushi chubanshe, 1988.

Chung, Jae Ho, "Studies of Central-Provincial Relations in the People's Republic of China: A Mid-Term Appraisal," *The China Quarterly* 142 (1995), pp. 487–508.

Clausen, Soren, "Party Policy and National Culture: Towards a State-Directed Cultural Nationalism in China?" in Brodsgaard and Strand (1998), pp. 253–279.

Cohen, Michael A., "The Myth of the Expanding Center: Politics in the Ivory Coast," *The Journal of Modern African Studies* 11 (1973), pp. 227–246.

Cohen, Paul A., "The Post-Mao Reforms in Historical Perspective," *The Journal of Asian Studies* 47:3 (August 1988), pp. 518–540.

The Commission of Economic Planning of Zhejiang, "Zhejiang guting zichan touzi" ("Fixed Asset Investment in Zhejiang"), annual report, 1986, in *Zhejiang jingji nianjian 1986* (Yearbook of Zhejiang Economy, 1986), Hangzhou: Zhejiang renmin chubanshe,1988, pp. 240–243.

The Commission of Economic System Reform of Jiangsu, "Jiangsu shinian jingji tizhi gaige huigu" ("Reviewing Economic System Reform in Past Ten Years in Jiangsu"), in The Commission of Economic System Reform of Jiangsu (1988), pp. 8–27.

The Commission of Economic System Reform of Jiangsu (ed.), *Shinian gaige zai Jiangsu* (Ten Years of Reforms in Jiangsu), Beijing: Gaige chubanshe, 1988.

The Compact Edition of the Oxford English Dictionary, Oxford University Press, 1987.

Concepcion, Juanito, "Gitic Fallout Hangs over Banking Sector," *Hong Kong Standard*, 2 January 1999.

Crane, George, "Special Things in Special Ways: National Economic Identity and China's Special Economic Zones," in Unger (1996), pp. 148–168.

Crane, George, *The Political Economy of China's Special Economic Zones*, Armonk, NY.: M. E. Sharpe, 1990.

Daedalus, Reconstructing Nations and States, special issue, Summer 1993.

Dahl, Robert A. & Charles E. Lindblom, *Politics, Economics, and Welfare*, 2nd Ed., Chicago: University of Chicago Press, 1976.

Dai Aisheng, "Jindai Guangzhou diqu rencai beichu de yuanyin chutan" ("A Preliminary Investigation into Why the Guangzhou Region Produced Enormous Talented People in Modern Time"), *Guangdong shehui kexue* (Guangdong Social Sciences) 2 (1986), pp. 102–106.

Dearlove, J., *The Politics of Policy in Local Government*, Cambridge: Cambridge University Press, 1973.

Deng Xiaoping, "Zai Wuchang, Shenzhen, Shanghai dengdi de tanhua yaodian" ("Main Points in the Speeches Made in Wuchang, Shenzhen, and Shanghai," 18 January– 21 February 1992), in Deng (1993), pp. 370–383.

Deng Xiaoping, *Deng Xiaoping wenxuan* (Selected Works of Deng Xiaoping), Vol. 3, Beijing: Renmin chubanshe, 1993.

Deng Xiaoping, *Jianshe you Zhongguo tese de shehui zhuyi* (Building Socialism with Chinese Characteristics), Beijing: Renmin chubanshe, 1984.

Deng Xiaoping, *Deng Xiaoping wenxuan* (Selected Works of Deng Xiaoping 1975–1982), Beijing: Renmin chubanshe, 1983.

Deng Xiaoping, "Guanyu nongcun zhengce wenti" ("On Policy Problems in Rural Areas"), in Deng (1983), pp. 275–276.

Di Palma, Giuseppe, *To Craft Democracies: An Essay on Democratic Transition*, Berkeley: University of California Press, 1990.

Diao Tianding, *et al.*, *Zhongguo difang guojia jigou gaiyao* (An Introduction to Local State Organizations in China), Beijing: Falu chubanshe, 1989.

Dimitrov, Martin, *Administrative Decentralization, Legal Fragmentation, and the Rule of Law: The Enforcement of Intellectual Property Rights in China, Russia, Taiwan, and the Czech Republic*, Ph.D dissertation, Stanford University, 2004.

Ding Jinhong & Luo Zude, "Lun woguo quyu jingji fazhan yu xingzheng quhua tizhi gaige" ("On Regional Economic Development and the Reform of Regional Administrative System in China"), The Development Research Center, the State Council, internal circulation, 1993.

Dittmer, Lowell & Samuel S. Kim (eds.), *China's Quest for National Identity*, Ithaca, NY.: Cornell University Press, 1993.

The Document Research Office of the CCP, *Shisida yilai: zhongyao wenxian xuanbian* (Selected Important Documents since the Fourteenth Party Congress), Beijing: Renmin chubanshe, 1998.

The Document Research Office of the CCP, *Shiyi jie sanzhong quanhui yilai dang de lici quanguo daibiao dahui zhongyang quanhui zhongyao wenjian xuanbian* (Selected Important Documents of the Party Congresses and its Plenums since the Third Plenum of the Eleventh Party Congress), Beijing: Zhongyang wenxian chubanshe, 1997.

Dong Liwen, *Lun Jiushi niandai de zhonggong minzu zhuyi* (Chinese Nationalism in the 1990s), doctoral dissertation, National Chengchi University, Taipei, 1997.

Dong Zhaocai, "Jin yibu shenru gaohao Wenzhou de gaige shinian" ("Deepening and Improving Wenzhou's Reform Experiment"), in Pan Shangen (1988), pp. 3–4.

Donnithorne, Audrey, "China's Cellular Economy: Some Economic Trends since the Cultural Revolution," *The China Quarterly* 52 (1972), pp. 605–619.

Donnithorne, Audrey, *China's Economic System*, New York: Praeger, 1967.

DOO (The Department of Organization of the Central Committee of the CCP), "Zhongyang zuzhibu guanyu xiuding 'zhonggong zhongyang guanlide ganbu zhiwu mingchengbiao' de tong zhi" ("Notice of the CCP Organization Department on Revision of the 'Job Title List for Cadres Managed Centrally by the Chinese Communist Party'"), 10 May 1990 (Zhongzufa (1990) No. 2), in The Office of Policy and Regulation of the Personnel Ministry (ed.), *Renshi gongzuo wenjian xuanbian* (Selection of Personnel Work Documents), Vol. 13, Beijing: Zhongguo renshi chubanshe, 1991, pp. 39–53.

Dorn, James A. & Wang Xi (eds.), *Economic Reform in China: Problems and Prospects*, Chicago: The University of Chicago Press, 1989.

Duchacek, Ivo D., *Comparative Federalism: The Territorial Dimension of Politics*, New York: Holt, Rinehart and Winston, Inc., 1970.

The Economic Institute of Zhejiang Academy of Social Sciences, "Zhejiang jin shinian (1979–1988) jingji fazhan de xitong fenxi" ("A Systematic Analysis of Economic Development in Zhejiang 1979–1988"), *Zhejiang xuekan* (Zhejiang Studies Monthly) 63:4 (1990), pp. 16–28.

The Economic Research Center of Suqian City Government, "Gengche zhen fazhan xiangzhen qiye de xintujing" ("New Ways to Develop Rural

Enterprises in Gengche Township"), in The Commission of Economic System Reform of Jiangsu (1988), pp. 80–88.

The Economist, "The Ostrich's View of the World," 19 December 1998.

The Economist, "A Survey of China: When China Wakes," 28 November–4 December 1992, pp. 1–18.

The Editorial Bureau of the Economic Management of Contemporary China (ed.), *Zhonghua renmin gongheguo jingji guanli dashiji* (Chronicle of Economic Management of People's Republic of China), Beijing: Zhongguo jingji chubanshe, 1987.

The Editorial Committee of the Journal of China's Economy (ed.), *Gaige, Kaifang yu zengzhang* (Reform, Open-Door and Growth), Shanghai: Sanlian shudian, 1991.

The Editorial Office of Jiangsu Yearbook, *Jiangsu jingji nianjian* (The Yearbook of Jiangsu Economy, 1987), Nanjing: Nanjing daxue chubanshe, 1987.

Elazar, Daniel J., *Exploring Federalism*, Tuscaloosa, AL.: The University of Alabama Press, 1987.

Elazar, Daniel J., "Federalism," *International Encyclopedia of the Social Sciences*, Vol. 5, New York: Macmillan, 1968.

Elkins, David J. & Richard E. B. Simeon, "A Cause in Search of Its Effect, or What Does Political Culture Explain," *Comparative Politics* 11 (1979), pp. 127–145.

Falkenheim, Victor C. (ed.), *Citizens and Groups in Contemporary China*, Ann Arbor: Center for Chinese Studies, The University of Michigan, 1987.

Falkenheim, V., "Provincial Leadership in Fukien: 1946–1966," in Scalapino (1972), pp. 199–244.

Fei Xiaotong, *Fei Xiaotong xueshu jinghualu* (Selected Works of Fei Xiaotong), Beijing: Beijing shifan xueyuan chubanshe, 1988.

Fei Xiaotong, "Wenzhou xing" ("Travelling around Wenzhou"), in Fei Xiaotong (1988), pp. 258–304.

Fei Xiaotong, "Xiao shangpin dashichang" ("Small Commodities and Big Markets"), *Zhejiang xuekan* (Zhejiang Studies Monthly) 38:3 (1986), pp. 4–13.

Fincher, John H., *Chinese Democracy: The Self-Government in Local, Provincial and National Politics, 1905–1914*, New York: St. Martin's Press, 1981.

Fitzgerald, John, " 'Reports of my death have been greatly exaggerated': the history of the death of China," in Goodman and Segal (1994), pp. 21–58.

Forster, Keith, *Rebellion and Factionalism in a Chinese Province: Zhejiang, 1966–1976*, New York: M. E. Sharpe, Inc., 1990.

Friedman, Edward, *National Identity and Democratic Prospects in Socialist China*, Armonk, NY.: M. E. Sharpe, 1995.

Friedman, Edward, "Reconstructing China's National Identity: A Southern Alternative to Mao-Era Anti-Imperialist Nationalism," *Journal of Asian Studies* 53:1 (1994), pp. 67–91.

Friedrich, Carl J., *Limited Government: A Comparison*, Englewood Cliffs, NJ.: Prentice-Hall, Inc., 1974.

Friedrich, Carl J. (ed.), *Totalitarianism*, Cambridge, MA.: Harvard University Press, 1954.

Friedrich, Carl J. & Zbigniew K. Brzezinski, *Totalitarian Dictatorship and Autocracy*, Cambridge, MA.: Harvard University Press, 1956.

Gao Shangquan, "Chongfen fahui zhongxin chengshi de zuoyong" ("To Make Full Use of Major Municipal Cities"), *People's Daily*, 21 October 1983.

Garnaut, Ross & Guonan Ma, "How Rich Is China?" *The Australian Journal of Chinese Affairs* 30 (1993), pp. 121–147.

Geertz, Clifford, "Thick Description: Toward an Interpretive Theory of Culture," in Geertz (1973), pp. 3–30.

Geertz, Clifford *The Interpretation of Cultures*, New York: Basic Books, 1973.

Geertz, Clifford "The Integrative Revolution," in Geertz (1964), pp. 105–157.

Geertz, Clifford (ed.), *Old Societies and New States*, New York: Praeger, 1964.

Goldstone, Jack A., "The Coming Chinese Collapse," *Foreign Policy* 99 (Summer 1995), pp. 35–52.

Goodman, David S. G. (ed.), *China's Provinces in Reform: Class, Community and Political Culture*, London: Routledge, 1997.

Goodman, David S. G., "Provinces Confronting the State?" in Kuan & Brosseau (1992), pp. 2–19.

Goodman, David S. G., *Center and Province in the People's Republic of China: Sichuan and Guizhou, 1955–1965*, Cambridge: Cambridge University Press, 1987.

Goodman, David S. G. (ed.), *Groups and Politics in the People's Republic of China*, Cardiff: University College Cardiff Press, 1984.

Goodman, David S. G., "Li Jingquan and the South-west Region, 1958–1966: The Life and 'Crime' of a 'Local Emperor'," *China Quarterly* 81 (March 1980), pp. 66–96.

Goodman, David S. G. & Gerald Segal (eds.), *China Deconstructs: Politics, Trade and Regionalism*, London: Routledge, 1994.

Gore, Lance L. P., *Market Communism: The Institutional Foundation of China's Post-Mao Hyper-Growth*, Hong Kong: Oxford University Press, 1998.

Gouldner, Alvin W., "The Norm of Reciprocity: A Preliminary Statement," *American Sociological Review* 25 (April 1960), pp. 161–178.

Gourevitch, Peter, *Paris and the Provinces,* Berkeley: University of California Press, 1980.

The Government of Jiangsu, "Guanyu fuyu Su, Xi, Chang, Tong, Lian wushi waimao zhigongsi chukou jingyingquan de yijian" ("About Authorizing Suzhou, Wuxi, Changzhou, Nantong and Lianyungang Five Cities Export Management," 31 October 1986a), in The Editorial Office of Jiangsu Yearbook (1987), Part I, pp. 183–185.

The Government of Jiangsu, "Guanyu guli duo chukou duo chuanghui jiangli banfa de tongzhi" ("A Notice about the Reward Methods to Encourage More Exports and Earn More Foreign Exchange," 14 January 1986b), in The Editorial Office of Jiangsu Yearbook (1987), Part I, pp. 64–66.

The Government of Jiangsu, "Guanyu guli duo chukou duo chuanghui jiangli banfa de buchong tongzhi" ("An Additional Notice about the Reward Methods to Encourage More Exports and Earn More Foreign Exchange," 15 April 1986c), in The Editorial Office of Jiangsu Yearbook (1987), Part I, pp. 64–66.

The Government of Jiangsu, "Guanyu banhao waishang touti qiye jiasu yinjin waizi de yijian" ("About Establishing Joint Ventures or Foreign Enterprises and Speeding Up Introducing Foreign Capital," 20 July 1986d), in The Editorial Office of Jiangsu Yearbook (1987), Part I, pp. 55–57.

The Government of Jiangsu, "Guanyu youguan fangmian zhichi liangshi yiqu jinyibu dui wai kaifang de yijian" ("On How the Departments Concerned to Support Two Cities (Lianyunguang and Nantong) and One Area (Changjiaguang) to Further Their Open Door Policy," 20 July 1986e), in The Editorial Office of Jiangsu Yearbook (1987), Part I, pp. 58–59.

The Government of Jiangsu, "Guanyu guli waishang touti de ruogan guiding" ("Some Regulations on Encouraging Foreign Investment," 11 November 1986f), in The Editorial Office of Jiangsu Yearbook (1987), Part I, pp. 180–181.

The Government of Jiangsu, "Subei shisan xian jingji fazhan gongzuo huiyi jiyao" ("A Summary of Working Conference of Economic Development of Thirteen Counties in N. Jiangsu," April 1986g), in The Editorial Office of Jiangsu Yearbook (1987), Part I, pp. 87–90.

The Government of Jiangsu, *Jianguo san shi wu nian lai de Jiangsu 1949–1984* (35 Years in Jiangsu Province Since the Establishment of PRC), Nanjing: Jiangsu renmin chubanshe, 1984.

The Government of Zhejiang, "Guanyu guli waishang touzi de buchong guiding" ("A Complementary Regulation about Encouraging Foreign Businessmen's Investment"), 1 May 1988a, in *Zhejiang jingji nianjian 1989* (Yearbook of Zhejiang Economy, 1989), Hangzhou: Zhejiang renmin chubanshe, 1989, pp. 91–92.

The Government of Zhejiang, "Guanyu shixing dui wai maoyi chengbao jingying zeren zi ruogan wenti de tongzhi" ("A Notice on Implementing the Contract System of Foreign Trade"), 6 April 1988b, in *Zhejiang jingji nianjian 1989* (Yearbook of Zhejiang Economy, 1989), Hangzhou: Zhejiang renmin chubanshe, 1989, pp. 88–90.

The Government of Zhejiang, "Zhejiang sheng jingji shehui fazhan zhanlue gangyao" ("A Summary of Economic and Social Development Strategy of Zhejiang, 1986–2000"), 10 September 1986a, in *Zhejiang jingji nianjian 1987* (Yearbook of Zhejiang Economy, 1987), Hangzhou: Zhejiang renmin chubanshe, 1988, pp. 52–60.

The Government of Zhejiang, "Zhejiang sheng guomin jingji he shehui fazhan de qi ge wunian jihua" ("The Seventh Five-Year Plan of Economic and Social Development of Zhejiang, 1986–1990"), 14 June 1986b, in *Zhejiang jingji nianjian 1987* (Yearbook of Zhejiang Economy, 1987), Hangzhou: Zhejiang renmin chubanshe, 1988, pp. 44–51.

The Government of Zhejiang, "Guanyu jiji kuoda chukou zengjia waihui shouru de baogao" ("A Report on Expanding Export and Increasing Foreign Exchange Revenue"), 2 January 1986c, in *Zhejiang jingji nianjian 1987* (Yearbook of Zhejiang Economy, 1987), Hangzhou: Zhejiang renmin chubanshe, 1988, pp. 89–91.

The Government of Zhejiang, "Guanyu xiangzhen qiye jingji zhengce de bucong guiding" ("A Complementary Regulation about Economic Policy toward Rural Enterprises"), 15 April 1985, in *Zhejiang jingji nianjian 1986* (Yearbook of Zhejiang Economy, 1986), Hangzhou: Zhejiang renmin chubanshe, 1988, pp. 63–64.

Gray, Jack (ed.), *Modern China's Search for a Political Form*, New York: Oxford University Press, 1969.

Grindle, Merilee S. (ed.), *Politics and Policy Implementation in the Third World*, Princeton, NJ.: Princeton University Press, 1980.

Gu Xiulian, "Fazhan shangpin jingji bixu zhongshi shichang de peiyu: Zhejiang kaocha jiqi qishi" ("Developing Commodity Economy Requires an Emphasis on Cultivating the Market: A Zhejiang Visit and Lessons from Zhejiang," 22 April 1986), in The Editorial Office of Jiangsu Yearbook (1987), Part VIII, pp. 1–6.

Gui Shiyong, *et al.* (eds.), *Lun Zhongguo hongguan jingji guanli* (On China's Macro-Economic Management), Beijing: Zhongguo jingji chubanshe, 1987.

Guo Xiaoming, *et al.*, "Sunan moshi de zai renshi" ("Reconsideration of the South Jiangsu Model"), *Jingji tizhi gaige* (Economic System Reforms) 24 (1987), pp. 31–34.

Hall, Peter, *Governing the Economy: The Politics of State Intervention in Britain and France*, New York: Oxford University Press, 1991.

Harding, Harry, *China's Second Revolution: Reform after Mao*, Washington, DC.: Brookings Institution, 1987.

Harding, Harry, "Political Development in Post-Mao China," in Barnett & Clough (1986), pp. 13–38.

Harding, Harry, *Organizing China: The Problems of Bureaucracy, 1949–1976*, Stanford: Stanford University Press, 1972.

Hasegawa, Tsuyoshi, "The Connection Between Political and Economic Reform in Communist Regimes," in Rozman (1992), pp. 59–117.

Hawkins, Joyce M. & Robert Allen, *The Oxford Encyclopedia English Dictionary*, Oxford: Clarendon Press of Oxford, 1991.

He Li, *et al.* (eds.), *Zhonghua renmin gongheguo shi* (A History of the People's Republic of China), Beijing: Guofan daxue chubanshe, 1989.

He Ruo-han, "Zhuzong jiuba tiewan: wajie Guangdong bang" ("Premier Zhu's Ironhanded Policies to Crack down on the Guangdong Gang in 1998"), *Ming Pao Monthly* 4 (April 1999), pp. 68–72.

He Tohong & Li Jianxin, "Zhejiang nongcun siren qiye fazhan gaikuang ji duice" ("Private Enterprise Development in Rural Areas in Zhejiang and Strategies"), *Zhejiang xuekan* (Zhejiang Studies Monthly) 50:3 (1988), pp. 29–32.

Hendrischke, Hans, & Feng Chongyi (eds.), *The Political Economy of China's Provinces: Comparative and Competitive Advantage*, London: Routledge, 1999.

Hicks, U. K., *et al.* (eds.), *Federalism and Economic Growth in Underdeveloped Countries*, New York: Oxford University Press, 1961.

Hong Kong Standard, 2 January 1999.

Hu Angang, *Zhongguo fazhan qianjing* (Perspectives of China's Development), Hangzhou: Zhejiang renmin chubanshe, 1999.

Hu Angang, "Difang ganbu ruhe kandai zhongyang difang guanxi zhiduhua" ("How Local Cadres View Institutionalizing Central-Local Relations"), in Hu Angang (1999), pp. 126–129.

Hu Angang, "Fenshuizhi: pingjia yu jianyi" ("On Tax-Division System: Assessment and Suggestions"), *Zhanlue yu guanli* 5 (1996), pp. 1–9.

Hu Angang, "Weishemo wo zhuzhang tequ bu te" ("Why I Am for No Preferential Treatment for SEZs"), *Ming Pao*, 23 August 1995, p. C6.

Hu Angang, "Shengdiji ganbu yanzhong de dongxibu chaju" ("Income Disparities between Eastern and Western China in the Eyes of Leading Cadres of the Provincial and Prefectural Levels"), *Zhanlue yu guanli* 5 (1994), pp. 88–90.

Hu Tonggong, "Bu fada nongye diqu xiangzhen qiye moshi — Gengche moshi" ("Township and Village Industrial Model for Underdeveloped Agricultural Areas — The Chengche Model"), in Chen Jiyuan *et al.* (1988), pp. 117–137.

Hua Sheng Pao, 22 May 1998.

Huang Yasheng, *Inflation and Investment Controls in China: The Political Economy of Central-Local Relations during the Reform Era*, New York: Cambridge University Press, 1996.

Huang Yasheng, "Administrative Monitoring in China," *The China Quarterly* 143 (1995a), pp. 828–843.

Huang Yasheng, "Why China Will Not Collapse," *Foreign Policy* 99 (Summer 1995b), pp. 54–68.

The Investigation Group of Industrial Efficiency, the Commission of Science and Technology of the Conference of Political Consultants of Jiangsu, "Jiangsu sheng gongye jingji xiaoyi kaocha baogao" ("An Investigation Report of Industrial Enterprise Economic Efficiency of Jiangsu"), *Nanjing shehui kexue* (Nanjing Social Sciences) 35:1 (1990), pp. 47–53.

The Investigation Group of the Office for Agricultural Policy Studies, "Jianshe shangping jidi fazhan chuanghui nongye: shi ge nongfu chanping chukou shangping jidi de diaocha" ("Building Commodity Bases and Developing Agriculture for Creating Foreign Exchanges: An Investigation into Ten Export Bases of Grain Productions and Sidelines"), *Zhejiang tongxun* (Zhejiang Correspondence) 19 (1985), pp. 1–5.

Jacobson, Harold & Michel Oksenberg, *China's Participation in the IMF, the World Bank, and GATT: Toward a World Economic Order*, Ann Arbor: University of Michigan Press, 1990.

Jain, Purnendra, *Local Politics and Policy Making in Japan*, New Delhi: Commonwealth Publishers, 1989.

Jenner, W. J. F., *The Tyranny of History: The Roots of China's Crisis*, London: The Penguin Press, 1992.

Jia Hao & Lin Zhimin (eds.), *Changing Central-Local Relations in China: Reform and State Capacity*, Boulder, CO.: Westview, 1994.

Jiang Taiwei, "Gailun Zhejiang jingji fazhan de san jieduan" ("On Three Stages of Economic Development in Zhejiang"), in *Zhejiang jingji nianjian*, 1988, pp. 431–432.

Jiang Yiwei, "Chongxin chengshi de zuoyong" ("On the Role of Major Municipal Cities"), *Jingji tizhi gaige zazhi* (Journal of Economic System Reforms) 1 (1983), pp. 10–18.

Jiang Zemin, "Zhengque chuli shehui zhuyi xiandaihua jianshe zhong de ruogan zhongda guanxi" ("Handle Correctly Some Important Relations in the Construction of Socialist Modernization"), in The Document Research Office of the CCP (1998), pp. 1460–1476.

Jiang Zemin, "Zhengque chuli shehui zhuyi xiandaihua jianshe zhong de ruogan zhongda guanxi" ("Correctly Handle Some Major Relationships in the Process of Socialist Modernization," 28 September 1995), *People's Daily*, 9 October 1995.

Jin Ji, *Lianbang zhi: Zhongguo de zuijia chulu* (Federalism: China's Best Way), Hong Kong: Baixin wenhua shiye chuban gongsi, 1992.

Joseph, Willian A., Christine P. W. Wong & David Zweig (eds.), *New Perspectives on the Cultural Revolution*, Cambridge: Harvard University Press, 1991.

Katzenstein, Peter J., *Cultural Norms and National Security: Police and Military in Postwar Japan*, Ithaca, NY.: Cornell University Press, 1996a.

Katzenstein, Peter J., "Introduction: Alternative Perspective on National Security," in Katzenstein (1996b), pp. 1–32.

Katzenstein, Peter J. (ed.), *The Culture of National Security: Norms and Identity in World Politics*, New York: Columbia University Press, 1996b.

Keji jingmao bao (News for Science, Technology, Economy, and Trade), 25 June 1993.

Kelliher, Daniel, "The Political Consequences of China's Reform," *Comparative Politics* 18:4 (1986), pp. 479–493.

Kenyon, Daphen A. & John Kincaid (eds.), *Competition Among States and Local Governments: Efficiency and Equity in American Federalism*, Washington, DC.: The Urban Institute Press, 1992.

Keohane, Robert O., "Reciprocity in International Relations," *International Organization* 40:1 (Winter 1986), pp. 1–27.

Keohane, Robert O., *After Hegemony: Cooperation and Discord in the World Political Economy*, Princeton, NJ.: Princeton University Press, 1984.

Kesselman, Mark, "Research Perspectives in Comparative Local Politics: Pitfalls and Prospects," *Comparative Urban Research* Spring 1972, pp. 10–29.

Kesselman, Mark & Donald Rosenthal, *Local Power and Comparative Politics*, Beverly Hills: Sage Publications, 1974.

Kraus, Willy, *Private Business in China: Revival Between Ideology and Pragmatism*, Honolulu: University of Hawaii Press, 1991.

Kuan, Hsin-chi & Maurice Brosseau (eds.), *China Review 1992*, Hong Kong: Chinese University Press, 1992.

Kuang Ji, *et al.*, *Dangdai Zhongguo de Guangdong* (Guangdong in Contemporary China), Beijing: Dangdai Zhongguo chubanshe, 1991.

Kumar, Anjali, "China's Reform, Internal Trade and Marketing," *The Pacific Review* 7:3 (1994), pp. 323–340.

Lampton, David M., "A Plum for a Peach: Bargaining, Interest, and Bureaucratic Politics in China," in Lieberthal & Lampton (1992), pp. 33–58.

Lampton, David M. (ed.), *Policy Implementation in Post-Mao China*, Berkeley, CA.: University of California Press, 1987.

Lardy, Nicholas R., *Agriculture in China's Modern Economic Development*, Cambridge: Cambridge University Press, 1983.

Lardy, Nicholas R., "Centralization and Decentralization in China's Fiscal Management," *China Quarterly* 60 (March 1975), pp. 25–60.

Lau, Yee-Cheung, "History," in Yeung & Chu (1994), pp. 429–447.

Leach, Richard H., *American Federalism*, New York: W. W. Norton & Company, Inc., 1970.

Lee, Hong Yung, *From Revolutionary Cadres to Party Technocrats in Socialist China*, Berkeley, CA.: University of California Press, 1991.

Leichter, Howard, *A Comparative Approach to Policy Analysis*, Cambridge: Cambridge University Press, 1979.

Levenson, Joseph L., *Modern China and Its Confucian Past: The Problem of Intellectual Continuity*, New York: Anchor Books, 1964.

Lewis, John, *Leadership in Communist China*, Ithaca, NY.: Cornell University Press, 1963.

Li Cheng, *The Rise of Technocracy: Elite Transformation and Ideological Change in Post-Mao China*, Ph.D. dissertation, Princeton University, 1992.

Li Cheng & David Bachman, "Localism, Elitism, and Immobilism: Elite Formation and Social Change in Post-Mao China," *World Politics* XLII:1 (October 1989), pp. 64–94.

Li Cheng & Lynn White, "The Fifteenth Central Committee of the Chinese Communist Party: Full-Fledged Technocratic Leadership with Partial Control by Jiang Zemin," *Asian Survey* XXXVIII:3 (March 1998), pp. 231–264.

Li Fang, "Du 'wenzhou shiqu geti gongshangye hu qingkuang diaocha'" ("Read 'An Investigation to Private Industrial and Commercial Businesses inWenzhou'"), *Zhejiang xuekan* (Zhejiang Studies Monthly) 3 (1985), pp. 25–30.

Li Guocheng, "Zhonggong lijie zhongyang weiyuan shengji fenxi" ("An Analysis of the Provincial Origins of the Central Committee Members of the CCP"), *Yazhou yanjiu* (Asian Studies) 22 (April 1997), pp. 28–101.

Li, Linda Chelan, *Center and Provinces: China 1978–1993*, Oxford: Clarendon Press, 1998.

Li Shaomin (ed.), *Zhongguo dalu de shehui, zhengzhi, jingji* (Society, Politics and Economy in Mainland China), Taipei: Guiguan tushu, 1992.

Li Yun, "Dui Jiangsu changye jiegou youhua zhanlue de sikao" ("Some Considerations about Improving Industrial Structure in Jiangsu"), *Jianghai xuekan* (The Journal of Jianghai) 3 (1990), pp. 30–32.

Li Zongji, "Fada nongye diqu xiangzhen qiye moshi — Sunan moshi" ("The Township and Village Enterprise Model in Developed Agricultural Area — the South Jiangsu Model"), in Chen Jiyuan *et al.* (1988), pp. 66–89.

Lianhe Zaobao (Singapore), 23 October 1998.

Lianhe Zaobao (Singapore), 25 February 1998.

Liberation Daily, "Wenzhou shangpin jingji de xin fazhan" ("New Development in Wenzhou's Commodity Economy"), 18 October 1986.

Lieberthal, Kenneth G., *Governing China: From Revolution Through Reform*, New York: W. W. Norton & Company, Inc., 1995.

Lieberthal, Kenneth G., "Introduction: The 'Fragmented Authoritarianism' — Model and Its Limitations," in Lieberthal & Lampton (1992), pp. 1–30.

Lieberthal, Kenneth G. & David M. Lampton (eds.), *Bureaucracy, Politics, and Decision Making in Post-Mao China*, Berkeley, CA.: University of California Press, 1992.

Lieberthal, Kenneth G. & Michel Oksenberg, *Policy Making in China: Leaders, Structures, and Processes*, Princeton, NJ.: Princeton University Press, 1988.

References 399

Lijphart, Arend, "Consociation and Federation: Conceptual and Empirical Links," *Canadian Journal of Political Science* XII:3 (September 1979), pp. 499–515.
Lin Ling, "Xu yan" ("Preface"), in Tang Zejiang (1986), pp. 1–5.
Lindbeck, J. (ed.), *China: Management of a Revolutionary Society*, London: Allen and Unwin, 1972.
Linz, Juan J. & Alfred Stepan, *Problems of Democratic Transition and Consolidation: Southern Europe, South America, and Post-Communist Europe*, Baltimore: The Johns Hopkins University Press, 1996.
Liu, Alan P. L., "The Wenzhou Model of Development and China's Modernization," *Asian Survey* XXXII:8 (August 1992), pp. 696–711.
Liu, Alan P. L., *Communications and National Integration in Communist China*, Berkeley, CA.: University of California Press, 1975.
Liu Dinghan, *et al.* (eds.), *Dangdai Zhongguo de Jiangsu* (China Today: Jiangsu Province), Beijing: Zhongguo shehui kexue chubanshe, 1989.
Liu Jun & Li Lin (eds.), *Xin quanwei zhuyi* (Neo-Authoritarianism), Beijing: Jingji xueyuan chubanshe, 1989.
Liu Qing & Tang Hai, "Wenzhou dui hua lu" ("Dialogues about Wenzhou"), in *Nongmin ribao* (Peasantry Daily), 4–8 August 1987, in Pan Shangen (1988), pp. 95–128.
Liu Yia-ling, "Reform From Below: The Private Economy and Local Politics in the Rural Industrialization of Wenzhou," *China Quarterly* 135 (September 1993), pp. 491–514.
Liu Yingshu & Wang Yi, "Guoji da xunhuan jingji fazhan zhanlue gaishu" ("A Summary of Grand International Circulation Development Strategy"), *Jingji xue qingbao* (Information for Economics) 3 (1988), pp. 5–10.
Livingston, William, "A Note on the Nature of Federalism," in Wildavsky (1976), pp. 20–30.
Lu Dadao, *et al.*, *Zhongguo gongye buju de lilun yu shijian* (Theory and Practice of China's Industrial Distribution), Beijing: Kexue chubanshe, 1990.
Lu Zhengfang, "Nongcun jiceng kaituo xing lingdao banzi de tedian: Suzhou shi jiu ge jingji fada diqu lingdao de tiaocha" ("Characteristics of Innovative Leadership at the Grassroots Rural Level: An Investigation of Nine Township Leaderships in Advanced Economic Areas of Suzhou"), *Suzhou daxue xuebao* (The Journal of Suzhou University) 3 (1986), pp. 23–27.
Lyons, Thomas P., "Planning and Interprovincial Co-ordination in Maoist China," *China Quarterly* 121 (March 1990), pp. 36–60.

Lyons, Thomas P., *Economic Integration and Planning in Maoist China*, New York: Columbia University Press, 1987.

Ma Hong, "Zhejiang sheng Wenzhou shi Leqing xian xiangzhen 7,000 ge wanyuanhu qingkuang diaocha" ("An Investigation into 7,000 Ten Thousand Yuan households in Leqing County of Wenzhou Shi"), in *Zhongguo xiangzhen qiye nianjian* (1978–1987) (China's Yearbook of Rural Industry), Beijing: Nongye chubanshe, 1989, pp. 239–241.

Ma Hong, "Yao chongfen fahui jingji zhongxin de zuoyong" ("To Make Full Use of Economic Centers"), *Wenhui Daily*, 19 February 1982.

Ma Hong & Sun Shangqing (eds.), *Zhongguo jingji xingshi yu zhanwang* (Economic Situation and Prospects in China, 1991–1992), Beijing: Zhongguo fazhan chubanshe, 1992.

Maass, Arthur (ed.), *Area and Power: A Theory of Local Government*, Glencoe, Illinois: The Free Press, 1959.

MacFarquhar, Roderick, *The Politics of China, 1949–1989*, Cambridge: Cambridge University Press, 1993.

MacFarquhar, Roderick, *Origins of the Cultural Revolution: The Great Leap Forward, 1958–1960*, Vol. 2, New York: Columbia University Press, 1983.

MacFarquhar, Roderick, *Origins of the Cultural Revolution: Contradictions Among the People, 1856–1957*, Vol. 1, New York: Columbia University Press, 1974.

Mackerras, Colin (ed.), *Dictionary of the Politics of the People's Republic of China*, London: Routledge, 1998.

Mao Zedong, "Ren de zhengque sixiang shi cong nali lai de?" ("Where Do People's Correct Ideas Come From?" May 1963), in *Mao Zedong zhuzuo xuandu* (Selected Works of Mao Zedong), Vol. 2, Beijing: Renmin chubanshe, 1986, pp. 839–841.

Mao Zedong, "Lun shida guanxi" ("On the Ten Great Relationships," 25 April 1956), in Mao (1977), pp. 267–288.

Mao Zedong, *Mao Zedong xuanji* (Selected Works of Mao Zedong), Beijing: Renmin chubanshe, 1977.

March, James G. & Johan P. Olsen, *Rediscovering Institutions: The Organizational Basis of Politics*, New York: Free Press, 1989.

Meynaud, Jean, *Technocracy*, New York: Free Press, 1969.

Mi Shuzu, "Wenzhou nongcun jingji moshi lilun taolun hui zhuyao guandian zongshu" ("A Summary of Major Views in the Conference of Economic Theories of the Wenzhou Model"), *Zhejiang xuekan* (Zhejiang Studies Monthly) 40:5 (1986), pp. 22–26.

Migdal, Joel S., *Strong Societies and Weak States: State-Society Relations and State Capabilities in the Third World*, Princeton, NJ.: Princeton University Press,' 1988.

Migdal, Joel S., Atul Kohli & Vivinne Shue (eds.), *State Power and Social Forces: Domination and Transformation in the Third World*, New York: Cambridge University Press, 1994.

Milch, Jerome E., "Influence as Power: French Local Government Reconsidered," *British Journal of Political Science* 4 (1974), pp. 139–172.

Miles, James, *Legacy of Tiananmen: China in Disarray*, Ann Arbor: University of Michigan Press, 1996.

Ming Pao, 14 May 1999.

Ming Pao, 4 February 1999.

Ming Pao, 12 December 1998.

Ming Pao, 1 October 1998.

Ming Pao, 30 September 1998.

Ming Pao, 24 September 1998.

Ming Pao, 3 September 1998.

Ming Pao, 26 July 1998.

Ming Pao, 25 July 1998.

Ming Pao, 16 July 1998.

Ming Pao, 9 July 1998.

Ming Pao, 4 February 1998.

Ming Pao, 9 August 1995.

Mo Yuanren & Liu Qinghuan, "Jiangsu xiangzhen qiye fazhan jianshi" ("A Brief History of Rural Industrial Development in Jiangsu"), in Wu Xiangjun (1990), pp. 899–900.

Montinola, G., Yingji Qian & Barry R. Weingast, "Federalism, Chinese Style: The Political Basis for Economic Success in China," *World Politics* 48:1 (October 1995), pp. 50–81.

Moore, Barrington, Jr., *Injustice: The Social Bases of Obedience and Revolt*, White Plains, NY.: M. E. Sharpe, 1978.

Morey, Roy D., "A Letter from Beijing: On Reform of China's Public Institutions," *Political Science and Politics* XXVI:1 (March 1993), pp. 117–119.

The Municipal Government of Wenzhou, "Wenzhou shi jingji de xinfazhan" ("New Developments of the Wenzhou Economy"), in *Zhejiang jingji nianjian 1988* (Yearbook of Zhejiang Economy, 1988), Hangzhou: Zhejiang renmin chubanshe, 1988, pp. 360–362.

The Municipal Government of Wenzhou, *Wenzhou shiqu geti gongshangye hu qingkuang diaocha* (An Investigation into Private Industrial and Commercial Businesses in Wenzhou), Wenzhou: The Municipal Government of Wenzhou, 1984.

Nakamura, Robert T. & Frank Smallwood, *The Politics of Policy Implementation*, New York: St. Martin's Press, 1980.

Nanfang Daily, 12 March 1999.

Nathan, Andrew J. & Robert Ross, *The Great Wall and the Empty of Fortress: China's Search for Security*, New York: W. W. Norton, 1997.

Nathan, Andrew J. & Kellee S. Tsai, "Factionalism: A New Institutionalist Restatement," *The China Journal* 34 (July 1995), pp. 157–192.

Nathan, Richard P. & Margarita M. Balmaceda, "Comparing Federal Systems of Government," in Bennett (1990), pp. 59–77

Naughton, Barry, *Growing Out of the Plan: Chinese Economic Reform 1978–1993*, New York: Cambridge University Press, 1995.

Naughton, Barry, "The Third Front: Defense Industrialization in the Chinese Interior," *China Quarterly* 115 (September 1988), pp. 351–386.

Naughton, Barry, "The Decline of Central Control over Investment in Post-Mao China," in Lampton (1987), pp. 51–79.

Nee, Victor, "Peasant Entrepreneurship and the Politics of Regulation in China," in Nee & Stark (1989), pp. 169–207.

Nee, Victor & David Stark (eds.), *Reforming the Economic Institutions of Socialism: China and Eastern Europe*, Stanford, CA.: Stanford University Press, 1989.

Nelson, Daneil N. (ed.), *Local Politics in Communist Countries*, Lexington: The University Press of Kentucky, 1980.

Nolan, Peter & Dong Fureng (eds.), *Market Forces in China: Competition and Small Business (The Wenzhou Model)*, Atlantic Highlands, NJ.: Zed Books Ltd., 1990.

North, Douglass C., *Institutions, Institutional Change and Economic Performance*, New York: Cambridge University Press, 1990.

O'Donnell, Guillermo & Philippe C. Schmitter, *Transitions from Authoritarian Rule: Tentative Conclusions About Uncertain Democracies*, Baltimore: Johns Hokpins University Press, 1986.

The Office of Coordination of International Economy of Zhejiang, "Zhejiang waixiang xing jingji fazhan gaikuang" ("A Summary of Export-Oriented Economy of Zhejiang"), 1988, in *Zhejiang jingji nianjian 1989* (Yearbook of Zhejiang Economy, 1989), Hangzhou: Zhejiang renmin chubanshe, 1989, pp. 285–287.

The Office of Local Chronicles of Changjiagang City, The Rural Industrial Bureau of Changjiagan City, *Changjiagang shi xiangzhen gongye zhi* (A Chronicle of the Rural Industry in Changjiagang City), Shanghai: Shanghai renmin chubanshe, 1990.

Oi, Jean C., *Rural China Takes Off: Incentives for Industrialization*, Berkeley, CA.: University of California Press, 1996.

Oi, Jean C., "Fiscal Reform and the Economic Foundations of Local State Corporatism in China," *World Politics* 45 (October 1992), pp. 99–126.

Pan Shangen, *Wenzhou shiyan qu* (Wenzhou Experimental Zone), Beijing: Zhonggong zhongyang dangxiao chubanshe, 1988.

Parish, Willian L. & Martin K. White, *Village and Family in Contemporary China*, Chicago: University of Chicago Press, 1978.

Parris, Kristen, "Local Initiative and National Reform: The Wenzhou Model of Development," *China Quarterly* 134 (June 1993), pp. 243–263.

People's Daily, 25 December 1998.

People's Daily, 4 December 1998.

People's Daily, 26 October 1998.

People's Daily, 1 September 1998.

People's Daily, 9 August 1998.

People's Daily, 16 September 1995.

People's Daily, 17 May 1995.

People's Daily, 23 June 1994.

People's Daily, 12 September 1987.

People's Daily, 17 March 1986.

People's Daily, 29 April 1985.

People's Daily, 27 November 1980.

Perkins, Dwight, *Market Control and Planning in Communist China*, Cambridge, MA.: Harvard University Press, 1966.

Perry, Elizabeth J. & Christine Wong (eds.), *The Political Economy of Reform in Post-Mao China*, Cambridge, MA.: Harvard University Press, 1985.

Powell, Walter W. & Paul J. DiMaggio (eds.), *The New Institutionalism in Organizational Analysis*, Chicago: University of Chicago Press, 1991.

Pressman, Jeffrey & Aaron Wildavsky, *Implementation*, Berkeley, CA.: University of California Press, 1973.

Prime, Penelope, "Central-Provincial Investment and Finance: The Cultural Revolution and Its Legacy in Jiangsu Province," in Joseph, Wong & Zweig (1991), pp. 189–209.

Pu Xingzu, *et al.*, *Zhonghua renmin gongheguo zhengzhi zhidu* (The Political System of the People's Republic of China), Hong Kong: Sanlian shudian, 1995.

Pun, Pamela & Reuters, "Gitic Officially Declared Bankrupt," *Hong Kong Standard*, 11 January 1999.

Putnam, Robert D., "Diplomacy and Domestic Politics: the Logic of Two-Level Games," *International Organizations* 42:3 (Summer 1988), pp. 427–460.

Pye, Lucian W., "Factions and the Politics of *Guanxi*: Paradoxes in Chinese Administrative and Political Behavior," *The China Journal* 34 (July 1995), pp. 35–53.

Pye, Lucian, "China: Erratic State, Frustrated Society," *Foreign Affairs* 69:4 (1990), pp. 56–74.

Pye, Lucian, *The Mandarin and the Cadre*, Ann Arbor: University of Michigan Center for Chinese Studies, 1988.

Pye, Lucian, *The Dynamics of Chinese Politics*, Cambridge, MA.: Oelgeschlager, Gunn & Hain, 1981.

Pye, Lucian, *The Spirit of Chinese Politics*, Cambridge, MA.: MIT Press, 1968.

Rabinoviz, Francine & Felicity M. Trueblood (eds.), *National-Local Linkages: The Interrelation-ships of Urban and National Politics in Latin America*, Beverly Hills: Sage, 1973.

Rao Yuqing & Xiao Geng, "Zhongguo zhen jiang fenbeng lixi ma?" ("Is China Really Going to Disintegrate?"), *Ershiyi shiji* 21 (February 1994), pp. 22–23.

Reagan, M. D. & J. G. Sanzone, *The New Federalism*, New York: Oxford University Press, 1981.

The Research Group of China's Private Economy during the Seventh Five-Year Plan (ed.), *Zhongguo de siying jingji: xianzhuang, wenti, qianjing* (China's Private Economy: Current Situations, Problems, and Prospects), Beijing: Zhongguo shehui kexue chubanshe, 1989.

The Research Office of the Central Committee, China Democratic Construction Association, "Wenzhou siren jingji mianmian guan" ("A Comprehensive Look at Wenzhou's Private Economy"), in The Research Group of China's Private Economy during the Seventh Five-Year Plan (1989), pp. 135–149.

Riggs, Fred, *Administration in Developing Countries*, Boston: Houghton Mifflin, 1964.

Riker, William H., *Federalism: Origin, Operation, Significance*, Boston: Little, Brown & Company, 1964.

Ripley, Randall & Grace Franklin, *Bureaucracy and Policy Implementation*, Howewood, Ill.: Dorsey Press, 1982.

Riskin, Carl, *China's Political Economy: The Quest for Development Since 1949*, New York: Oxford University Press, 1988.

Robson, W. A., *Local Government in Crisis*, London: Allen & Unwin, 1966.

Rose, Richard, *Politics in England*, Boston: Litter & Brown, 1964.

Roy, Jayanta (ed.), *Macroeconomic Management and Fiscal Decentralization*, Washington, DC.: The World Bank, 1995.

Rozman, Gilbert (ed.), *Dismantling Communism*, Washington, DC. and Baltimore: The Woodrow Wilson Center Press & The Johns Hopkins University Press, 1992.

Sahlins, Marshall, *Stone Age Economics*, Chicago: Aldine-Atherton, 1972.

Samuels, Richard J., *The Politics of Regional Policy in Japan: Localities Incorporated?* Princeton: Princeton University Press, 1983.

Scalapino, Robert, "The CCP's Provincial Secretaries," *Problem of Communism* 25:4 (1976), pp. 18–35.

Scalapino, Robert (ed.), *Elites in the People's Republic of China*, Seattle: University of Washington Press, 1972.

Schapiro, Leonard, *The Government and Politics of the Soviet Union*, London: Hutchinson, 1967.

Schoppa, R. Keith, "Province and Nation: The Chekiang Provincial Autonomy Movement, 1017–1927," *Journal of Asian Studies* 36:4 (1977), pp. 661–674.

Schoppa, R. Keith, "Local Self-Government in Zhejiang, 1909–1927," *Modern China* 2:4 (October 1976), pp. 503–530.

Schroeder, Paul E., "Territorial Actors as Competitors for Power: The Case of Hubei and Wuhan," in Lieberthal and Lampton (1992), pp. 283–307.

Schroeder, Paul E., *Regional Power in China: Tiao-Tiao Kuai-Kuai Authority in the Chinese Political System*, Ph.D. dissertation, Ohio State University, 1987.

Schulz, Ann, *Local Politics and Nation-States*, Santa Barbara, California: Clio Books, 1979.

Schurmann, Franz, *Ideology and Organization in Communist China*, 2nd Ed., Berkeley, CA.: University of California Press, 1968.

Schurmann, Franz, *Ideology and Organization in Communist China*, 1st Ed., Berkeley, CA.: University of California Press, 1966.

Schwartz, Benjamin, *In Search of Wealth and Power*, New York: Harper Torchbook, 1964.

Scott, Anthony (ed.), *Natural Resource Revenue: A Test of Federalism,* Vancouver: University of British Columbia Press, 1976.

The Secretariat of ECASC, *Lianhe xiezuo chengguo zhanshi* (Exhibition of Achievements of Cooperation and Coordination of the ECASC), Kunming: Government Print, 1999.

The Secretariat of ECASC, *Lu sheng qu shi qifang jingji xietiao hui di shisi ci huiyi wenjian ziliao huibian* (Collected Documents of the 14th Conference of the ECASC), Guiyang: Government Print, 1998.

The Secretariat of ECASC, "Zou Jiahua fuzongli dui lu sheng qu shi qifang jingji xietiao hui di shisan ci huiyi de jidian zhishi" ("Some Instructions by Vice Premier Zou Jiahua over the 13th Conference of the ECASC"), in *Lu sheng qu shi qifang jingji xietiao hui de shisan ci huiyi wenjian ziliao huibian* (Collected Documents of the 13th Conference of the ECASC), Chengdu: Government Print, 1997, pp. 105–106.

The Secretariat of ECASC, *Wushengqu qifang jingji xietiao hui di shi'er ci huiyi wenjian huibian* (Collected Documents of the Twelfth Conference of the ECASC), Lasha: Government Print, 1996.

The Secretariat of ECASC, *Wushengqu qifang jingji xietiao hui dijiuci huiyi wenjian huibian* (Collected Documents of the Ninth Conference of ECASC), Kunming, Government Print, 1992.

The Secretariat of ECASC, *Wushengqu qifang jingji xietiao hui dibaci huiyi wenjian ziliao huibian* (Collected Documents of the Eighth Conference), Chongqing: Government Print, 1991.

The Secretariat of ECASC, *Wushengqu qifang jingji xietiao hui diqici huiyi wenjian huibian* (Collected Documents of the Seventh Conference of ECASC), Guiyang: Government Print, 1990.

The Secretariat of ECASC, *Wushengqu lufang jingji xietiao hui diluci huiyi wenjian huibian* (Collected Documents of the Sixth Conference of the ECASC), Lasha: Government Print, 1989.

The Secretariat of ECASC, "Guanyu jiaqiang hengxiang jingji lianhe cujin shaoshu minzu diqu jingji fazhan de yijian" ("Agreement on Strengthening Horizontal Economic Cooperation and Promoting the Economic Development in the Minority Areas"), in The Secretariat of ECASC (1989), pp. 30–34.

The Secretariat of ECASC, *Wushengqu lufang jingji xietiao hui disici huiyi wenjian huibian* (Collected Documents of the Fourth Conference of ECASC), Chengdu: Government Print, 1987.

The Secretariat of ECASC, "Guanyu jingji xietiao hui disici huiyi zhuyao qingkuang de baogao" ("A Report on Main Themes of the Fourth Conference of ECASC"), in The Secretariat of ECASC (1987), pp. 1–3.

The Secretariat of ECASC, *Xinan jingji xietiao hui diyici huiyi wenjian huibian* (Collected Documents of the First Conference of Economic Coordination Association Southwest China), Guiyang: Government Print, 1984.

Segal, Gerald, *China Changes Shape: Regionalism and Foreign Policy*, Adephi Paper 287, London, Brassey's for IISS, March 1994.

Shang Jingcai, *et al.* (eds.), *Dangdai Zhongguo de Zhejiang* (Contemporary Zhejiang), Beijing: Zhongguo shehui kexue chubanshe, 1989.

Shao Jun, "Dui Jiangsu jiagong gongye de zai renshi" ("Rethinking the Processing Industry in Jiangsu"), *Jianghai xuekan* (The Journal of Jianghai) 1 (1991), pp. 31–34.

Shen Liren & Dai Yuanchen, "Woguo 'zhuhou jinji' de xingcheng jiqi biduan he genyuan" ("The Formation of the Economy of Dukedom, Its Defects and Roots in China"), *Jingji yanjiu* 3 (1990), pp. 12–20.

Shi Tianjian, "Village Committee Elections in China: Institutional Tactics for Democracy," *World Politics* 51:3 (April 1999), pp. 385–412.

Shijie jingji daobao (World Economic Herald), 8 August 1983.

Shirk, Susan, *The Political Logic of Economic Reform in China*, Berkeley, CA.: University of California Press, 1993.

Shirk, Susan, "The Politics of Industrial Reform," in Perry & Wong (1985), pp. 195–221.

Shue, Vivienne, "State Power and Social Organization in China," in Migdal, Kohli & Shue (1994), pp. 65–88.

Shue, Vivienne, *The Reach of the State: Sketches of the Chinese Body Politic*, Stanford, CA.: Stanford University Press, 1988.

Sing Tao Daily, 18 November 1998.

Sing Tao Daily, 26 July 1998.

Skilling, H. G., "Interest Groups and Communist Politics Revisited," *World Politics* 36:1 (1983), pp. 1–27.

Skilling, H. G. & F. Griffiths (eds.), *Interest Groups in Soviet Politics*, Princeton, NJ.: Princeton University Press, 1971.

Skilling, H. G., "Interest Groups and Communist Politics," *World Politics* 18:3 (1966), pp. 435–451.

Smiley, Donald V., "The Political Context of Resource Development in Canada," in Scott (1976), pp. 61–72.

Snead, William, "Self Reliance, Internal Trade and China's Economic Structure," *China Quarterly* 62 (1975), pp. 302–308.

Solinger, Dorothy J., *China's Transition From Socialism: Statist Legacies and Market Reforms 1980–1990*, Armonk, NY.: M. E. Sharpe, 1993.

Solinger, Dorothy J., "Politics in Yunnan Province in the Decade of Disorder: Elite Factional Strategies and Central-Local Relation, 1967–1980," *China Quarterly* 92 (December 1982), pp. 628–662.

Solinger, Dorothy J., *Regional Government and Political Integration in Southwest China, 1949–1954*, Berkeley, CA.: University of California Press, 1977.

Solomon, Richard, *Mao's Revolution and the Chinese Political Culture*, Berkeley, CA.: University of California Press, 1971.

Special Correspondent, "The Important Role of Bureaucrat-Businesses in the Economic Development of Guangdong," *IEAPE Background Brief* No. 64, Singapore, the Institute of East Asian Political Economy, 2 June 1994.

The Standing Committee of the Seventh Congress of Zhejiang, *Zhejiang sheng zhongwai hezi jingying qiye laotong renshi guanli tiaoli* (Regulations on Labor and Personnel Management in Joint Ventures in Zhejiang Province), 23 July 1988.

The State Council, "Xinan he huanan bufen shengqu quyu guihua gangyao" ("Essentials of Regional Planning for Some Provinces and Autonomous Regions in Southwest and Southeast"), the State Council Document No.56, 1993.

The State Statistical Bureau, *Zhongguo jingji nianjian* 1990 (Yearbook of China's Economy), Beijing: Jingji guanli chubanshe, 1990.

The State Statistical Bureau, *Yanhai jingji kaifangqu jingji he tongji siliao* (Economic Studies and Statistical Data of Coastal "Open" Economic Areas), Beijing: Zhongguo tongji chubanshe, 1989.

The Statistical Bureau of Jiangsu, *Jiangsu tongji nianjian 1998* (Statistical Yearbook of Jiangsu), Beijing: Zhongguo tongji chubanshe, 1998.

The Statistical Bureau of Jiangsu, *Jiangsu tongji nianjian 1990* (Statistical Yearbook of Jiangsu), Beijing: Zhongguo tongji chubanshe, 1990.

The Statistical Bureau of Jiangsu, "Dui Jiangsu shishi yanhai fazhan zhanlue de sikao" ("Reflections on Implementing the Coastal Development Strategy in Jiangsu"), in The State Statistical Bureau (1989), pp. 42–55.

The Statistical Bureau of Jiangsu, *Jiangsu tongji nianjian 1988* (Statistical Yearbook of Jiangsu), Beijing: Zhongguo tongji chubanshe, 1988.

The Statistical Bureau of Zhejiang, "Zai 'jie' de guonei xuqiu yali xia fazhan Zhejiang sheng waixiangxing jingji de duice sikao" ("Considerations on Strategy to Develop an Export-Oriented Economy in Zhejiang under a 'Hungry' Domestic Demand Pressure"), in The State Statistical Bureau (1989), pp. 69–82.

The Statistical Bureau of Zhejiang, *Zhejiang tongji nianjian 1989* (The Statistical Yearbook of Zhejiang), Beijing: Zhongguo tongji chubanshe, 1989.

The Statistical Bureau of Zhejiang, *Zhejiang tongji nianjian 1988* (The Statistical Yearbook of Zhejiang), Beijing: Zhongguo tongji chubanshe, 1988.

The Statistical Bureau of Zhejiang, *Zhejiang tongji nianjian 1986* (The Statistical Yearbook of Zhejiang), Beijing: Zhongguo tongji chubanshe, 1986.

The Statistical Bureau of Zhejiang, *Zhejiang tongji nianjian 1981* (The Statistical Yearbook of Zhejiang), Beijing: Zhongguo tongji chubanshe, 1981.

Stein, Michael, "Federal Political Systems and Federal Societies," *World Politics* 20:4 (July 1968), pp. 721–747.

Steinmo, Sven, Kathleen Thelen & Frank Longstreth (eds.), *Structuring Politics: Historical Institutionalism in Comparative Analysis*, Cambridge: Cambridge University Press, 1992.

Suleiman, Ezra, *Politics, Power, and Bureaucracy,* Princeton: Princeton University Press, 1974.

Sun Yusheng, *Dongfang xiandaihua qidongdian: Wenzhou moshi* (A Starting Point of Oriental Modernization: The Wenzhou Model), Beijing: Shehui kexue wenxian chubanshe, 1989.

Sun Zulun, "Guanyu wosheng jingji fazhan zhanlue de yixie sikao" ("Some Reflections on Our Province's Economic Development Strategy"), a lecture in the conference of studying the documents of the Thirteenth Congress of the CCP, 24 December 1987, in *Zhejiang jingji nianjian 1988* (Yearbook of Zhejiang Economy, 1988), Hangzhou: Zhejiang renmin chubanshe, 1988, pp. 49–52.

Swilder, Ann, "Culture in Action: Symbols and Strategies," *American Sociological Review* 51:2 (1986), pp. 273–286.

Ta Kung Pao (Hong Kong), 12 December 1998.

Tang Zejiang (ed.), *Daxinan ziran jingji shehui ziyuan pingjie* (An Evaluation of Natural, Economic and Social Resources in Southwest China), Chengdu: Sichuan shehui kexueyuan chubanshe, 1986.

Tang Zhimin, "Special Economic Zones: Still Special?" *IEAPE Background Brief* No. 19, 14 September 1995.

Tao Youzhi (ed.), *Sunan moshi yu zhifu zhidao* (The South Jiangsu Model and the Road to Wealth), Shanghai: Shanghai shehui kexueyuan chubanshe, 1988.

Tarrow, Sidney, *Between Center and Periphery: Grassroots Politicians in Italy and France*, New Haven: Yale University Press, 1977.

Taylor, Bruce, "Regional Planning for Reciprocal Benefit in South China," in Kwan-yiu Wong *et al.* (1990), pp. 18–27.

Teiwes, Frederick C., "The Establishment and Consolidation of the New Regime, 1949–1957," in MacFarquhar (1993), pp. 5–86.

Teiwes, F., "Provincial Politics in China: Themes and Variations," in Lindbeck (1972), pp. 116–189.

Thelen, Kathleen and Sven Steinmo, "Historical Institutionalism in Comparative Politics," in Steinmo, Thelen & Longstreth (1992), pp. 1–32.

Thurston, Anne F., *Muddling Toward Democracy: Political Change in Grassroots China*, Washington, D. C., United States Institute of Peace, 1998.

Ting Wang, *Li Changchun yu Guangdong zhengtan* (Li Changchun and the Guangdong Political Scene), Hong Kong: Celebrities Press, 1998.

Tong Dalin, "Kaizhan shehui zhuyi fazhan jingji de yanjiu" ("Study of Opening a Socialist Development Economy"), Preface to *Huan bohai wan jingji yanjiu* (A study of the Bohai Bay Circle Economy), Ma Ye (ed.), Beijing: Zhongguo jihua chubanshe, 1990, pp. 1–3.

Tong Dalin, *et al.*, "Jiaqiang hengxiang jingji lianhe shi fazhan shehui zhuyi shangpin jingji de biyou zhilu" ("The Only Way to Develop Socialist Commercial Economy is to Strengthen Horizontal Economic Cooperation"), *People's Daily*, 8 November 1985.

Toonen, Theo A., "Administrative Plurality in a Unitary System: The Analysis of Public Organizational Pluralism," *Policy and Politics* 11:3 (July 1983), pp. 247–272.

Triska, Jan F., "Introduction: Local Communist Politics, An Overview," in Nelson (1980), pp. 1–18.

Tsou, Tang, "Chinese Politics at the Top: Factionalism or Informal Politics? Balance-of-Power Politics or a Game to Win All?" *The China Journal* 34 (July 1995), pp. 95–155.

Ulam, Adam, *The New Face of Soviet Totalitarianism*, Cambridge, MA.: Harvard University Press, 1963.

Unger, Jonathan (ed.), *Chinese Nationalism*, Armonk, NY.: M.E. Sharpe, 1996.

Vogel, Ezra, *One Step Ahead in China: Guangdong Under Reform,* Cambridge, MA.: Harvard University Press, 1989.

Vogel, Ezra, *Canton Under Communism,* New York: Harper & Row, 1969.

Walder, Andrew G., "Local Governments as Industrial Firms: An Organizational Analysis of China's Transitional Economy," *American Journal of Sociology* 101:2 (September 1995), pp. 263–301.

Walder, Andrew, *Communist Neo-Traditionalism: Work and Authority in Chinese Industry,* Berkeley: University of California Press, 1986.

Waldron, Arthur, *From War to Nationalism: China's Turning Point, 1924–1925,* New York: Cambridge University Press, 1995.

Waldron, Arthur, "Warlordism versus Federalism: The Revival of a Debate," *China Quarterly* 121 (1990), pp. 116–128.

Wang Fang, "Zai quansheng nongcun gongzuo huiyi shang de jianghua" ("Talk in a Conference of Rural Work of the Province," 1 February 1985), in *Zhejiang jingji nianjian 1986* (Yearbook of Zhejiang Economy, 1986), Hangzhou: Zhejiang renmin chubanshe, 1988, pp. 3–14.

Wang, Gungwu, *The Chinese Way: China's Position in International Relations,* Oslo: Scandinavian University Press, 1995.

Wang Hongmo, *et al.* (eds.), *Gaige kaifang de licheng* (The Evolution of Reform and Open-Door), Zhengzhou: Henan renmin chubanshe, 1989.

Wang Huaichen, "Zai lu sheng qu shi qifang jingji xietiao hui di shisi ci huiyi shang de jianghua" (Speech at the 14th Conference of ECASC), in The Secretariat of ECASC (1998), pp. 7–15.

Wang, James C. F., *Contemporary Chinese Politics,* Englewood Cliffs, NJ.: Prentice Hall, 1989.

Wang Shaoguang, "China's 1994 Fiscal Reform: An Initial Assessment," *Asian Survey* XXXVII:9 (September 1997), pp. 801–817.

Wang Shaoguang, "Guojia zai shichang jingji zhuanxing zhong de zuoyong" ("On the Role of the State in the Transition to a Market Economy"), in Wu Guoguang (1994), pp. 19–32.

Wang Shaoguang, "Jianli yige qiangyouli de minzhu guojia" ("Building a Strong Democratic State"), in Li Shaomin (1992), pp. 93–138. The paper was originally published by the Center for Modern China in 1991.

Wang Shaoguang & Hu Angang, *The Political Economy of Uneven Development: The Case of China,* Armonk, NY.: M. E. Sharpe, 1999.

Wang Shaoguang & Hu Angang, *Zhongguo guojia nengli baogao* (A Report of State Capacity in China), Hong Kong: Oxford University Press, 1994a.

Wang Shaoguang & Hu Angang, "Zhongguo zhengfu jiqu nengli de xia-jiang jiqi houguo" ("The Decrease in the Extractive Capacity of the Chinese Government and Its Consequences"), *Ershiyi shiji* 21 (February 1994b), pp. 5–10.

Wang Suijin, "Jindai Ningbo bang qiyejia weishenme neng jueqi" ("Why Could Modern Entrepreneurs of Niangbo Natives Rise"), *Zhejiang xuekan* (Zhejiang Studies Monthly) 54:1 (1989), pp. 41–45.

Wang Xu, "Lun sifaquan de zhongyanghua" ("Centralization of China's Judicial System"), *Zhanlue yu guanli* (Strategy and Management) 5 (2001), pp. 28–36.

Watson, James L., "Rites or Beliefs? The Construction of a Unified Culture in Late Imperial China," in Dittmer & Kim (1993), pp. 80–103.

Wedeman, Andrew H., *From Mao to Market: Rent Seeking, Local Protectionism, and Marketization in China*, New York: Cambridge University Press, 2003.

Wheare, K. C., *Federal Government*, 4th Ed., New York: Oxford University Press, 1964.

White, Gordon (ed.), *The Chinese State in the Era of Economic Reform: The Road to Crisis*, London: Macmillan, 1991.

White, Lynn T., III, *Shanghai Shanghaied? Uneven Taxes in Reform China*, Hong Kong: Center for Asian Studies, 1989.

White, Lynn T., III & Cheng Li, "China Coast Identities: Regional, National, and Global," in Dittmer & Kim (1993), pp. 154–193.

Whitney, Joseph B. R., *China: Area, Administration, and Nation Building*, Department of Geography, The University of Chicago, 1970.

Wildavsky, Aaron (ed.), *American Federalism in Perspective*, Boston: Little, Brown and Company, 1976.

Williams, Walters, *Studying Implementation: Methodological and Administrative Issues*, Chatham, NJ.: Chatham House Publisher, 1982.

Wong, Christine (ed.), *Financing Local Government in the People's Republic of China*, Hong Kong: Oxford University Press, 1997.

Wong, John, et al., *China After the Ninth National People's Congress: Meeting Cross-Century Challenges*, Singapore and London: World Scientific, 1998.

Wong, John, et al., *China After the Fifteenth Party Congress: New Initiatives*, EAI Occasional Paper No. 1, Singapore: World Scientific & Singapore University Press, 1997.

Wong, John & Zheng Yongnian, *Political Reform in China*, a report submitted to the Ministry of Foreign Affairs, Singapore, 1999.

Wong, Kwan-yiu, *et al.* (eds.), *Perspectives on China's Modernization*, Hong Kong: The Chinese University of Hong Kong Press, 1990.

The World Bank, *China: Macroeconomic Stability and Industrial Growth Under Decentralized Socialism*, Washington, DC., 1990.

The World Bank, *China: Investment and Finance*, Washington, DC., 1988.

Wu Bo & Rong Zihe (eds.), *Dangdai Zhongguo caizheng* (China Today: Finance), Beijing: Zhongguo shehui kexue chubanshe, 1988.

Wu Guoguang (ed.), *Guojia, shichang yu shehui: Zhongguo gaige de kaocha yanjiu* (The State, Market and Society: An Investigation into China's Reform Since 1993), Hong Kong: Oxford University Press, 1994.

Wu Guoguang, *Zhongguo shisida hou de renshi: quanli jiegou yu zhengzhi jiaoli* (Leadership, Power Structure, and Possible Policy Conflicts of the CCP After its 14th Congress), Papers of the Center for Modern China, Princeton, NJ.: Center for Modern China, 4:27 (1993), pp. 1–12.

Wu Guoguang & Zheng Yongnian, *Lun zhongyang difang guanxi* (On Central-Local Relations), Hong Kong: Oxford University Press, 1994.

Wu Jiaxiang, *Lianbang hua: Zhonghua desan gongheguo zhilu* (Federalization: The Road to the Third Republic of China), Hong Kong: The Mirror Press, 2004.

Wu Jiaxiang, "Quanqiuhua yu lianbanghua" ("Globalization and Federalization"), *Zhanlue yu guanli* (Strategy and Management) 3 (2003), pp. 95–100.

Wu Jiaxiang, "Jijin minzhu haishi wenjian minzhu?" ("Radical or Gradual Democratization?"), in Liu & Li (1989), pp. 27–33.

Wu Xiangjun (ed.), *Jiangsu xiangzhen qiye guanli jingnian qianli xuan* (1376 Cases of Management Experience of Rural Industry in Jiangsu), Beijing: Zhonggong zhongyang dangxiao chubanshe, 1990.

Xie Liping, "Shichang xing xiangzhen qiye moshi — Wenzhou moshi" ("The Market Type of the Rural Industry — The Wenzhou Model"), in Chen & Xia (1988), pp. 90–116.

Xin Bao (Hong Kong Economic Journal), 10 December 1998.

Xinhua News Agency, 22 January 1988. In *Zhejiang jingji nianjian* (The Yearbook of Zhejiang Economy, 1988), Hangzhou: Zhejiang renmin chubanshe, 1988, pp. 3–6.

Xu Gongmin, "Ping Yan Jiaqi de 'lianbangzhi' zhengzhi zhuzhang" ("Commenting on Yan Jiaqi's Political Advocacy of Federalism"), *Liaowang* (Outlook) overseas edition, 3 (15 January 1990), pp. 4–5.

Xue Jiaji, "Jiyu, yunxing jizhi, xin de shengchangdian" ("Opportunity, Operating Mechanism, and New Initiative"), *Jianghai xuekan* (The Journal of Jianghai) 5 (1988), pp. 3–7.

Yan Huai, "Organizational Hierarchy and the Cadre Management System," in Zhao & Hamrin (1995), pp. 39–50.

Yan Jiaqi, *Lianbang Zhongguo gouxiang* (The Conception of a Federal China), Hong Kong: Minbao chubanshe, 1992.

Yan Wenguang, "Wenzhou gouyou qiye shuaibai yuanyin ji chulu de tantao" ("On the Causes of the Decline of the State Enterprises and Outlets"), *Jingji yu guanli yanjiu* (Economy and Management Studies) 3 (1988), pp. 53–54.

Yang Dali L., *Beyond Beijing: Liberalization and the Regions in China*, New York: Routledge, 1997.

Yang Dali, "China's Special Economic Zone Policy: The Debate Continues," *IEAPE Background Brief* No. 102, Singapore, 11 October 1996.

Yang Dali, "Dui 'bin wei lun' de jidian fanbo" ("Refuting the 'Imminent Crisis' Thesis"), *Ershiyi shiji* 21 (February 1994), pp. 15–18.

Yang Dali & Zheng Yongnian, "Regional China," in Mackerras (1998), pp. 33–37.

Yang Jianxiang, "Smuggling Has Dire Influence on Economy," *China Daily*, 26 October 1998.

Yang Mu, "The Stock-Buying Fever in China and its Background," *IEAPE China News Analysis* No. 8, Singapore, 20 August 1992.

Yang, Richard H., *et al.* (eds.), *Chinese Regionalism: The Security Dimension*, Boulder, CO.: Westview Press, 1994.

Yazhou zhoukan (Asian Weekly), 16–22 November 1998.

Yeung, Y. M. & C. T. Chang, "Kungtung," in *The New Encyclopedia Britannica*, 15th Ed., Vol. 10, Chicago: Helen Hemingway Benton, 1974, pp. 553–558.

Yeung, Y. M. & David K. Y. Chu (eds.), *Guangdong: Survey of a Province Undergoing Rapid Change*, Hong Kong: The Chinese University Press, 1994.

Yi Jiafu, "Dui Jiangsu gongye sudu yu xiaoyi fanchai de sikao" ("Some Reflections on the Gap between Industrial Growth and its Efficiency in Jiangsu"), *Jianghai xuekan* (The Journal of Jianghai) 1 (1990), pp. 35–37.

Yu Guan, "Shilun Jiangsu gongyehua de jincheng" ("On the Process of Industrialization in Jiangsu"), *Jianghai xuekan* (The Journal of Jianghai) 1 (1990), pp. 28–34.

Yu Guan, *et al.*, "Shilun Jiangsu sheng chanye jiegou yu chanye zhengce" ("On Industrial Structure and Industrial Policy in Jiangsu"), *Jianghai xuekan* (The Journal of Jianghai) 6 (1990), pp. 38–43.

Yu Guan & Zhu Jun, "Cong Jiangsu de shijian kan fahui difang tiaojie gong-neng" ("Knowing Local Regulative Functions Through Examining Jiangsu's Practice"), in Gui *et al.* (1987), pp. 814–824.

Yuan Enzhen (ed.), *Wenzhou moshi yu fuyu zhilu* (The Wenzhou Model of Economy and the Road to Affluence), Shanghai: Shanghai shehui kexueyuan chubanshe, 1987.

Zang Xiaowei, "Provincial Elite in Post-Mao China," *Asian Survey* XXXI:6 (June 1991), pp. 512–525.

Zeitz, Gerald, "Interorganizational Dialectics," *Administrative Science Quarterly* 25:1 (1980), pp. 72–88.

Zeng Weiyuan & Jiang Yaochu, "Shenhua gaige zourenmin fuyu zhilu" ("Deepen the Reforms and Go along the Road of Getting Rich"), *Minzhu yu fazhi* (Democracy and Legal System) 8 & 9 (1987), pp. 4–9.

Zhang Mingtao, "Guanyu 'xinan diqu guotu ziyuan zonghe kaocha he fazhan zhanlue yanjiu' de zongji gongzuo huibao" ("A Report on An Comprehensive Examination of Natural Resources and Development Strategy in Southwest China"), in The Secretariat of ECASC (1989), pp. 64–86.

Zhang Xin, "Xindai, huobi jinrong he quyu jingji zhizi" ("Credit, Currency, Finance and Regional Economic Autonomy"), *Modern China Studies* 1–2 (1995), pp. 106–117.

Zhang Xin, "Lun quyu jingji zizhi" ("On Regional Economic Autonomy"), in The Editorial Committee of the Journal of China's Economy (1991), pp. 65–73.

Zhang Zhicheng, "Zhanhou ouzhou huaqiao huaren jingji bianhua chutan" ("A Preliminary Analysis of Economic Changes of Chinese in Europe After World War I"), *Zhejiang xuekan* (Zhejiang Studies Monthly) 58:5 (1989), pp. 31–38.

Zhao Chenggang, *et al.*, *Jiangsu duiwai jingji maoyi fazhan zhanlue yu duice* (Foreign Trade Development Strategy and Its Measures in Jiangsu), Nanjing: Nanjing daxue chubanshe, 1989.

Zhao Deqing (ed.), *Zhonghua renmin gongheguo jingji shi* (An Economic History of People's Republic of China), 2 volumes, Zhengzhou: Henan renmin chubanshe, 1988.

Zhao Suisheng, "Deng Xiaoping's South Tour: Elite Politics in Post-Tiananmen China," *Asian Survey* XXXIII:8 (August 1993), pp. 739–756.

Zhao Suisheng & Carol Lee Hamrin (eds.), *Decision-Making in Deng's China: Perspectives from Insiders*, Armonk, NY.: M. E. Sharpe, 1995.

Zhao Ziyang, "Advance Along the Road of Socialism with Chinese Characteristics," Report Delivered at the Thirteenth National Congress of the Chinese Communist Party, 25 October 1987, in The Document Research Office of the CCP (1997), Vol. 1, pp. 439–496.

Zhao Ziyang, A talk in a plenary session, the State Council of P. R. China, in Chong & Xiang (1988), pp. 362–363.

Zheng Yongnian, "Institutionalizing *de facto* Federalism in Post-Deng China," in Hung-mao Tien and Yun-han Chu (eds.), *China Under Jiang Zemin*, Boulder, Colorado: Lynne Rienner Publishers, 2000, pp. 215–232.

Zheng Yongnian, *Discovering Chinese Nationalism in China: Modernization, Identity, and International Relations*, Cambridge: Cambridge University Press, 1999.

Zheng Yongnian, *Zhu Rongji xinzheng: Zhongguo gaige xinmoshi* (New Deal of Zhu Rongji: A New Model of Reform China), Singapore: World Scientific, 1999.

Zheng Yongnian, "Lun ganbu jiaoliu zhidu de juxianxing" ("On the Limitations of the Cadre Transfer System"), *Xin Bao*, 23 February 1999, p. 13.

Zheng Yongnian, "Jingguan shenru difang nengfou jiaqiang zhongyang quanli?" ("Can the Transfer of Central Officials to Localities Strengthen Central Power?"), *Xin Bao*, 17 February 1998a.

Zheng Yongnian, "Difangguan jinjing dui Zhongguo zhengzhi de yingxiang" ("The Impact of Promoting Local Officials to the Central Leadership on China's Politics"), *Xin Bao*, 26 February 1998b.

Zheng Yongnian, *Institutional Change, Local Developmentalism, and Economic Growth: The Making of Semi-Federalism in Reform China*, Ph.D. thesis, Department of Politics, Princeton University, 1995.

Zheng Yongnian, "Fenquan zhanlue yu ban lianbangzhi de yanjin" ("The Strategy of Decentralization and the Evolution of Semi-Federalism"), in Wu (1994), pp. 72–81.

Zheng Yongnian, "Perforated Sovereignty: Provincial Dynamism and China's Foreign Trade," *The Pacific Review* 7:3 (1994b), pp. 309–321.

Zheng Yongnian & Li Jinshan, "China's Politics After the Ninth People's Congress: Power Realignment," in Wong *et al.* (1998), pp. 51–92.

Zheng Yongnian & Wang Xu, "Lun zhongyang defang guanxi zhong de jiquan he minzhu wenti" ("Centralization, Democracy and China's Central-Local Relations"), *Zhanlue yu guanli* (Strategy and Management) 3 (2001), pp. 61–70.

Zheng Yongnian & Zou Keyuan, "China's Politics in 1998," *EAI Background Brief* No. 26, East Asian Institute, National University of Singapore, 11 January 1999.

Zhong Liqiong, "Should SEZs Retain Privileges?" *Inside China Mainland* 18:4 (1996), pp. 61–63.

Zhongguo Tongji Nianjian 1991 (Statistical Yearbook of China), Beijing: Zhongguo tongji chubanshe, 1992.

Zhou Jingfen, "Zhejiang ji zibenjia xingqi tanwei" ("A Study of the Rise of Capitalists in Zhejiang"), *Zhejiang xuekan* (Zhejiang Studies Monthly) 56:3 (1989), pp. 34–40.

Zhou Taihe (ed.), *Dangdai Zhongguo de jingji tizhi gaige* (The Reform of Economic System in Contemporary China), Beijing: Zhongguo shehui kexue chubanshe, 1984.

Zhou Yifeng, "Sunan moshi de xingcheng yu fazhan" ("The Formation and Development of the South Jiangsu Model"), in Tao (1988), pp. 11–30.

Zhu Jialiang, "Gaosu zengzhang de jiyu chengyin he bianhua qushi: Zhejiang gongye shinian zengchang de huigu yu fansi" ("Opportunity, Cause and Trend of Changes of Fast Growth: Reflections on Zhejiang's Fast Industrial Growth of Past Ten Years"), *Zhejiang xuekan* (Zhejiang Studies Monthly) 61:2 (1990), pp. 24–28.

Zhu Jialiang, "Ziyuan xiaosheng he jingji dasheng" ("The Province with Little Resource and Big Economy"), in *Zhejiang jingji nianjian* (Yearbook of Zhejiang Economy, 1988), Hangzhou: Zhejiang renmin chubanshe, 1988, pp. 417–419.

Zhu Jialiang, "Ziyuan xiaosheng he jingji dasheng: dui Zhejiang jingji fazhan zhanlue de yidian sikao" ("Poor Resource and Big Economy: Some Reflections on Economic Development Strategy of Zhejiang"), *Zhejiang jingji* (Zhejiang Economy) 11 (1987), pp. 417–419.

Zhu Rongji, "Tongji sixiang, jiaqiang lingdao, xunsu er yanli di daji zousi fanzui huodong" ("To Crack Down on the Criminal Activities of Smuggling Immediately and Forcefully by Unifying Thoughts and Strengthening the Leadership"), *People's Daily*, 1 September 1998, p. 1.

Zou Ziying, "The Impact of Deng Xiaoping's Talks in South China," *IEAP China News Analysis* No. 7, Singapore, 18 March 1992.

Zuo Chuntai & Song Xinzong (eds.), *Zhongguo shehui zhuyi caizheng jianshi* (A Brief History of Chinese Socialist Finance), Beijing: Zhongguo caizheng jingji chubanshe, 1988.

Index